W9-CFK-676

DIVER'S ALMANAC

GUIDE TO THE BAHAMAS AND CARIBBEAN

A great deal of effort has been made to obtain accurate information for this publication. The information was obtained from numerous sources. Due to the sheer magnitude of the task, not all of the information presented herein has been confirmed, but has been accepted as presented by area contacts. For this reason, this book is intended for use as a guide only. Additional information should be obtained for areas visited. The editors and publishers assume no liability for its use, and encourage caution and prudence in application of information presented. Remember, diving is an inherently dangerous sport.

HDL COMMUNICATIONS
650 Town Center Drive
Costa Mesa, CA 92626

Editor
Stephen F. Guettermann

Research Editor
Jeff M. Tabler

Medical Editor
Dr. David E. Boaz

Contributing Editor
William Holdeman

Contributing Writers
George S. Lewbel
Ellworth Boyd
Janet Felix-Harper
Steve Bowden

Editorial Assistants
Theresa M. Owen
Michelle Lowery

Cover Photograph
Alan Williams

Production
Angela Wilson, New York

Design & Layout
Bhob

Maps
Jack Ashcraft
Design and Illustration

Typesetting
BPE Graphics, Inc.
Spring Valley, New York

SPORTS ALMANACS, INC.

President
Robert C. Robertson

Vice-President
Thomas M. Owen

Secretary/Treasurer
Joyce E. Robertson

Administrative Assistant
Barbara J. Feinstein

Staff Assistant
Shelli M. Ross

Co-Published By
HDL Communications, Inc.

Foreword

The *Diver's Almanac: Guide to The Bahamas and Caribbean* is the first attempt ever to compile a dive travel book which covers these two major dive destinations under one cover. The work has been a learning experience for us and we hope paging through the book will be educational and entertaining for you. We tested several ways of organizing the book in order to best present the information. However, because of culture, geography, government and history, the Caribbean defies being "organized." We respect the Caribbean for that. We respect the individual countries and island groups for maintaining their individuality and integrity. Diversity and differences are what make The Bahamas and Caribbean so dynamic, so alluring and such a prime dive destination.

We have tried to highlight some of the area differences so the dive/traveler could make a choice as to where he or she would like to explore. The Bahamas, for example, offer never-ending excitement and relaxation. First there is Bimini. Only 50 miles off the Florida coast, it is a springboard to world-class fishing. There are the casinos and nightclubs of Nassau, the nightlife and subtropical golf courses on Grand Bahama Island, and sailing in the Exumas. Or choose the out-island of San Salvador, where Columbus first made landfall in the New World, or the open-water seclusion of Rum Cay. The common bond among these islands and others in The Bahamas is that they all have excellent diving supported by comfortable resorts and qualified people.

South of The Bahamas is the Caribbean Sea. One of the world's great Seven Seas, it covers over 970,000 square miles. A veritable basin of clear, warm water fed by tropical currents from the Atlantic Ocean, the Caribbean offers a host of pleasures we can only hope we are wise enough to preserve and sane enough to enjoy. Fortunately, the people of the islands and the mainland countries which fringe the Caribbean are aware of the processes which maintain the sea and its life. Dive-service operators and dive-resort owners have pioneered preserving the reefs in particular and the sea in general. Even the most remote areas, such as Belize and the Bay Islands which are making it into the 21st century relatively unscathed by the 20th century, are extremely conscientious of how their guests interact with the environment. We can learn a lot from some of these resorts. They are built in ways which allow the dynamics of the area to be enjoyed as well as to continue unfettered. They have been woven into the landscape and become a part of it, yet guests are tastefully supplied with the amenities of fine food and drink, quality accommodations, friendly people, excellent diving and a pristine environment. We thank them for their foresight.

Special thanks go to all the operators and staff of the dive resorts through The Bahamas and Caribbean. Without their cooperation and support we would never have been able to bring you this book.

How to Use This Book

Because of The Bahamas' proximity to and popularity with the United States, we felt that they and Turks and Caicos, a British Colony which is part of the same archipelago as The Bahamas, should be the first dive destinations we discussed. The Bahamas share many characteristics with the Caribbean, but geographically they are in the Atlantic Ocean, rather than the Caribbean Sea. By treating The Bahamas and the Caribbean in separate sections and by using the same descriptive headings in each section, we felt we could present information in the most attractive and useful way. The Caribbean section includes those countries which, at this time, have the greatest appeal to the American dive/traveler.

Each introduction to an island or country begins with a bit of history and topographical information. The **Getting There/Getting Around** heading lists the major airports, modes of island and interisland travel and how feasible it is to tour that particular island or area.

The **Topside Attractions** section describes areas of interest to travelers who want to get a feel for the unique aspects of that particular island. Some people travel to dive. Others dive when they travel. Topside activities can be an important determinant when considering where they want to go or give them a reason to go there.

A description of **Area Diving** follows the **Topside Attractions** piece. This section gives the dive/traveler an idea of the dive specialties available in each place. It will discuss its major features, such as blue holes or popular shipwrecks, as well as special conditions of which divers need to be aware while considering that area's diving.

This piece leads into the **Dive Site Descriptions**. There are literally thousands of dive sites in The Bahamas and the Caribbean. We have listed a sample of them to give divers an idea of what to expect at specific locations or what to ask for when diving the area. Many of these sites have been popular for a long time and continue to attract divers; for example, a rare species of fish or coral may be there. There may be giant sponges, intricate patterns of surge channels, schools of fish, or it could be a favorite night dive site. We also list some recently discovered sites, since dive instructors and guides are constantly looking for new places which other services do not yet know about. This usually friendly competition between the services helps keep the diving fresh.

The final part of each island/country chapter is the list of **Dive Services**. We made every effort to visit personally with these services. Many of the visits were followed up with phone calls so we could go to press with the most updated information possible. We keyed upon talking to the resorts and services which specifically offered diving from highly accredited people. Some of the dive services listed provide diving for guests of merely one resort, usually the resort with which that service is affiliated. Other services are affiliated with a resort and are located on the resort's premises, but also provide diving to guests of nearby hotels, condominiums and villas. Finally, there are services which have no resort affiliation. These shops are independent and offer services and dive packages in association with any of several nearby resorts, resorts which may be on the beach or may be in the downtown area of a larger city. Or the service may specialize in doing trips with cruise-ship passengers. We have tried to list that information with each service.

Though we tried conscientiously to contact each legitimate service, we probably overlooked some. But we know we also found a few services which were so new that the paint on their sign had not dried yet. We feel good about finding those, apologize to those we missed, and will continue to update our information. *Any service which is not in this book may contact us and we will pass your information to our readers.* Each reader is also welcome to contact us for any new information we receive.

In addition to material on the countries and their dive services, the Almanac includes articles on dive travel and preparation, medical and emergency information, weather, shipwrecks and creatures of the coral reefs. These articles should serve as a good primer for people new to the areas as well as people new to diving. The articles should also be useful to experienced divers who may need a refresher on how to plan and enjoy a dive vacation.

Much more than the words do, it is the photographs which tell the story of the Caribbean. The photographers who contributed to the selection presented here did a masterful job with a tricky task. Coping with currents, constantly changing light, shy fish and other secretive subjects, as well as hazards embodied in everything from urchins to caves to sharks, the photographers present an image of a world seen by few. Each underwater photo is a gift from the sea. Each topside shot creates a feeling that says "I want to go there." We hope the photos entice you to take a Bahama or Caribbean dive vacation and to learn about what awaits you there.

Stephen Gutterman

Acknowledgments

I thank all the dive-shop managers, dive guides, photographers, artists and tourist-board representatives who supplied so much of the information and talent needed to create this book. But there are three friends who deserve special mention. First is Tom Owen, who believed in the project, pulled the people together to make it happen, and tirelessly supported it when many others would have quit. Next is Bill Holdeman who, through his work as editor of the West Coast Diver's Almanac, designed the format for this Almanac and established a standard of quality we have tried to meet. Finally, I want to thank Research Editor, Jeff Tabler, a man who became a valued, trusted friend when the going was the toughest. I couldn't have done it without you, Jeff.

CONTENTS

Vacation Tips For The Occasional Diver

Are you looking forward to a great vacation, but somewhat apprehensive about your rusty diving skills

Dive services may expect a great deal from anyone with a C-card. They will want to see the card, and, may even want a look at your log book to see how often and where you have dived recently. Divemasters carry heavy legal liability, and tend to be very conservative. To protect both of you, divemasters give a fundamental skills review test.

Who do they spot as potential trouble?

Divers arriving without having prepared their gear properly; it doesn't fit, or hasn't been serviced, or the weight is wrong, etc.

Divers who can't control buoyancy properly, maintain comfortable posture in the water, respond to correct hand signals, or consume air rapidly.

Divers who find it difficult to become part of a functioning buddy pair or dive group, to share the experience, help others, or socialize before and after the dives.

There are many ways that traveling divers can avoid this kind of ineptitude.

First, take at least some of your own equipment. You'll be more at ease, and you'll know it has been maintained properly. Keep it in a sturdy bag and mark everything

clearly. Try it for fit before you leave, in a pool if necessary.

Before the trip, take a refresher course and continue to dive locally.
• Stay physically fit.
• Review all the information you can before leaving, including talking with divers who have been there, so you know what to expect.
• At the resort, pay attention to the dive guides and obey reasonable instructions. Ask questions until you are satisfied about procedures that seem unclear, about hazardous marine life, or other aspects of the dive plan.
• Be part of the dive group; helping, diving together, pointing out interesting things.
• Underwater, relax and move slowly over the bottom; maintain near-neutral buoyancy to keep from damaging life on the bottom with elbows, knees or fins; keep aware of where the boat or shore exit point is.
• Monitor your instruments regularly and compare your status with your buddy.
• If diving from a boat, when you leave the water, clear the boarding ladder area quickly, doffing your gear in a spot where you won't interfere with others trying to get out of the water. As you remove your gear, place it immediately in your bag.

Dive guides are forced to deal with many ill-prepared divers every day. Don't be one of them.

Planning Your Trip

Questions to ask yourself:
1. What type of diving do I have in mind? (boat, beach, reef, kelp, island, etc.)
2. Am I qualified or do I need some instruction in that phase of diving? (beach entry, surf, current night, etc.)?
3. What's my price range?
4. Do I want to dive all day or have time to sightsee and lie around?
5. What equipment will I want to take? (What can I get there?)
6. How many days and/or nights of diving do I want?
7. How will I get there?
8. Who will make the travel arrangements? (me or an agent)
9. How long will I stay in the area?
10. Will there be any special arrangements — babysitters, etc. — at my destination?
11. What are the qualifications of all those going?
12. What purchases of equipment and repair items do I need to budget?
13. Can I make air reservations far enough in advance to take advantage of discount rates?
14. What sources of information will I need? (travel guides, brochures, magazine articles, books, maps, etc.)
15. And last, is all of this planning going to be worth the trouble? Of course it is!

Things you need to know:
Diving
1. Diving type offered.
2. Best time of year.
3. Visibilities.
4. Marine life.
5. Fish and Game laws.
6. Wrecks to dive on.
7. Land photography.
8. Are there reefs, drop-offs, caves.

Boats
9. Common dangers.
10. Type available.
11. Fitted with diving facilities: ladders, platforms, compressors, tanks, weights, etc.?
12. Maximum passengers.
13. Hot showers.
14. Bunks or cabins.
15. Galley with a full-time cook.
16. Boat size.
17. Dive masters per number of divers.
18. Crew's qualifications. How many years in service in that area. Licensed?
19. Facilities for cleaning gear.
20. Game cleaning and storage facilities.
21. Electrical outlets — AC/DC.
22. Boat's registration and certification dates.
23. How many tanks per guest — how long between fills.
24. Dives included per day.
25. How long to dive site.
26. All tank dives?
27. Any shore and boat dives.
28. Boat put into other than home ports.
29. Night dives available.
30. Is instruction offered.
31. What gear to bring.
32. What gear is available for rental or purchase. (sundries, snacks, suntan lotion, etc.)
33. Best source of information on visiting and diving the area.
34. Best way to get to departure point.
35. Check-in and boat departure point.
36. Valuables and camera gear storage.
37. Safety record.
38. Costs for all of the services offered.
39. If we come in by air, what is the least costly way to get to the resort or departure point? Do they offer airport pickup service?

Colorful depths, floating sensations and majestic underwater scenery are the diver's world. But that world is no longer restricted to a few hardy souls covered with muscles. Advances in equipment and technique since self contained underwater breathing apparatus (SCUBA) was invented forty years ago have opened the field to virtually all comers, and now it is hailed as one of the newest family sports.

The camaraderie, the interdependence, and the shared joy of discovery that exist in the underwater world can surpass any other group activity, as devoted divers are quick to point out. Deep in azure waters the family finds a whole new form of inter-action, a whole new excitement to their relationship. From planning the dive to discussions over dinner afterwards, diving as a family sport offers the best of opportunities for individual and group effort.

SCUBA diving is accessible to almost anyone. The sport no longer requires exceptional physical strength or coordination, just average good health and physical stability. The equipment is easy to use. New styles and

R.H. McPeak

DIVING WITH THE
FAMILY

colors of wetsuits and accessories offer "high fashion" to the sport, creating a panorama of undersea travelers who are almost as colorful as the marine life itself.

Many families start by learning to dive together, often after becoming enchanted with the undersea world through a snorkeling experience. A trip to a local dive shop or an introductory

course at a resort begins their training, and they soon realize this family sport is comparable in cost to most others like skiing, kayaking or camping. It can, in fact, be less expensive, since initial costs for training and equipment rentals are most reasonable, and further investment is spread over the time it takes for the family to improve their techniques and experience.

The rewards are countless. Whether exploring a calm tide-pool and thrilling at each other's discoveries or sharing the challenge of an ocean reef, the resulting bond of spirit is priceless.

SCUBA diving has changed in other ways, also. Formerly the domain of underwater hunters and scientists, a new conservation ethic has emerged. SCUBA diving holds the opportunity for learning and appreciating the interdependence of sea life and its importance to land-bound humans. It is, in short, an entrance to another world, a world we increasingly realize is critical to the earth's survival. What better way for a family to rediscover their own interdependence than by exploring new thoughts, ideas — new worlds?

Equipment Tips

CAUTION:

Depth gauges and decompression meters may be damaged when travelling in the unpressurized holds of aircraft. Either carry them in your carry-on luggage or check with the manufacturer to see whether you can adjust to compensate or should use a sealed travelling case.

NOTE:

Putting dive gear or camera gear in special bags or containers marked with all those beautiful, eye-catching decals really lets the world know who and what you are, though you might find that's not such a good idea after all. Conservative, more anonymous containers are recommended as less of an invitation to theft.

FAA Regulations on Baggage

One aspect of travel often overlooked when planning a trip is the luggage volume restrictions imposed by the Federal Aviation Administration. The measurements prescribed for carry-on type luggage are approximately 9 x 13 x 23 inches. The Safety Regulations set by the Administration also state that luggage which does not fit in an expressly designed baggage compartment or underneath a seat must be checked with owner identification clearly marked on the exterior.

Transportation of breakables or items subject to spoilage must be appraised upon boarding or they are carried at the traveler's own liability. Tariff Regulations include set limits to the amount of liability for claims regarding checked luggage.

In cases involving nearly all international travel, and the homeland segments of such journeys, submission must be in written form within 21 days for delay or loss of property claims, and within 7 days for damage claims.

Within the United States or between the United States and St. Thomas, St. Croix or San Juan, all claims must be submitted in written form and within 45 days of occurrence.

In Canada, the United States and many Caribbean countries, charges are waived for luggage weighing under 70 pounds in the following assigned size groups:

For excess, large or heavy pieces of luggage, contact the airlines for information.

Since international travel allowances are determined according to destination, travelers should consult the airlines for specifics.

Sporting gear (such as diving equipment and golf bags) is excluded from no-charge luggage policies but usually subject to lower rates than ordinary baggage.

Airlines stipulate that diving tanks should be completely empty when transported; however, the diver who bleeds a tank to 0 psi does run the risk of

damaging it. Because of this, many divers will attempt to persuade the airlines that a tank is empty when in actuality it still holds 100 or 200 psi.

Size of Luggage (L + W + H)	Quantity Allowed
Exterior area 62 inches or less	One.
Exterior area 55 inches or less	One.
Combined area of 45 inches or less	One or more pieces with total weight under 70 pounds.

THE
BAHAMAS

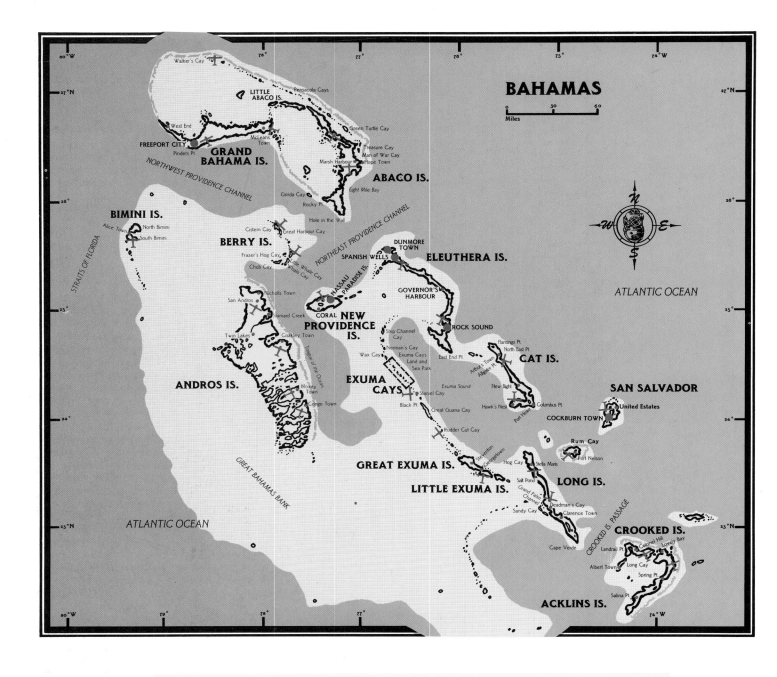

Information

Common Name:
The Bahamas

Official Name:
Commonwealth of the Bahamas

Area:
5,382 sq mi

Population:
240,000

Language:
English

Currency:
Bahama Dollar of 100 cents (B$)

Electric Current:
110 volts, 60 cycle (Same as U.S.)

Taxes:
Departure Tax—Adults $5; Children 2 to 12 $2.50; under 2 yrs exempt.
The international norm of 15% is generally added to food and beverage checks.

Entry Requirements:
U.S. and Canadian citizens need proof of citizenship: voter's registration, Social Security card, or birth certificate.
All other visitors need a passport. All visitors are required to have an onward or return ticket.

Tourist Information:
For General Information and Reservations call The Bahamas Reservation Service at (800) 327-0787.

For sports or private pilot information contact:
Sports Information 255 Alhambra Circle—Suite 415,
Coral Gables, Florida 33134
(800) 323-7678.
For other assistance contact:
Ministry of Tourism, Nassau Court, P.O. Box N 3220,
Nassau, Bahamas (809) 322-7505.

The Bahamas

David McCray

General Description

The Bahamas are comprised of more than 700 islands lying in a 600–mile northwest-southwest arc which begins 125 miles north of the tip of Florida and angles southeast to just north of Haiti. Bimini is the closest island to the U.S. mainland at approximately 50 miles east of Miami. Together, the islands have a total land area of 5,382 square miles, which is comparable in size to the state of Connecticut. Tens of thousands of square miles of warm, clear sea water flow between them and provide for year-round recreation. The islands are predominantly flat with small hills. Cat Island has the highest point in The Bahamas—Mt. Alvernia at 207 feet.

Geologic & Oceanographic Influences

The word Bahamas is taken from the Spanish "baja mar" and means shallow sea. Millions of years ago, when the sea bed was uplifted, the warm, shallow waters provided an environment in which colonies of coral animals could thrive. Coral animals feed upon microscopic ocean plants. These plants grow on the coral itself, and it is the chlorophyll and other pigments of the plants which gives coral its color. Without plants growing upon it virtually all coral would be white. The Bahama Islands are composed mainly of calcium carbonate limestone (and sandstone) cemented together by shell chips, crushed coral, and other fragments of calcium carbonate that settle into crevices. The coral of what is now

The Bahamas islands was exposed thousands of years ago when the sea level was lowered during the last Ice Age. In some places the foundation of these coral islands exceeds 12,000 feet, which is testimony to how long the cycles of coral formation, sea level changes and shifts in the Earth's crust have been occurring. Within the coral reefs around the islands the waters are calm, clear, and seldom reach a depth of more than 60 feet. Outside the reefs, depths plunge in excess of 6,000 feet.

Shore Life

Grasses and forbs were the first types of vegetation to come to these islands. Later, as the soil gradually became deeper, other types of plants were able to become established from seed brought by winds and birds. Today, dense forests of Caribbean Pine grow on Andros, Grand Bahama, New Providence, and Abaco. On a few of the islands, hardwood forests, cascarilla, logwood, horseflesh, and lignum vitae trees grow. Red mangrove forests root in shallow water and cover many of the shorelines of protected bays and inlets. Palms frequently provide a background for island beaches. Most of the vegetation of the smaller islands and cays is made up of dense shrubs and small trees. Agricultural quality land is sparse in The Bahamas and is usually found only in places where wind and rain do not erode it.

A number of colorful tropical birds call The Bahamas home. The West Indian flamingo is the national bird of The Bahamas and is protected by The Bahamas National Trust. The roseate spoonbill, Ba-

hama parrot, and Bahama woodstar humming bird are also found here. Small reptiles and rodents inhabit many of the islands and include the rock iguana, a harmless vegetarian lizard, and the almost extinct Bahama hutia, a cat-sized rodent once prized by native Indians for its meat. The Bahamas have no poisonous snakes.

Climate

Each island, of course, has slight variations in climate. Generally speaking, The Bahama islands north of the Tropic of Cancer have slightly more rain, more lush vegetation, and are slightly cooler than the islands south of that line. Seasons are based not on temperature, but rather on rainfall. High temperatures from November to May average between 70°F and 77°F. June through September is warmer and more humid with average temperatures nearing 85°F. Most of the rain falls as showers between June and October at a monthly average of six to nine inches. The hurricane season starts in July and may last until November.

There are three main influences on the Bahama climate: the trade winds, ocean currents, and fairly constant day length throughout the year. A continuous flow of warm, equatorial water enters the Caribbean basin from the Atlantic Ocean mainly through gaps in the Lesser Antilles. The water flows between these islands, then sweeps westward across the Caribbean, and moves into the Gulf of Mexico through the narrow passage between Yucatan and Cuba. This current also mingles with warm water from the Gulf Stream and continues north through the Straits of Florida.

Warm water moves from east to west north of the Caribbean Basin, too. This stream flows between The Bahamas and joins the Gulf Stream near the tip of Florida then continues north. The Bahamas, then, are constantly bathed with warm water. The warm water helps make for constant year-round temperatures with water temperature averaging 75°F in the winter and 80°F in the summer. Trade winds blow almost always from an easterly direction and help mix the air over the water so temperatures do not build. The Bahamas average about 320 days of sunshine a year. All this combines to make a dive-traveler haven through most of the year, but especially in the winter months. From November through April, when cold rules the north, the dry air and the warm water of The Bahamas attract the largest numbers of divers and other tourists.

The extremes in temperature are between 60°F and 90°F, so it is a good idea to pack a sweater or a light jacket. Clothing is casual, but decent, in the major resort areas and cities. Depending upon your tastes in evening entertainment, you may also want to pack more formal attire for casinos and the more luxurious spots.

History

The Bahamas were inhabited by Arawak Indians for at least 600 years before Columbus first made landfall in the New World at San Salvador on October 12, 1492. The Spanish quickly discovered The Bahamas had virtually no mineral wealth, so they made no serious effort to colonize them. The native Indians were enslaved and exported to work in the silver and gold mines of Hispaniola and Cuba. Within a few decades the Arawaks had been almost exterminated.

The English Navy as well as pirates used The Bahamas as a base from which to harass treasure ships of Spain and other colonial powers that sailed north upon the Gulf Stream Current near the coast of Florida. Frequently, pirates served as part of the British Navy, but soon became an embarassment to the Crown as well as a threat to British merchants. With Spain occupied in the Caribbean and the American mainland, England claimed The Bahamas in 1629. The first permanent settlement was established in 1648 when English Puritans seeking religious freedom fled Bermuda and made their home on Eleuthera.

Pirates ruled New Providence and dominated The Bahamas during the late 17th and early 18th centuries. Edward Teach, or Blackbeard, as he is commonly remembered, is one of many English pirates who

called New Providence island his home port. Though Spanish and French warships blasted back at the pirates, it was not until 1718 when Woodes Rogers was appointed Royal Governor of The Bahamas and began hanging pirates, that order came to New Providence. Today, topside fortifications and sunken ships give silent testimony to colonial warfare and piracy.

In 1776, during the American Revolution, United States naval units and marines twice captured Nassau in bloodless invasions. After that war, about 8,000 American Loyalists brought their slaves and settled in The Bahamas. The soil did not sustain agriculture long, so many of the white settlers freed their slaves and left the islands. Slaves were officially freed on August 1, 1834 when the Emancipation Act was signed.

Wrecking was another Bahama industry, which was sometimes practiced by luring vessels into the reef at night with shore lamps. When passing merchant ships struck the reef or were lost in storms, much of the cargo was salvaged by wreckers to be sold or traded later.

The U.S. Civil War brought prosperity to The Bahamas, which served as a transfer point for munitions and medical supplies to be run through the northern blockade of southern ports. At this time the first hotel was built in The Bahamas, the Royal Victoria in Nassau.

During Prohibition, The Bahamas again prospered from their close proximity to the U.S. mainland. This time the islands served as a liquor supply point for American rum-runners and Nassau became a gambling and vacation haven for wealthy Americans who wanted to escape the restrictions at home. The worldwide depression of the 1930s limited tourist development in the Bahamas and the local people again turned to the sea for their livelihood.

During World War II, The Bahamas was an important naval training area. The United States Navy has a base on Andros and does submarine tests and research in the Tongue of the Ocean.

After World War II The Bahamas became one of the world's foremost vacation spots. In 1950, the first year of intensive tourist promotion, 45,000 visitors came to the islands. Now The Bahamas serve over 2,000,000 vacationers annually and tourism accounts for over 70 percent of the nation's gross national product, with dive travel as a growing part of local economies. International banking and investment management are becoming major industries, as well.

In 1964 Britain granted The Bahamas

self-government. The country achieved full independence on July 10, 1973, and is now a member of the British Commonwealth of Nations. A Governor-General represents the Queen of England as head of state. The country follows a democratic constitution similar to England's, with the Prime Minister as the head of government.

How History and Natural History Influence Diving

The history and natural history of The Bahamas have combined to create some of the best diving in the world. As mentioned in the oceanographic section, climate, depths, and clear, warm-water currents create an ongoing dynamic diving environment in which divers have easy access to experience colors, life and secrets unavailable to land dwellers. The water flowing through The Bahamas originates near equatorial Africa. As it flows east, virtually all the sediment drops from it and the water picks up extra heat from the sun. By the time it reaches The Bahamas it is incredibly warm and clear with visibility frequently surpassing 100 feet. So little rain runs off the islands that the waters are seldom cloudy except after high winds and major storms. Many of the undersea cave systems formed when the sea was shallower and underground water courses dissolved the limestone of the reefs. As the sea became deeper, these caves and tunnels were flooded, and now provide a fantastic haven for sea life that can be observed by experienced divers who know how to navigate through such mazes.

The Bahamas are coral islands built upon the same continental shelf as the eastern United States, an area which has only recently been submerged by gradually rising seas. From the island beaches the sea bottom slopes gradually until a depth of about 60 to 80 feet. Here, the continental shelf plunges into deep trenches and basins of the Atlantic Ocean, such as The Tongue of the Ocean east of the coast of Andros. Along these drop-offs are hundreds of miles of barrier reef, which can be over 50 yards wide. The reefs can be followed down in excess of 150 feet or as long as there is adequate sunlight to sustain its life. In the protected waters between the barrier reefs and islands, many species of tropical marine animals and plants thrive.

Virtually every type of coral which is found in the Caribbean is found in The Bahamas. In shallow water, the most common corals are often the staghorn and elkhorn. These coral are more stout and can recover faster from storm and wave damage than coral located deeper, because of the greater availability of sunlight needed for photosynthesis by their internal plants.

In deeper water there is usually a mixture of corals. In relatively protected areas, and on shallow patch reef, leaf coral and ribbon corals often predominate. They are thin and somewhat fragile and need quiet waters to survive. Their close relatives, the plate corals, are even more fragile, and form large sheets in deeper water or under overhangs and in caverns.

Star corals are the main reef builders in most areas of The Bahamas as undersea terraces of coral and white sand approach drop-offs such as the Tongue of the Ocean, where wall diving originated. Star corals can form huge mounds in shallower depths, or large flattened plates in deeper water. As you swim downward along their faces you can see the star corals gradually change from mounds to plates.

There are miles of undersea gardens in which coral, sponges, and fish abound. There are more than 55 species of gorgonians on the coral reefs. Gorgonians include sea fans, sea rods, and sea fingers. Similar in appearance to some of the gorgonians are black coral. Brain corals abound, and rare species thrive in micro-environments created by caves, overhangs of limestone, and coral chimneys cut through the barrier reefs. (Take a flashlight while diving during the day. Sponges need artificial light upon them for their colors to show, otherwise they'll appear gray.)

Fire coral which, strictly speaking, is not a coral—it is more closely related to the Portugese Man-of-War—grows on its own as flat sheets or boxlike formations, or encrusts gorgonians and coral heads. Fire coral has nematocysts that can cause a painful sting. If you don't touch anything that looks like dull tan paint, you'll avoid most fire coral.

Closely related to fire coral are the stinging hydroids, a group which forms lacy, black fan-like colonies. Stinging hydroids usually grow under overhangs and in caves.

The Bahamas are a great place to experience some of the finest thrills of diving. Each island which has dive services offers unique underwater and topside attractions. For example, off the Great Barrier Reef east of Andros, a diver can sense the ocean's immenseness, tranquility, and power as he hovers above the 6,000 foot plunge of the Tongue of the Ocean. There, great pelagic fish can be seen cruising along the deep shadows of the reef. Sea turtles are always a thrill to see and favor several sites in The Bahamas, especially the submerged plains of turtle grass.

Colonial warfare, piracy, shallow reefs and storms have all contributed to the shipwrecks which divers explore around The Bahamas. Shipwrecks are another 'watch-out' place. These areas should always be explored with a little extra caution so that a grouper coming out of the dark in front of your face mask doesn't make you bump into a rusty nail.

Current dives along reef walls and through tunnels give divers the sensation of flying. Many resorts offer current dives and some are specifically mentioned in the Dive Services section.

Current dives and night dives will help you learn new skills so you can take in new wonders. Much of the life in the water of The Bahamas only comes out at night. Sites you dive during the day will look totally different at night and the excitement of the unexpected can make you use a lot of air in a hurry. Prepare yourself before you go down to stay calm and alert as you float through the quiet ecstasy. Most services offer night dives and you will certainly see a bounty of species and action that are just not there during the day.

Dive service facilities range from fully equiped dive resorts and local dive shops serving several resorts, to live-aboard dive adventure boats. In general, Bahamian diving operations are modern and well run, with high safety standards and well-maintained gear. The Bahamas Diving Association sponsors a Diving Awards Programme which promotes its member diving resorts and facilities through its Diving Passport. Awards are given based upon the number of days you dive The Bahamas and the number of diving destinations you visit in a three-year period.

General Information
Entry Requirements

U.S. citizens do not require a passport or visa to enter The Bahamas for visits up to eight months. Proof of citizenship is required though, such as birth certificate, voter's registration card, or Social Security card. Immigration will not accept a driver's license as proof of citizenship. Canadians may also enter The Bahamas with only proof of citizenship, but only for visits up to three weeks. *All* visitors must have an onward or return ticket.

Customs

Baggage declaration by visitors upon entry into The Bahamas is verbal, but

David McCray

luggage is subject to Customs inspection. The Bahamas does not have income or corporate taxes. Most government revenue is by import duties charged on nearly all imported items. As a visitor, all your personal effects, including your dive equipment, are duty-free provided you take them with you upon returning home. Expensive items such as photographic systems may attract customs scrutiny. Officials will want to be satisfied you are not attempting to import and sell valuable items without paying import duty. Be sure to register expensive cameras and watches with customs in your country before leaving. This is to prove you did not buy the item at lower prices in The Bahamas. U.S. and Canadian customs provide this service at all international airports.

U.S. regulations limit to $400 the amount of merchandise its citizens can bring home duty-free, provided that the resident has been out of the States for at least 48 hours and has not claimed the exemption within the previous 30 days.

Bahama Tourist

Canadian citizens who have been out of their country for 48 hours or more may bring back up to $100 (Canadian)–worth of duty-free merchandise, which must accompany the passenger. The exemption, which must be claimed through written declaration, is allowed once per quarter. A person who has been outside Canada for seven days or more may claim duty-free goods valued at not more than $300 once each calendar year. Goods acquired in The Bahamas or any area outside continental North America may be shipped separately, but must be declared upon arrival in Canada.

Getting There

Nassau on New Providence and Freeport on Grand Bahama both have international airports. Other major islands have airfields which are official ports of entry too, plus there are over 40 more air strips and flying boat harbors at which both commercial and private planes land. Air carriers and schedules vary, but it is easy to make flight connections from major U.S. airports on the Gulf and Southeast Coasts.

Bahamasair is the national airlines and provides service between The Bahamas and the U.S., as well as providing many inter-island flights. Other services provide passenger and cargo service and are listed under specific island sections. We suggest always consulting with your travel agent when scheduling flight connections.

For the private pilot coming to The Bahamas, contact your nearest Bahamas Tourist Office for your fact-filled Flight Planner, or in the U.S. call (800) 327-7678 or (305) 442-4867.

Arriving by Sea

Maybe the best way to enjoy The Bahamas is cruising among the islands on your live-aboard dive boat. Well-equipped marinas are on every major island and many cays. Boats must check with Customs at the first Port of Entry and get a cruising clearance permit to The Bahamas. There are Ports of Entry in: Abaco, Andros, Berry Island, Bimini, Cat Cay, Eleuthera, Exuma, Grand Bahama, Inagua, and New Providence.

An excellent reference is "The Yachtman's Guide to The Bahamas," available from Tropic Isle Publishers, P.O. Box 866, Coral Gables, Florida 33134.

Mail boats serve all the main islands and will carry passengers. For the person not in a hurry who wants to travel this way, contact the Dock Master at Potter Cay Dock in Nassau at 809/323-1064 for schedules and costs.

Bahamian Fisheries Laws that Affect Diving

1. No living marine product (conch, crawfish, scalefish, coral, etc.) may be taken with the use of scuba.
2. A snorkel diver may only use a Hawaiian sling or pole spear. Any other powered speargun may not be used. It is illegal to bring a powered speargun into the country.
3. The export of any marine product is illegal unless a permit is issued.
4. No toxic product may be used to kill or catch fish.
5. The Bahamas National Trust is establishing many protected areas within The Bahamas. Within these areas there are specific restrictions on either commercial fishing, or the taking of any marine product. To obtain up-to-date information on the status of protected areas and the regulations, contact The Bahamas National Trust, P.O. Box N-4105, Nassau 809/322-8333. Local dive operators may also provide this information.

When we spoke to the dive operators in The Bahamas and asked them for something unique about their service or of what they were the most proud, almost without fail they said, "We have the best diving and the best people working here." We feel this is a fine situation to walk into for the traveler who must, to a large extent, put his trust and life in the hands of strangers. The safety records of these services show they are competent; people who enjoy their work usually are. The occasional sport diver is much more likely to get complacent and hence, careless, than the divemasters we met. For as many times as these people have taken groups of divers to the depths, their experience will not allow them to be complacent. The divemasters constantly monitor the divers and the conditions in order to be aware of a situation before it becomes a problem. Listen to them and trust them, but take full responsibility for yourself being there. When you are with a group of divers either onshore, in a boat, or underwater, do as the divemaster says. Once the situation is over there will be time to ask questions.

Many of the operators listed are members of The Bahamas Diving Association and cooperate with one another to help protect dive sites as well as ensure customer safety. They also offer an Awards Programme which can reduce costs to divers who frequently dive The Bahamas. For information concerning the Awards Programme call: 800/327-0787.

ABACO ISLANDS

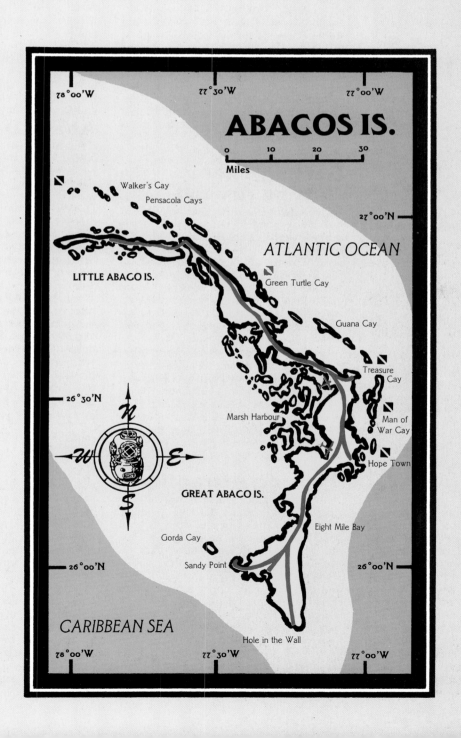

ABACOS IS.

0   10   20   30
Miles

78°00'W   77°30'W   77°00'W

Walker's Cay
Pensacola Cays

27°00'N

ATLANTIC OCEAN

LITTLE ABACO IS.

Green Turtle Cay

Guana Cay

Treasure Cay

26°30'N

Marsh Harbour

Man of War Cay

Hope Town

GREAT ABACO IS.

Eight Mile Bay

Gorda Cay

26°00'N   26°00'N

Sandy Point

CARIBBEAN SEA

Hole in the Wall

78°00'W   77°30'W   77°00'W

Bahama Tourist

The Abacos are a group of islands and cays in the northeast part of The Bahamas approximately 150 miles from Palm Beach and 180 miles from Miami, Florida. The boomerang-shaped chains of islands and cays extend 130 miles from Walker's Cay in the north to "Hole-In-The-Wall" in the south. The two main islands are Great Abaco and Little Abaco and all the surrounding cays are frequently referred to merely as Abaco. Great Abaco and Little Abaco are linked by one major road which runs almost their entire length, with side roads connecting the settlements.

The best sailing, diving, and scenery is between the eastern shores of Abaco and the many cays which are protected from the open Atlantic Ocean by barrier reefs. The Abacos are a favorite of mariners and have a number of excellent marine facilities and resorts which serve not only yachtsmen and fishermen, but divers as well. At Marsh Harbour, Hope Town, Green Turtle Cay, Treasure Cay and Walker's Cay there are full-service marinas and guides.

The west coast of Abaco slopes into a shallow sea, while central Abaco is a large area of shallow water over mud called "The Maris." It is an important part of the sealife cycle as it is a major breeding spot for fish and shellfish.

Settled by British colonists and American Loyalists during the sixteen and seventeen hundreds, the towns of The Abacos are reminiscent of New England fishing villages. The fishing industry has given way largely to tourism, though agriculture is important. Some of the mahogany that grows there is used for local shipbuilding and some is exported to America.

The population of The Abacos is approximately 7,000, with 4,000 people living in Marsh Harbour. The Abacos are well serviced by tourist facilities, with at least twenty resorts dotting the beaches of the major islands and cays. These range from the luxury accommodations such as those on Treasure Cay to guest cottages on Green Turtle Cay. All water sports are available throughout the islands and the abundance of small, uninhabited cays near the resorts makes finding a private beach easy and desireable.

Getting There/ Getting Around

The Abacos have three airfields, all of which are ports of entry, and two sea ports of entry, one on Turtle Cay, the other at Cross Harbour. Most passengers arrive on the daily flights from Nassau to Marsh Harbour on Bahamasair Airlines. Smaller carriers also serve The Abacos and asking your travel agent to check on these may help you make the best possible connections, but be aware that schedules and carriers vary.

Treasure Cay has frequent direct service from Miami. Walker's Cay has charter flights for their guests and will help you make connections from Fort Lauderdale.

Car rentals are available at Marsh Harbour and the major dive resorts assist their guests who want to tour the area with making connections on ferries and taxis.

Topside Attractions

Among the places to see while on The Abacos include Marsh Harbour, a vibrant town in which to tour and dine. Several good restaurants are in the Marsh Harbour area. Pelican Cays National Park, an underwater preserve, lies south of Marsh Harbour. It winds through reefs, islets, and cays. You can tour it topside or go there for some easy day or night diving. It is a good place to identify marine life you may encounter elsewhere while diving. Two other favorite stops are a trip to Man-O-War cay to observe how fishing boats are crafted by hand, and the port of Hope Town on Elbow Cay. Ferries run frequently between the cays and everything

on the small isles is within easy walking distance, but wear comfortable shoes.

The people of Abaco are committed to tourism. There is everything here, from luxury resorts to seaside guest cottages. As mentioned, quality marine services abound and the resorts are spread around the major cays, so it's easy to avoid crowds. There are many small uninhabited cays throughout the protected waters, making it easy to find a private beach for the afternoon. The ease with which to privately explore these waters is one of the things we like best about The Abacos. If you rent a boat we suggest you set a course back to the marina before twilight, though. Twilight does not last long in the Bahamas, and you will want enough light to navigate through the reef and home to port.

Abaco Diving

For the diver, much awaits to be explored below the surface of the water. Reefs wind among the cays from Walker's Cay in the north to the deep subsurface caves off the southern coast near Hole-In-The-Wall. Experienced divers can drift dive along walls of coral and other reef formations along the outer cays and reef more exposed to ocean currents. Coral caves, grottos, and blue holes offer a challenge to all skill levels of diver. Large, sea-going fish cruise the fringes of reef. Throughout the inner coral terraces are most of the popular Bahama fish, including giant amberjack, grouper, barracuda and manta rays. Shipwrecks of many nations and several eras are found throughout the reef. Add to this the great variety of color, marine life, and wall diving and the Abacos provide underwater excitement that is not soon exhausted.

Abaco Dive Sites

Sandy Cay Reef, located about seven miles south of Hopetown at the south end of Pelican Cay Nation Preserve, is a beautiful coral garden well inside the barrier reef line. Elkhorn coral, amberjack, spotted eagle rays, moray eels and other marine life can be seen. The entire 2,000 acre National Preserve is a fine place for underwater photography, with the average site at 30 feet.

Six miles north of Hopetown is Fowl Cay, part of a barrier reef which offers splendid photographic possibilities. Large coral heads rise to the surface from a depth of 25 feet in calm, protected water. Among the coral heads is a structure known as **The Towers**. These coral pinnacles are located in the center of Fowl Cay Reef. They have a 50-foot diameter base and break the surface of the water 30 feet above.

At **Maxi Cave** divers follow a ravine down 25 feet to a grotto area and cave which burrows 20 feet into the reef. Hatchetfish, groupers, and shellfish are found around this site. Two steam locomotives lost from a barge lie atop the barrier reef in 10 feet of water. They make an excellent fish-feeding and photography station.

About thirty miles north of Marsh Harbour is Treasure Cay, a popular luxury resort with some fine diving nearby. One of the most intriguing sites is **The Catacombs**, a coral maze running underneath the reef. It consists of about 100 caves interconnected by tunnels and arches in just 10 to 25 feet of water. Near Treasure Cay are also a number of inland blue holes including **Devil's Hole**. About 80 feet in diameter and 200 feet deep, the site provides good diving for all levels of expertise. There is an inversion layer at 65 feet. Fish and crab live throughout the upper areas of the caves and stalactites hang from undercuts along the wall.

Guana Cay Reef is composed of 50 acres of coral gardens alive with groupers, rays, and sponges. Between Snake Cay and Great Abaco lies **Rouse's Hole**, a

sixty-mile-long trench carved by ocean currents which, at times, make diving tricky. The hole is 75 feet wide and at least 200 feet deep. Coral ledges and holes are a haven for shellfish, groupers and spotted eels.

Two popular shallow dives are the wreck of the **U.S.S. Adirondack**, a federal war ship lost off Man-O-War Cay during the American Civil War, and **Top Tree Reef**, an excellent snorkeling area with schools of fish and coral. Both sites are in 20 feet to 30 feet of water.

Near Walker's Cay, the northernmost island of The Abacos as well as the Bahamas, is **Tom Browns**, a thriving coral garden in 25 feet of water. **Old Wreck** is a shipwreck that is home for octopus, angel fish, sergeant majors and trigger fish. **Charlie's Cannons** is a shallow dive near the dock of Walker's Cay resort where it is said cannons can be found in the reef or covered by sand.

At always-popular **Nick's Reef**, unbelievable numbers of fish cruise and school in the pockets, overhangs, and fissures of the reef. Tunnels are illuminated by sunlight coming through the porous coral, which gives enough light by which to

identify some of the fish-life there. **White Hole** is a site popular for fish feeding and presents divers with a chance to photograph grouper and angelfish. A few minutes from Walker's Cay and 50 feet down you'll find the base of **Queen's Reef**, an unusual bowl-like formation of coral heads which provides good visibility for viewing parrotfish, rays, and sometimes lobsters. Farther out, at **Queen's II**, you're on the outer edges of the Little Bahama Banks, and may see any of the pelagic fish including kingfish, amberjack, and mackerel.

Broad Bottom offers limestone caverns and tunnels to a depth of 30 feet. Shellfish, including lobster and the tiny arrow crab, are often seen on the coral wall and stands of coral.

Abaco Dive Services

BRENDAL'S DIVE SHOP
   Owner: Brendal Stevens
Service Address:
   Green Turtle Cay; Green Turtle Club; Marina, Bahamas
Mailing Address:

Susan Speck

Same as above
Service Telephone:
809/367-2572
Reservation Telephone:
809/367-2572 or 305/833-9580
Hours Service is Open:
8:30 am–5 pm Seven days a week
Resort Affiliation:
Green Turtle Club
Rooms:
40
Cottages/Villas:
Several

Guests fly in from West Palm Beach or Ft. Lauderdale, Florida, to Treasure Cay Airport on Abaco, then take a short ferry-boat ride to Green Turtle Cay. The Green Turtle Club is right on the waterfront and is popular with divers and non-divers alike.

Brendal's Service caters to all levels of diver and they do offer resort diving courses. Instruction is done in shallow water near the resort. Brendal's is affiliated with NAUI, but other than offering a resort instruction course, no other certification is offered. "C" cards are not required.

Brendal's has a full line of rental equipment. Dives are conducted from a 29-foot dive boat with a 15-diver capacity; most dives are within 20 minutes of shore. You can even treat yourself to an all-day dive trip with a picnic on the beach of one of the uninhabited nearby cays.

There are coral garden dive sites for both snorkelers and novice divers. Intermediate and advanced divers can explore the deeper reefs and wrecks. The coral catacombs are favorite sites to dive through, and excellent wall diving begins at 90 feet. The area is popular for photography, with abundant stands of coral as well as parrot fish, rays, eels, dolphins and turtles often being subjects. Brendal's offers one morning dive, one afternoon dive, and frequent night dives. Pop-

Margo Nelson

ular dive sites include: Coral Condos, Pelican Park and Coral Pillars, all reef dives which begin in about 45 feet; Brendal's Wreck at 55 feet, and Catacomb Caverns.

Packages range from four days to 14 days, which include lodging at the Green Turtle, diving, meals and ferry rides. Leaders of eight or more divers dive free.

There is plenty to do between dives while at the Green Turtle. The cay is surrounded by beaches. The resorts also offers boat rentals, fishing, windsurfing, and tennis. The amenities of Abaco are just across the bay and easy to get to by ferry.

DIVE ABACO, LTD
Owner: Skeet LaChance
Service Address:
P.O Box 555; Marsh Harbour; Abaco, Bahamas
Mailing Address:
Same as above
Service Telephone:
809/367-2787 or 367-2014
Reservation Telephone:
Same as above. Ask for Skeet.
Hours Service is Open:
8:30 am–7 pm Seven days a week
Resort Affiliation:
Provides dive services for guests at area hotels.

Guests arrive at Marsh Harbour from Ft. Lauderdale and West Palm Beach Florida, flying either Bahamasair or Aero Coach. By making dive reservations in advance with Dive Abaco, and letting them know where you will be staying, transportation can be arranged to take you to the dive service whenever you wish to make your first dive. Dive Abaco has full rental services and does some repairs.

Dive Abaco can handle all divers, but Skeet caters to novices and the older divers who enjoy the shallow and medium depths they dive. Skeet has been diving since 1950. As he no longer guides wall dives, and his day dives run between 9:30 am and 2 pm, he recommends hard-core divers go to one of the other services for more action. Dive Abaco offers PADI certification.

Divers head to sites aboard Skeet's 30-foot dive boat, which he built himself. They explore reefs, such as Grouper Alley, a site 40 feet down where Skeet's trained groupers come out to greet divers. Tunnel dives are popular and include The Tunnels and Medusa's Lair, two tunnel and cave dives which cut into the reef. Maxy Cave Bay is an area of four caves with Barry the Barracuda at 30 feet. The

Cathedral is an inspiring cave dive at 35 feet. Skeet says they try to do it on Sunday because of its name.

At 85 feet, Uncle Skeeter's Reef is a site where there are many remains of broken-up sailboats and mystery objects. Skeet also dives the **U.S.S. ADIRONDACK**.

Between dives, divers can enjoy most other watersports, tennis, and the shopping and sightseeing available on and around Abaco.

GALE'S ISLAND MARINE
Owner: Dave Gale
Service Address:
P.O Box G; Hopetown; Abaco, Bahamas
Mailing Address:
Same as above
Service Telephone:
809/367-2822
Reservation Telephone:
Same as above
Hours Service is Open:
Open for custom dive trips
Resort Affiliation:
Divers stay at any of the nearby resorts

After taking divers out for over 25 years, Dave Gale is limiting his services to small, custom dive trips. He does both day and night dives from his 23-foot dive boat to sites within ten miles of his service.

Gale's offers no rental or repair service.

HOPETOWN CHARTERS, LTD.
Owner: Dave Malone
Service Address:
Hopetown, Elbow Cay; Abaco, Bahamas
Mailing Address:
Same as above
Hours Service is Open:
8 am–6 pm Seven days a week
Resort Affiliation:
They recommend divers to Hopetown Harbour Lodge

Divers to Elbow Cay land at Marsh Harbour Airport from West Palm Beach or Ft. Lauderdale, Florida, on Bahamasair, Aero Coach, or Transair. A ferry runs between Marsh Harbour and Hopetown on Elbow Cay. Hopetown Charters recommends staying at the Hopetown Harbour Lodge, but will serve guests of all nearby resorts.

They are affiliated with NAUI and cater to all level of divers. Presently they do offer resort courses, and hope to soon be certifying divers through NAUI.

Hopetown Charters rents scuba gear, but can only handle very limited repairs on personal dive gear. They make both morning and afternoon dives, with night diving on request. Divers have several small dive boats available to them, as well as a 25-foot dive boat.

Their more popular dives include Sandy Cay Reef, which is part of the island's underwater park. Dave Malone says there are so many reef fish in the park you literally have to push them away. They also do cave dives near Fowl Cay at depths from 25 feet to 70 feet. The majority of their dives for the experienced diver are wall dives, caves, and three blue holes. One of the better wrecks is the **ADIRONDACK,** a large ship in 75 feet of water. Hopetown Charters has many sites from which to choose, including over 100 wall dives.

Dave Malone opened Hopetown Charters in June of 1986. As we go to print Dave had not yet installed his phone, but his number should be available through the Abaco operator. He says you can send a telegram if you can't get through, otherwise to let him know you are coming. Dave has been in the dive business for seven years and has worked with Dave Gale at Gale's Island Marine.

Through Hopetown Charters you can also charter a boat for guided fishing. Other watersports are available, and Elbow Cay has miles of protected beaches. The ferry which runs between Elbow Cay and Marsh Harbour puts the other amenities of Abaco at your disposal.

TREASURE CAY DIVERS
Service Address:
    Treasure Cay; Abaco, Bahamas
Mailing Address:
    4050 SW 11th Terrace, Ft. Lauderdale, FL 33315
Reservation Telephone:
    305/763-5665
Hours Service is Open:
    800/327-1584
Resort Affiliation:
    Treasure Cay Beach Hotel & Villas
Rooms:
    Accommodations for 450 guests
Cottages/Villas:
    Privately owned villas are available

Guests are chartered a flight on Gulf Stream Pacific Airways and land at the Treasure Cay Airport from Ft. Lauderdale, Florida. Treasure Cay is no longer separate from the rest of Abaco, so you don't take a ferry ride from the airport to get to this treasure.

Treasure Cay Divers accommodate all divers, but are especially appealing to vacation divers. Their resort courses includes pool as well as shallow water instruction, and they offer NAUI certification.

Treasure Cay has full rental services.

They have both one- and two-tank morning dives, and one-tank afternoon dives. Night dives are held upon request.

Shallow reef dives are done on Lighthouse Reef and the Whale, which are 20 feet to 40 feet deep. Other popular dives include The Catacombs and Guana Gardens, two dives winding through a system of caverns. Divers will see turtles, butterfly fish, angelfish, stingrays, morays, and barracudas at sites along the reefs. They have no real wall diving.

The between-dive attractions at Treasure Cay revolve around fishing, sailing, tennis, and golf. They have entertainment along with seclusion. Kathi, our contact, told us Treasure Cay is great for honeymoons.

WALKER'S CAY DIVE SHOP
Service Address:
    Walker's Cay; Abaco, Bahamas
Mailing Address:
    700 SW 34th St., Ft. Lauderdale, FL 33315
Service Telephone:
    800/326-3714 or 305/522-1469
Reservation Telephone:
    Same as above
Hours Service is Open:
    8 am–6 pm Seven days a week
Resort Affiliation:
    Walker's Cay Resort
Rooms:
    62

Cottages/Villas:
    3

Walker's Cay is a 100 acre-isle at the northern part of the Abacos chain. The resort has a private charter for its guests which makes the one-hour flight out of Ft. Lauderdale directly to the resort's airfield.

Walker's Cay Dive Shop offers a resort course as well an open-water PADI training for divers who want certification. The shop will rent all the equipment you need. They offer two-tank morning dives and single-tank dives in the afternoon. If you can get five other divers to go, a dive master will take you night diving.

Most of their sites are along the Upper Bahamas Barrier Reef from 30 feet to 50 feet of water. Since the sites are far out, pelagics can be sighted cruising inside the reef, plus turtles, snappers and groupers. The reefs have excellent coral formations, including black coral and star coral, and many of the dives wind through tunnels and caves cut into the reef. Drift dives begin at 100 feet for more advanced divers. Average size of dive parties is 15. Dive packages are available.

Walker's Cay is a one-resort island and totally self-contained. The resort also has a full-service marina and offers bonefishing, reef fishing, and big game fishing. There is tennis and nighttime entertainment.

Margo Nelson

ANDROS

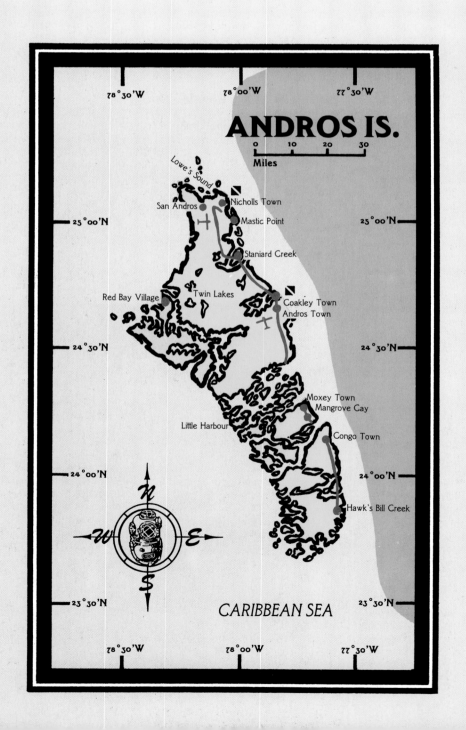

ANDROS IS.

0   10   20   30
Miles

Lowe's Sound

San Andros •   Nicholls Town

Mastic Point

25°00'N   25°00'N

Staniard Creek

Twin Lakes

Red Bay Village   Coakley Town
Andros Town

24°30'N   24°30'N

Moxey Town
Mangrove Cay

Little Harbour   Congo Town

24°00'N   24°00'N

Hawk's Bill Creek

23°30'N   23°30'N

CARIBBEAN SEA

78°30'W   78°00'W   77°30'W

Andros is the largest and least explored island of The Bahamas. At 104 miles long and 40 miles wide, it supports tropical forests of mahogany, pines, lignum vitae, and madeira. Palm trees stretch for miles along the sand beaches of the east coast. The west coast is a marshy area and borders a long, low bank called "The Mud." Tricky shoals over "The Mud" make the island almost unapproachable from that side. Birdwatchers and botanists have a special paradise on Andros with an unmatched diversity of tropical birds and over 40 species of wild orchids thriving throughout the island.

Andros is 170 miles southeast of Miami and 50 miles southwest of Nassau, New Providence. Andros and New Providence are about 20 miles apart at their closest point.

Andros, though usually referred to as one island, is actually divided into three parts: North Andros, Central Andros, and South Andros. Collectively, they have a population of approximately 5,000, with most of the development on North Andros. Fresh water percolates throughout the island's interior and is an important resource shipped to Nassau. Central Andros is actually composed of several large and many small cays surrounded by bights of fresh water.

North Andros is dotted with fishing settlements along the east and north shores and has the major towns of Nicholl's Town, Majestic Point, and Andros Town. There are airstrips near San Andros and Andros Town. Most of the island's resorts and restaurants are found on North Andros, but here, as throughout all of Andros, there is little entertainment outside of resort activities or private pursuits.

The visitor action on Central Andros revolves around the settlements of Lisbon Creek and Moxey Town on Mangrove Cay. Central Andros is separated from the North Andros by several miles of open water speckled with small cays, and there is about a five-mile-wide channel between it and South Andros. Mangrove Cay also has an airstrip and is a port of entry.

Central Andros has some of the least expensive tourist accommodations in The Bahamas. They are limited to guest houses with few amenities, but they provide the experience some people want as well as access to the fine bonefishing, sailing, and diving of Andros. This is the place for the economical adventurer.

Tourists of South Andros are adequately served by a selection of resorts near Congo Town. On South Andros there really are miles of palm-fringed beaches that can be claimed for a private afternoon. Tourism is developing slowly on South Andros, but topside amenities are coming. Buffets and barbecues fill and nourish hungry divers, most water sports are available, and there are cocktail lounges where you can chase down the seawater and get to know the people of Andros.

Getting There/ Getting Around

Bahamasair has frequent, though not necessarily daily, service to all four airstrips on Andros from Nassau. Taxis usu-

David McCray

ally are available for each incoming flight and are shared between passengers. It's expensive and slow trying to navigate between North, Central, and South Andros, so double-check your connections and destination. Normally you will want to land at the airstrip closest to your resort.

There is not much touring done on Andros. Unmetered taxis and tour cars are available on North and South Andros, as are scooters and bicycles. These can be arranged for from your resort. The main road, which runs along the east coast, is poorly maintained, but it does give access to beaches and the coastal settlements. Small groups of tourists frequently travel the coast and spend time with the people who live in the coastal settlements, but they are advised against traveling far into the interior of the island.

Topside Attractions

There are two main reasons why people come to Andros: fishing & diving. Andros is appropriately termed the "Bonefish Capital of the World." Lowe Sound, four miles north of Nicholl's Town, is the most popular place to hire a guide to stalk these fighters. Bonefish inhabit the clear shallow flats around Andros and fight like no fresh water fish can. Andros also gets high marks for deep sea fishing. All large sport fish in The Bahamas are caught beyond its barrier reefs.

Andros Diving

Andros diving is legendary. A few hundred yards off the east shore, and running almost the entire length of the island, are 142 unbroken miles of barrier reef. At widths which vary from ten to 50 yards, it offers some of the best and most diverse diving in the world on both sides of its wall. Visibility inside the reef averages in excess of 100 feet except near The Bight of Central Andros where runoff reduces it to 60 to 80 feet.

There are sites and services for all levels of divers. Most of the diving inside the reef is between 25 and 60 feet and gives beginners many excellent sites and marine life to explore. More experienced divers can tune up behind the reef before taking one of many challenging wall dives or drift dives outside the reef which borders the 6,000-foot deep trench of The Tongue of the Ocean, affectionately referred to as TOTO. This is where wall diving began over 25 years ago. In places the barrier reef is exposed to the surface of the water. Elsewhere divers may have to go down as deep as 70 feet before reaching the reef. Most diving is within the top 100 feet, though a few dive masters will take experienced divers for special trips to sites as deep as 190 feet.

The Andros Blue Holes are another draw of this area. Most services take divers to any number of blue holes and caverns which permeate the coral reefs. Some of the blue holes have caverns and tunnels within their walls showing formations from when these same areas were above water. The diversity of life within some of the blue holes is enhanced by cool, fresh water mixing with warmer sea water.

Andros Dive Sites

Elkhorn Park and **Domais Pass** provide an excellent array of shallow water corals, thereby introducing novice divers to the intricacies of coral garden life. The white sand, representative of the sea bottom most common inside the reef, gives a bright, reflective background from which to observe sea plants and animals. **Red Shoals** is another shallow dive. It begins in about 15 feet of water and features a huge coral head approximately 200 feet across. Shellfish abound in the crevices found throughout the area. These sites and others, such as **Cowry Reef**, make for interesting night dives, too.

Shipwrecks dot the ocean bottom around Andros. Among them include **THE BARGE**, a well-preserved U.S. Navy assault landing craft in 75 feet of water. At those depths, tan-colored fire coral and other stinging hydroids can often be seen. This wreck does have some fire coral on it, but it's easy to avoid even while feeding resident Nassau Groupers and other fish. Another wreck is the **POTOMAC**. This cargo ship was lost in 35 feet of water over 40 years ago and gives novices a crack at wreck diving.

Several sites in The Bahamas are named **The Wall**, but off Andros **The Wall** refers to an area of coral tunnels, chutes, and fissures in the barrier reef less than a mile offshore from Andros Town. These sites are for intermediate and advanced divers. Sites range from 75 to 190 feet.

Also not far offshore from Andros Town is an area known as the Andros Blue Holes. Two of the most famous and deepest are **Benjamin's Blue Hole**, discovered by George Benjamin in 1967 during some of the early scuba explorations from Andros, and **Charlie's Hole**, which was charted by Jacques Cousteau and members of his dive team. These holes are blessed with incredible clarity which sometimes approaches 200 feet. Formations associated with above-ground caves are found in tunnels which wind deep within the coral. Sponges, shellfish, and cave fish abound.

The Crater is a 100-foot-deep blue hole which exposes sensational rock formations, caves, and the creatures which live there. Near it are **The Catacombs**, an aptly named dive site at the north edge of the reef wall. At its deepest depth of 90 feet, visibility still approaches 100 feet. There are tunnels to explore, black coral and large coral heads.

Paw Paw Cay near Mastic Point also has many blue holes near it. One of the most interesting has a small opening at ten feet which leads to a deeper coral cavern. A huge blue hole is the opening to **King Kong's Cave**, an enormous underwater cavern southwest of Paw Paw Cay. Divers could spend their entire vacation at this site alone. It is rated as one of the area's most exciting dives.

Joultier's Cay, off the north coast of Andros, provides access to areas inside and outside the great reef. It is a good place for underwater photography and spotting pelagic fish.

Valley of Sponges lives up to its name. At its deepest it is 75 feet and provides a haven for a multitude of shallow and intermediate water sponge species. Light currents here help the sponges thrive.

Jeff's Ladder, in 30 feet to 60 feet of water, offers a colorful array of corals, sponges and shellfish. **The Giant Staircase** steps down from 80 feet to 120 feet. This is a spectacular dive for the experienced and many secretive species can be hiding on coral ledges and in crevices. **The Elevator Shaft** is another formidable experience for divers who know how to handle themselves in coral tunnels. It starts at 70 feet and drops to 120 feet. It's a rewarding dive that will stimulate your imagination with its reality. It combines colorful coral formations with unexpected sightings of anemones and other invertebrates.

The Coral Caverns reach a depth of 90 feet. They have several 40- to 50-feet tall coral pillars. There are mazes of walls between which divers swim and it's fun to explore them closely to discover what different species thrive in adjacent microenvironments created by changes in light and depth.

Sea Turtle Ridge is a favorite of turtles and divers alike. Sea turtles are often seen in the 30 feet to 60 feet of water of this site. Excellent visibility helps to make this a fun dive.

Near Nicholl's Town the barrier reef comes within a quarter mile of shore. Known as **Nicholl's Town Wall**, this part of the reef begins in 70 feet of water and in places is 30 yards wide. This area equals any wall diving around. Many dive sites are popular on both sides of the

wall with visibility averaging 100 feet.

Klein's Deli, off Long Cay, is a good dive for novices ready for more of a challenge. At 50 feet deep, its sand bottom is graced with coral heads and sponges.

Conch Alley follows corridors of coral 40 feet to 60 feet down. It is a good place to find shells, sea fans, and shellfish. It's also a place where novices can practice moving gently and cautiously to avoid kicking sand up to the face masks of dive buddies.

Caverns and Caves is another site that hooks novices on diving. High visibility in 25 feet of gentle water allows divers to cruise through coral mazes and begin to experience that relaxed-alert state needed to fully enjoy diving.

Chinatown gets its name from the plate coral there which resembles Chinese hats. These high coral mounds grow in 70 feet to 80 feet of water.

These two sites we saved for last. The first is the **Great Stalactite Blue Hole**. Guides won't usually take you there unless you ask them to. It is a challenge to the intermediate and advanced diver. Located on the south end of the island, it takes a good truck to get there, but is a must-dive during the off-season when tropical storms may make the rest of the area rough. The hole is 250 feet deep with visibility at approximately 100 feet. Magnificent stalactites and a diversity of sea life caused by the mixing of fresh and salt water make this a super dive.

And for the really adventurous diver is **Cay Sal Bank**. It's southwest of Andros and about 30 miles from Cuba. It has coral life and formations much different from anything near Andros. Visibility usually is around 100 feet, so you can easily see plane wrecks, shipwrecks, black coral, invertebrates, barracuda, shark, and more. Depths average 30 feet to 70 feet.

Andros Dive Services

ANDROS UNDERSEA ADVENTURES
   Owner: Neal Watson
Service Address:
   Nicholl's Town; Andros, Bahamas
Mailing Address:
   P.O. Box 21766; Ft. Lauderdale, Fl 33335
Service Telephone:
   305/763-2188 (Florida & Canada)
   800/327-8150
Reservation Telephone:
   Same as above Call 9 am–5 pm Mon–Fri
Hours Service is Open:

8 am–5 pm Seven days a week
Resort Affiliation:
Andros Beach Hotel
Rooms:
24
Cottages/Villas:
Several

Besides taking Bahamasair, divers to Andros can take a charter plane to Nicholl's Town Airport from Ft. Lauderdale and Nassau. Andros Undersea offers a resort course as well as NAUI certification for all levels of training.

Andros Undersea takes divers to nearby reef sites along the 142-mile barrier reef off the east coast of Andros. It is packed with good diving and divers will go to a different type of site each day. Most of the dives range from 15 feet to 70 feet, with wall diving along the face of the barrier reef to sites as deep as 110 feet overlooking the Tongue of the Ocean. The variety of sites available through Andros Undersea includes exploring some of the most fascinating blue holes in the area.

Shorter boat rides and diving diversity are enhanced since this service has five 30-foot to 40-foot custom dive boats. One two-tank dive is offered in the morning, and there is a one-tank afternoon dive. There are frequent night dives. Most divers sign up for an all-inclusive dive package. Andros Undersea Adventures is convenient. It is competitive. And it provides everything the diver needs.

Between dives, guests fish, sail, or take off to one of the nearby beaches.

SMALL HOPE BAY LODGE
Service Address:
Fresh Creek; Andros, Bahamas
Mailing Address:
P.O. Box 21667; Ft. Lauderdale, Fl 33335
Service Telephone:
809/368-2014 or 368-2015
Reservation Telephone:
800/223-6961 or 305/463-9130 (Florida)
Hours Service is Open:
8 am–5 pm Seven days a week
Resort Affiliation:
Small Hope Bay Lodge
Rooms:
NA
Cottages/Villas:
20 villas, all built on the beach

Small Hope Bay has charter plane service out of Ft. Lauderdale, in addition to Bahamasair landing at Andros Town Airport. The field is a ten-minute taxi ride away from the resort.

Small Hope Bay Lodge enjoys an excellent reputation for the service it gives divers above and below the water. Owned and operated by Richard and Rosi Birch since its beginning 26 years ago, Small Hope has a friendly ambience which provides both comraderie and solitude.

They offer a resort training course for novices. Every other diver is required to go through their modest, open-water check out. They have complete rental services and do some repair work, specializing in Sherwood equipment. They have two dive boats and keep dive parties at 15 or less.

The dive sites from Small Hope Bay appeal to all skill levels. They offer two morning dives and one afternoon dive. Special features include all-day dive trips, and an early bird wall dive. They will make night dives for a minimum of six divers.

Beginning divers and snorkelers will enjoy such shallow dives as Trumpet Reef, Love Hill Channel, and Clarinet Cut. Intermediate and advanced divers explore the Coral Caverns at 90 feet, wrecks, such as The Barge, and blue holes. Wall dives over the Tongue of the Ocean range from 70 feet to an incredible 185 feet. Recently, their divers found a huge coral pillar with an opening at 50 feet leading to vertical tunnels which cut through the coral to within ten feet of the surface. If you want to dive this one, ask for Brad's Mountain.

Small Hope Bay Lodge is a family resort. They offer other water sports and rent bikes for touring the island. The resort's nightlife centers around the patio and bar.

Margo Nelson

BIMINI

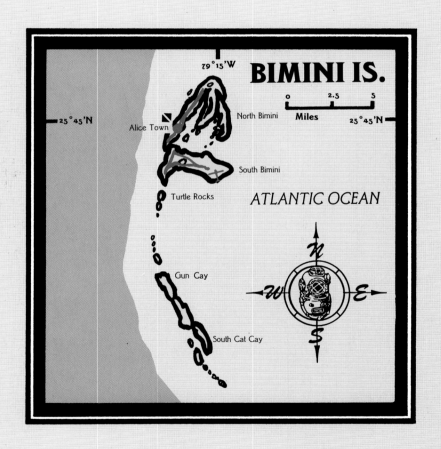

BIMINI IS.

29°15'W

North Bimini

Alice Town

South Bimini

Turtle Rocks

ATLANTIC OCEAN

Gun Cay

South Cat Cay

25°45'N

25°45'N

0   2.5   5

Miles

Bimini is another group of islands and cays referred to under one name. The two main islands, North Bimini and South Bimini, have a combined surface area of 11 square miles and are separated by a narrow channel of water. Bimini is about 50 miles from Miami and 105 miles from Nassau.

Much of the population of 1,600 lives in Alice Town, which is the main tourist center. Bailey Town and Porgy Bay are the other prominent settlements. The local economy is almost totally supported by recreation.

Getting There/ Getting Around

Chalk's Airlines serves North Bimini with daily seaplane flights from Miami, Fort Lauderdale, and Nassau. Chalk's has a 30-pound limit on luggage, so travel light to Bimini or pay for the extra baggage. The seaplanes land off Alice Town and most of the resorts are nearby. A minibus is usually waiting on shore to transport tourists to their resort, if necessary. There is also a 5,000 foot-long airstrip on South Bimini. On Bimini, most people walk to wherever they need to go. A ferry boat provides service between North and South Bimini; the ride takes about ten minutes.

Topside Attractions

Known as the "Big Game Fishing Capital of the World," the waters off Bimini have yielded many world record big game fish records. There is also excellent panfishing and bonefishing in the flats around the islands.

The Gulf Stream passes between Bimini and the Florida coast making sailing a popular sport. Fishing and sailing combine with diving to give Bimini a three-pronged attack with which to satisfy the pursuits of the water sports enthusiast. Bimini's marinas can provide full services and provisions for your boat, or rent boats to you, with or without guides. It is best to bring as much of your personal fishing gear as possible.

Bimini's accommodations are more than adequate in providing tourist services at various prices. There are more than a half dozen good restaurants and lounges serving Bahamian food and rum, along with meat and liquor flown in from the U.S.

The main islands have several good beaches. Calm waters make it appealing to rent a boat and go to a small uninhabited cay for an afternoon.

Bimini Diving

More and more divers are discovering the undersea of Bimini. Easy access to the island, with an off-season during the winter months when most of the other islands are the busiest, help make Bimini attractive. Because Bimini is so small, all popular dive sites are a quick boat ride away. For those who plan to dive from a private boat, remember that a cruising permit is required while in Bahamian waters.

Bimini's most enticing wall dives and drift dives are off its west coast in an area known as the continental shelf. Within the barrier reefs which surround the islands and cays are black coral gardens, vintage wrecks, valleys of sponges and blue holes. Sunken formations of stone, which appear to be cut and set in place, beckon many divers to explore them and speculate about their origins.

Bimini Dive Sites

Hawksbill Reef, a 45-foot dive inside the barrier reef, is home for tube sponges, sea fans, cup sponges, and a host of small, mobile invertebrates and fish.

The **Continental Shelf** is a 2,000-foot drop-off into the trench between Florida and the west edge of the Great Bahamas Bank. The drift diving is great. Drift diving is about all that divers do because of the two- to three-knot Gulf Stream Current which constantly flows through here.

Twenty feet down are the **Bimini Walls**, a formation of huge square stone blocks set together in a 300-foot wall. The stones are of unknown origin and age. It is not even known for sure if the rocks came from near Bimini.

The Kinks is a hot spot for spotted eagle rays, sting rays, grouper and jewfish. Moray eel hide in the coral canyons and crevices among the coral heads.

Two giant brain corals are the prominent feature of a coral garden known as **Turtle Heads**. Seawhips and sea fans abound. There are sponges growing upon ledges of limestone and mounds of coral.

THE SAPONA is a shipwreck that sits upright 20 feet down. Fish and divers swim through the holes in its concrete hull. There is good coral and many reef fish nearby.

Bimini Dive Services

BIMINI UNDERSEA ADVENTURES
Owner: Neal Watson
Service Address:
Alice Town; North Bimini, Bahamas

Mailing Address:
P.O. Box 21766; Ft. Lauderdale, FL 33335
Service Telephone:
305/763-2188 (Florida and Canada)
800/327-8150 (U.S.A.)
Reservation Telephone:
Same as above. Call from 9 am–5 pm Mon–Fri
Hours Service is Open:
8 am–5 pm Seven days a week
Resort Affiliation:
Bimini Big Game Fishing Club and Hotel
Rooms:
35
Cottages/Villas:
16
Brown's Hotel:
30

Most people who fly to Bimini take one of Chalk's seaplanes from Miami to the seaplane ramp off Alice Town, Bimini. Some divers make the 60–mile trip by boat and tie in at the Alice Town marina. If you want to do that, reserve a slip first from the marina.

This service has comparable dive packages and services similar to Neal Watson's other ventures. By calling the dive service number listed above, you can get the prices on any of Neal's operations. Room reservations as well as dive reservations can be made directly through Neal without having to contact the resorts with which he is affiliated.

Two fine examples of Bimini diving are the Gulfstream Wall, an exciting drift dive off the Bimini Wall facing Florida, and the wreck of the Sapona, a popular dive also with good coral and shell life.

The appeal of Bimini diving is twofold. It is extremely easy for divers to get there from Florida, and Bimini is a resort island with accommodations at various levels and meals which is attractive to a wide variety of people.

Steve Rosenberg

CAT ISLAND

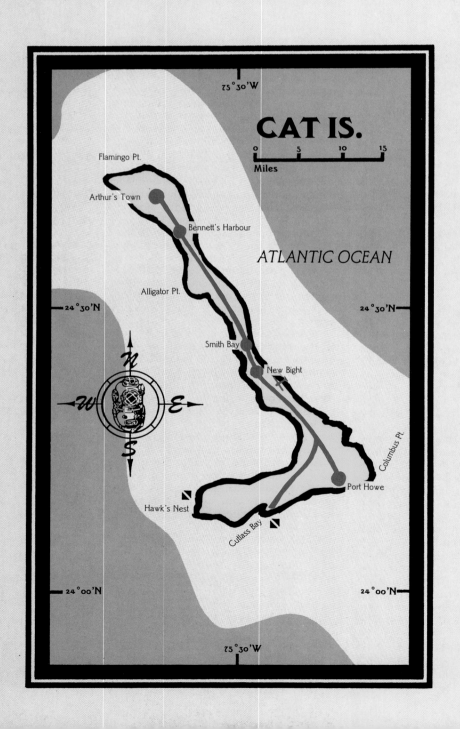

CAT IS.

0   5   10   15

Miles

75°30'W

Flamingo Pt.

Arthur's Town

Bennett's Harbour

ATLANTIC OCEAN

Alligator Pt.

24°30'N   24°30'N

Smith Bay

New Bight

Columbus Pt.

Port Howe

Hawk's Nest

Cutlass Bay

24°00'N   24°00'N

75°30'W

N

W   E

S

Undeveloped and unspoiled, Cat Island lies near the middle of The Bahamas island chain. The island is 48 miles long and has an area of about 150 square miles. Located 130 miles southeast of Nassau and 325 miles southeast of Miami, Cat Island also boasts the highest point in The Bahamas—the 207-foot summit of Mt. Alvernia.

Native plants cover the relatively steep hills on the coast of the island. Farther south, tropical forests are dominant. Cat Island is the most fertile of The Bahamas. American Loyalists settled here with their slaves in the seventeen hundreds. The Bahamaian soils, however, could not tolerate intensive culture for long. After disease ravaged the cotton crop, most of the owners abandoned the island and left their slaves behind. Plantation ruins still dot the countryside which had been cleared to grow cotton and other crops.

On Cat Island, visitors do not have to sail to an uninhabited cay to find a private beach. The west coast beaches are protected from the Atlantic to the east. The main road, though poorly maintained, traverses almost the full length of Cat and provides access to long, private stretches of white sand beaches backed with palm trees and small coastal settlements.

Cat Island. has a population of nearly 2,000 with most of the residents living on the south one-third of the island in the villages of Port Howe, Moss Town, and The Bight. Near the north end is Arthurs Town, which serves as a base from which tourists can explore the wild north coast.

Getting There/ Getting Around

There are airports near The Bight and Arthurs Town. Bahamasair serves both fields with Monday and Thursday flights. Taxis are available to meet incoming flights.

Topside Attractions

Miles of secluded beaches are Cat Island's main topside attraction; however, major towns such as The Bight and Port Howe have good restaurants, shops and local entertainment. The major resorts also have restaurants and lounges.

For an island tour, visit the Armbrister Plantation ruins and The Hermitage on Mount Alvernia. From The Hermitage, a retreat built by the late Father Jerome, you can get a great view of the ocean and island. Another sightseeing stop are the caves on the south tip of the island which were inhabited by Arawak Indians.

Cat Island Diving

Cat Island's reefs contain great numbers of fishes and corals. The one active dive service on the island is adding to the list of known sites, which include terraces and coral gardens inside the barrier reefs. Steep walls, such as Hawk's Nest Wall, plunge down to 1,200 feet. Groupers and barracuda frequent the shipwrecks and caves. Hawksbill turtles and rays cruise through some of the grassy flats.

In short, Cat Island has satisfied many divers in the past. With support services topside, it will do so again.

Cat Island Dive Sites

The Amphitheatre, located on the wall off the southern part of the island, is a bowl scooped into the reef. Beginning at 60 feet, it has sides of coral over which dangle several different types of sponges. It slopes down to 100 feet and a bottom of white sand where groupers and horse-eye jacks gather around the coral. Coral canyons are cut in the reef above; some are wide enough for divers to explore.

Marine life on the quarter-mile-long ridge known as **The Ledge** has giant basket sponges, brain coral, gorgonians and pillar corals. It is an excellent sample of how different coral and sponge species grow together.

Ball Rock Reef is a site where divers frequently see hawksbill turtle. It begins in 20 feet of water and has stands of elkhorn and staghorn coral, quite a few small baitfish, anemones, and some giant red starfish.

Cat Island Dive Services

CUTLASS BAY CLUB
Service Address:
Cutless Bay; Cat Island, Bahamas
Mailing Address:

Same as above
Service Telephone:
305/462-4420
Reservation Telephone:
305/584-7487
Resort Affiliation:
Cutlass Bay Club
Rooms:
13

This service offers no instruction or certification. This is a small resort which is more into fishing and boating than diving. It is commonly listed as a dive resort, so we wanted to tell you that it no longer offers much. The resort still has a compressor, however.

HAWK'S NEST CLUB
Service Address:
Devil's Point; Cat Island, Bahamas (Extreme southern end)
Mailing Address:
P.O. Box 3190, Ocala, FL 32678
Service Telephone:
800/426-4222 (U.S.A.) 904/368-2500 (FL)
Reservation Telephone:
Same as above
Hours Service is Open:
Open any hours the customers want.
Resort Affiliation:
Hawk's Nest Club
Rooms:
10
Cottages/Villas:
One guest house

Most Hawk's Nest guests get to this resort either via private charter or Bahamasair. Flights depart from Ft. Lauderdale.

This resort has been closed for a while, but is now open and developing a solid commitment to the sport and vacation diver. They are getting a full rental shop in order and plan to have full-time dive personnel on staff. These people really bend over backwards to provide for their customers. We feel their dive service, with the comraderie and joy the staff has toward one another and to the customer, will bloom into a high-quality service which will receive high marks both underwater and topside.

At the moment, Hawk's Nest does diving inside and outside the Cat Island Reef. They have some special cave dives and do wreck diving. Boat dives are reached from either a 24-foot or a 31-foot dive boat, with duties handled by a part-time dive master.

Hawk's Nest has tennis courts, fishing, *great* food and small, friendly crowds. If you are looking for a place you can fall into and feel at home, this is it.

BERRY ISLANDS
CHUB CAY

This arc of islands, located about 20 miles northeast of Andros and 35 miles north of Nassau, is made up of over 30 cays which run predominantly north to south. The total land mass of these islands is just 12 miles. There are two main stops—Great Harbour Cay and Chub Cay, which are at opposite sides of this island group. Chub Cay, located at the southern tip, is a full-service resort and offers the only scuba diving in the area.

The Berry Islands have never supported many people, though today a few fishermen live throughout them. Much of the land is privately owned and privately used, but secluded beachfronts on a few of the small cays can be secured for an afternoon.

The islands lie upon the Great Bahama Bank. Bonefishing, small game and large game fishing is topped only by Bimini. The reefs to the islands' east lie on the edge of the Tongue of the Ocean.

Getting There/ Getting Around

Chub Cay Resort has a marina and an airstrip. Flights are available between Nassau and Chub Cay via a charter through Lucayan Air Service on Mondays, Wednesdays, and Saturdays. At Chub's full-service marina, boats can be rented and supplied for island cruises. Essential services are available for private planes at its airstrip.

Topside Attractions

The resort's amenities, including many sports, are the prime topside pastimes. There are a few sites to see on the other cays, but sailing, fishing and socializing are the prime pursuits.

Berry Island Diving

Miles of wall diving along the barrier reef bordering the Tongue of the Ocean are accessible from Chub Cay. Inside the reef divers go as deep as 100 feet to explore lairs of marine animals hidden among coral gardens, tunnels, and fissures of coral and rock. Within and beyond the barrier reef visibility is almost always in the 100-foot range as there is no measureable runoff from these small islands.

Sites are plentiful for beginners, intermediate, and expert divers. There are many good photographic sites around the smaller cays. The area is a favorite of people who enjoy solitude and intimacy both above and below the water.

Berry Island Dive Sites

Chub Cay Wall has schools of horse-eye jack, some angelfish and eagle rays along its almost vertical face. **The Salad Bar** slopes from 60 feet to 100 feet. Sponges and black coral are part of the wide variety of life found here.

Mama Rhoda Rock is part of a shallow reef thick with elkhorn and staghorn corals. Starfish and shellfish are often found near or at the base of the coral formations. Excellent visiblity benefits photographers and snorkelers.

Canyons and Caves is an area of small caves and fissures which honeycomb the reef. Eels are occasionally lured from their holes while other fish voluntarily come to investigate divers. **Angelfish Reef** features corals which thrive in 40 feet to 70 feet of water. This area is more open than Canyons and Caves, making it less likely for divers to bump into coral and more likely to see some of the larger small game fish.

Chub Flats Snorkel is a shallow drift dive through an area that is dotted with shellfish and shells. Shallow water fish abound and, as the name implies, it is also a favorite of snorkelers.

Chub Cay Dive Services

CHUB CAY UNDERSEA ADVENTURES
Owner: Neal Watson
Service Address:
  Chub Cay; Berry Islands, Bahamas
Mailing Address:
  P.O. Box 21766; Ft. Lauderdale, FL 33335
Service Telephone:
  305/763-2188 (Florida and Canada)
  800/327-8150 (U.S.A.)
Reservation Telephone:
  Same as above. Call 9 am–5 pm Mon–Fri
Hours Service is Open:
  8 am to 5 pm Seven days a week

Resort Affiliation:
  Chub Cay Hotel 809/325-1490
Rooms:
  20
Cottages/Villas:
  NA

Chub Cay Undersea Adventures, along with Andros Undersea and Bimini Undersea, is owned by Neal Watson. As mentioned earlier, guests to Chub Cay are chartered a flight out of Ft. Lauderdale and land at the island's airfield.

Chub Cay rests on the Great Bahama Bank and practically looks down into the north end of the Tongue of the Ocean. Divers of all levels come to Chub Cay where seclusion and excellent diving are both easily accessible. Chub Cay Undersea offers a two-tank morning dive and a one-tank afternoon dive. Night diving is available on request. A range of options is available through the service's all-inclusive dive package.

Resort courses plus NAUI certification are available, as are full rental services and repair services. Their services can accommodate up to 40 divers, but they have several dive boats in order to keep the diving parties small.

Undersea also has a complete photo lab for underwater photography and their professionals can help you get the most out of that part of sport diving. Each year Chub Cay offers one week underwater photography courses taught by some of the world's top experts.

The Chub Cay Wall is the sight of some of the most exciting dives around the Tongue of the Ocean. Mama Rhoda and Canyons and Caves, two sites described above, show outstanding color and sealife. Flash Point and Shutterbug Reef feature angelfish, sea fans, gorgonians and sergeant majors.

Chub Cay Resort offers a full-service marina, secluded beaches, and excellent fishing to complement the diving.

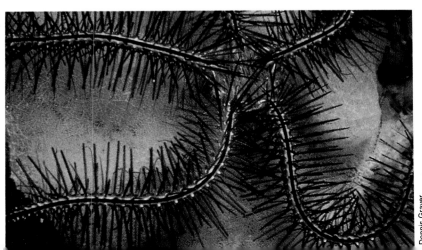

Dennis Graver

CROOKED ISLAND

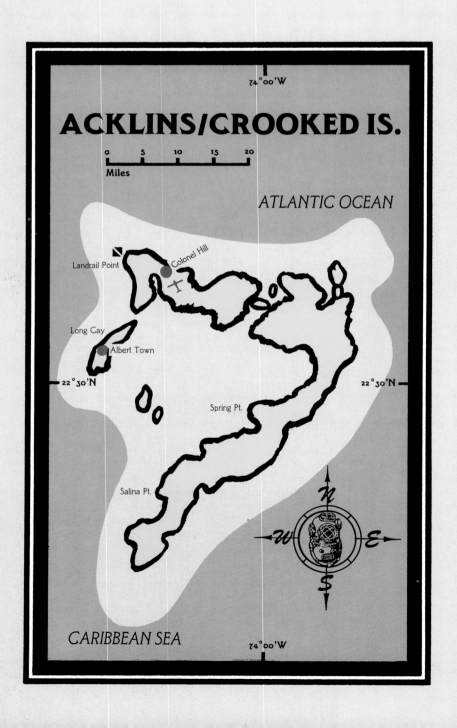

ACKLINS/CROOKED IS.

74°00'W

0 5 10 15 20
Miles

ATLANTIC OCEAN

Landrail Point

Colonel Hill

Long Cay

Albert Town

22°30'N

22°30'N

Spring Pt.

Salina Pt.

N
W E
S

CARIBBEAN SEA

74°00'W

Acklins and Crooked Island are two small islands in the southern Bahamas. Separated by a narrow channel, Crooked Island Passage, they are so close to one another that they are almost always referred to together.

Crooked Island, the smaller of the two islands, is north of Acklins and about 220 miles southeast of Nassau. It is about 22 miles long and five miles wide, encompassing an area of less than 90 square miles. Known as one of the "Fragrant Isles," it was named by Columbus as he sailed by and smelled an aromatic blend of herbs and spices. Acklins Island is about 120 square miles.

The Windward Passage runs along the northwest coast of Crooked Island. During the colonial period when the passage was a prominent shipping lane, Acklins and Crooked Island, along with their surrounding cays, were a favorite hideaway for pirates from which to plunder merchant ships. Later, American Loyalists settled here. For a short time their cotton plantations thrived, until wiped out by a cotton blight. Some of the owners and freed slaves stayed on and made a living sponge fishing and mining sea salt. Today, the 2,200 residents of the two islands make their living from the land, the sea, and tourism.

Though there are tourist facilities on both these islands, only Pittstown Point Landing on Crooked Island has dive services.

Getting There/ Getting Around

Pittstown Point Landings has a private, full-service airstrip for guests. The resort also arranges charter flights from Fort Lauderdale. Except for flying in with your private plane, this option is, by far, the most convenient way to get there. Bahamasair also flies to the airfield at Colonel Hill on Crooked Island twice a week from Nassau. Taxis meet incoming flights.

There is also an airstrip at Spring Point on Acklins Island.

A ferry runs between Browns Crooked Island and Lovely Bay, Acklins. Most resorts will help you find transportation, from taxis to bicycles. The main roads are adequate and make access to fine beaches, the settlements and hamlets, and historical sites easy. Boats are available for you to rent to explore the coastlines of the main islands or to cruise about the cays.

Topside Attractions

Until recently, these islands were overlooked by nearly every tourist. Long stretches of beaches, as well as ones nestled within a small bay, offer seclusion and scenery.

The excellent fishing within the reefs and in the open water is one secret about Crooked Island which has not gotten out yet. These waters have not been fished heavily and everything from bonefish to pelagics are taken.

Tropical bird life is more abundant and colorful here than is found on other islands. The cliffs and caves provide a haven for other creatures as well as giving visitors enticing places to explore. The Caves of Crooked Islands, for example, is a favorite stop, with interiors resembling the ruins of churches and castles.

Other places of interest include the Bird Rock Lighthouse and the Castle Island Lighthouse. Bird Rock was built in 1872 and guards Crooked Island Passage, the passage between Crooked and Acklins islands. Castle Island Lighthouse is on Castle Island, near the southern tip of Acklins.

Hope Great House is another attraction many visitors make a point to see while on Crooked Island. A relic from the era of George V of England, its maintained orchards and gardens are a sanctuary for birds.

Crooked Island Diving

Wall, canyon and wreck diving are the dive specialties of Crooked Island. And, as virtually all the divers who come here are experienced, the guides are prepared and knowledgeable enough to ensure that the diving is challenging and novel. It is also possible to rent small dive boats and explore some of the excellent sites along parts of the barrier reef few people have seen.

The medium dives and deep dives hold an excellent variety of coral formations. Tropical angelfish and grouper are two fish which are frequent diving companions. Other fishlife inside the reef ranges from large eagle rays to the small, shy squirrelfish.

Crooked Island Dive Sites

Thunderball Alley is the best known site of Crooked Island. Teeming with small tropical fish and shellfish which inhabit coral crevices and rock ledges, this site provides divers with countless canyons to explore.

Barracuda City is a dive which drops from 35 feet to 100 feet through coral gardens and ledges.

The Deep is a wall dive that begins in medium depth and offers hard coral formations, some sponge colonies and rock openings which hold many different species of small shellfish and other invertebrates.

The Bathtub is a reef dive through elkhorn and staghorn coral five feet to 20 feet deep. It's a favorite for a tune-up dive and gives divers a chance to identify shallow water marine life.

Crooked Island Dive Services

PITTSTOWN POINT LANDING
Service Address:
 Landrail Point; Crooked Island, Bahamas
Mailing Address:
 P.O. Box 9831; Mobile, Alabama 36691
Service Telephone:
 205/666-4482
Reservation Telephone:
 Same as above
Hours Service is Open:
 8 am–5 pm Seven days a week
Resort Affiliation:
 Pittstown Point Landing
Rooms:
 12 beach front and beach view rooms
Cottages/Villas:
 NA

Pittstown Point justifiably says it is perfect for the private pilot. After landing at its private, full-service airstrip on the island's north coast, pilots can taxi to within 100 feet of their room. Bahamasair lands twice a week at Colonel Hill Airport. Flights are met by taxis which take guests to the resort.

This service is for certified divers only; they do no instruction or certification. Bring your "C" card. They have rental service, but recommend you bring your personal gear, especially your regulator. Their repair work is pretty much limited to maintaining their own equipment.

They offer one two-tank dive in the morning and a two-tank dive in the afternoon. There is no night diving as of this writing. They specialize in diving the 45-mile-long reef wall facing 600-foot deep Crooked Island Passage. Best wall sites include Thunder Alley, The Deep, and Barracuda City. Divers board one of their two 18-foot boats to explore any of several wrecks. Dive parties are small, and a minimum of two divers is all the guide needs to take you to a site.

Pittstown Point Landing offers fishing, windsurfing, and can arrange tours to Acklins and Crooked Island sights. Socializing focuses around the private beach or their small restaurant and lounge. Pittstown Point has a comfortable, uncrowded family atmosphere.

ELEUTHERA

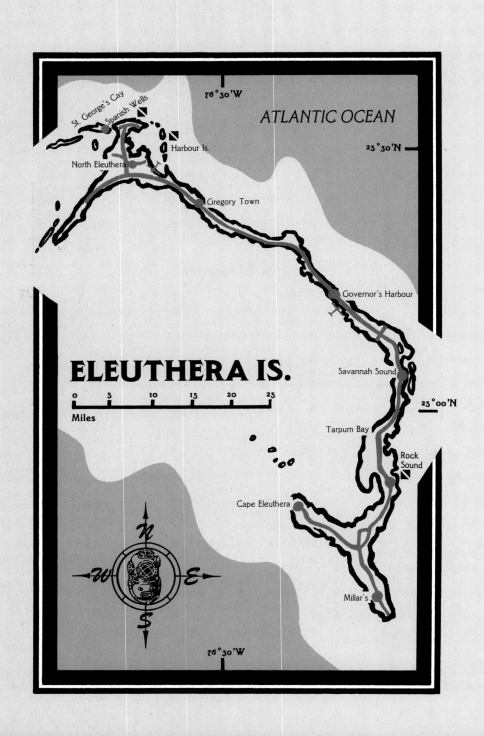

76°30'W

ATLANTIC OCEAN

25°30'N

St. George's Cay
Spanish Wells
Harbour Is.
North Eleuthera

Gregory Town

Governor's Harbour

ELEUTHERA IS.

0   5   10   15   20   25

Miles

Savannah Sound

25°00'N

Tarpum Bay

Rock
Sound

Cape Eleuthera

Millar's

N
W   E
S

76°30'W

Eleuthera is a slender curve of an island 100 miles long and less than two miles wide. It is cherished as one of the most beautiful Bahama Islands. Eleuthera's white beaches and sheltered coves on the west shore of the island and pink-white beaches and limestone cliffs on the Atlantic Coast offer vacationers a chance to experience the pleasures of two distinctly beautiful coastlines.

Eleuthera, with a population of 9,000, along with the resort islands of Spanish Wells and Harbour Island, is the most developed of the Outer Islands. Towns are far enough apart to provide room to roam quiet stretches of beach, yet accommodations and other services are ample throughout the island.

Eleuthera also holds the claim to being the western world's first true democracy, established by a band of settlers who left Bermuda seeking religious freedom. The settlers were shipwrecked on the north coast and managed to survive until a ship of Virginians happened upon them and shared the meager supplies. The first settlers named their new home Eleuthera, the Greek word for freedom.

Slowly, a mixture of people developed Eleuthera into a moderately prosperous agricultural island. As throughout The Bahamas, however, intensive, prolonged farming cannot sustain many people for long. Though fishing and agriculture are still part of the local economic base, visitors are fortunate that the islanders have combined a bounty of recreational pastimes with the natural allure of Eleuthera and its nearby cays.

Harbour Island and Spanish Wells, two major island resort centers off North Eleuthera, add to Eleuthera's appeal. Harbour Island still shows the influences of colonists from New England who settled the island in the 17th century. Many who stay on Eleuthera come to Harbour Island just to experience one of its pink sand beaches. A goombay smash at twilight is a favorite way to enjoy them.

Spanish Wells gets its name for once being an anchorage for Spanish ships to fill up with fresh water. It looks out over the scenic north waters of Eleuthera and is a favorite of modern seafarers and other travelers.

Getting There/ Getting Around

Bahamasair serves all three of Eleuthera's airports. The North Eleuthera Airport is the stop for travelers who are staying near Gregory Town or on Harbour Island and Spanish Wells. Governour's Harbour, near the center of the island, and Rock Sound Airport, near the

prime resort area and main town of Rock Sound, are the other two airports. All three are official ports of entry.

Topside Attractions

Eleuthera's excellent resorts are well supplied with recreational amenities. There is surfing off the east coast where warm Atlantic waves curl into the beaches. All other watersports are available throughout the island and cays.

Eleuthera has a fair system of roads connecting its villages, beaches and resort areas, so touring is a popular topside pastime. Rental cars are available throughout the main island and on Harbour Island. Many of the amenities, such as tennis courts and golf courses, located at resorts, are free to guests and open to visitors for a fee. Restaurants and lounges abound. Quality seafood is served at many of the resorts and town restaurants. No matter where you go you can find someone to suggest a good place nearby at which to eat. The nightlife is not bright, but there is a lot of music and live entertainment especially on weekends.

Among the places to see include the Glass Window Bridge. Dividing North Eleuthera from Central Eleuthera, the Glass Window is the narrow place on the island. A rock arch once stood where the road now passes, separating the blue Atlantic from the turquoise water of the Sound on the West coast. It is just wide enough for one car at a time to drive over.

The 2,500-acre Hatchet Bay Plantation near Hatchet Bay is the largest dairy and poultry farm in The Bahamas. It also grows vegetables for markets through the outer islands.

Preacher's Cave is where the first Eleutheran adventurers sought shelter after being shipwrecked off the north coast.

Tarpum Bay is one of the older settlements and is a favorite of painters and photographers. Its setting includes fishing boats lined along its beach, a church and graveyard, and an odd hilltop castle.

Located at Hatchet Bay, The Cave is a mile long and filled with luminous stalagmites and stalactites. Torchlight gives it the appearance of an underground cathedral.

Near Rock Sound, the most populous center of the island, is Ocean Hole. This "bottomless" hole is a salt water lake with many tropical fish which come to the surface to be fed. If you are near Rock Sound, it is worth the stop.

Eleuthera Diving

Most of the Eleuthera diving is around North Eleuthera, Spanish Wells and Harbour Island. The dive sites range from 10

feet to 100 feet through a tremendous variation of coral. The reefs and shallow waters brought many ships to their demise, leaving an abundance of wrecks, named and unnamed, throughout these waters. There are probably more wrecks per square mile off Harbour Island, than anywhere else in the world. Many of these wrecks have sunk along the 12-mile-long reef known as Devil's Backbone, which runs between Harbour Island and Spanish Wells.

There are outstanding coral arches, tunnels, and rock formations. If you make ten different dives you will feel as though you have experienced ten different parts of the world.

There is no real wall diving here, but the north waters of Eleuthera offer some of the best current diving in the world as the Atlantic swirls between the islands and outer reef formations. The **Current Cut**, for example, carries divers along in a seven- to 10-knot current when the tides are moving.

Divers can expect to see many variations of coral formations and other marine life off Eleuthera. Sea plumes, sea fans, and other soft corals frequently cover coral ridges. Small caves abound with shellfish and other crustaceans. There is a thrilling mix of fish life, from small shark to rays to parrot fish.

Eleuthera Dive Sites

Twelve-mile-long Devil's Backbone, though a terror to boaters, is a diver's delight. This shallow reef has broken and sunk many steel-hulled and wooden-hulled ships. At low tide, heads of elkhorn coral rise above the water's surface. Below these formations are hard corals and fire coral. Divers should be cautious of the fire coral which grows on some of the wrecks listed below. All are off the Devil's Backbone.

David McCray

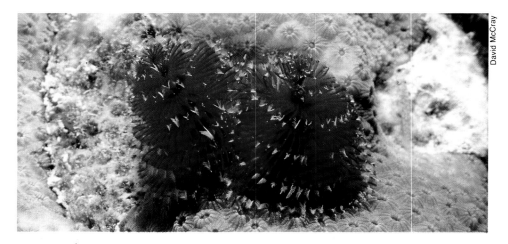

David McCray

THE POTATO AND ONION WRECK, a small coastal freighter, is in 15 feet of water. Sunk in a storm in 1969, she was tossed about the rocks and reef until she settled down to where she is now.

THE CARNARVON is an old 200-foot-long steel freighter with coral formations on it and good fish life around and in its intact stern. Sunk in 1916, it gives divers a good feel for how the sea reclaims steel.

CIVIL WAR TRAIN WRECK is the encrusted remains of a train which fell overboard when its barge hit the reef. It is one of several sites where divers feed grouper, angelfish, and other tropicals.

The Plateau is a large coral plateau cut with deep crevices and populated with tame groupers and snappers that eat out of your hand. It blends hard and soft corals with all kinds of sponges on top of and around the plateau. Its base is in about 90 feet of water.

Miller's Reef is an excellent site for photography. A coral archway leads to the reef's plateau, where eagle rays and jacks are often seen cruising through the formations.

The Current Cut, as mentioned, is the most popular and thrilling of the current dives in The Bahamas. Its depth varies from 30 feet to 60 feet and winds by rock and canyons of coral. Barracuda, rays, and horse-eye jacks watch as divers cruise through the narrow channel between North Eleuthera and Current Island.

Split Reef is a great example of the types of coral tunnels and crevices which curve through this area. Located a half-mile from Current Cut, this site has rope sponges and other sponge species which grow with the hard coral along the formation's walls.

The Arch is a deep dive from 80 feet to 110 feet. Divers see various large fish species here, and visiblity is good enough to watch and photograph them. The deepwater corals combine with the rock formations to provide a dive site with more to see than one dive can hold. This is a good one to come back to.

Eleuthera Dive Services

COTTON BAY CLUB
Service Address:
P.O. Box 28; Rock Sound, Eleuthera, Bahamas
Mailing Address:
Same as above
Service Telephone:
809/334-2101 or 334-2156
Reservation Telephone:
800/843-2297 (U.S.A.)
Hours Service is Open:
8 am to 4 pm Seven days a week
Resort Affiliation:
Cotton Bay Club
Rooms:
77

Guests land at Rock Sound Airport via Bahamasair or one of the other commercial lines which provide occasional service. Taxis or rental cars are available at the airport.

The Cotton Bay Club does offer diving, but it does not have a full dive service or dive shop. Their rental services are adequate, but you are encouraged to bring your personal dive gear. Diving is a small part of what Cotton Bay offers, and, as they give no instruction, only certified divers can dive here. They have one dive boat with a capacity of ten.

Jimmy Wilson is the dive master. He takes divers to sites along the shallow reef to outside the barrier wall.

Cotton Bay Club's emphasis is on fishing, boating, golf, and tennis. For the occasional diver who wants a plush, tropical getaway, Cotton Bay is worth considering.

ROMORA BAY CLUB
Service Address:
Harbour Island; Eleuthera, Bahamas
Mailing Address:
P.O. Box 7026; Boca Raton, FL 33431
Service Telephone:
809/333-2324 and 333-2325
Reservation Telephone:
800/326-8266 (U.S.A.) 305/997-9699 (Florida)
Hours Service is Open:
7:30 am–5:30 pm Seven days a week
Resort Affiliation:
Romora Bay Club
Rooms:
30
Cottages/Villas:
Available

Taxis meet guests at the North Eleuthera Airport, then it's a one-mile ride to the dock where guests board a ferry for a trip direct to the Romora Bay Club dock two miles across the bay.

Romora's dive team conducts both resort courses and open water PADI and YMCA certification. Certification is available to those only with a referral letter verifying they've done the classroom and close water dives.

All levels of diver come for fun to the Romora Bay Club. Romora's specialties are deep reef dives including The Plateau down to 90 feet, and The Arch from 80 feet to 110 feet and, of course, the Current Cut drift dive. An abundance of wreck dive sites and coral gardens for beginners and novices take less than 15 minutes to get to by boat.

Romora's dive center has full rental and repair services. They dive in the morning and afternoon, with night diving on request. Dive packages are offered.

Between dives, Romora offers a full selection of watersports. Guests not only enjoy themselves at Romora's waterfront lounge in the evening, but also at a couple of Harbour Island's local spots for seafood, an ocean view, and a party.

SPANISH WELLS BEACH RESORT
Service Address:
Spanish Wells; Eleuthera, Bahamas
c/o Win Chesley Associates, Inc.
Mailing Address:
4316 W. Broward Blvd., Suite 5; Plantation, FL 33317
Service Telephone:
809/332-2645
Reservation Telephone:
800/327-5118 (U.S.A.) 800/432-1362 (FL) 791-5118 (Local)
Hours Service is Open:
8 am–10 pm Seven days a week
Spanish Wells Beach Resort

Spanish Wells Harbour Club

(Note—These two resorts are run to-gether and guests have access to both)

Guests of these resorts land at North Eleuthera Airport via Bahamasair or Transair from Ft. Lauderdale or West Palm Beach. After short taxi and ferry rides, they are left off at the Beach Resort dock.

At Spanish Wells, resort courses, PADI certification and advanced open-water training are offered. They have full rental and repair services. Dive packages include morning and afternoon dives, with night diving available on request.

Divers are assured of well-planned, quality diving through Spanish Wells. Trips are planned to make use of the area's many opportunities for underwater photography. They have overnight E-6 film processing.

As mentioned, the North Eleuthera area has as many or more wrecks per square mile of reef as anywhere in the world. Spanish Wells dives many of these including the Potato and Onion Wreck, The Cienfuegos, and The Civil War Train Wreck. They dive the gardens and crevices off the Lighthouse Reef and Devil's

Backbone. The Current Cut is also in their repertoire.

This full-service resort area also has tennis, bicycling, excellent beaches, and puts a strong emphasis on fishing and most other watersports.

VALENTINE'S DIVE CENTER
Service Address:
P.O. Box 1; Harbour Island, Bahamas
Mailing Address:
3928 Shelbyville Road; Louisville, KY 40207
Service Telephone:
809/333-2309
Reservation Telephone:
800/662-2255 (after first ring dial 832); 502/897-6481
Hours Service is Open:
8 am–5 pm Seven days a week
Resort Affiliation:
Valentine's Hotel

Guests arrive at North Eleuthera Airport from either Florida or Nassau on Transair, Aero Coach or Bahamasair. They take the ferry and go ashore at Government Dock, near the Valentine Hotel, on Harbour Island.

Valentine's is a full-service resort combining the amenities of a unique island

with fine underwater sites that the staff makes more thrilling with special dives. They will supply everything the diver needs, including resort courses and SSI open-water training, equipment, and photography instruction and film processing. Their dive boat fleet includes a 36-foot custom-built Thompson Trailer complete with fresh water shower and sink for camera rinsing. Qualified divers can take one of the resort's smaller boats and do their own diving.

They offer one-tank dives in the morning, afternoon and evening. They have sites along 38 miles of reef, including The Arch, The Plateau, The Current Cut and cave dives. They do the thrilling Dutch Bars Shark Dive beyond the barrier reef, where divers in floating cages watch as their dive guides chum the water and lure sharks in from the deep.

For years the staff of Valentine's has prided themselves on friendly, quality service. Their thoroughness enhances the diving; they are always helpful and never meddlesome. This attractive resort has a full line of watersports, tennis, the pink sand beach on the Atlantic side of the island, and helps you enjoy the pleasures and sites on Eleuthera, just across the bay.

Bahama Tourist

EXUMA

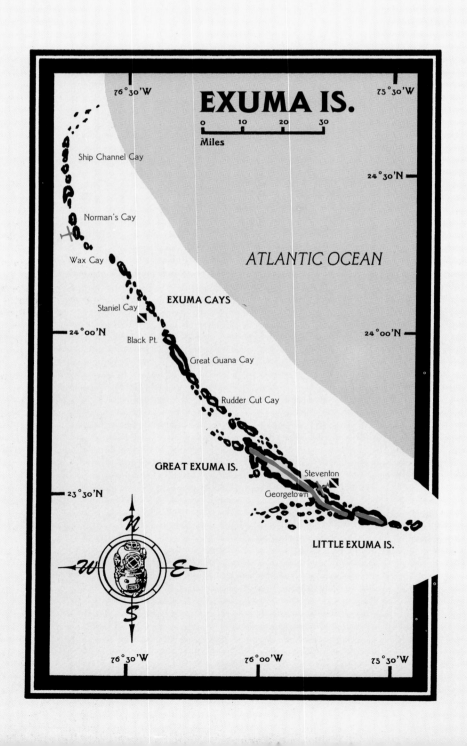

EXUMA IS.

0 10 20 30
Miles

76°30'W

75°30'W

24°30'N

Ship Channel Cay

Norman's Cay

ATLANTIC OCEAN

Wax Cay

EXUMA CAYS

Staniel Cay

24°00'N

24°00'N

Black Pt.

Great Guana Cay

Rudder Cut Cay

GREAT EXUMA IS.

Steventon

23°30'N

Georgetown

LITTLE EXUMA IS.

N
W E
S

76°30'W

76°00'W

75°30'W

The Exumas are a chain of 365 isles which begin 35 miles south-southeast of Nassau and run for 100 miles down to Hog Cay. The vast majority of the isles are unnamed, with Staniel Cay, Great Exuma and Little Exuma being the islands of major interest to most tourists.

Together, Great Exuma and Little Exuma have an area of 130 square miles. Residents grow enough fruits and vegetables to export their surplus to other islands. Fish, conch and lobster are other island mainstays, and the sponge fishing industry is making a comeback as a commercial venture.

Though some of these islands are in the tropics, a subtropical climate dominates throughout the year. The islands are hilly with long, sloping beaches and excellent shelling on some of the more secluded ones. The calm waters around isolated, uninhabited cays create one of the yachtsman's favorite cruising areas.

The Exumas have a population of just about 4,000. There are small settlements along both the east and west coasts. Georgetown, the capital, is on the east coast of the southern part of Great Exuma. It has a large part of the islands' 4,000 residents and is the center of business and tourism. Georgetown had once been considered as the capital of The Bahamas due mainly to its fine deep-water port, Elizabeth Harbour.

Getting There/ Getting Around

Most dive travelers will get to Exuma via Bahamasair which has daily flights into Georgetown Airport. The other airstrip of interest to travelers is the runway on Staniel Cay which serves the resorts there.

You can count on a taxi being at Georgetown Airport to meet the plane and you will be able to rent a car in Georgetown, and a bike or scooter at most of the resorts.

Topside Attractions

Georgetown and vicinity are the key to most of the topside activity. Its 5-mile-long harbor has full-service marinas, and a good number of private boating parties stop there for supplies and shore leave. Across the bay is Lee Stocking Island, a long, thin island with pure beaches; a favorite of sunbathers and divers. More will be mentioned about Stocking in the dive-site section.

Boating is the biggest draw of the Exumas, be it for bonefishing, big game fishing, yachting, or exploring. A place well worth mentioning is the Exuma

Land and Sea Park, which is accessible only by boat. Lying northwest of Staniel Cay, it is a 22-mile-long protected area of land and sea encompassing many small cays, coral gardens and is a sanctuary for rare tropical birds, fish and other animals.

The Queen's Highway runs from the south end of Little Exuma to the north tip of Great Exuma, with the two islands being connected by a bridge, but the roads are poor and touring is not the reason to go to Exuma. This is no reflection upon the people who live there. Most are friendly, but the farther you get from Georgetown the less maintained most stretches of road tend to be.

Touring the cays by boat is a totally different story, however. There are many private beaches and secluded coves available and accessible. As elsewhere, though, if you see "No Trespassing" signs, or other evidence that you are approaching privately owned land, keep sailing because there are places to go where no one will disturb you, nor will you disturb anyone.

Besides boating and fishing, most other watersports are available. Bahamian food and local entertainment are offered with pride in the resort areas.

Exuma Diving

Exuma has an excellent selection of challenging dives off its north and west coasts and new sites are being discovered as dive boats explore along the outer reefs and cays. Blue holes and deep and shallow caves which tunnel into reef and rock dominate sites off Lee Stocking Island. Elsewhere there is wall diving at sites which start anywhere from 45 feet to 140 feet. Experienced divers head for open water and dive along formations bordering Exuma Sound, a 5,000-foot drop-off.

Throughout the coral gardens and gently sloping undersea terraces, shellfish, sponges and other invertebrates offer a bounty of underwater photographic opportunities. Some of the sites near shore have a visibility of 50 feet and more while farther out it can exceed 100 feet.

The main areas of resort diving are around Norman's Cay and Staniel Cay, both in the north part of the chain, Lee Stocking Island, and the walls and open water near Stocking Island.

The closer we look at Exuma the better it gets.

Exuma Dive Sites

Eagle's Eyrie and **Black Forest** are two excellent sites on the wall north of Norman's Cay. At **Eagle's Eyrie** the wall starts at 65 feet and drops vertically to 100 feet. The wall then slopes steeply down to 145 feet, to where it drops into the deep. For most divers the 100 foot to 145 foot levels offer the site's most interesting diving where tube, candelabra and other sponges grow on the wall and shelter the small marine life from the large amberjack and snapper which come to feed.

Black Forest gets its name from the trees of black coral which grow around 70 feet down. This site has deep crevices and tunnels cut into the reef wall. Much of the fish life indicative of the waters north of Norman's Cay abound here.

South of Norman's Cay is **Wax Cut Cay**, a drift dive through currents averaging one to three knots.

Moving south to near Stocking Island is **Stingray Reef**, a large barrier that runs between the north end of Stocking Island and Lily Cay. Covered with coral heads, sea fans and gorgonians from 35 feet to 50 feet, it also has starfish, lobster, and other reef dwellers, including rays.

Mystery Cave is a treat for experienced cave divers. It is reached through a large blue hole through the Hurricane Harbour

Mike Mesgleski

Lagoon at Stocking Island. The cave entrance is at 15 feet. The cave angles slightly to 60 feet. It levels out, then runs straight under the island for 400 feet. Tide currents flow through the cave, restricting the diving to slack or ebb tide.

Angelfish Blue Hole is in the same lagoon as Mystery Cave. The entrance is on the floor 20 feet down. The tunnel slopes to 95 feet, then it tapers close as it levels off. Visibility is less here than at Mystery Cave because the current keeps things stirred up, but there are many cave-dwelling fish which help make this a good site.

Crab Cay Blue Hole is a cave system off Crab Cay near Stocking Island that goes down to 95 feet. Its tide currents are not quite as strong as those at Mystery Cave and gives divers a different look as it winds through a maze of rock.

Exuma Dive Services

EXUMA AQUATICS, LTD.
Service Address:
Hotel Pieces of Eight; P.O. Box 49, Georgetown, Exuma
Mailing Address:
Same as Above
Service Telephone:
809/336-2672
Reservation Telephone:
809/336-2600
Hours Service is Open:
9 am–5 pm Seven days a week
Resort Affiliation:
Hotel Pieces of Eight & Out Island Inn, a sister hotel
Rooms:
33 at Pieces of Eight
Cottages/Villas:
NA

Dive travelers to the Pieces of Eight Resort usually fly from Ft. Lauderdale to Georgetown via Bahamasair, Aero Coach or Transair. Taxis and rental cars are waiting at the airport.

Exuma Aquatics, Ltd. is an established, two-year-old service with a growing operation. They have a five-boat fleet, including a 22-foot North American and two 34-foot flattops. Dive parties vary in size for their two-tank morning dives and three-tank full day boat dives. They do night diving on request for a minimum of six divers.

Their resort course is available to guests from all nearby hotels and they offer PADI and SSI open water instruction. They have rental and repair services, including a full service photo shop.

Exuma Aquatics does it all—everything from beach entry dives to 140-foot wall dives. Much of the island's barrier reef is virtually unexplored, but they have charted a variety of phenomenal sites. Popular dive sites include Stingray Reef, Lobster Alley, Mystery Cave and the blue holes of Hurricane Harbour lagoon on Stocking Island. They are trying to get through the red tape of sinking a 200-foot passenger freighter, and soon they will offer live-aboard dive trips to other islands and seldom seen dive sites.

Topside, vacationers have access to the Georgetown Harbour and resort area. Bonefishing, big game fishing, and boating are available through the resort. The food is great and they have picnics and parties to some of the pristine uninhabited cays around the Exumas.

EXUMA DIVERS–Owner: Wendle McGregor
Service Address:
P.O. Box 110; Georgetown, Exuma, Bahamas
Mailing Address:
Same as above
Service Telephone:
809/336-2710
Reservation Telephone:
Same as above
Hours Service is Open:
8:30 am–4:30 pm Monday through Sunday
Resort Affiliation:
Peace & Plenty
Rooms:
32

Also arranges dives for guests of the Two Turtles Inn

Many private boats come to Georgetown Harbour, but most guests fly in from Ft. Lauderdale or Miami to the Georgetown Airport where taxis meet incoming flights.

Wendle McGregor, owner and divemaster of Exuma Divers, has operated in Exuma's underwaters for years. Exuma Divers offers a resort training course,

Alan Davis

PADI certification up to assistant instructor, and rental equipment. Their 38-foot houseboat serves larger dive parties, with a 23-footer and a 17-footer also available. Wendle offers a two-tank morning dive, a one-tank afternoon dive, and if you want night diving, you got it!

Their specialties include the best of Exuma's diving—reef, wall, blue holes and high-color coral gardens especially for u/w photographers. In addition to popular Stingray Reef, they dive the wall on the open-water side of Stocking Island. Reef dives off Guana Cay and a 100-foot wall off Conch Cay are worth asking for by name. Shark Reef is a 30-mile boat trip from Georgetown where sharks and other pelagics cruise. The Angelfish Blue Hole of Stocking Island is a favorite of divers here, too.

The Peace and Plenty is a waterfront resort with fine beaches, bone and big game fishing, and is a favorite of yachtsmen who put in to Elizabeth Harbour. The resort helps guests arrange island tours, keeps abreast of what entertainment is appearing locally and shuttles guests to and from Stocking Island where it maintains a beach club.

STANIEL CAY YACHT CLUB
Service Address:
   Staniel Cay; Exumas, Bahamas
   c/o TransMar International, Inc.
Mailing Address:
   1640 SE 7th St., Ft. Lauderdale, FL 33316
Service Telephone:
   809/336-2170
Reservation Telephone:
   305/467-6850
Hours Service is Open:
   As needed
Resort Affiliation:
   Staniel Cay Yacht Club
Cottages/Villas:
   4 cottages
   1 house

Staniel Cay has a private airstrip and marina. Upon making reservations, TransMar International will assist you in making flight connections.

This self-contained resort shares Staniel Cay with private land owners, another resort, and local fishermen. The superb diving includes reefs, walls and caves. All dive parties are small and for experienced divers. Rental gear is available, but most divers who come here bring as much of their personal equipment as they can except for tanks, weight belt, B.C. and/or back pack.

Guided trips for bone, reef, and big game fish are part of the resort's draw.

GRAND
BAHAMA

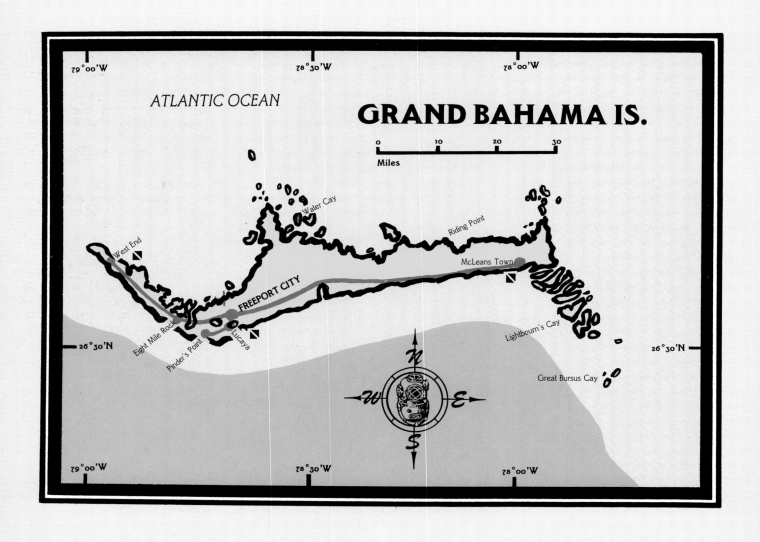

GRAND BAHAMA IS.

ATLANTIC OCEAN

79°00'W

78°30'W

78°00'W

0   10   20   30
Miles

Water Cay

Riding Point

West End

McLeans Town

Eight Mile Rock

FREEPORT CITY

Pinder's Point

Lucaya

Lightbourn's Cay

26°30'N

26°30'N

Great Bursus Cay

79°00'W

78°30'W

78°00'W

Grand Bahama sparkles. Development upon Grand Bahama in general, and Freeport/Lucaya in particular, have always been aimed at providing the best resort facilities and services possible. Everything from city walks to the golf courses has been integrated into the island's natural order to preserve its subtropical setting.

Grand Bahama had only been lightly settled until the mid-1950s, when Wallace Groves and others began full-scale development of the island. Freeport, with its deep-water harbor, is the island's primary industrial and commercial center; Lucaya is the resort center. Freeport/Lucaya is second only to Nassau in terms of population and economic importance. The city complex is set inland in order to preserve nearby beaches. It is the only inland city in The Bahamas.

Grand Bahama is the fourth largest island in The Bahamas. It has three major sections: East End, with its small villages and secluded beaches; West End, in itself a premiere resort area, and Freeport/Lucaya. The island is approximately 90 miles long and two to eight miles wide. Grand Bahama is in the northern part of The Bahamas and lies about 60 miles west of Palm Beach, Florida, and 115 miles north-northwest of Nassau.

Topside Attractions

Good roads from end to end of Grand Bahama make it easy to explore the towns and beaches along the island's popular south coast. There are at least two 'must sees' on Grand Bahama: The Garden of the Groves, an eleven-acre botanical garden of rare tropical and subtropical plants, and the International Bazaar, a ten-acre shopping mecca with good buys and products from around the world, if you know what to look for.

The Underwater Explorers Society (UNEXSO), based in Lucaya, is one of the premiere diving research and training centers in the world. Not only is it a full-service dive facility, it also has a diver-oriented library and the Museum of Diving History, a feature which appeals to non-divers, as well.

There are marinas at Freeport/Lucaya and 50 miles up the Queen's Highway to West End at the Jack Tar Village. Water sports are available through most of the resorts and include sailing, fishing (everything from bone fishing to night fishing for shark) and wind surfing. There are beaches from the East End town of McLeans Town to West End. Six well-groomed golf courses give six different challenges and an ample number of tennis courts are available at several resorts

for guests and nonguests, including courts at the Jack Tar.

At night, the Freeport/Lucaya area is alive with casinos and entertainment. One of the favorite spots on the island for many visitors is the Bahamas Princess Casino, adjacent to the International Bazaar. It is one of the largest casinos in The Bahamas and Caribbean. Two other night spots are the Casino Royale Theatre, and The Jack Tar Village for dancing and live entertainment.

Good restaurants and lounges are found in the major tourist centers as well as in the small coast settlements. With the ease with which Grand Bahama can be toured, it's possible to have a variety of social and cultural experiences every evening.

Getting There/ Getting Around

Grand Bahama is probably the most convenient stop in The Bahamas for visitors. Several carriers make daily flights to Freeport International Airport and to West End from the U.S. and Canada. Bahamasair provides flights from the mainland as well as from numerous ports throughout the Bahamas.

Freeport/Lucaya is a major port of call for cruise ships.

The design of the island and cities makes getting around quick and easy. Metered taxis are plentiful on Grand Bahama. Motorscooters, bicycles, and cars can be rented from either the airport or major resorts.

Grand Bahama Diving

In addition to a great variety of coral reefs offshore, divers can explore walls, caves, wrecks and blue holes. Night diving is one of the greatest attractions and the quality facilities on Grand Bahama help you get the most from that experience. Marine life is abundant, ranging from the smallest coral reef dwellers to large pelagic fish coming near shore from the depths.

As throughout The Bahamas, the sites around Freeport/Lucaya offer challenges for all skill levels of diver, as three distinct levels of reef terrace down gradually from 20 feet to 80 feet. Sites off the south shore include Bell Channel and the "Edge of the Ledge," a 2,000-foot drop-off where the Grand Bahama Ledge falls into the trench of the continental shelf. These areas have wrecks, coral caves and deep tunnels with some current diving along selected parts of the reef.

Grand Bahama Dive Sites

THEO'S WRECK is one of the best known sites in The Bahamas. Deliberately sunk in 1983 to provide an artificial reef, the 230-foot steel ship lies on its port side 100 feet down, on the rim of the Grand Bahama Ledge. You can stand on the dive boat and see both the wreck and the 2,000-foot plunge into the trench of the continental shelf.

Surge channels cut through coral formations known as **The Caves**, a site which begins near 50 feet. Colorful sponges cover much of the area and large groupers and angelfish cruise among the ledges.

Little remains of the treasure ship found in **Treasure Reef**. Found in 1965, divers have sifted through the area and probably found most of the booty, but brain coral and elkhorn coral abound. Schools of fish provide good subjects for photography. This is a popular snorkeling spot.

The Cup Handle is a deep dive for experienced divers. The Handle juts out from a vertical wall like the handle of a tea cup. The wall plunges into the ocean depths. Large enough for a diver to swim through, the arch is covered with sponges and coral fans.

Little Hale's Lair is a coral cave which frequently fills with schools of baitfish. The lip of the reef is covered with gorgonians, sponges, and plate corals, giving refuge to many kinds of large fish and hard-to-spot anemones.

Ben's Cave is a popular blue hole east of Freeport. Divers use a ladder to descend to and through the top of the hole to water ten feet below. Not all of the tunnels which lead off the main cavern have been fully explored. Rare species, including the blind cave fish, live in Ben's.

Zoo Hole is a spectacular blue hole. At 30 feet, it drops vertically for 65 feet, then splits into two coral-rimmed tunnels which continue to drop for hundreds more. Sponge colonies, gorgonians and encrusted coral are part of the many things experienced divers come to the Zoo to explore.

PAPA DOC is the wreck of a Haitian gunrunner in 40 feet of water. Military hardware has been recovered by divers in the nearby reef.

Hawksbill Creek Blue Hole is another dive-site favorite. Located near the center of Hawksbill Creek, divers swim to the opening from shore. The hole starts at 40 feet, then descends and divides into two horizontal caves. The varieties of coral hold fish, lobster and crab.

Grand Bahama Dive Services

SUNN ODDESSEY
Owner: Nick Roe
Service Address:
P.O. Box F-4166; Freeport, Grand Bahama
Mailing Address:
Same as above
Service Telephone:
809/352-8776 (This is Nick's home phone)
Reservation Telephone:
809/373-5700 (Silver Sands Hotel)
Hours Service is Open:
8 am–5 pm Seven days a week
Resort Affiliation:
Silver Sands Hotel
Rooms:
164 studio apartments and suites
Cottages/Villas:
NA

Guests of Sunn Oddessey can take a metered taxi from Freeport International and ride seven miles to the Silver Sands Hotel. Nick Roe operates Sunn Oddessey at the beach about 100 yards from the hotel.

At the moment, Sunn Oddessey is Nick's one-man operation for certified divers only. He offers a morning dive, two in the afternoon, and night dives on request. Sunn Oddessey provides scuba gear rental and repair.

Nick operates from three dive boats, two in the 24-foot range and one 44-footer. His customers' favorite sites include the very popular Theo's Wreck 100 feet down, Orson Wells Reef, and Pigmy Caves. He does shallow and medium depth dives throughout the coral and rock formations of the Grand Bahama's "Edge of the Ledge," which hold many snappers, horse-eye jacks, turtles, barracudas, corals and sponges.

Nick likes operating out of Freeport not only because of the diving, but because Freeport is a clean, small city that is alive morning, noon, and night. The Silver Sands Hotel itself is close to all Freeport offers, plus it has many watersports, tennis courts, a poolside snack bar, yet you can walk down the beach and get away from all of it.

UNDERWATER EXPLORERS SOCIETY, LTD. (UNEXSO)
Service Address:
P.O. Box F-2433; Freeport, Grand Bahama
Mailing Address:
Same as above
Service Telephone:
809/373-1244
Reservation Telephone:
Same as above
Hours Service is Open:
8 am–5 pm Seven days a week
Resort Affiliation:
They provide services to many Freeport/Lucaya hotels

Located next to the Lucayan Bay Hotel, UNEXSO is one of the world's premiere dive training centers. It is a NAUI facility where everyone who works here is an instructor. The staff provides many types of training, from resort courses to open water and will soon conduct dive master certification. UNEXSO have a complete rental shop and repair shop. They recently installed a new, state-of-the-art recompression chamber and have the only recompression facility in The Bahamas.

For sport divers UNEXSO has three boats for 12-to-18-person dive parties. The instructors are very flexible in accommodating divers. They do three one-tank dives a day and will dive every night. Excellent sites lie off the south of Grand Bahama on the coral terraces which step down to, then drop off, over the Edge of the Ledge of the continental shelf. Popular reef dives are Little Hale's Lair, Photo Fantasy, Octapussy Garden and Rainbow Reef. They also dive the Pigmy Caves, The Orson Wells, and Theo's Wreck.

Part of UNEXSO's facilities include a Diver's Museum and a library. And, as they provide dive services to the nearby resorts, they have a good idea of what is happening and where in topside entertainment.

DEEP WATER CAY CLUB
Service Address:
Box F-39; Freeport, Grand Bahama, Bahamas
Mailing Address:
P.O. Box 1145, Palm Beach, FL 33480
Reservation Telephone:
809/348-2112
Hours Service is Open:
305/684-3958
Resort Affiliation:
Deep Water Cay Club
Rooms:
11
Cottages/Villas:
5

Located on the East End of Grand Bahama, guests arrive at The Deep Water Cay Club via private charter from Miami and West Palm Beach, Florida.

The Deep Water Cay Club no longer emphasizes diving as it once did. But offshore, there is excellent reef and near-vertical wall diving, as well as many blue holes and underwater caverns. Michael Quinn tells us the Club specializes in fishing now and though divers are welcome, they must bring all their own gear and can only rent fishing boats (which are very expensive) for diving. Deep Water Cay Club still has two compressors and a dive boat, but the boat is for sale.

WEST END DIVING CENTER
Service Address:
West End; Jack Tar Village, Grand Bahama Island
Mailing Address:
c/o UNEXSO P.O. Box F-2433; Freeport, Grand Bahama
Service Telephone:
809/373-1244 and 809/346-6211
Reservation Telephone:
800/527-9015 (U.S.A.) 800/472-7212 (Texas)
Hours Service is Open:
8 am–5 pm
Resort Affiliation:
Jack Tar Village
Rooms:
800
Cottages/Villas:
2

To get to Jack Tar Village, guests land at the 2,000-acre resort's commercial airport. All reservations for the village and diving go through Adventure Tours, which provided the toll-free telephone numbers above.

UNEXSO also handles the diving instruction and trips for Jack Tar. They do morning and afternoon dives, with night diving on request. Much of the diving off the West End focuses on diving along the ledge where the Gulf Stream flows. There are current dives and dives through coral formations on the wall and in the shallow to medium deep reefs. They also do a day-long dive to Memory Rock, a magnificent area of huge coral jutting up from 80 feet to within 20 feet of the surface.

Jack Tar Village is a plush, self-contained resort that includes golf, tennis, all watersports and a full-service marina, night club entertainment, shopping and several bars. It is about 32 miles from Freeport.

LONG ISLAND

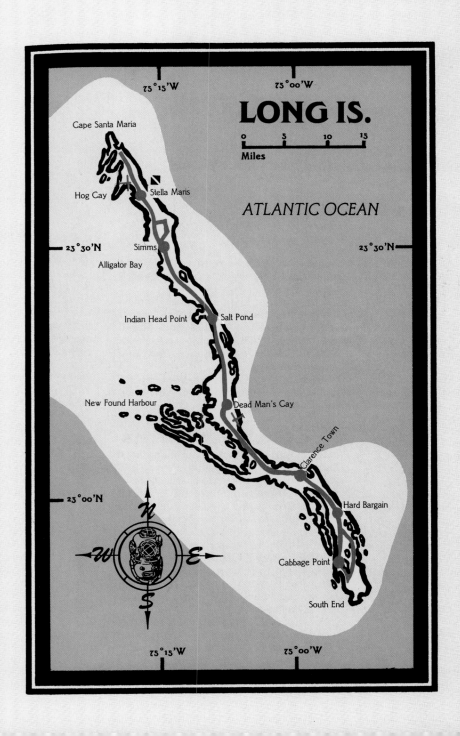

Karl Wallin

Long Island is a 60-mile-long coral island averaging 1.5 miles wide. It is about 160 miles southeast of Nassau and has a land area of about 230 square miles. On a good day you can see parts of the Exumas, about 25 miles to the west, from Long Island's northwest shore. Columbus landed on Long Island during his first voyage to The Bahamas and found Lucayan Indians there. After the Lucayans lost out to the Spanish, Long Island remained relatively quiet for 450 years, with the Indians being succeeded by plantation owners, then freed slaves, until the 1960s when the island and tourism discovered one another.

Long Island's population of 3,500 lives in small villages spread along both coasts. The island's west shore is calm. The east coast, where the Atlantic rolls in, kicks up with the incoming tide. Coral rock cliffs, protected coves and long, white sand beaches characterize the island. One of the more remote Bahama Islands, its coastlines encompass hills and flat land which supports some small farms.

Getting There/ Getting Around

There are two airfields on Long Island which handle four flights a week from Nassau via Bahamasair and, when arranged, other carriers. The north field includes a 4,200-foot runway that serves the Stella Maris resort; the other field is near Clarence Town in the south.

A network of poor roads runs almost the length of the west shore of the island and branches into the interior. Rutted trails do run along the east, with better sections serving the Clarence Town and Stella Maris areas.

Taxis can be hailed at either airport. Rental car, scooters and bikes are available from Stella Maris.

Topside Attractions

Technically, most of Long Island is in the tropics, but, of course, the winds and water maintain a constant climate most of the year. There is less rain and a shorter rainy season during the summer months than on the islands farther north.

Stella Maris is the hub of tourist activity for the island, though, to the south, Deadman's Cay, Thompson Bay and Clarence Town have some facilities, shopping, and restaurants. Fishing, boating, tennis, and other watersports are available at Stella Maris.

Long Island has a number of caves which visitors frequently explore with guides. Some of the caves were homes for the Lucayans and were also used by pirates. Deadman's Cay Cave is one of the largest and most interesting, showing stalagmites and stalactities, as well as Indian wall drawings.

Father Jerome, mentioned earlier from Cat Island, had an impact on Long Island, too. He was the guiding force behind two gothic churches built in Clarence Town: St. Peter's and St. Paul's.

Long Island Diving

There are scores of boat dives and several beach entry dives which divers have access to from Stella Maris. Sites are off both the Atlantic coast and the more protected west coast. They include dives ranging from ten-foot coral gardens to deep wall dives into Exuma Sound, which is between Long Island and the Exumas.

Divers explore several old and recent wrecks off the island. A 135-foot freighter was intentionally sunk recently and is already attracting fish and other marine life.

On the Atlantic side are sites which shelter many pelagics, including shark, and large grouper, snapper and barracuda.

Long Island Dive Sites

Off Long island is **Shark Reef**, a dive that the people at Stella Maris have made famous. Shark Reef begins at 35 feet in clear waters where six-foot to 12-foot sharks are fed fish on spears held by divemasters. The coral is of secondary importance, here, as the sharks cruise in from the aqua haze. A few will slow down long enough to make for some thrilling photos.

Barracuda Heads is another spot divers have enjoyed for years. Grouper appear throughout the coral heads, and shiny barracuda frequently hover motionless near divers before they (the 'cudas) dart away.

Deep Reef is a sloping reef 80 feet to 125 feet deep. Coral life changes as the water gets deeper and the sunlight gets fainter. Deep water gorgonians, sea whips and tube sponges are part of this reef. Coral crevices hold pockets of other colorful sponges.

Conception Island Wall is a favorite that begins in 55 feet of water. The wall varies in width and depth. Coral chimneys are fractured in the wall and give divers places to observe secretive reef dwellers. The wall slopes, then plunges, almost straight down thousands of feet.

South Hampton Reef is a nine-mile-long reef with sloping gardens of coral in depths ranging from ten to 100 feet. An early 20th century British freighter sank on this reef, as have other wrecks, which now rest amid stands of giant elkhorn and other corals.

Long Island Dive Services

STELLA MARIS INN
Service Address:
    P.O. Box 105; Stella Maris, Long Island
Mailing Address:
    Same as above
Service Telephone:
    809/336-2106
Reservation Telephone:
    305/467-0466
Hours Service is Open:
    Daily and as needed
Rooms
    60
Cottages/Villas
    Variable, depends on season

The Stella Maris airfield and marina can accommodate and service just about any private craft. Bahamasair also lands at the resort's field from Nassau and Florida coast cities.

Stella Maris has a strong commitment to the sport diver which novices benefit from while learning to dive in the service's training pool. There is also PADI certification available and rentals, though they recommend you bring personal dive gear.

Divers take two-tank dives in the morning and afternoon on sites off the east, north, and west coasts of Long Island. Night dives are offered, too. Sites are reached via one of Stella Maris's four boats, including their pride and joy, a new 65-foot, specially equipped dive boat. Being able to dive off three distinct coasts gives Stella Maris an excellent variety of dives. They include Shark Reef, Barracuda Heads, and the Santa Maria Deep Reef, an 80-foot to 125-foot dive. Among their favorite wall dives are Conception Island Wall, which starts at 55 feet and plunges for thousands, and the Rum Cay Northwest Wall off Rum Cay. They also dive the South Hampton Wreck and a new dive, a 135-foot freighter which went down recently.

Stella Maris is a 3,500-acre estate which sits on a ridge with a view of the ocean on three sides. Fishing, windsurfing, tennis, excellent fishing and boating, as well as plane rentals add to the resort's appeal. Their evenings are filled with live native music and dances, cave parties and barbecues, and nightclub tours of various island establishments.

David McCray

NEW PROVIDENCE/ PARADISE ISLAND

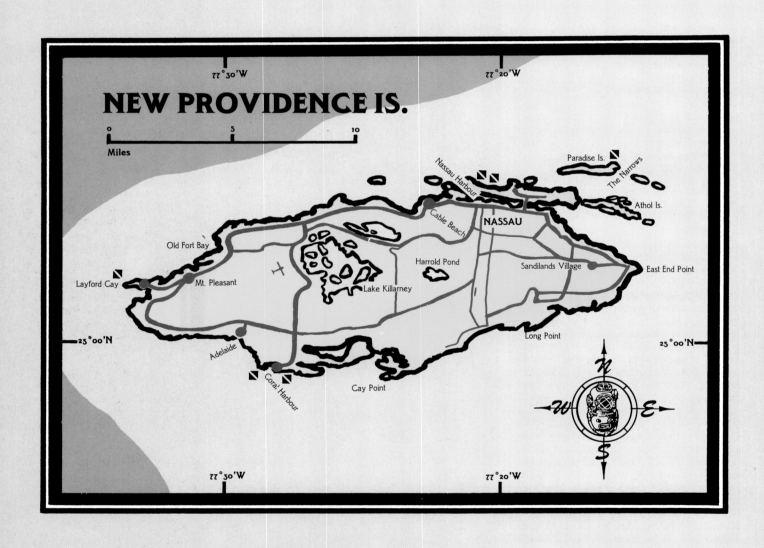

NEW PROVIDENCE IS.

77°30'W

77°20'W

Miles
0   5   10

Paradise Is.

The Narrows

Nassau Harbour

Athol Is.

Cable Beach

NASSAU

Old Fort Bay

Harrold Pond

Sandilands Village

East End Point

Layford Cay

Mt. Pleasant

Lake Killarney

Long Point

25°00'N

25°00'N

Adelaide

Coral Harbour

Cay Point

77°30'W

77°20'W

New Providence is located near the center of The Bahamas and is also the center of commerce, tourism, and government. The capital city of Nassau is on New Providence and has 135,000 of the island's 140,000 residents. A short bridge connects Nassau with the resort haven of Paradise Island. New Providence, approximately 20 miles long and six miles wide, is 150 miles east by southeast of Miami.

Nassau was an important deep-water port for the early colonial powers on the north coast of the island. Later, the port and city became a refuge for pirates until they were evicted by the British. Because of the island's close proximity to major shipping lanes, Nassau and New Providence began to grow as heads of industry became acquainted with them. Nassau is also a prominent center for international banking. These cosmopolitan influences have all left their marks on this island. They combine with The Bahamian culture and the country's commitment to tourism to create a distinct environment which spans everything from world-renowned resorts to quiet beaches to virgin stands of timber.

Getting There/ Getting Around

International flights arrive at Nassau International Airport daily from Miami, Fort Lauderdale, Chicago, from cities throughout the Northeast U.S., Toronto, and Montreal. Cruise ships make a port of call at Nassau several times a week.

Keep your head after arriving at Nassau International. It will probably be crowded, and you will appreciate traveling light if you have to find transportation. Of course, the easiest and most expensive way of getting around is with a rental car. If you are planning to be in Nassau for a while and want to do some touring and night clubbing, renting a car may be the best way to go. Major car rental agencies are located across the street from the main airport terminal. Metered taxis will also be cruising the airport. Some resorts do have bus services, but no public bus transportation is available from the airport to Nassau.

During the day, the best way to see and get to know Nassau is to walk. Buses, the cheapest way to ride, and horse-drawn surreys, about the most expensive, can take you through town, to Paradise Island, or to outlying areas. At night, many people prefer taxis while hitting the hot spots between Cable Beach and Paradise Island.

Bahama Tourist

Topside Attractions

Most of the two million annual visitors to The Bahamas come through Nassau. Many of the vacationers stay to enjoy the casinos, sports, and entertainment available at the major resort centers of Nassau, Paradise Island, and Cable Beach.

Products created throughout The Bahamas and the world find their way to Nassau. Bay Street, which parallels Nassau's waterfront, is the site of the International Bazaar. There, many countries have exhibits and shops where certain goods can be bought at substantial savings, if you know what to look for.

There are also vintage forts and colonial homes which can be toured. Among these include three forts built by the British: Fort Charlotte, the largest and most impressive, guarded the west harbour entrance; Fort Montagu, the oldest and is located near the east entrance of the harbour; and Fort Fincastle a small fortification which served primarily as a signal tower.

The Seafloor Aquarium and the Botanic Garden are both located near Fort Charlotte. Combined, they allow the visitor to view much of the tropical life that can be found in The Bahamas. For people who enjoy knowing what it is they are looking at, these are two good places to see species which may be encountered above and below the water elsewhere in The Bahamas. Ardastra Gardens, which feature The Marching Flamingoes, include five acres of tropical garden replete with exotic animals. At Ardastra, sometimes a dress code which bans women wearing shorts, is enforced.

Guided tours are available for many of the top attractions and can be arranged for through many resorts.

Good restaurants and clubs, which are a reason in themselves for visiting New Providence, are plentiful along the north coast from Cable Beach and along the waterfronts of Nassau and Paradise Island. Many specialize in certain types of food and entertainment. Entertainment may include music, dancing, and night club acts. Local food and native music is popular, too.

Virtually all land and water sports are available on New Providence/Paradise Island. One thing which should be stressed is that as modern as this island is, it is very diverse. Its tropical setting enhances the modern atmosphere rather than being dominated by it. Though people do not come to New Providence for seclusion, uncrowded beaches can be found around the island away from the Cable Beach-Nassau-Paradise Island area.

New Providence/ Paradise Island Diving

Often bypassed by divers who want less developed islands, New Providence has an outstanding choice of dive sites that range from 10-foot reefs, to caves and fissures beginning at 40 feet, to wall diving. It is not always realized that the western reefs of New Providence border the Tongue of the Ocean; the wall dives there are equal to any in The Bahamas. In addition, Clifton Wall to the south has many sites which have not been thoroughly explored. New Providence, then, offers divers a vacation experience unlike most islands; both crowded casinos and seldom-seen gardens of coral.

Shipping, rum running and piracy have left an abundance of ships in the waters off New Providence. The film industry has made a contribution, too. At least half a dozen wrecks and others sites, including a few specifically created for James Bond, were set in place as movie props and remain as dive sites today.

Topsiders have also been too busy to fish near shore. Groupers, snapper, lobsters, sponges and an occasional nurse shark are among the residents off New Providence.

New Providence/ Paradise Island Dive Sites

Porpoise Pens is a shore dive off Clifton Point. *Flipper* and *Day of the Dolphin* were filmed here and some of the dolphin pens still remain. But this is much more than just a movie set. There are fabulous bushes of black coral here, which virtually all divers, so far, have respected as the rare beauty they are and left them alone. The best diving is in the 40-foot to 90-foot range where there are other coral and sponges.

Lost Ocean Hole is a blue hole pocked with caves. This bell-shaped cavern opens in 40 feet of water and drops to nearly 200 feet. Fish love this place as well, and divers should keep a look-out for what's looking at *them* while exploring these formations.

THE LCT WRECK is a 20-foot dive in clear, bright water that's good for beginners. Coral is growing on and around the wreck, making this craft more colorful than it ever was on the surface. Fish are attracted to it and make cooperative photo subjects.

Rose Island and **Athol Island** are two popular sites for new divers and dive boats will also make the trip for snorkelers. Natural light pictures can be taken of the coral here.

Love Beach Wall starts in shallow water and slopes steeply to 100 feet, creating places to explore all along its face. Black coral, tube sponges, and rope sponges can be easily found.

Elkhorn and staghorn coral pattern the bright sand bottom of this 40-foot to 60-foot dive known as **Green Cay Reef**. 20-foot- and 30-foot-tall pillar corals are its dominant feature.

Paradise Island Caves, in 50 feet of water, is found north of Paradise Island. Undercut ledges have formed caves in several reef outcrops. The larger caves hold rare limestone formations and coral unique to the area.

THE MAHONEY is a wreck that, while afloat, never had that name. It was called the Candance, Firebird, Firequeen, and maybe once or twice My Honey, but never The Mahoney. Whatever its name, this wreck, lost in 40 feet of water, affords a challenge for the serious dive photographer. Parts of the ship hold grouper, triggerfish, parrotfish, and lobster. One hundred yards away in deeper water is a section of stern from the same wreck with even more fish nearby.

Lyford Cay Dropoff is a wall dive that borders the Tongue of the Ocean near Lyford Cay off the west tip of New Providence. The lip of the reef starts at 45 feet. The wall, past which run strong currents, and the reef ridge, have given divers incredible thrills. Pelagic fish, plate corals, and rope sponges are a few of the sights.

Goulding Cay is a tiny island which lies near Lyford Cay Dropoff. A grove of giant elkhorn grows within a protected cove; in 20 feet to 40 feet of water.

Clifton Wall is over five miles of pristine reef which begins in 35 feet of water about a mile from the west tip of New Providence. The wide shelf has a variety of hard and soft corals and sponges. Interlaced with tunnels and fissures it provides a hunting ground for large pelagic fish which cruise by searching for prey.

Divers can often see lobsters, jack, and triggerfish.

Tunnel Wall is deeply etched with fissures and tunnels running throughout this vertical wall. Brain coral, gorgonians, and colonies of sponges make this a colorful dive. Fire worms, star fish, and shellfish are here, too.

Sea fans abound in 20-foot deep **Cannon Reef**. This site was named for an old British cannon found here. Smaller invertebrates thrive among some of the other coral formations.

A 110-foot freighter was sunk as a prop for the movie *Never Say Never Again* and is still intact. You can glide in and around the wreck checking for creatures which prefer the dark. Located within the Bahamas Marine Park, and near the sunken freighter, is **Thunderball Reef**, where location shots for the movie *Thunderball* were filmed. This entire area is a favorite of divers not only becasue of the props, but also for the large number of tame groupers, triggerfish and other fish which call this reef home.

New Providence Dive Services

BAHAMA DIVERS, LTD.
Service Address:
 P.O. Box SS 5004; Nassau, Bahamas
Mailing Address:
 Same as above
Service Telephone:
 809/326-5644
Reservation Telephone:
 Same as above
Hours Service is Open:
 8 am–5 pm Seven days a week
Resort Affiliation:
 Serve divers from nearby hotels

Bahama Divers offer dive services to guests of several Nassau area resorts. It is best to call to let them know when and where you will be while in Nassau and how many are in your dive party. From that information they can handle all the logistics and arrange to pick you up on the days you want to dive. They are a PADI affiliated service and provide resort courses at the different hotels. They offer no other certification.

Bahama Divers offer one- and two-tank morning dives and a one-tank dive in the afternoon. Night diving is on request. They accommodate as many as 30 divers on their 42-foot and 44-foot custom built dive boats.

Their popular sites include Treasure Island, a garden of coral and sponges teeming with reef life east of New Providence, and Green Cay Reef, an excellent spot for

soft coral beginning at 35 feet. Travellers' Rest is a deep reef and wall dive. Barracudas and rays are frequently seen. They dive wrecks, caves and blue holes as well as the wall overlooking the Tongue of the Ocean.

CORAL HARBOUR DIVERS
 Owner: Stuart Cove
Service Address:
 P.O. Box SS6635; Lyford Cay Resort; Nassau, Bahamas
Mailing Address:
 Same as above
Service Telephone:
 809/326-4171
Reservation Telephone:
 Same as above
Hours Service is Open:
 8:30 am–6:30 pm Seven days a week
Resort Affiliation:
 Lyford Cay Resort/Orange Hill Hotel

Lyford Cay is a very exclusive resort located on the western tip of New Providence. Guests come in by private boat, private plane, or a commercial flight into Nassau International.

Coral Harbour is a full-service center providing a resort training course as well as PADI certification. They rent all you will need and can repair some personal dive equipment.

They offer two-tank dives in the morning and afternoon, and will dive every night. Their fleet includes a 30-foot and 45-foot boat, plus a 20- and 25-footer for private parties.

Coral Harbour's dive sites include the Tunnel Wall, which has many tunnels and crevices cut into the barrier reef, and sites along the North and South Walls of New Providence. Most of the sites, from shallow coral gardens to the walls, are less than a ten-minute boat ride away. Due to their location and diversity of sites, they can almost always dive somewhere where it's calm.

Other watersports are available from Lyford Cay, and the Nassau/Paradise Island area is easily accessible by car.

NEW PROVIDENCE DIVERS, LTD.
Service Address:
 South Ocean Beach; New Providence, Bahamas
Mailing Address:
 N87 W16459 Appleton Ave; Menomonee Falls, WI 53051
Service Telephone:
 809/326-4391 ext 269
Reservation Telephone:
 404/955-1496
Hours Service is Open:
 8 am to 5 pm Seven days a week
Resort Affiliation:

South Ocean Beach Hotel and Club
Rooms:
120
Cottages/Villas:
NA

The South Ocean Beach Resort, located on the southwest coast of New Providence, is a ten-minute taxi ride from Nassau International.

This is a dive service new to South Ocean Beach, a resort center which is becoming known and respected for its diving as well as topside allures.

New Providence divers offer a resort course as well as PADI and P.D.I.C. open-water training. They have a new, fully equipped dive shop with rental and repair services. Underwater photographers are coming here for a springboard to excellent offshore photo opportunities.

Ideally situated to dive the caves of Lyford Cay Wall to Clifton Wall south of the island, New Providence Divers' three dive boats provide action for beginning, intermediate and expert divers. Popular reefs include The Fishbowl and Goulding Cay, which include massive columns of elkhorn and staghorn breaking the surface of the water from 35 feet down. Porpoise Wall is named for the porpoises which cruise the area. It begins in 45 feet and drops over the Tongue of the Ocean. Clifton Wall is less than ten minutes from the hotel. It begins in 30 feet, giving novice divers a chance to see its white and pink sponges, lobster, jacks and triggerfish.

South Ocean Beach Hotel is famous for its 18-hole golf course, tennis, and nightlife. Fishing, skiing, and five-and-a-half miles of beach are available. Public buses make the half-hour trip into Nassau several times a day. Dive packages are available.

SEA & SKI OCEAN SPORTS
Service Address:
Paradise Island, Bahamas
Mailing Address:
P.O. Box N-4754; Nassau, Bahamas
Service Telephone:
809/326-3371
Reservation Telephone:
809/326-2011 which is for the Grand Hotel
Hours Service is Open:
9 am–5 pm Seven days a week
Resort Affiliation:
Grand Hotel
Rooms:
350
Cottages/Villas:
NA

Sea & Ski Ocean Sports is fairly new, but has efficiently served guests of the Grand Hotel as well as other patrons. They pride themselves on the personal attention they give and intend to keep dive parties small, even as they grow.

The staff gives resort courses and PADI certification, if you arrange that ahead of time. They have full rental services, but do no repairs on personal gear as yet. Their dives include one- and two-tank dives to the reefs and nearby coral gardens from either their 21-foot or 24-foot dive boat. Divers also go to the farther walls such as Porpoise Pens, Lyford Cay, and Clifton Wall.

All the nightlife splendor of Nassau/Paradise Island is available to divers who stay at the Grand Hotel. The hotel also offers many watersports and the amenities associated with a major population center.

SMUGGLER'S REST DIVE RESORT
Service Address:
Coral Harbour; New Providence Island, Bahamas
Mailing Address:
P.O. Box N-8050; Nassau, Bahamas
Service Telephone:
809/326-1143 or 326-1401
Reservation Telephone:
800/328-8029 ext. 246
Hours Service is Open:
7 am–7 pm Seven days a week
Resort Affiliation:
Smuggler's Rest Dive Resort
Rooms:
0
Cottages/Villas:
5

Smuggler's Resort is located on the protected beach of Coral Harbour on the south coast of New Providence. Most guests take a taxi for the ten-minute ride from Nassau International to the resort. Smuggler's will also pick up guests of other resorts on the north shore and bring them here to dive.

The clientele of Smuggler's Resort is almost exclusively divers, and they like it that way. The operation is also known as Dive-Dive-Dive on the island. They offer a resort course within the harbour's shallows as well as PADI certification. They have all rental services, including underwater photography equipment, but provide only limited repairs on personal dive gear. They offer two-tank morning and afternoon dives, and night diving on request.

Within reach of their dive boats are the walls, wrecks, reefs, and caves of sites on both sides of the barrier reefs off the south and west coasts. Their favorites include Golden Cay, a 30-foot coral garden dive, Porpoise Pens, sites along the Tongue of the Ocean and Thunderball Reef. Fish life includes a bounty of parrot fish, moray and spotted eels, queen angelfish, manta and eagle rays, dolphin, flying fish and pelagics. They plan to press a new dive boat into service soon.

The people of Smuggler's Rest enjoy the remote beauty they have above and below the water. They know, though, that some divers like it hot, so part of their service includes busing divers to the Nassau/Paradise Island area for the nightlife.

SUN DIVERS, LTD.
Owner: Lambert Albury
Service Address:
Sherton Bay Street; Nassau, Bahamas
Mailing Address:
P.O. Box N-10728, Nassau, Bahamas
Service Telephone:
809/322-3301
Reservation Telephone:
Same as above
Hours Service is Open:
8:30 am–5:30 pm Seven days a week
Resort Affiliation:
The Sheraton-British Colonial Hotel
Rooms:
325
Cottages/Villas:
NA

Guests of Sun Divers stay at the Sheraton-British Colonial, an eight-acre resort in the center of Nassau with a private beach and dock. Sun Divers is a full service operation, providing pool training and checkouts for novices, PADI certification, and rental and repair service. They dive almost 50 different sites, which accommodate all skill levels of diver. In winter they tend to cater more to professional and experienced divers.

Sun Divers do a shallow reef dive in the morning for novices and photographers, and a deeper afternoon dive for the more experienced. This dive ranges from 45 feet to 90 feet. They offer night dives in the summer for certified divers only.

Divers board either their 30-foot or 42-foot dive boat at the hotel dock and cruise to sites off Paradise Island and the north and west coasts. A few of the places they dive are: Paradise Caves, Goulding Cay, Twin Ledge Drop-off, Green Cay Reef, Lyford Cay Drop-off as well as some blue holes, The Mahoney and other wrecks.

Lambert Albury of Sun Divers has a friendly, competent staff who attract many return customers year after year. From the Sheraton, guests have access to all watersports, deep sea fishing, and the shopping, dining, and casinos of Nassau/Paradise Island.

Tools for the underwater explorer.

Helix has the tools for the underwater explorer, whether professional or amateur. Our staff of diver/photographers knows the equipment and supplies used below the water line and can help you make the best choice. Before you dive, call us. Helix makes the dive more rewarding.

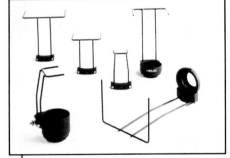

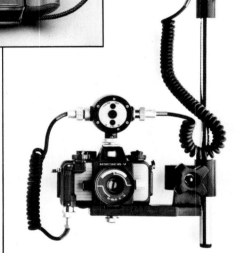

Now you can take your autofocus camera underwater or in all weather conditions with an affordable Helix Auto-Marine II Housing. Featuring a built-in viewfinder and patented prism I.R. regulator. The Auto-Marine II is constructed of durable acrylic resin and stainless steel and is pressure tested to 100 feet. Specify Nikon One-Touch, Nikon L35AF, Canon AF35M, Canon AF35MII or Canon AF35ML.

Helix sponsors frequent dive trips and seminars. For information call 1-800-33/HELIX.

There are many underwater strobes available at a wide range of prices. But no other flash unit, no matter what the price, offers as many features as our Aquaflash units. Dedicated for the Nikonos IV and V, the Aquaflash 28TTL and 28 feature automatic and manual exposure control down to 165 feet, wide-angle coverage up to 15mm lens with optional diffuser and built-in sensor. In addition, the 28TTL offers convenient TTL auto exposure control with the Nikonos V. Both strobes come complete with everything necessary to take the plunge. And. they're backed by our comprehensive Helix 2-year limited service plan, the most complete warranty in the industry!

Our unique extension tube system is designed to help you build the most versatile set of tubes and framers available. With just 3 basic tubes, you can develop up to 7 different tube, framer, and lens combinations for your 35mm or 28mm Nikonos lenses without having to buy 7 different tubes and framers! You can even use the Helix Extension Tube System to expand a basic Subsea or Nikonos extension tube set.

These and other outstanding Helix underwater products are available at professional dive shops throughout the world.

HELIX ®

310 South Racine Avenue, Chicago, IL 60607
312/421-6000

Live outside of Illinois? Call our underwater department toll free: 1-800-33/HELIX.

Please send me a FREE copy of the current Helix Underwater Catalog and Booklist ($2.00 value).

Name _____

Address _____

City, State, Zip _____

DA87

Ever Since You Were a Kid You`ve Wanted to Try It

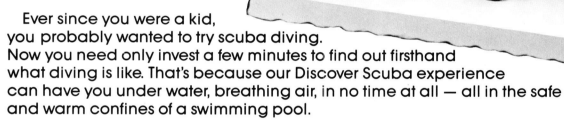

Ever since you were a kid,
you probably wanted to try scuba diving.
Now you need only invest a few minutes to find out firsthand
what diving is like. That's because our Discover Scuba experience
can have you under water, breathing air, in no time at all — all in the safe
and warm confines of a swimming pool.

Discover Scuba is simple, easy and fun. It's the most convenient way we know to experience the actual sensation of scuba diving. And if you would like to find out how easy it is to continue diving once you've tried it, we'll be happy to explain that, too.

To find out where you can start, just look in the Yellow Pages under *Skin* or *Scuba Diving* for a local PADI Training Facility. For a complete list of PADI Training Facilities world wide, write PADI, 1243 East Warner Avenue, Santa Ana, CA 92705.

RUM

CAY

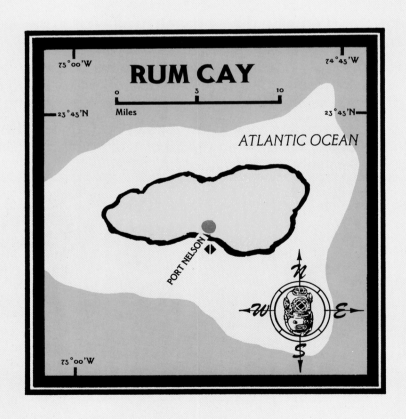

Luxury and isolation is the appeal of Rum Cay. A small island located between Long Island and San Salvador, this island resort was developed in the early 1980s exclusively for the dive traveler. Rum Cay measures approximately four miles by nine miles, and has a resident population of less than 100. Port Nelson is the only settlement.

Rum Cay's history was only slightly tinted by explorers, colonists, and pirates. Salt mines were operational until a hurricane wiped them out in 1853, leaving the isle to bask in the sun for over 100 years until developers began plans for a resort.

Today, more than ever, Rum Cay is an adventure diver's haven. New amenities have been added, however, and other lovers of luxury and isolation are beginning to explore the sites on and around Rum Cay.

Getting There/ Getting Around

Rum Cay has a 2,400-foot runway served by Associated Air Service, a private charter, and Aero Coach. Flights leave Ft. Lauderdale for Georgetown on Exuma where passengers are cleared through customs, then take a commuter to Rum Cay. The 340-mile trip from the Florida coast to Rum Cay can take as little as three hours. Most of the flights come in and leave on Saturday, but the resort can make other arrangements as needed.

Guests travel the island on foot, bicycle, or resort-supplied electric trams. Longer trips to the island's north beach area are made in jeeps.

Topside Attractions

The resort and the water provide the base for Rum Cay fun. The maximum number of guests on Rum Cay at any one time is seldom over 40, so the miles of beach which fringe this 30-square-mile isle are more than ample to assure privacy.

Other offerings provided by Rum Cay include bonefishing and deep sea fishing, catamaran sailing, and a club house complete with bar, boutique, and library. Island style drinks go well with highly acclaimed Bahamian and American meals.

Hiking trails lead inland to Hartford Cave where there are Pre-Columbian Indian drawings on the walls.

Rum Cay Diving

Rum Cay diving covers the coral gamut with beach entry dives to shallow coral gardens, to dives exceeding 110 feet to explore deep water corals along the drop-offs. Rum Cay is especially well known for its spectacular wall dives.

Coral heads, fractures, caves, wrecks and exotic marine life are all here. Divers explore a number of seldom-seen sites in the waters near other cays, such as uninhabited Conception Island.

The people who have dived these sites over the years have respected them and the life they' hold. Consequently, fish feeders and photographers get a chance to enjoy themselves with the action down under Rum Cay.

Rum Cay Dive Sites

Snowfields has been a popular site for years. For some of the people who live here it is as close as they will ever get to seeing snow. Coral heads are laced with delicate white formations brimming with life. Visibility is excellent, helping divers spot some of the smaller, more reclusive reef dwellers.

The Chimney is a vertical tunnel which descends from 50 feet to 100 feet. It leads to a coral cavern. Coral heads rise from the floor and there are encrusted forms along the sides. From the cavern a ravine leads to a drop-off at 130 feet.

Dynamite Wall is a fine example of the diveable tunnels which cut deep into the reef walls near Rum Cay. Staghorn and other species hang from the wall and sides of the canyons.

Rum Cay Dive Service

RUM CAY CLUB, LTD.
Owner: David Melville
Service Address:
Port Nelson; Rum Cay, The Bahamas
Mailing Address:
701 SW 48th Street, Ft. Lauderdale, FL 33315
Service Telephone:
305/467-8365
Reservation Telephone:
800/326-0787
Hours Service is Open:
8 am–5 pm Seven days a week
Resort Affiliation:
Rum Cay Club Resort
Rooms:
14
Cottages/Villas:
3

The Rum Cay Club has been designed to support the adventures of serious sport divers. It offers a resort course, a PADI four- to five-day open-water course and underwater photography classes.

Full gear rentals, including camera equipment, film processing and repairs are part of this club's services.

Their two 36-foot flattop boats take small diving parties to the reefs, wrecks and walls three to four times a day. Two-tank wall dives are offered in the morning and a shallow reef dive is in the afternoon. They have night diving twice a week.

The Snowfields Reef is not only one of Rum Cay's best-known sites, it is also a favorite of the dive masters. On Rum Cay's Northwest Wall deep sites such as Pinder Reef hold predictable sightings of sharks, rays, and barracuda. Elsewhere divers explore tunnels and canyons which cut into the reef base under Rum Cay.

The Rum Cay Club is less than a stone's throw from the beach on the protected south coast. The entire island is virtually surrounded by fine, white coral sand, making it very easy to walk away from it all. Boating, windsurfing and fishing are popular pastimes and there is a lot of socializing centered around the lounge and beachside patio. The management and guests combine for impromptu island tours and parties, helping make a stay at Rum Cay both educational and entertaining.

Alan Williams

SAN SALVADOR

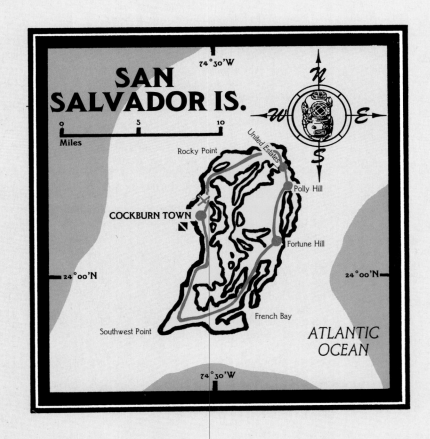

San Salvador sits alone atop the east edge of the Bahama Bank. Located about 175 miles east-southeast of Nassau, San Salvador is reportedly the island upon which Columbus first made landfall in the New World, on October 12, 1492. White beaches, hills, and subtropical trees and shrubs are in much the same pristine condition as they were 500 years ago. The island is about 68 square miles with a good part of its interior filled with lakes.

Cockburn Town, on the protected west coast, is the island's main center for its 1,200 residents. Fishing and agriculture villages are speckled along the coast. The U.S. Coast Guard has a station at Graham's Harbour on the north shore.

Getting There/ Getting Around

Bahamasair lands at San Salvador's 4,500-foot runway twice a week from Nassau and the airport serves as an official port of entry. The Riding Rock Inn has charter flights each Saturday from Ft. Lauderdale. Rental cars, motorbikes, and bicycles are available through the Riding Rock. The minimum age to rent cars or motorbikes is 25.

Roads fringe the entire island and give access to miles of pure white beaches and the settlements and historic sites on the island.

Topside Attractions

After studying the evidence, the Bahamas Government has accepted that San Salvador is the most likely island for Columbus to have first discovered. While touring about you can view any of the four monuments dedicated to being the site of Columbus' landfall, but the Cross Monument, about three miles south of Cockburn Town, is probably closest to any actual spot.

Second to the Columbus monuments, visitors are most interested in seeing Dixon Hill Lighthouse. Built by the Imperial Lighthouse Service, it is one of the last hand-operated, kerosene-powered lighthouses in operation in the world. Its light can be seen from up to 90 miles away at sea.

San Salvador is a popular stop for boaters. There is a marina at Riding Rock through which guided bonefishing and big game fishing can be arranged. Some record bonefish have been taken in the flats. A tennis court is also available at Riding Rock.

Other attractions include Farquharson's Plantation, an old relic from the cotton growing era. The site has the ruins of a house, prison, and kitchen.

San Salvador once went by the name Watling's Island because the pirate George Watling took over the island in the 1600s and built one of his castles there. The castle's ruins are located at the south end of the island on a bluff overlooking the sea.

Cockburn Town has The New World Museum with some artifacts from the Lucayans and the colonial period. The resort can call ahead for you to make sure someone will be there.

San Salvador Diving

With the re-opening of the Riding Rock Inn, adventure divers again have access to the spectacular walls and deep coral canyons off San Salvador. Reefs, drop-offs, and coral caves dominate the diving from French Bay and Southwest Point in the south and up along the west coast north of Riding Rock Inn. The deep canyons and fissures at 40 feet to 140 feet hold all of the usual Bahama fish and coral life and more. The coral formations have a wildness about them which brings out the undersea nightlife in a massive array of colors and quantities. Jutting out into the Atlantic as it does, San Salvador has some species which are a rarity to the inner islands.

San Salvador's waters offer excellent u/w photography possibilities especially at medium depths where there is excellent water clarity to spy eagle rays, black coral, many types of sponges, or photograph small marine animals throughout fissures splitting the walls. Hawksbills turtles, eels and octopuses are all frequently seen.

San Salvador Dive Sites

At 45 feet, the **Telephone Pole** wall dive starts with a coral canyon that winds through the reef. At 100 feet it opens onto the vertical face of the drop-off. After leaving the canyon (a telephone pole lies on the wall above the canyon's mouth), divers explore the wall down to 130 feet.

Sandy Point is a wall cut with crevices in its rim reef and tunnels bored into its face. Home to a myriad of sponges, it also has shellfish, starfish, and a host of smaller invertebrates living within the wall from 40 feet to 130 feet. Spotted rays cruise among the coral and white sand at the site's shallower depths.

Snap Shot Reef has long been popular with u/w photographers. Divers with food easily coax groupers and eels out of hiding. Beginning at 30 feet, the reef quickly becomes a favorite of novice and intermediate divers. Its abundant marine life and coral are also stimulating to the more advanced who take it as an afternoon dive. Lobster, arrow crab and sea star are around the rocks and sponges.

Sand Castles is indicative of how sand falls cut fissures through drop-offs of a reef, providing places for new life as they wear away the old. There are sights all along this site, with corals and sponges intermingling along the rim and the wall.

FRESCATE WRECK is one of the better known wrecks off San Salvador. A freighter which ran onto the reef and sank in 1902, it was later blasted away to keep it out of the way of other ships, as well as to salvage some of its copper. Pieces of the 260-foot-long wreck are scattered over a couple of acres, with the boilers being some of the largest identifiable chunks.

San Salvador Dive Services

GUANAHANI DIVE, LTD.
Service Address:
Cockburn Town; San Salvador, Bahamas
Mailing Address:
c/o Out Island Service Corp, Inc., 701 SW 48th Street; Ft. Lauderdale, FL 33315
Service Telephone:
809/332-2631
Reservation Telephone:
800/272-1492 (USA) 305/761-1492 (FL)
Hours Service is Open:
8:30 am–5 pm Seven days a week
Resort Affiliation:
Riding Rock Inn
Rooms:
24
Cottages/Villas:
NA

Back in action after being closed for two-and-a-half years, The Riding Rock Inn, in conjunction with Guanahani Dive, boasts a newly refurbished dive resort and new dive equipment to help ensure a quality time.

Guanahani Ltd., once known as Island Water Sports, offers a resort course as well as a PADI certification program. Rentals and repairs are available. They do a two-tank dive in the morning, a single-tank in the afternoon, and night dives along the reefs and wrecks. Guanahani's fleet includes a 30-foot, 41-foot, and a 47-foot dive boat. Most of the sites are five to 15 minutes away from the resort.

For years, novice to expert divers have come to dive the waters of San Salvador, once known as Guanahani. The resort staff has many years of experience between them, with most of the people who work at Riding Rock now having been there when it was open before. It's friendly. It's quiet. There's excellent, fresh seafood and plenty of it.

Other activities include tennis, swimming and island tours.

TURKS & CAICOS

The Turks and Caicos are two groups of islands which begin approximately 400 miles southeast of Nassau. A crown colony of Britain since 1976, these islands are governed by an Executive Council comprised of eleven duly elected members, three who are appointed by the Governor, and three ex-officio members. The Governor is appointed by the Queen and presides over the Council.

(The name Caicos is derived from the Spanish cayos, which means island.)

The Caicos group consists of these main islands: Providenciales, Middle Caicos, and South Caicos. West Caicos and East Caicos are uninhabited, as are many of the smaller cays. Flowing between the Caicos Islands and The Bahamas is the deep, 30-mile-wide Caicos Passage. The Caicos are atop the shallow water of the Caicos Bank, which is surrounded by a barrier reef and deep water, making the area of special interest to divers.

The Turks are separated from the Caicos by the 22-mile-wide, 7,000-foot-deep channel called the Turks Island Passage. This group gets its name from the Turk's Head Cactus, whose blossom resembles a Turkish fez. The main islands are Grand Turk and Salt Cay. As is the Caicos group, these are also protected from the deep Atlantic by barrier reef. The combined area of both islands groups is approximately 160 square miles.

The Turks and Caicos Islands are a blend of tropical wilderness and semi-arid desert. Savannahs and headlands carpeted with thatch palm and cactus cover the larger Caicos Islands. These get 30 to 40 inches of rain a year and, as such, have a fairly good water supply and support some agriculture. Dry, low-lying salinas make up the smaller islands like Grand Turk and Salt Cay, where sea salt production is still part of the economy. These islands receive 20 inches of rain annually and water conservation is essential. The stormiest part of the year is during the summer.

Besides the salt industry, many of the other 8,000 residents sustain themselves on fishing and tourism. The large majority of the people live on the islands named above, with the capital city of Cockburn Town on Grand Turk Island being the prime population and tourist center. Tourism is being developed by people who know how to serve guests as well as protect the beauty and tranquility found here.

Though it is uncertain whether Columbus discovered Turks and Caicos, Arawak Indians did live on them for centuries before Ponce de Leon landed upon Grand Turk in 1512 during his quest for the Fountain of Youth. Soon thereafter, the French and Spanish battled one another, pirates, and Bermudian colonists for them. Eventually, both The Bahamas and Bermuda claimed them. The English were finally able to establish control and decided The Bahamas should have jurisdiction over them. Later, that control was passed to Jamaica, but when Jamaica was granted independence in 1962, Turks and Caicos became a separate British colony, and remains so today.

Getting There/ Getting Around

Three airfields serve as official ports of entry: The airfield on Grand Turk Island outside Cockburn Town; the one on South Caicos near Cockburn Harbour; and the airfield serving Providenciales Island. After passing through immigration and customs at any of these ports, private planes or charters can fly to any of the five airfields serving other parts of Turks and Caicos.

To pass through immigration, U.S. and Canadian citizens do not require passports, but should carry some form of identification such as a birth certificate or voter registration card. A driver's license is not considered valid. Citizens of other countries do require a passport. All visitors must have a round-trip or onward ticket. If they find you trying to bring in a speargun, they will take it. If they find you trying to bring in drugs, they will take you.

Each person is required to pay a $5 departure tax when leaving the country. Persons entering these islands on a private boat must obtain a cruising permit from a port of entry.

Taxis are usually available to meet incoming commercial flights and the rates are fixed to most resorts. There are no car rental agencies here yet, but your resort can help you find a car to rent. There are also no ferries running between the islands, but the Turks & Caicos National Airlines (TCNA) provides island hopping service. Have your resort make and confirm your reservation, and always find out in advance how much baggage you can take. Though it is possible, do not count on being able to rent a boat or hire someone to drop you off and pick you up from the outlying cays.

Topside Attractions

People come to Turks and Caicos to dive, fish and tan. The fishing is equal to many of the best places in the Caribbean and The Bahamas. Everything from bonefishing to big game fishing is available and often prolific, with a little help from your guide and his boat.

Around the major islands there is well over 200 miles of white and gold sand beaches. As the resorts and dive services are small, privacy and intimacy are the real attractions. The restaurants and lounges, since most cater to hungry and thirsty boaters and divers, offer excellent drinks and food. Meals are entertainment in themselves, and are sometimes enhanced with local music and dancing.

Turks and Caicos Diving

New sites are going to be discovered around Turks and Caicos for a long time. Some of the people with whom we visited just before this book went to print will be exploring virgin areas along the walls which surround the islands to find the best of the best. As mentioned, the Turks and the Caicos, as two separate island groups, are surrounded by barrier reef and are bordered by deep ocean channels. The walls off the west and north coasts of Providenciales, the west coast of West Caicos, the west coast of Grand Turk Island, and the east coast of South Caicos are, at this time, the prime dive areas.

The wild walls of South Caicos and Grand Turk are on opposite sides of the Turks Island Passage. Since Turk-Cai Watersports closed, there are no dive services operating on South Caicos at the time of this writing, although the area is too exciting for this void to last long. On both sides of the reef wall offshore from South Caicos and Long Cay there is good diving. Caves, wrecks, and walls are the prime attractions. Generally, the area along the outer wall is more of a challenge for the experienced divers because it is more exposed to Atlantic currents flowing through the Turks Island Passage.

There are many charted wall and canyon dives which begin in 40 feet. Visibility inside and outside the reef ranges from 80 feet to close to 200 feet. The water is seldom clouded by runoff, currents, or tides. Eagle rays, manta rays, turtles, dolphin, trumpet fish, sunfish, tropical angels, and other reef fish and pelagics abound. During January, February, and March, it may be possible to glimpse migrating humpback whales which pass within a quarter of a mile from Grand Turk Island.

Currents and sand have cut channels through the reef walls. There are coral gardens, coral heads and plateaus with

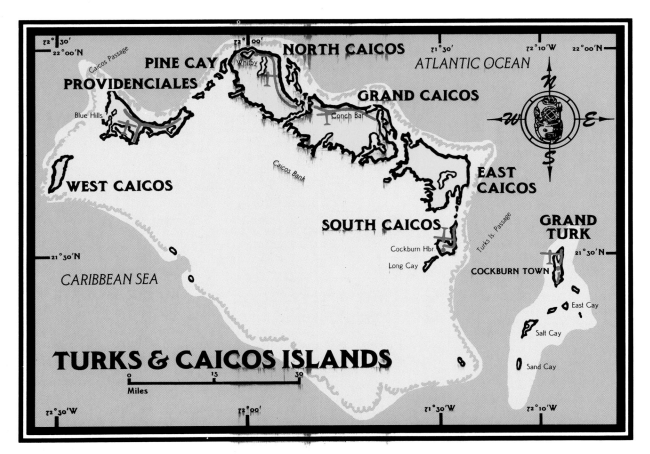

TURKS & CAICOS ISLANDS

barrel sponges and tube sponges, sea whips and shellfish. Branches of black coral are found at 70 feet. Occasionally, storms pile ships onto the reef and, more than once, salvaging operations have led to newfound old wrecks.

Turks and Caicos Dive Sites

Steller's Cut Wall and **The West Wall** are two areas off Providenciales that are for intermediate and advanced divers. Beginning in 35 feet divemasters take divers as deep as 130 feet to areas still largely unexplored. These walls have formations of rock and coral which hang over the 6,000 foot depths of the Caicos Passage. The West Wall is especially dynamic. It is a vertical edge of the U.S. Continental Shelf at which divers frequently see sharks and rays cruising about the shadows. A specific site on The West Wall is **The Laurel Canyon**, a site ranging from 45 feet to 110 feet. With elkhorn coral and sponges dangling from its sides, this narrow, vertical canyon cuts back into the Continental Shelf about 150 feet. It has a white sand bottom opening into a white sand plain dotted with garden eels, coral heads, and sponges.

The Pinnacles is an excellent 35-foot to 60-foot dive which features coral mounds and coral ridges separated by a white sand bottom that cuts through gullies and valleys. It is a colorful spot in which to find reef fish and invertebrates.

For novice divers, there are many sites inside the reef. For example, **Eagle Ray Run** is a 20-foot dive with coral heads and many shallow water coral species, such as brain and elkhorn. Abundant sealife lurks among the coral, making this spot a popular night dive, as well.

One of the newer wrecks is the **SOUTH WIND SHIP WRECK**. Down in 50 feet to 60 feet of water, this 80-foot cargo carrier sunk in 1985 off the north coast of Providenciales is becoming a home to groupers and puffers and is still well intact.

Northeast of Providenciales are **Pine Cay** and **Fort George Cay**, two small isles which lie on the coral ridge between Provo and North Caicos. Aside from the abundant reef fish, sponges and other invertebrates, divers occasionally find artifacts in the sand from the pirate-colonial era. Outside the reef there is superb wall diving over the Caicos Passage.

Wall dives off Grand Turk Island begin in 25 feet of water, making parts of the wall and ridge accessible to novice divers. **The Amphitheatre** is a bowl of white sand fringed with coral. In places, sand has cut through the ridge, giving divers vertical crevices to explore as deep down as 80 feet.

The Tunnel is another wall dive with some features similar to The Amphitheatre. It is a deep crevice which directs divers through the reef wall and then opens up at about 80 feet, providing access to the outer wall which faces the Turks Island Passage. Pelagics are a frequent sight for divers hovering above the depths of the passage.

The Black Forest is a pristine and abundant stand of black coral, mixed with other coral and many different kinds of sponges. The forest starts in about 50 feet of water and slopes down gradually to 100 feet.

Turks and Caicos Dive Services

BLUE WATER DIVERS
Service Address:
   Cockburn Town; Grand Turk Island, British West Indies
Mailing Address:
   P.O. Box 124; Grand Turk, British West Indies
Service Telephone:
   809/946-2432
Reservation Telephone:
   Same as above
Hours Service is Open:
   No specific hours, but open seven days a week
Resort Affiliation:
   The Turk's Head Inn
Rooms:
   7
Cottages/Villas:
   The Salt Raker Inn
   10

Mitch Rolling, divemaster at Blue Water Divers, enjoys working with small dive parties and tailoring the trips to their desires, with particular consideration to underwater photographers. Blue Waters caters to beginning as well as advanced divers. The service offers a resort course and PADI certification. Rental gear is available, but they recommend you bring as much personal dive gear as possible.

Twice a day Blue Waters takes divers aboard the 23-foot dive boat to sites along the protected wall west of Grand Turk. The wall starts in 25 feet to 30 feet of water. Divers go down to 80 feet and overlook the Turk Passage. Their wall sites include the Black Forest, Amphitheatre, Library and The Tunnel. They will also do all-day dives to the uninhabited cays southeast of Grand Turk. Night dives are arranged on request.

The advantage of Blue Waters diving is that the dive parties are usually limited to eight and, since few divers have seen this area, the coral life, including a bounty of sponges and shellfish, is intact and plentiful.

Mitch says Grand Turk is a great getaway place. The beaches are empty and clean. They want to keep it that way for the diver who wants it that way.

PROVO AQUATICS CENTER
Service Address:
   Providenciales Island, Turks & Caicos
Mailing Address:
   P.O. Box 526002; Miami, FL 33152
Service Telephone:
   809/946-4455
Reservation Telephone:
   Same as above
Hours Service is Open:
   8 am–6 pm Seven days a week
Resort Affiliation:
   Local hotels

Provo Aquatics Center is a watersports center which opened in December, 1985. They offer a novice resort course and are PADI affiliated. The only equipment they rent are tanks, packs and weights. They do no equipment repairs.

This service has a growing commitment to diving. Not only do they have a 53-foot sailboat which they use for dive trips to the West Caicos Wall ten miles away, but they are checking out the reefs closer to their port to find new, untouched sites. Often their sailboat parties consist of a handful of divers, with other passengers along for snorkeling and beachcombing.

In addition to diving, Provo Aquatics has boat rentals, windsurfing, fishing, and guided boat trips.

PROVO TURTLE DIVERS
Service Address:
   Providenciales, Turks & Caicos
Mailing Address:
   P.O. Box 526002; Miami, FL 33151

David McCray

Service Telephone:
809/946-4230
Reservation Telephone:
800/323-7600
Hours Service is Open:
Variable hours; seven days a week
Resort Affiliation:
Third Turtle Inn
Rooms:
15
Cottages/Villas:
NA

The Third Turtle Inn has been popular with divers for years. The dive service enhances the Provo's topside adventure with a selection of prime sites.

A resort course is offered as well as both PADI and NAUI instruction. They have a full line of rentals and repair some personal dive equipment. Divemasters Felix and Carol Swann guide one-tank dives in the morning and afternoon. Night diving is available with a minimum of three people. They have two dive boats, a 20-footer and a 22-footer; seldom do they have more than eight divers at a time.

Their reef sites include Eagle Ray Run, which is a checkout and night dive, The Aquarium and The Grouper Hole. The reefs have eels, coral heads, lobster, grouper and sponges. Steller's Cut is a wall dive from 35 feet to 110 feet. They are still

exploring the West Wall, a vertical edge of the continental shelf which starts at 35 feet and drops into the Caicos Passage. They dive the South Wind Shipwreck at 60 feet, an 80-foot cargo carrier lost in 1985.

The Third Turtle features strictly gourmet dining prepared and served by the friendliest people you can hope to find anywhere. The resort also has tennis, guided fishing and other watersports, but its main emphasis is on diving.

OMEGA DIVING SERVICES
Service Address:
Grand Turk Island
Mailing Address:
P.O. Box 119; Grand Turk, Turks & Caicos
Service Telephone:
809/946-2232
Reservation Telephone:
Same as above
Hours Service is Open:
9 am–5 pm Seven days a week
Resort Affiliation:
Hotel Kittina and other island hotels
Rooms:
43
Cottages/Villas:
NA

Mike Spillar has been a part owner-manager of this service for the past eight years. He is now teamed with Gene Al-

berti. Between them, they have many years of diving Turks & Caicos waters. Omega Diving has three PADI instructors and they cater to all divers, from novice to the advanced. The service is outfitted with new and complete sets of dive gear. They also rent cameras and do film processing.

Their dive boat, a 32-foot Island Hopper, comfortably carries 22 divers to the reefs and walls along Grand Turk. Inside the east coast reef they dive The Cathedral, Gibb's Cay Reef and Horseshoe. On the west side the top of their barrier reef averages from 25 feet to 45 feet. The wall offers great diversity with over 30 sites where canyons and tunnels run through the drop-off of the Turks Passage. They dive The Tunnels, The Amphitheatre and The Black Forest, which have been described earlier. Scientists from the Smithsonian have said that the coral along that wall is probably the oldest and best developed in this part of the world. The sites hold virtually all tropical and subtropical fish species that can be found anywhere nearby. Divers may also catch sight of humpback whales during their migration.

There is little planned for between dives. Aside from great watersports and beachcombing, people come to Omega Diving Services for its competent, experienced and personal service.

Mike Mesgleski

Bahama Live-Aboards

Blackbeard's Cruises

P.O. Box 661091
Miami Springs, FL 32266
305/888-1226 or 800/327-9600

Blackbeard's has three 65-foot live-aboard sail/motor boats which cruise The Bahamas. On the average, they dive three times a day. They usually spend the night at a calm, secluded anchorage at which divers can dive, snorkel or beachcomb. Each boat will spend one night of the week-long cruise in port at Bimini, Freeport or in the Berry Islands. All the passengers have to do is eat, drink and dive; the crew does the rest.

Bottom Time Adventures

P.O. Box 11919
Fort Lauderdale, FL 33339-1919
305/561-0111 or 800/345-3483

Bottom Time Adventures has two boats. The Bottom Time 1 is a 65-foot power boat which can hold 14 divers. The Bottom Time 2 is an 87-foot-long powered catamaran with room for 30. It has 16 cabins and a darkroom. Both boats leave from Port Everglade and cruise throughout The Bahamas. If they are going to the Exumas, they have an option to pick up passengers at Nassau, Grand Bahama.

The Bottom Time 2 is a magnificent luxury boat, with two 800-horse-powered, turbo-charged Rolls-Royce diesel engines. It represents the first marine application for Rolls-Royce diesels.

Island Fantasy

301 E. Blue Heron Blvd.
Rivera Beach, FL 33404
305/848-7632 or 800/848-7632

The Island Fantasy is 90 feet of floating luxury. Offering customized Bahama dive trips, this ship can carry as many as 32 people, but tries to limit it to 16 divers and a crew of eight. That ratio makes for a very laid-back trip for divers.

The six-day-six-night trips include a stop in port almost every night so passengers can fully experience the topside nightlife of the larger Bahama cities. When cruising to the more remote islands, however, passengers usually stay on board.

E-6 processing is available on board and can be done by a staff member, or they will teach the diver how to develop his/her own pictures.

Sea Aggressor

c/o Sea & See Travel
50 Francisco St., Suite 205
San Francisco, CA 94133
415/771-0077 or 800/348-9778

Sea & See Travel is the world's first and largest travel agency for scuba divers. The 100-foot-long Sea Aggressor is just one ship in its growing live-aboard fleet. Offering week-long Bahama dive trips, the Sea Aggressor can support divers in almost any environment, be it 50 miles from land or just offshore from a casino. The diving is virtually unlimited. All are one-tank dives, since it is easy to strap on a fresh tank.

Sea Fever

P.O. Box 39-8276
Miami Beach, FL 33139
305/531-3483 or 800/443-3837

The Sea Fever cruises many prime sites in the Bahamas, of which three areas are customer favorites: The Western Bahamas, Berry Islands and the Cay South Bank area. The boat does five- six- and seven-day trips, with usually one night a trip in port.

This 90-foot-long, customized dive cruiser has room for 24 passengers. The Sea Fever has been supporting divers for over 15 years. Its congenial, courteous crew assures each group of guests receives as much diving and as much topside rest and relaxation as it wants.

Sea Dragon

2200 South Andrews Ave.
Ft. Lauderdale, FL 33316
305/522-0161

The 65-foot-long Sea Dragon offers some of the most complete yet economical live-aboard diving in The Bahamas. Specializing in cruising the Exumas, the Sea Dragon offers unlimited diving to walls, reefs, caves and currents.

You Can Train Better Divers

using the Jeppesen 4th Edition Manual

Most good divers are equal in underwater skills. What separates the better diver from the good diver is knowledge and judgement.

Train Better Divers With Latest Information
Every instructor knows diving skills and judgement are based on the student's learning important need-to-know information. Jeppesen materials make teaching easy and student learning easy by providing the latest need-to-know information combined with many illustrations and photographs. Student insight is much faster and is retained longer with a well illustrated manual and workbook.

Diving Knowledge Moves Forward with The 4th Edition
Once again Jeppesen moves diving knowledge forward with the revised 4th Edition of its Open Water Manual, Workbook, and Final Exam. Many subjects are added so instructors can train safer, more confident, thinking divers.

Existing Subjects

* Seeing & Swimming
* Warmth & Buoyancy
* Breathing Underwater
* Tools & Accessories
* Sensations
* Breathing
* Descending & Ascending
* Depth & Time Limits
* Repetitive Dives
* The Worlds of Diving
* Water Movement
* Ocean Life
* Fresh Waters
* Ecology
* Food from the Sea
* Photography
* Specialty Diving
* Careers

Revised Subjects

* Dive Planning
* Safe Diving Standards
* New Equipment Photographs
* Protecting Your Ears
* Emergency Ascents
* Dives Tables
* Medical Aspects

Added Subjects

* Natural Navigation
* Compass Use
* Tidal Current Table Use
* Weather Information
* Nutrition
* Considerations for Women
* Heat & Aluminum Tanks
* High Tech Dive Computers
* Hypothermia

Other Products by Jeppesen

Open Water Slide/Cassette Course, Open Water Video Course VHS, Advanced Slide/Cassette Course, Advanced Video Course VHS, Advanced Kit (Manual & Workbook), Open Water Diver Logbook, Hard Plastic Dive Table, Skin Diving Manual, Promotional Slide/Cassette Program

How to Order

Instructors and Dive Stores only call toll free **1-800-525-7379** to place your order. All Jeppesen products are satisfaction guaranteed.

VISA & MasterCard Accepted

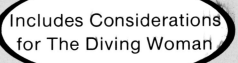
Includes Considerations for The Diving Woman

JEPPESEN

55 Inverness Dr. East Englewood, CO 80112-5498
(303) 799-9090   Texex 4322029

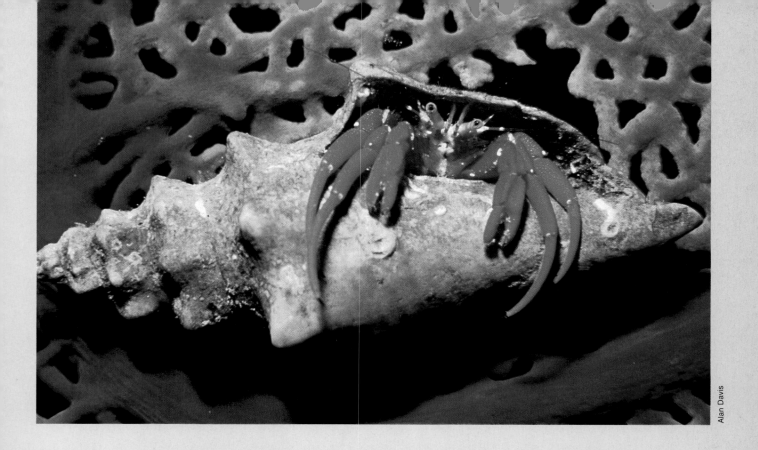

THE
CARIBBEAN

Belize

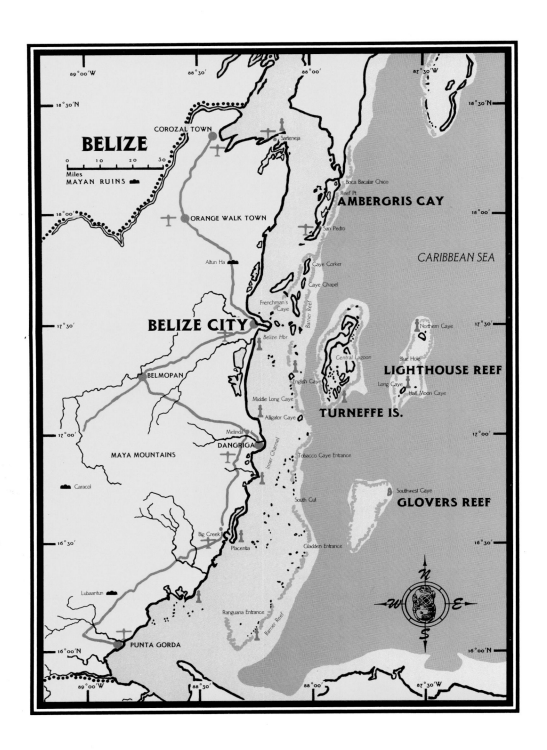

Belize

Entry Requirements
Proof of Citizenship for USA, Canada & U.K. citizens. Passports for all others

Language
English, Spanish, Creole

Airport
Belize International; 10 mi from Belize City, the nation's captial

Departure Tax
US $5

Electricity
110 volts; 60 cycles

Size
8,866 sq. mi.

Population
150,000

U.S. Tourist Office
Belize Embassy, Washington, D.C.
800/368-5909
Belize Tourist Board
P.O. Box 325
12 Regent Street
Belize City, Belize C.A
02-72-13

Belize borders the Caribbean Sea along the eastern shore of Central America, just below the Yucatan Peninsula. It is bounded on the north and west by Mexico and on the south and west by Guatemala. The coastline has swampy flats as well as sand beaches. Inland, the terrain rises gradually toward the low peaks of the Maya Mountains in the south. The highest point is Victoria Peak at 3,680 feet. The climate is hot and humid, but along the coast and the cays, heat and humidity are tempered by sea breezes. Offshore is the incredible 175-mile-long Great Barrier Reef of Belize. The reef, plus the many cays inside the reef and the three coral atolls, account for the diver's main attraction to this country.

The Mayan Indian civilization flourished in the area known as Belize between 1500 B.C. and 1000 A.D. Several archeological sites, notably those at Altun Ha and Xunantunich, reflect the civilization of this period. European contact began in 1502 when Columbus sailed along the coast. The first recorded European settlement was begun by shipwrecked English seamen in 1638. Over the next 150 years, more English settlements were established. This period was also marked by pirating, indiscriminate logging and plant collecting, and sporadic battles between the Indians, Spaniards and English.

Spain recognized Great Britain's authority over the territory in several 18th century treaties. Britain sent its first official representatives to the area in the late 18th century, but Belize was not formally termed the "Colony of British Honduras" until 1840. It became a crown colony in 1862 and became independent on September 21, 1981.

Guatemala, however, claims Belize as part of its territory. Consequently, there is tension between Guatemala and Belize. Britain maintains a small military force in Belize to help preserve its security.

Getting There/ Getting Around

Belize International Airport receives flights from the U.S. via TACA, TAN/SAHSA and Challenge Airlines. TAN/SAHSA has special baggage allowances for dive equipment. It is approximately two hours by air from Miami and Houston and five hours from San Francisco and New York. Unmetered taxis are available at the airport and rental cars are available there, as well as in Belize City. The airport is open during *daylight hours only!* Private craft need to get landing clearance 48 hours ahead of time.

By car, the drive to Belize by all-weather roads takes three to five days from Texas, and about one week from California.

How to get to the dive resorts located on the major islands and cays will be mentioned in the dive service section.

Topside Attractions

Many sport divers to Belize enjoy spending some time touring Mayan Indian archeological sites. As mentioned above, the ruins of Altun Ha and Xunantunich are well-preserved examples of the architectural genius of the Mayans. No digging or removal or artifacts from the country is allowed.

There is much natural glory still left in Belize. Large cats roam the jungles, tropical forests hold over 500 species of birds and countless rare flowering plants. There are many caves, which, themselves, are archeological sites, and suggest to the adventure diver some of the mysteries which awaits those who dive the caves and blue holes along the Great Barrier Reef.

While touring the country, there is a good chance you will be approached by someone who wants to sell you something. We encourage you to get souvenirs from department stores, hotels, specialty stores or other legitimate outlets. Removing black coral or buying black coral novelties from any unauthorized person is illegal.

Belize Diving

Belize has hundreds of miles of diveable reef and coral atolls. The 175 mile wall of the Great Barrier Reef parallels the mainland from ten miles to 30 miles from shore. Within the barrier are scores of coral islands and cays. The major cays there serve as a resort base for adventure divers, including some who take liveaboards to the outer coral atolls of Turneffe Reef, Lighthouse Reef and Glover's Reef. Divers who come to Belize, then, have access to three of the four true atolls in the entire Atlantic Ocean, which help make Belize diving the thrill it is. Turneffe is about twenty miles south of Ambergris Caye and Lighthouse Reef is about ten miles east of Turneffe. Glover's Reef begins approximately 20 miles to their south.

Ambergris Caye is a few hundred yards from the southern tip of the Yucatan Peninsula. It was the first area of Belize to be developed as a dive destination and now has the majority of the country's dive services. San Pedro, the island's main community, is a combination resort town/

fishing village. San Pedro is quaint and friendly; even the police don't carry guns. Going to San Pedro is like stepping back in time. There are no phones or television. The only pavement on the island is the landing strip at the airport. All resorts here complement the peace and solitude of Ambergris Caye.

The barrier reef begins about a mile east of Ambergris. Its wall characterizes that which is found along the length of the Great Barrier Reef. The top of the reef is near the water's surface and actually breaks it in many places. The reef slopes toward the open Caribbean. Then between 40 feet and 50 feet deep is a formation known as the shallow wall. Many east-west canyons have been carved into it. The canyons themselves have near-vertical walls, colored with trophy-size sponges, sea fans and other gorgonians, soft corals and encrusting corals. Divers sometimes encounter mild currents while going through them. They also see many schools of reef fish, sharks, tarpons, barracuda and solitary members of some of the more shy species. The canyons usually bottom out anywhere from 80 feet to 125 feet. Most diving is done in these canyons and along the face of the shallow wall. At the bottom of the shallow wall is a terrace of sand and deep-water corals. The sand terrace slopes seaward then joins the top of the deep wall at 125 feet to 150 feet. The deep wall drops vertically to the ocean bottom for at least several hundred feet.

Inside the barrier reef are many good 30-foot sites which are dived in the afternoons and at night. There are many sponge-covered patch reefs between the barrier and the coast of Belize. Together with the clear waters, coral gardens, white sand and sea grass bottom, these patches hold many of the largest shellfish and reef fish in the Caribbean.

Beginning about 15 miles south of Ambergris is a string of large cays inside the barrier. The wall runs parallel to and about a mile from their east shore. Caye Corker and Caye Chapel are home to growing dive operations. A 15-mile to 22-mile boat ride from Belize City, they have access to comparable coral structures and depths as that available anywhere, as well as pure white sand beaches, excellent bird life and fishing. Sites to the north and south of the barrier reef are easily accessible from the services here, which also take multi-day boat trips to the coral atolls. The other two cays of interest to divers in this area are Moho Caye and St. George's Caye, both offshore from Belize City and less than a five-minute boat ride to the wall.

The exotic undersea formations along the Great Barrier Reef create many different challenges. Grottos, tunnels and blue holes abound. As the tides change, divers can find themselves drifting through rock caves or forests of black coral. Most of the caves are only for skilled and experienced cave divers.

The adventure of Belize is enhanced for those who travel beyond the barrier reef for several days of diving to the coral atolls: Turneffe Reef, also known as Turneffe Islands, Lighthouse Reef and Glover's Reef. Everything around these atolls seems to be magnified—the color, the diversity of coral and sponges, the size and number of the pelagics, the vertical slope of the walls and the thrill of the unknown and unexplored. Here, the top of the wall can begin at 25 feet. Within the atolls and near other shallow patch reefs are caves and blue holes. Divers usually dive here from a live-aboard, or stay at one of the small resorts on Turneffe or Glover's Reef.

The undersea around Lighthouse Reef, east of Turneffe, has two unique formations: The Great Blue Hole and Half Moon Caye Drop-off. The Great Blue Hole, located in the center of Lighthouse Reef, was first explored by the 1972 Cousteau expedition that plumbed its depth to over 400 feet. The blue hole angles under the reef to form a giant cave resplendent with coral overhangs, stalactites and side tunnels.

Half Moon Caye Drop-off is one of the most liberating wall dives in the Caribbean. Part of the Lighthouse Reef system, Half Moon has a maze of coral formations which begin about 25 feet from the surface and angle and slope toward the open sea. The visibility is seldom anything but excellent. These areas, though, are more subjected to the whims of the weather and wind. The bigger boats which come out here give experienced divers stability and support when the water gets choppy.

Divers have access to the southern part of the Great Barrier Reef via a dive service at Placencia. There are patch reefs and formations around the smaller cays here, as well as virgin sites on the wall to dive.

Belize Dive Sites

Belize has a multitude of dive sites on, within and beyond its Great Barrier Reef, however, few have been named. The sites which are titled and described below are some with which we are familiar and are a good sample of Belize diving. The descriptions should give visiting divers an idea of what to expect and where to find it.

Mexico Rock is a popular shallow coral garden dive off Ambergris Caye. It has some of the best formed coral canyons and terraces to be found in any shallow site known. The reef is populated by a bounty of tube sponges, orange sponges, and vase sponges growing among the bases of stands of elkhorn coral and clumps of brain coral. Plumes of soft corals grace the sides of canyon walls. Hogfish, blennies, yellowtails and butterfly fish are a few of the many reef fish found here.

The top of the mouth of **Mexico Cave** is ten feet down. Inside the cave are schools of small barracuda and yellowtails. Along the walls are lobsters, shrimp and other shellfish. Divers explore this cave to a depth of about 60 feet where it gets too clogged to be fun.

Holchum Reef, offshore from Ambergris Caye, is a site which offers two distinct types of diving inside the reef and outside the reef. At **Inner Holchum Reef**, 25 feet down, there is a V-shaped cut filled with shellfish, damselfish, Spanish hogfish, French grunts, and schooling yellowtail snappers. Divers need to be aware of the mild currents they are likely to encounter coursing through this formation. Finger corals grow among stands of brain and star corals on the floor. Throughout the chutes and crevices packed into this site are many places from which big green moray eels and trumpetfish can appear. It is a prime night-diving area. On the outer side of Holchum Reef is an area cut with surge channels and mini drop-offs. Sponges feed well on nutrients carried in the mild currents. Large tarpons, rays, barracudas and sharks frequently dive this area, too.

The Plateaus is another area of the reef near Ambergris Caye that offers a lot of diving. In most places, cuts in The Plateaus begin in 50 feet of water and are covered with encrusting coral and sponges. The cuts, or canyons, have vertical walls which descend down to the edge of the Continental Shelf. There are magnificent caves and tunnels laced throughout where divers descend to approximately 125 feet.

Pine Canyon is a site just offshore on the barrier reef from San Pedro on Ambergris Caye. It is a large canyon-filled area with overhangs and ledges with a lot of coral and sponge colonies. There are basket sponges, fluorescent vase sponges colored hues of blue, lavendar, pink, orange and yellow. They literally look as if they have a candle in the middle of them. Rose coral, plumes of gorgonian, hydrocorals and other soft corals abound. The groupers, snappers and yellowtails here

give divers an idea of just how big these fish can get.

Punta Arena Reef is an area where numerous caves penetrate the walls of the reef and canyons and exist at the top of the structure in 55 feet of water. The merging of walls and tunnels form micro-environments where the ranges of many fish, sponges and corals overlap.

Morgan's Cut runs through the barrier reef and is a magnificent winding formation through and between crevices of rock and coral. Schools of yellowtail, parrotfish, and chromis scurry through them, as do bands of barracuda and tarpon.

Caye Corker is a reef dive blanketed with brilliant sponges, making it a popular u/w photography site. Soldier fish, some bat fish, angels and triggerfish combine with shellfish and corals to be a good identification site for divers interested in learning and photographing Caribbean reef species.

RAGGEDY ANN BOAT WRECK is down in more than 80 feet of water, two and a half miles southwest of Caye Corker. This was a 50-foot Chris Craft, which was sunk on purpose to train divers in shipwreck diving.

St. George's Caye, seven miles east of Belize City, is an area rich in coral garden, deep reef and wall diving. **Little Finger**, for instance, bottoms out at 120 feet, but has many shelves and ravines that run like terraces about its depths. In one place, the Little Finger reef starts in shallow water and slopes to a shelf about 40 feet down. The shelf drops over a mini-wall to 120 feet where there is another shelf and drop-off. Divers here see large snappers, groupers, sand sharks, sea turtles and an occasional dolphin.

Eileen's Ravine is a valley between two mountains of coral. It is a great location especially for large nurse sharks, as well as eagle rays, triggerfish, hogfish and queen angels.

Dived by only a few is the **Great Blue Hole**, in the center of the Lighthouse Reef Atoll. The topside diameter of the hole is 300 feet across and at least 400 feet deep. Several dive services make a trip here, and guide divers down to 100 feet where the wall curves into the rock to form an enormous cave with stalactites formed when the cave was above sea level.

Belize Dive Services

BLUE MARLIN LODGE
Service Address:
    South Water Caye, east of Dangriga
Mailing Address:
    South Water Caye, Belize, C.A.
Resort Affiliation:

Blue Marlin Lodge
Rooms:
30

This is a new resort which opened for the 1986–87 season. At the time we went to press, the resort had no phone, but it should have a working number at this time.

Most guests of the Blue Marlin will take a commuter flight from the Belize International Airport to the airfield at Dangriga, on the coast of south-central Belize, then boat to South Water Caye and the resort. The cay, ideally situated, sits right on top of the barrier reef midway between Dangriga and Glover's Reef Atoll.

More information on the service should be available by calling the resort direct, or check with Sports Almanacs and we'll let you know if we have an update.

CAPTAIN MORGAN'S RETREAT

Service Address:
About 3 mi. north of San Pedro, on Ambergris Caye
San Pedro Post Office, Belize, C.A.

Mailing Address:
Captain Morgan's Retreat, 5629 FM 190 West, Suite 113, Houston, TX 77069

Service/Reservation Telephone:
800/527-1137

House Service is Open:
24 hrs. a day, Seven days a week

Resort Affiliation:
Captain Morgan's Retreat

Rooms:
9

Most guests of Captain Morgan's take a Tropic or Maya Airlines commuter from Belize International to the San Pedro airfield. A boat from the resort will pick them up at San Pedro.

The dive service here serves only certified divers and offers no resort training or certification. They have enough rentals to supply small groups of divers, but each diver is urged to bring at least a regulator. They rent no u/w camera gear.

Captain Morgan's offers a one-tank dive in the morning and afternoon, with night diving on request. They have three small, fast dive boats: a 16–footer, 18–footer and a 22–footer, which can carry eight divers.

The sites that Captain Morgan's Retreat dives depends, to a large extent, on the competence of the divers in the party. For example, there are some major caves between Caye Corker and Ambergris Caye, but a diver must be a certified cave expert before entering one. Incompetent divers make dives more difficult than they need

Margo Nelson

David McCray

to be, and not every diver who has gone into these caves has come out alive.

This service goes to Mexico Rock, Morgan's Cut and Holchum Reef. There are no major wrecks here, but there is a small wreck in front of the hotel which is used as a check-out dive on the first day. Divers also take trips to the more distant sites of Lighthouse Reef, including The Great Blue Hole, and the Turneffe Islands, as well as many sites up and down the barrier reef.

The resort is associated with International Expeditions, a company which specializes in challenging nature trips and studies. Captain Morgan's people guide some of these trips and are familiar with the area's animals, reptiles and birds. Fishing, food and relaxation are also available in ample quantity and quality at Captain Morgan's Retreat.

DIVE SHOP LIMITED
Service Address:
  5 minutes from San Pedro Airport on Ambergris Caye
Mailing Address:
  P.O. Box 1140, Belize City, Belize C.A.
Service Telephone:
  011-501-02-44632
Reservation Telephone:
  800/331-2458
Hours Service is Open:
  7:30 am to noon; 1 pm to 5 pm and as needed
Resort Affiliation:
  San Pedro Holiday Hotel
Rooms:
  12
Cottages/Villas:
  2

After people confirm their trip to San Pedro Holiday Hotel, the staff makes connections for them via Tropic Air from Belize International to San Pedro Airport. Established around 1965, this is one of San Pedro's oldest resorts.

San Pedro Holiday Hotel serves only certified divers and they are required to bring "C" card and log book. The operation is well stocked with essential rental equipment, but has no u/w photography gear.

They specialize in taking groups of five to six divers in one of their 22-foot boats to dive the canyons outside of the barrier reef, virtually to any depth the divers are able. Outside the wall, rays, nurse sharks, large groupers and barracuda are common sites. The service offers a one-tank morning and one-tank afternoon dive, with night dives on request. Sites include the more distant areas, such as trips to the Great Blue Hole. Between dives, most guests stroll about the grounds of the resort and San Pedro, go fishing or relax along the sea.

OUT ISLAND DIVERS
Service Address:
Their boats are docked at the Sun Breeze Hotel
Mailing Address:
P.O. Box 7, San Pedro, Ambergris Caye, Belize, C.A.
Service Telephone:
011-501-026-2151
Reservation Telephone:
800/826-9834 (Boulder Scuba Tours) or 800/426-0226 (Triton Tours)
Resort Affiliation:
Serve guests staying on Ambergris Caye

Out Island Divers have two live-aboard boats in dock at Ambergris Caye. The boats are an eight-diver capacity 45-foot Celestial and a 16- to 20-diver capacity 50 foot Roamer. This service offers two day/one night trips to Turneffe Islands, the Lighthouse Reef area and Glover's Reef. During this trip they make a minimum of four dives. Divers have the option to dock and spend a night at Half Moon Caye, a beautiful and remote out-island on Lighthouse Reef popular among photographers. The cay includes a nature sanctuary for the rare Red-Footed Booby bird and other tropicals. The boat can also be chartered for longer trips; Captain Ray Bowers will take divers wherever they want.

This service is for certified divers who want to dive everything from 30-foot virgin reefs, to sites along Lighthouse Wall facing the open Caribbean, to maximum depths at the Great Blue Hole. Guests of any of the Ambergris Caye resorts can reserve space aboard the Out Island Divers boats.

PYRAMID ISLAND RESORT
Service Address:
On Caye Chapel
Mailing Address:
P.O. Box 192, Caye Chapel, Belize, C.A.
Service Telephone:
011-501-44-409
Reservation Telephone:
Same as above
Hours Service is Open:
8 am to 5 pm or as needed Seven days a week
Resort Affiliation:
Pyramid Island Resort
Rooms:
32

Visitors to Caye Chapel fly from Belize International to the Caye Chapel airstrip, or take a boat from Belize City and travel about 15 miles northeast to Caye Chapel.

Pyramid Island Resort is an exclusive, secluded resort, the only one on this privately owned cay. The dive service caters heavily to certified divers and offers challenging one or two tank dives in both the morning and afternoon. Night diving is on request.

Divers to Caye Chapel have the full gamut of Caribbean tropical marine life nearby. Among the reefs are green turtles, dolphins, squirrelfish, hamlets, triggerfish, shellfish and jacks. The resort guides specialize in diving the surge channels and canyons cut into the reef as well as numerous sites along the Great Barrier drop-off.

Guests of Pyramid Island Resort are supported by a fine restaurant and lounge. There are wide open and private stretches of magnificent beach. Fishing, most other watersports and tennis is available, and there are plans to build a golf course on the island.

REEF DIVERS, LTD.
Service Address:
North end of Ambergris Caye
Mailing Address:
Ramon's Reef Resort, Amerbris Caye, Belize, C.A.
Service Telephone:
011-501-026-2071
Reservation Telephone:
800/426-0226 (Triton Tours)
504/522-3382 (Triton Tours Louisiana number) or 601/693-1304
Hours Service is Open:
8 am to 5 pm Seven days a week
Resort Affiliation:
Ramon's Reef Resort
Cottages/Villas:
30 cabanas

After landing at San Pedro Airfield, guests board a boat and cruise north to Ramon's Reef Resort.

Ramon's caters to all level of divers, including novices. A resort course is offered as well as PADI and NAUI certification, advanced open-water and advanced rescue training. They have a full line of dive equipment, but recommend divers bring personal dive gear. They have no u/w photography equipment at this time.

Ramon's offers one-tank morning and one-tank afternoon dives. Night diving, to such photogenic spots as Mexico Rock, is available on request. They also dive Holchum Reef, The Plateaus and other parts of the wall. Dive sites are a two to 25-minute boat ride away.

Larry Parker runs the service here, and does an excellent job training his guides and maintaining the equipment. Ramon's has access to one of the Out Island Divers boats whenever needed and the guides use the personal boats to shuttle divers to and from sites.

Between dives the resort offers windsurfing and sailboating. There are good beaches to stroll and the birdwatching is fabulous. Bicycles, glass-bottom boats and Land Rovers are for rent. Other visitors go to the mainland to see Mayan ruins and some of the other wild and scenic areas of Belize. Mainland tours and river trips can be arranged through the resort.

Ramon also has a small dive shop at the Victoria House in San Pedro. The number there is 011-501-026-2180. Its stateside reservation number is 713-529-6800. Victoria House guests have just about all the amenities available to them as do those who stay at Ramon's Reef Resort.

RUM POINT INN
Service Address:
A south coast beachfront resort near Placencia
Mailing Address:
Rum Point Inn, Placencia, Belize, C.A.
Service Telephone:
011-501-06-2017
Reservation Telephone:
415/752-8008
Hours Service is Open:
6 am to midnight; depending on the weather
Cottages/Villas:
4 cabanas

People traveling to Placencia can fly into Belize International, then board a charter or a Maya Airlines flight to the Placencia airfield. The resort usually has a ride waiting there for its guests.

The resort dives only with certified divers, but offers a NAUI certification course. Divers should bring as much personal gear as possible, except for weight belts, tanks and packs.

Divers to the Rum Point Inn have a lot of adventure awaiting. The Rum Point dive boat, a fast 30-foot open launch, takes divers to the seldom-seen underwater of Laughing Bird Caye, Round Caye and Long Caye. The most royal of all is Queen Caye, a must site with a lot of variety. Each cay offers a little different form, a little different ecology and a little different diving.

In the shallower waters are an abundant store of shellfish such as lobster and conch. Gorgonians, florescent sponges, and gardens of hard corals grow about the reefs and throughout the sharp crevices and channels which perforate the wall. There is even some wreck diving on the Great Barrier Reef.

The Maya Mountains are directly west of Placencia and the Mayan ruins at Lubaantum are to the south. You can charter a truck with some friends, kick back on the sofa secured into the truck bed, and be chauffeured about the countryside.

ST. GEORGE'S LODGE
Service Address:
On St. George's Caye, 7 mi. from Belize City
Mailing Address:
P.O. Box 625, Belize City, Belize, C.A., or Travel Directions, 9550 Skillman Ave., Dallas, TX 75243
Service Telephone:
800/631-0032
Reservation Telephone:
214/341-5577
Hours Service is Open:
Any time there is a need
Resort Affiliation:
St. George's Lodge
Rooms:
12
Cottages/Villas:
4

For years, St. George's Lodge has been ranked as one of the best adventure dive destinations in the world. Quality abounds in the people, the gear and the diving. The lacquered hardwood of the thatch-covered cottages and buildings makes guests feel as if they are aboard a yacht. The lodge is the only one on St. George's Caye and provides transportation for guests from Belize International to the resort.

St. George's offers a resort course, NAUI certification up to assistant instructor and a specialty class in advanced deep diving. The rental shop includes a full line of scuba equipment, but u/w camera gear is not available. Repairs can be done on some personal gear divers bring.

Most of the dives are a five-minute boat ride from the lodge; seldom does a trip take more than 15 minutes. They do a morning and afternoon one-tank dive at a leisurely pace to ensure maximum enjoyment. Night dives are available on request. Special trips are planned in advance to Lighthouse Reef, Turneffe Islands, Mauger Caye and Northern Two Cayes.

A favorite site is at Little Finger Reef, to places as deep as 120 feet along the face of the wall. Sightings of reef sharks, eagle rays, dolphins and sand sharks are common. Guides take divers as deep as they want, after being assured they can handle what they ask for. The emphasis is always on safety, with divers being briefed and debriefed before and after each dive. The usual ratio is one guide to every four divers.

The pace on St. George is very relaxed. Between-dive action centers around the resort's lounge and sundeck. Bonefishing and big game fishing is excellent. The resort will arrange a guide and ride for mainland tours.

TRITON DIVE SHOP
Service Address:
North end of San Pedro, on Ambergris Caye
Mailing Address:
Paradise Resort Hotel, San Pedro, Ambergris Caye, Belize
Service Telephone:
011-501-026-2083
Reservation Telephone:
800/231-0629 ext. 176 (US); 800/392-4900 ext. 786 (TX)
Hours Service is Open:
7 am to 6 pm Seven days a week
Resort Affiliation:
Paradise Resort Hotel
Rooms:
10
Cottages/Villas:
13 cabanas

Immediately after clearing customs at Belize International, guests who have a package with the Paradise Resort Hotel board a Tropic Air plane for the 15- to 20-minute flight to San Pedro Airport and will be shown to the nearby beachfront resort.

The Triton Dive Shop, which operates out of Paradise Resort Hotel, caters to all levels of divers. They offer a resort course and NAUI certification. The dive package includes all gear rentals, but divers should bring their mask, fins, snorkel and camera equipment.

The service follows no pre-set dive schedule. Guests may dive in the morning and afternoon virtually any time they want and choose a one-tank or two-tank dive. No night diving is offered, however.

Triton Dive Shop has several dive boats ranging from 20-footers to a 31-footer for full-day trips. Two divers and a guide are all that is needed to make a dive party. The Barrier Reef is located just offshore from them. They dive Mexico Rocks and Holchum Inner Reef, two sites which have abundant stands of elkhorn, brain and star corals, rose coral and schools of tropical fish in addition to being good places for shells. They also go to the large coral canyon known as Pine Canyon, which cuts through the wall, and the canyons and wall of Palmetto Reef from 55 feet to 100 feet. They boat to Half Moon Caye on the southeast side of Lighthouse Reef and dive the outer part of that atoll. Cave dives include Mexico Cave and some of the caves and tunnels 17 miles away around Caye Corker. Visibility throughout their sites is in excess of 100 feet.

The Paradise Resort Hotel is one of the island's most established services. Guests have their choice of reef fishing or deep-sea fishing. Other watersports are available as are trips to the Mayan ruins on the mainland. When divers aren't diving, the San Pedro environment beckons many of them to just eat, drink and lie on the beach in the sun.

TURNEFFE ISLAND LODGE
Service Address:
Southernmost end of Turneffe Islands, on Caye Bokel
Mailing Address:
P.O. Box 480, Belize City, Belize, C.A.
Service Telephone:
011-501-2331
Reservation Telephone:
800/772-1002 or 713/659-3232
Hours Service is Open:
Hours as needed
Resort Affiliation:
Turneffe Island Lodge
Rooms:
9

As the crow flies, the Turneffe Islands are between 20 and 30 miles from Belize City. From Belize International, guests of the Turneffe Island Lodge take a taxi to the Belize City marina where a water taxi is awaiting to take them on the two-and-a-half-hour, 30-mile boat trip to Caye Bokel.

Turneffe Island Lodge works with only certified divers. No resort course or open water certification is available at this time. Instructors, however, are PADI certified.

Turneffe Island Lodge has four boats: a 38-foot cruiser and three small open launches. The lodge accepts no more than 18 divers at a time and, aided by its boat fleet, accommodates virtually every diving desire. There is challenging open-water diving here as well as shallow diving within the protection of the reefs. Large pelagics and reef fish abound. There are sea turtles, sand sharks, morays, porcupinefish, hamlets, filefish and schools of others. Sponges practically illuminate the coral walls. Depending upon the weather and wind they do either one or two-tank dives during the day, and night diving on request.

They dive the Turneffe and Lighthouse Reef Atolls and many sites along the tremendous wall of the barrier reef. There are a few good diveable wrecks off Turneffe, including an old island cruiser 65 feet down off Caye Bokel known as the Sayonara. Guides will also take experienced divers to selected caves and The Great Blue Hole.

Most divers to Turneffe dive as much as their strength and decompression limits allow, but those who fish around these islands bring in good catches of both reef and big game fish. The lodge is a well-known base for some of the world's best open-water and shallow-water fishing.

Dave Bennett owns and manages this full-service lodge. He and his people pride themselves on giving personal, friendly, competent service. Providing good food and drink in a happy, relaxed atmosphere is part of the way they like to operate.

BELIZE DIVING SERVICES

Service Address:
Caye Corker, 22 mi. northeast of Belize City
Mailing Address:
P.O. Box 667; Belize City, Belize, C.A.
Service Telephone:
011-501-45937 ext. 143
Reservation Telephone:
Same as above

Hours Service is Open:
8:30 am to 4:30 pm and as needed
Resort Affiliation:
Serves guests of most resorts on Caye Corker

The boats of Belize Diving Services are docked at Caye Corker, which is primarily a remote fishing village. Boat taxis run the 22 miles back and forth between Belize City and Caye Corker daily. There is also boat traffic to Caye Corker from Caye Chapel and Ambergris Caye. Caye Corker is untouched by heavy tourism. The cay has about a dozen resorts for guests who enjoy sailing, fishing, diving and bird watching. It really *is* the way the Caribbean was thirty years ago.

Frank Bounting owns and operates this complete dive service. Frank offers resort training, PADI certification, and specialty classes in wreck diving, advanced open water and deep diving. All equipment that divers need is included in the cost of the dive, so there is no extra charge for rentals. They also have a limited supply of u/w camera gear. Divers should bring their "C" card and log book.

Frank runs a very flexible, customer-oriented service. He has a 27-foot V-bottom cruiser, a custom dive boat and two fast skiffs to get small dive parties to the special places. Parties usually head out between nine and ten in the morning

for a two-tank deep-and-shallow dive. Sometimes they will do just a one-tank deep-dive in the morning so they can do another deep-dive in the afternoon. Night diving is on request. They dive the barrier wall from six miles north of Caye Corker to Long Caye, which is about ten miles south of the dock, giving them over 16 miles of sites behind, in and on the barrier reef. Canyons predominate on the outer parts of the barrier, most of which run east and west through coral beds. The lip of the canyons is usually at 50 feet and goes down as deep as 110 feet. The canyon walls are sheer, mini-dropoffs bright with sponges and corals. Divers also explore the near vertical face of the barrier wall.

Turneffe and Lighthouse atolls are dived on request, but divers should make arrangements for that ahead of time. Only very skilled divers are taken to dive the caves here, which are extremely dangerous and demanding. Belize Diving Services also does the Raggedy Ann Shipwreck, an intentionally sunk, beyond-repair 50-foot Chris Craft.

Frank and his people are very safety oriented, which is a necessity for those who operate in Belize. He and others are working with the government to establish some type of association or regulation to assure the country's dive guides and services operate in a professional manner.

Wes Wright

ENGLISH-METRIC CONVERSIONS

Length			
	1 inch	=	2.540 centimeters
	1 foot	=	0.304 metres
	1 yard	=	0.914 metres
	1 fathom	=	1.828 metres or 6.0 feet
	1 statute mile (5280 feet)	=	1.609 kilometres
	1 nautical mile (6080 feet)	=	1.853 kilometres
	1 centimetre	=	0.393 inches
	1 metre	=	3.280 feet
	1 metre	=	1.093 yards
	1 metre	=	0.546 fathoms
	1 kilometre	=	0.621 statute miles
	1 kilometre	=	0.539 nautical miles
Capacity	1 cubic inch	=	16.378 cubic centimetres
	1 cubic foot	=	0.028 cubic metres
	1 cubic foot	=	28.317 litres
	1 cubic yard	=	0.764 cubic metres
	1 pint	=	0.568 litres
	1 gallon	=	4.546 litres
	1 cubic centimetre	=	0.061 cubic feet
	1 cubic metre	=	35.314 cubic feet
	1 cubic metre	=	1.308 cubic yards
	1 litre (1,000 c.c.)	=	0.035 cubic feet
	1 litre	=	0.220 gallons
	1 litre	=	1.760 pints
Weight	1 ounce	=	28.349 grams
	1 pound	=	0.454 kilograms
	1 long ton	=	1.016 metric tons
	1 long ton	=	1.016 kilograms
	1 kilogram	=	2.205 pounds
	1 metric ton	=	0.984 long tons
	1 metric ton	=	2,205 pounds

1 pound per square inch	=	0.073 kilograms per square centimetre
1 kilogram per square centimetre	=	14.223 pounds per square inch
1 atmosphere	=	14.7 pounds per square inch
1 atmosphere	=	1.033 kilograms per square centimetre

THE
CAYMAN ISLANDS

Steve Rosenberg

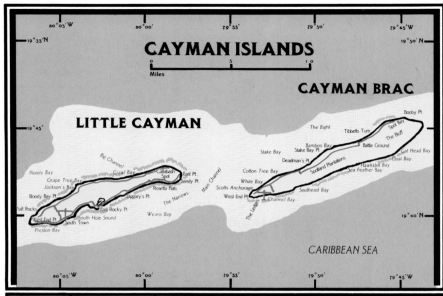

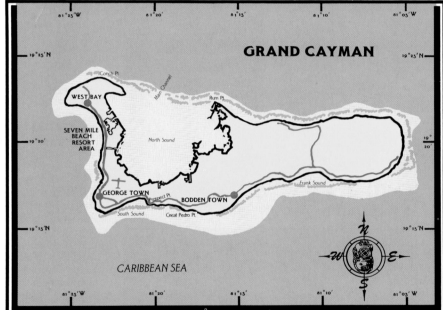

The Caymans

Entry Requirements
  Proof of citizenship and return ticket for U.S. & Canadian citizens. Passports and return ticket for all others.

Language
  English

Airlines
  Cayman Airways, Air Jamaica and Republic

Airport
  Owens International at George Town; Gerald Smith International on Cayman Brac

Departure Tax
  $5

Electricity
  110 volts; 60 cycles

Size
  Grand Cayman 76 sq mi.; Cayman Brac 15 sq mi.; Little Cayman 11 sq. mi.

Population
  18,750 Total
  Grand Cayman 17,000

Tourist Office
  Cayman Islands Dept. of Tourism
  Government Building
  P.O. Box 67
  George Town, Grand Cayman
  9-84-44

  Tourist Office
  250 Catalonia Avenue
  Suite 604
  Coral Gables, FL 33134
  305/444-6551

The Cayman Islands, composed of Grand Cayman, Little Cayman and Cayman Brac, are a British Crown Colony located in the northwest part of the Caribbean Sea. They lie approximately 480 miles south of Miami, with Grand Cayman at 76 square miles being the largest island and the center of business and tourism.

The first recorded sighting of the Caymans was made by Columbus in May, 1503 during his fourth voyage. He named the islands "Las Tortugas," which means "The Turtles" for the large quantities of turtles he saw nesting there and swimming about. The Cayman Islands were acceded to England by Spain as part of the Treaty of Madrid in 1670.

Early inhabitants included shipwrecked sailors, army deserters, debtors and pirates, but no serious settlement took place until the early 1700s when Scottish immigrants, most of them fishermen, settled here. In 1788 a fleet of ten British merchant ships ripped their hulls on Grand Cayman's eastern barrier reef and sank. The people onshore put to sea in their fishing boats, rescued the tattered passengers and crew and brought them to shore. King George III was so impressed by their bravery and kindness that he exempted the Cayman Islands forever from income tax and wartime conscription.

In two respects life on the Caymans has been happy ever after: taxshelters and shipwrecks are now two of their main commodities. The islands' underwater terrain is a third, for though the topside of the Caymans are flat deposits of sand and coral limestone they are built upon submerged mountain ridges which drop off over 6,000 feet to the ocean floor, creating an exciting system of coral archways, tunnels and walls. All three islands are surrounded by barrier reefs.

The sunken treasures of The Caymans are no secret. Nearly 70,000 sport divers dive the Caymans annually. As a unit the Cayman dive operators are conscientious and competitive; most belong to the Cayman Islands Watersports Operators Association (C.I.W.O.A.). As individuals their specialties range from supporting dive parties who stay at such places as Seven Mile Beach, Grand Cayman's major resort area, to accomodating the needs of the adventure diver who wants to dive the seldom seen underwater walls of Little Cayman, the least populated of these islands.

Although hurricane season officially is June through December, none has struck since 1932 when Cayman Brac was laid waste. The wet season, which drops about 60 inches of rain annually, is usually benign, falling most heavily in June, and September through November. The temperatures of Cayman are stable year round, with winter highs averaging 75° F and summer temperatures to 85° F. Daily lows can be 20 degrees lower and nights can be cool.

Wes Wright

Getting There/ Getting Around

Cayman Airways, Air Jamaica and Republic are the major airlines which serve the Caymans. Most flights come in from Miami, Houston and Kingston, Jamaica. Owen Roberts International Airport is near the islands' capital of George Town on Grand Cayman. Little Cayman and Cayman Brac also have airports and there are frequent flights between the three islands which usually take less than ten minutes. There are no public buses and just a few resort limousines at the airport because Cayman law allows only licensed taxis to carry commercial passengers to most places. The more remote resorts, however, can provide transportation for their guests. Taxis are metered. Several car rental companies for cars, jeeps and mopeds are on Grand Cayman.

Roads run along the shores of all three islands, but most visitors do very little touring and it is only done to any extent on Grand Cayman. Sand beaches, old coral reefs called ironshore, broken rocks and bluffs are parts of all these islands' coastlines.

Topside Attractions

Life ashore is calm compared to the exotic underwater world. Caymanians are rather sedate by comparison with their Caribbean neighbors. But as people who are attracted by the Caymans' tax laws invest into the country, resort complexes are being developed, especially upon Grand Cayman. For now though, the appeal of 15-square-mile Cayman Brac (brac is Gaelic for bluff) and 11-square-mile Little Cayman, is their solitude. These two rocky islands have some tourist services and entertainment, and the government is working on roads and other developments, but for the most part the smaller islands are very quiet. Most visitors to them are nature lovers who come to see some of the islands 150 bird species, or they are divers. Nature lovers and divers have at least one thing in common: they are well-treated guests of the islands' people who make their living from the land and sea.

At the other end of the Cayman spectrum is Grand Cayman's Seven Mile Beach, the island's version of Waikiki. Fifty hotels, condominium complexes and apartment buildings line this sandy stretch and its edges along the West Bay Anchorage. Advantages of the Seven Mile Beach hotels include the best beach of the few sand beaches on the islands and a plethora of dive sites within a half-hour's boat ride, though many are within ten minutes.

Other dive resorts are on the east coast. These attract divers looking for a quiet, self-enclosed resort environment as well as privacy at dive spots.

Local flavor is dished out in most of the 60 restaurants in Grand Cayman's George Town/West Bay/Seven Mile Beach area. Conch fritters, turtle steaks, fried plantains and fresh seafoods are the specialties. Other meats and most vegetables are imported, and as a result, somewhat expensive. Bodden Town and East End are two other major coastal settlements with protected beaches, accomodations and restaurants. Cayman Kai on the north coast's Rum Point is a growing development for fishermen and divers.

One of the more popular local enterprises is the Cayman Islands Turtle Farm, located north of West Bay, a town second in population only to George Town. The Turtle Farm raises thousands of sea turtles a year for meat, leather, jewelry and cosmetics.

Bone fishing and deep-sea fishing are good. Fishing is promoted through events such as the Million Dollar Month competition held every June. It will pay one million U.S. dollars to anyone who breaks the existing blue marlin record with a marlin caught in Caymanian waters. Many dive services and resorts either provide or can arrange guided fishing trips.

Cayman Diving

Unusual geographical features create exceptionally good diving on all three islands. A shallow bank reef system hugs most of the shoreline, composed mainly of elkhorn corals. In deeper waters staghorn and 50 other species of coral take over, creating narrow canyons, caves and tunnels, as well as a wall of coral ridges running at right angles to the shore. This type of formation is known as spur-and-groove, meaning it has long coral fingers extending out from the main body of the reef. In many places the coral has fused together, creating caves of a sort, referred to as grottos. Some of this type of diving requires lines, lights and cave dive training.

An array of colorful sponges starts appearing at 25 feet, and further down, at between 40 and 60 feet, the spur-and-groove system forms a terrace that drops abruptly at the Wall of Cayman at about 70 feet. (The barrier reef wall is called the Cayman Wall around all three islands, with descriptive names assigned to specific sites and locales.) This formation of long coral mounds divided by white sand gulleys provides an ideal setting for seeing both coral creatures and big fish

which seek out the sandy chutes for napping. Giant basket sponges live at 50 feet, providing homes for a variety of fish. Frequently this part of the reef is within a few minutes' boat ride from the shore.

The drama of the wall, so sheer a drop-off that it slants inward in some places, is the big attraction for many divers. Grand Cayman's North Wall sites require comparatively deep dives, but in some sections, such as Little Cayman's Bloody Bay, the reef begins to drop only 18 feet below the surface.

A number of good sites can be reached from shore, particularly south of George Town on Grand Cayman. However, instead of sandy beaches, ironshore—the sharp and jagged remnants of an ancient coral reef—edges most of the islands' perimeters. This uneven terrain can make shore entries tricky.

There is no official count for the number of shipwrecks around these islands, although some estimate that at least a few hundred have foundered along the edges of the Cayman walls. Several lie in less than 60 feet of water, and one, the **Oro Verde** ("Green Gold"), was purposely sunk off Seven Mile Beach as a dive attraction.

These waters are clear of industrial pollution and silt, and visibility sometimes exceeds 200 feet. The quality and quantity of sea life in the Caymans are high, in part due to the Cayman Islands Watersports Operators Association which enforces restrictions on ocean products har-

vesting and random anchorage. The association is also one of the sponsors of the annual Scuba Bowl, a five-day program especially for dive-shop owners and operators. The program features Cayman diving in addition to helping participants become aware of how to create and market dive packages.

The Caymans also are pioneering a concept in marine park management to protect the reefs and sea life. The marine park around Grand Cayman has widespread local approval. The park and its regulations are designed to maintain and replenish fisheries and shellfisheries, enhance diving by protecting ocean products and regulating their harvest, and it regulates boating. The specific management zones are to be reviewed every year to ensure that they are being properly administered and to determine when controls should be changed.

Cayman Dive Sites
Grand Cayman

Grand Cayman's west shore off Seven Mile Beach has many good shallow reef sites, but it also has wall diving at Northwest Point and Spanish Bay. This area is closest to most of the island's hotel rooms, restaurants and shopping.

Big Tunnels starts at 60 feet, but is one of the favorite dives on the island. Spiralling tunnels, a vertical labyrinth and canyons create an exciting deep dive.

David McCray

Near Big Tunnel is **Orange Canyon.** Named for its giant elephant-ear sponges, it is also a dramatic dive of canyons cutting into the wall. Divers follow the canyons to the face of the wall and can explore deep water sponges and coral there.

Also called **Tri-Caves, Trinity Caves** has three sandy ravines lying in 70 feet of water as well as an opening through an L-shaped canyon. Black coral trees decorate its vertical walls.

At **Peter's Reef** pillar coral feed during the day, extending their soft fur-like polyps from their hard exteriors. The spur-and-groove formation goes down to about 50 feet.

Multitudes of angelfish and other tropicals give **Angel Reef** and **The Aquarium** their names. Schools of fish looking for food swarm around divers and sometimes dive buddies lose sight of one another until the fish can be pushed away.

In the waters off the Turtle Farm, **Hepp's Pipeline** attracts crustaceans, tropicals and luxuriant sponge and coral life along its small wall. Hundreds of garden eels live near the sandy bottom at 60 feet.

It may be that no other wreck has been explored as thoroughly as the **BALBOA,** a small freighter spread out along the sand at about 25-foot in Hog Sty Bay. Christmas tree worms, hard corals and sponges are thick on its steel grid columns. Resident Sergeant Majors are known to nip visitors whether they have food or not. The 25-foot depth makes this wreck a popular night dive, too.

Sunset Reef features large coral heads, caves and caverns active with life. The reef is an easy kick away once you get off the ironshore. Green morays, trumpet fish and shy spotted trunkfish are in the area.

Eagle Ray Rock is known for its huge curving canyon with 30-foot-high walls and narrow passages. Orange elephant-ear sponges and long finger sponges are found here.

An eight-mile-long North Wall between Conch Point and Rum Point is Grand Cayman's biggest attraction for most. The relatively high winds of May through September can make this area inaccessible, however, and even during the rest of the year this area is dived "weather permitting." Some resorts charge extra for the longer boat trip to this area.

There are barracuda and cruising eagle rays, a vertical plunge with undercut ledges, and deep, tight ravines. Tunnels are cut throughout the reef's terraces. Divers occasionally spot swimming sea turtles or a nurse shark sleeping in a sand

chute. Each operator has a favorite site, and some are listed in the dive service section.

A well-known site in this area is **Tarpon Alley** where schools of sleek silver tarpon glide through the maze of crevices cut in the reef. The overhangs have plate corals and sponges. Schooling with the tarpons through the ravines makes this an exciting dive.

No Name Wall, which is four parallel ravines cracked into the wall, lies in 50 feet to 90 feet of water. Stands of black coral abound along the ravines.

Grand Canyon is an arched cut in the wall just west of Rum Point Channel. Black coral is thick here, too, and large basket sponges thrive in 50 feet to 70 feet of water.

Wind permitting, the east coast of Grand Cayman offers some interesting shipwreck sites, including the **METHUSLAN** and **MARIBELL,** which lie in 15 feet to 25 feet of water. These steel sailing ships lie near coral ravines and coral heads filled with blue striped grunts, eel and hogfish.

Black tip sharks and bull sharks are often sighted during 70-foot dives off East End Reef at **Shark Alley** and nearby **Three Sisters** where pinnacles rise from a ledge parallel to the wall.

The Maze is a concoction of deep, narrow crevices winding through the South Channel Wall at 60 feet and into the drop-off.

Cayman Brac

The diving possibilities offshore of this long, narrow island are seemingly limitless, but the moderate and deep sites usually dove are between Stake Bay to the north to midway along the southern coast where the south bluff starts.

Wave action on the south side is a bit more rugged than to the north and west. There are many coral caverns and deep gulleys along the wall. The sites off Cayman Brac are dived according to what direction the seasonal trade winds are blowing.

Greenhouse Reef off Stake Bay lies at 35 feet to 40 feet and can be reached from shore, but it is usually done from a dive boat. This spur-and-groove area is thick with fish and the occasional sting ray.

Cemetery Wall starts at only 45 feet below the surface, rather than at 60 or 70 feet as it usually does off Brac. Much of the interesting life is found at the lip, under which black coral and sponges are thickly growing. Yellow sponges, basket sponges and lavender vase sponges also characterize this site.

Further west lies **The Chute,** a dive

with a long tunnel starting at 50 feet and sloping down to emerge on the wall's face at 150 feet. Jacks sometimes pass the wall, and deep sea fans and tube sponges are found.

Schools of large silver tarpons live at **Tarpon Reef,** swimming in and out of the grooves of this tightly connected formation.

Divers pass beneath an encrusted nine-foot-long anchor wedged in a cut at **Anchor Reef** to approach a wall off the government dock at 100 feet. Great pink and orange sea fans and other soft corals sift the waters here.

Angel Reef's elkhorn forest is massive, with some arms over a dozen feet long. They start at 15 feet and go to the sand floor 40 feet down.

A hundred year old sail/steamer called the **PRINCE FREDERICK** lies about ten miles east of the dive boat dock, with large anchors, masts and a pile of chain.

Little Cayman

One reason some consider Little Cayman to have the best diving in the Caribbean is that its infrequently dived sites are in pristine condition. A small area from **Spot Bay** through **Bloody Bay** to **Jackson's Point** is riddled with unexplored chimneys, tunnels, reef invertebrates, sponges, large grouper, hogfish and pelagics. Trees of black coral and masses of deep water gorgonians are anchored in the cracks of the wall.

Bloody Bay's sheer wall, starting in less than 25 feet of water and forming a broad, sheer mural of sponges, sea whips and sea fans is one of the best known areas. One small section, **Three Fathom Wall,** starts at only 15 feet. It is close to shore and because it starts at such a shallow depth it is an excellent u/w photography sight which yields exquisite shots especially at night.

There are no dive services on Little Cayman at this time, but special boat trips are made to dive there. Cayman Brac has one dive resort which is continuing to explore and name new sites along its wall.

Cayman Dive Services

There are 16 dive operations now serving sport divers in the Caymans. All are professionally staffed and run with high standards set by the Cayman Islands Watersports Operators Association. The C.I.W.O.A. publishes a magazine called *Splash* which updates and reviews watersports happenings on the islands including fishing, boating, the marine parks

Karl Wallin

and diving. It is published for the Watersports Industry. Professional divers can receive a complimentary copy of the magazine from the Cayman Tourist Board or the Cayman Free Press, P.O. Box 1365 Grand Cayman BWI; 809/949-5111.

As outlined in the following dive-service section in the back of this chapter, many operators offer dive training programs. They range from resort courses, especially favored by cruise-ship passengers, to certification programs, to instructor training.

There are dive trips especially for the u/w photographer which are led by divemasters who are photography instructors. Intensive u/w photography classes are offered by dive services as well as specialty schools.

The islands' dive boats must meet strict safety requirements governing first aid, radio, oxygen and other emergency facilities. The British Sub-Aqua Club owns and operates the Compression Chamber in George Town. The chamber, managed by Dr. Jim Polson, is staffed 24 hours a day.

Grand Cayman Island Dive Services

BOB SOTO'S DIVING, LTD.
Service Address:
   Seven Mile Beach
   P.O. Box 1801, Grand Cayman, BWI
Mailing Address:
   Same as above
Service Telephone:
   809/947-4631
Reservation Telephone:
   800/262-7686
Hours Service is Open:
   8 am to 5 pm
Resort Affiliation:
   Cay Islander Hotel & Grand Pavilion Hotel
Rooms:
   68   60
Cottages/Villas:
   4

Bob Soto's Diving, Ltd., owned by Ron Kipp, is located on Seven Mile Beach on the west end of Grand Cayman. The re-

sort caters to all divers and has been designated both a PADI Five Star Facility as well as a NAUI Pro Facility. Their dive training ranges from resort classes to instructor certification and specialty courses in wreck- and cave-diving and underwater photography.

Certified divers should bring their "C" card and log book. Full equipment rental is available, but bring as much personal gear as possible. They do Sherwood regulator repair, but other repair work is limited.

Ron Kipp offers a lot of diving to a lot of divers, who are accommodated by his fleet of seven boats. They do two one-tank dives in the morning, but twice a week they do two morning wall dives, which is known as their "Double Deep" and is a unique aspect of this service. They offer a one-tank dive every afternoon and night dive several times a week. They take dive trips three times a week to sites along the North Wall.

Afternoon reef diving covers many sites along the reef parallel to Seven Mile Beach with depths ranging from 30 feet to

50 feet. The reef sites include The Aquarium, Peter's Reef, Hammerhead Hole and Killer Puffer Canyon (named so because a puffer bit off a diver's fingertip, so the ·story goes). Lobsters, shrimp, anemones and many species of tropical fish are found.

Wall dives off the west, north and south coasts are guided down to about 100 feet for 20 minutes of bottom time. Most wall diving is from 80 feet to 90 feet to maximize bottom time. Near the northwest point of Cayman Wall they dive Trinity Caves, Orange Canyon, the archway of Big Tunnels and Sand Chute. These sites have barrel sponges, archways, grottos, black coral, turtles, rays and pelagics.

Their prime wrecks are the Oro Verde and the Balboa, lost in the George Town Harbor during the hurricane of 1932.

This is the Cayman's largest watersports service. Windsurfing, jet skiing, and parasailing are available as is the duty-free shopping in George Town and the glitter of Seven Mile Beach.

CAYMAN DIVING LODGE
Service Address:
East end of island
P.O. Box 11, East End, Grand Cayman, BWI
Mailing Address:
Same as above
Service Telephone:
809/947-7555
Reservation Telephone:
800/262-7686
Hours Service is Open:
8 am to 5 pm Seven days a week
Resort Affiliation:
Cayman Diving Lodge
Rooms:
16

The Cayman Diving Lodge is another of Ron Kipp's services and provides for the experienced diver who is more interested in diving than night life. Located on the east end of Grand Cayman, the resort provides transportation for guests to the lodge after they land at Owen Roberts.

The Cayman Diving Lodge does provide PADI and NAUI instruction and certification. They rent equipment and do some repairs, but recommend divers bring as much personal gear as possible.

A lot of reef, wreck and wall diving is available here, including the two morning wall dives known as the "Double Deep." They dive inside and outside the barrier reef wall at sites off the north, south and east coasts, depending upon the wind and weather. Some of their favorites are Cinderella's Castle and the Tunnel of

Love. Wall dives are done as deep as 110 feet. They make several night dives a week.

Cayman Diving Lodge has a friendly atmosphere. The rooms are clean and comfortable. The cooking is family style and a bit on the native side. The food gives ample power to divers exploring the wilderness of the reefs. Night life centers around the Bitter End Bar.

CAYMAN KAI RESORT
Service Address:
On the north coast at Rum Point
P.O. Box 1112, Grand Cayman, BWI
Mailing Address:
Cayman Kai Resort Ltd., 3201 S.W. 94th Ave., Miami, FL 33165
Service Telephone:
809/947-9555 or 947-9556
Reservation Telephone:
800/223-5427
Hours Service is Open:
Open daily except for seasonal closing in September
Resort Affiliation:
Cayman Kai Resort
Rooms:
42
Cottages/Villas:
Many apartments, beach villas and condos available

Cayman Kai Resort is a diver resort located at Rum Point on the north coast. For guests staying three days or more, manager Georg Kienberger told us that the resort provides transportation to and from Owens International, which is 45 minutes away. Car rentals are available at the resort.

Cayman Kai is known as the North Wall resort and is one of Grand Cayman's most remote services. They offer resort courses, NAUI and PADI certification and will soon offer instructor training courses. Their specialties include underwater photography and video classes. They are closed for at least four weeks every year, usually in September, so they will be ready to dive again by October. Check with them for the exact dates of closure. Their best times to dive are from April through July and October and November. Divers should bring personal dive gear, but no tanks or weights.

This full-service dive resort dives day and night on both sides of the north wall. Their two flattops take divers to such sights as 100-foot deep Tarpon Alley. They dive through the coral tunnel known as Long Tunnel and follow it to the face of the wall 90 feet down. Gopher's Garden is a shallow dive where

black tip sharks are often seen cruising at 25 feet.

The remote tranquility of this resort appeals to adventure divers, but new divers and non-divers need not feel out of place. The resort has a full line of watersports, secluded beaches, picnics and live entertainment twice a week at the bar.

DIVERS WORLD, LTD.
Service Address:
Seven Mile Beach
P.O. Box 917, Grand Cayman, BWI
Mailing Address:
Same as above
Service Telephone:
809/949-8128
Reservation Telephone:
Same as above
Hours Service is Open:
7:45 am to 6 pm Mon–Sat
Resort Affiliation:
None

Divers World is a full retail dive shop which works with nearby dive services to equip and train divers. Located on the main hotel strip of Seven Mile Beach, it is about a mile north of George Town. They will do resort training and PADI certification for groups of four or more. They offer full rentals and repair.

At this time the only type of diving they do is guided shore entry dives.

FISH EYE PHOTOGRAPHIC SERVICES
Service Address:
West Bay Road, Trafalger Square
Mailing Address:
Seven Mile Beach
P.O. Box 2123, Grand Cayman, BWI
Service Telephone:
809/947-4209
Reservation Telephone:
Same as above
Hours Service is Open:
8:15 am to 5:30 pm Mon–Sat

Fish Eye specializes in training underwater photographers and videographers. They rent and sell u/w photography and video gear as well as rent dive equipment. Their u/w photography courses are sanctioned by PADI and NAUI. The training and guided dives, however, accommodate all levels of diver. They are the only World NAUI sanctioned underwater photography college. Training sites range from shallow reef gardens, which start 50 feet offshore, to weekly 110-foot wall dives of the north coast. Though the store is not open Sundays, they do an afternoon trip that day. Divers not interested in u/w photography or video are welcome to dive with them.

To arrange training with Fish Eye, it is

best to contact them for information on the best resort for you to stay in. They can book the accommodations for you.

DON FOSTER'S DIVE
Service Address:
Seven Mile Beach
P.O. Box 151, Grand Cayman, BWI
Service Telephone:
809/949-5679
Reservation Telephone:
809/949-7025
Hours Service is Open:
8 am to 5 pm Seven days a week
Resort Affiliation:
Royal Palms Hotel
Rooms:
124
Cottages/Villas:
some condos
Rooms:
124
Cottages/Villas:
some condos

Owned by Don Foster and managed by Alan Bloomrosen, this service is five minutes from George Town and ten minutes from the airport. Transportation from the airport is included in dive packages.

Don Foster's offers a resort course and certification through PADI, NAUI, SSI and NASDS. Other resort amenities are: a full rental shop, including photo center, Scuba Pro sales, u/w photography instruction, and repairs on personal dive gear.

This is a major service with a fleet of six dive boats which serve anywhere from eight to 22 divers per boat. Two of the boats are deluxe 52-foot flattops which Don designed himself. They offer two-tank morning dives, one-tank afternoon dives, a special two-tank afternoon dive on Wednesday, evening dives twice a week and u/w treasure hunting.

Paradise Reef and The Aquarium are two examples of their reef dives. They dive the Cayman Wall on both the west and north sides, going to Tarpon Alley, Big Tunnels, Trinity Caves, and Orange Canyon, which is dominated by black coral and orange elephant-ear sponges.

Between dives, guests have access to other watersports, shopping in George Town, or special tours such as exploring the undersea aboard the submersible "Atlantis", or on the surface via a glass bottom boat. Evening entertainment centers around the nightclubs at the Holiday Inn and the Cayman Islander. Don's motto: personalized service to give divers as much or as little service as they want.

QUABBIN DIVERS, LTD.
Service Address:
North Church Street, George Town
Mailing Address:
P.O. Box 157 George Town, Grand Cayman, BWI
Service Telephone:
809/949-5597
Hours Service is Open:
7:30 am to 5 pm Seven days a week
Resort Affiliation:
Serve guests of several condos on Seven Mile Beach

Quabbin Divers is a small, but experienced, dive service which specializes in training and diving with individuals and small dive parties. It is best to call them to recommend accommodations that suit your needs.

Their instruction includes resort courses as well as open-water training and certification under the PADI, NAUI and YMCA systems. They rent dive equipment, but recommend divers bring personal dive gear, including a wet suit. They rent no camera equipment, but go

Dennis Anderson

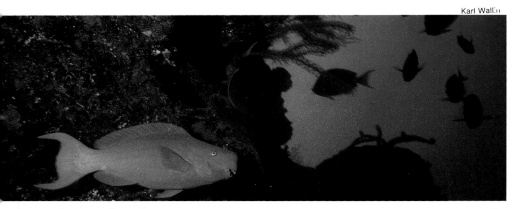

Karl Wall:n

to sites excellent for u/w photography. They will provide an u/w photographer to go on the trips to take pictures of and for divers.

Their first dive in the morning is to any number of sites along the west and north wall to depths approaching 110 feet. Sites include Tarpon Alley, Jimmy's Wall, Trinity Caves and the Eagle's Nest. More shallow dives include the wreck of the Oro Verde, Fisherman's Reef and Harbor Heights Reef, all prime sites for u/w photography. Dive parties are kept small and normally range from 15 to 25 divers on either of their two custom-built dive boats.

Quabbin Divers are especially proud of two aspects of their service: many of the people who come to them are return customers and they have one of the premiere deep-sea fishing operations on Grand Cayman.

EDEN ROCK DIVING CENTER
Service Address:
  South Church Street, George Town
Mailing Address:
  P.O. Box 1907, Grand Cayman, BWI
Service Telephone:
  809/949-7243
Reservation Telephone:
  Same as above
Hours Service is Open:
  8 am to 5:30 pm Seven days a week
Resort Affiliation:
  No resort affiliation

Eden Rock is a beachfront dive center which includes a retail equipment store. Their emphasis is on scuba instruction and diving Eden Rocks and Devil's Grotto, the only site they dive. Eden Rocks and Devil's Grotto combine to create one of the world's most highly acclaimed shallow dives. Together they form a system of caves and tunnels with a plethora of fingerling fish so thick they can block the light. There are also gardens of sponges and coral heads. The site is just a five-minute kick from shore and

has exciting maze-like passageways that go as deep as 40 feet, giving divers a maximum amount of down time.

Eden Rock Diving Center offers resort courses, PADI, NAUI and British Aqua Club School certification up to instructor training. They will soon have u/w photography classes. The center also has a scuba gear repair service.

RIVERS SPORT DIVERS, LTD.
Service Address:
  West Bay Road, Seven Mile Beach
Mailing Address:
  P.O. Box 442, West Bay Post Office, Grand Cayman, BWI
Service Telephone:
  809/949-1181
Reservation Telephone:
  Same as above
Hours Service is Open:
  8 am to 5 pm
Resort Affiliation:
  Carry dive packages with Villas of the Gallion, Plantation Village and Island House Resort

Rivers Sport Divers is owned and operated by Lynn and Wallace Rivers. They specialize in taking small groups of divers to sites along the north, west and south walls, depending upon the weather and customer interest. Dive parties are limited to 14, and carried aboard their 34-foot flattop, equipped with camera table and other amenities.

They rent all necessary gear and have recently upgraded it, including expanding their operation to include photography rentals. It is best to let them know what gear you need ahead of time, though, so they can make sure it is available. They do make some repairs on personal dive gear. Rivers Sport Divers also offers resort courses and PADI certification.

The small size of their dive parties allows them to give divers careful consideration. They pay particular attention to people new to diving and u/w photography.

Some of the more popular sites they dive are: Chinese Gardens, a 50-foot reef-dive on the south side of Grand Cayman excellent for photography; Sentinel Rock and Orange Canyon, two 80-foot to 100-foot dives off the west wall; and Tarpon Alley on the north side. They also dive the wreck of the Oro Verde. They offer a two-tank morning dive, one-tank afternoon dive and night diving on request.

They will also help you decide where you want to stay on Seven Mile Beach and put you in contact with the resorts for which they carry dive packages.

SEASPORTS
Service Address:
  Harbor Heights, Seven Mile Beach
Mailing Address:
  P.O. Box 1516, Grand Cayman Islands, BWI
Service Telephone:
  809/949-3965
Reservation Telephone:
  Same as above
Hours Service is Open:
  8 am to 5 pm; open 'til 8 for night dives
Resort Affiliation:
  They arrange dives for Beachcomber, Harbor Heights and Harpoon Manor

SeaSports, owned by Captain Butch, has been serving divers for 12 years and is the oldest independent dive operation on Grand Cayman. Guests who stay in the resorts with which SeaSports works are picked up on the beach by one of Butch's dive boats.

Because SeaSports has been operating here for years they have many return customers. As such, they cater a bit more to the advanced diver, but they do offer resort training and special dives for novices. They also offer PADI and NAUI open-water certification. All divers should make reservations in advance and bring personal dive gear as equipment rentals are limited. They do no repairs on other divers' equipment.

SeaSports takes only six or seven divers on either of their two 24-foot fiberglass boats. Captain Butch says, "Ours are the fastest dive boats on the island." The boats' speed, together with the small dive parties, allows SeaSports great flexibility to dive where the divers want to go and to get to the sites first. Normally, the two boats cover four different sites a day, with night diving available on request. They do their best to help divers get the most from their dive vacation. Captain Butch says, "Their vacation is my responsibility."

SeaSports dives Angel Reef, Pete's Ravine, Pillars, Grave Yard and Bay Reef.

They dive wall sites on the north, south and west including Chain Letters, The Maze, Gills' Grotto, Cayman Haven, Gall's Mountain and Tarpon Alley. Their wreck dives include the Oro Verde, Balboa and Palace.

SPANISH COVE DIVE RESORT

Service Address:
Spanish Bay Road, West Bay, Grand Cayman

Mailing Address:
P.O. Box 1014, George Town, Grand Cayman

Service Telephone:
809/949-3765

Reservation Telephone:
800/231-4610

Hours Service is Open:
8 am to 5 pm Seven days a week

Resort Affiliation:
Spanish Cove Resort

Rooms:
55

Cottages/Villas:
some available

On the beach of Spanish Cove north of West Bay, Spanish Cove Dive Resort is the only service in the immediate vicinity. Located 12 miles from George Town, they provide a free shuttle to and from town.

At Spanish Cove they offer novice training, but cater to the intermediate and advanced diver. They offer PADI, YMCA, SSI, and NAUI certification and are rated as a NAUI dream resort. The service also offers u/w photography instruction and certification, which complements the u/w photography center available on the premises.

Rental equipment is available, such as tanks, packs, weights and belt, but experienced divers should bring personal dive gear. They are in the process of upgrading their compressors and soon will have three to fill their tank bank. They have a two-tank morning dive, one-tank afternoon dive and dive on Tuesday, Thursday and Sunday nights.

They specialize in diving the north wall and the formations cut into it. Their four boats, with a 20-diver maximum, are custom-designed to handle the weather and situations of the north wall. Popular sites include the ravines of Tarpon Alley, the black coral of Pete's Ravine, Big Tunnels, Hole in the Wall, and the challenging Dragon's Hole.

They also dive some of the sites and wrecks of the west wall.

The resort activities center around diving, but volleyball, windsurfing and other watersports are available. Diving and non-diving packages are available.

SUNSET DIVERS

Service Address:
Seven Mile Beach

Mailing Address:
P.O. Box 479, Grand Cayman, BWI

Service Telephone:
809/949-7111

Reservation Telephone:
800/854-4767

Hours Service is Open:
9 am to 5 pm Mon–Sat, except holidays

Resort Affiliation:
Sunset House

Rooms:
45

The Sunset House is located within walking distance of George Town. Sunset Divers is the name of this in-house dive service. They provide many types of training and certification including a resort course, PADI, NAUI, YMCA and NASDS open water instruction. They have rentals and repairs, but recommend experienced divers bring the usual personal dive gear.

Sunset offers boat diving and unlimited shore entry dives. Their four dive boats take divers on a two-tank morning dive to depths ranging from 50 feet to 100 feet to sites such as Orange Canyon, Trinity Caves and Bonnie's Arch, which is a huge coral arch with many types of sponges, parrotfish and yellowtails. The one-tank afteroon dive has a 50-foot limit and they go to any of the many reef sites off the west wall, depending upon what the customers want. They try to keep dive parties at 20 or less.

Steve Rosenberg

Between dives guests enjoy drinks on the beach or at the waterfront bar. Guided fishing and sailing charters are available at the resort, and there are bars, restaurants and shopping nearby.

SURFSIDE WATERSPORTS
Service Address:
Seven Mile Beach
Mailing Address:
P.O. Box 891, Grand Cayman, BWI
Service Telephone:
809/947-4224
Reservation Telephone:
800/468-1708
Hours Service is Open:
8 am to 5 pm Seven days a week
Resort Affiliation:
Le Club Cayman
Rooms:
32

Surfside Watersports is the most complete watersports facility on Grand Cayman which includes not only a strong emphasis on diving (they supply air fills to many of the other services), but also everything from snorkel trips to private boat charters. They can provide shuttle service from the airport for groups, if arranged ahead of time. It's about a ten-minute trip from the airport. Surfside Watersports also has a facility at Rum Point called Rum Point North Side.

Diving comes in the form of a two-tank morning dive and a one-tank afternoon dive to sites on the west and north walls. Snorkelers and passengers are also welcome aboard any of their nine dive boats, space permitting, but parties are limited to between ten and 20. Either beach or car pick-up is available for customers along the seven-mile beach area. Instruction in all aspects of diving is offered, as well as the daily resort course. Open water and advanced open water training is sanctioned by PADI and NAUI. They offer rentals, including u/w cameras, and repairs.

They offer a deep and shallow two-tank morning dive, which ranges from 50 feet to 100 feet, then a one-tank afternoon dive to about 50 feet. They have night-diving three times a week.

Their reef dives include The Aquarium, Three Trees, Spanish Anchor, Wildlife Reef, Eden Rock and Devil's Grotto. They dive wall sites and spur-and-groove formations on the west and north sides, sometimes giving divers a chance to work out of their Rum Point facility where there are more big fish than those found on the west side. Wall and tunnel dives are Orange Canyon, Sentinel Rock, Trinity Caves, Big Tunnels, Sand Chutes, Big

Dipper and Little Tunnels.

Surfside Watersports offers a deluxe, commercial operation to give vacationers what they want without being over commercialized. They have glass-bottom boats to carry groups on picnics and day trips about the island, offer private boat charters and guided deep-sea fishing.

TORTUGA DIVE SHOP
Service Address:
Northeast corner of Grand Cayman; 25 miles from airport
Mailing Address:
P.O. Box 496, George Town, Grand Cayman, BWI
Service Telephone:
809/949-2022
Reservation Telephone:
809/947-7551
Hours Service is Open:
7:30 am to 5 pm Seven days a week
Resort Affiliation:
Tortuga Club
Rooms:
14

For guests who stay with the Tortuga Club three nights or longer, the resort will provide bus transportation to and from Owens International.

This small and friendly service is a complete dive center, providing resort courses and basic PADI certification. Rental and repairs are available, but bring the usual, well-maintained personal dive gear.

Dive parties are small and the marine life found off the east wall are larger and more exotic than what is usually seen in the more crowded areas. Tortuga has one dive boat that takes divers on morning, afternoon and night dives. Depending upon weather and diver desire, Tortuga also dives the east and south walls.

Most of the sites are from 30 feet to 100 feet and include everything from coral gardens, inside the reef and close to shore, to caves and blue holes. They dive Snapper Hole, Underwater Castle, Garden of Eels and The Maze, to name a few. One of their popular wrecks is the Wreck of the Ten Sails.

Fish life off the east end includes stingrays, barracudas, sharks, red band parrotfish, midnight parrotfish, many types of angels and other tropicals. There is abundant green coral and trees of black coral.

Between dives, guests can enjoy many of the other watersports offered by the resort. It is a relaxed, tranquil setting for adventurers who want another scene besides Seven Mile Beach waterfront. There is a tennis court, fishing and beachside bar.

DIVE TIARA
Service Address:
Southwest coast of Cayman Brac
Mailing Address:
P.O. Box 238, Cayman Brac, Cayman Islands, BWI
Service Telephone:
809/948-7313
Reservation Telephone:
800/367-3484
Hours Service is Open:
8 am to 5 pm Seven days a week
Resort Affiliation:
Tiara Beach Hotel
Rooms:
32

Dive Tiara is a Peter Hughes operation owned by Debbie Hotels and managed by Craig Burns, who is also head divemaster. Dive Tiara is the only dive resort on Cayman Brac at this time, giving divers access to seldom-dived sites off the island's south, west and north coasts. They also dive Little Cayman twice a week. Divers fly in on Cayman Airways, usually after a stop on Grand Cayman, and land at Gerald Smith Airport, just a short distance from the Tiara Beach Hotel.

Dive packages are available which include a two-tank morning dive, a one-tank afternoon dive and night dives on request. The first part of the morning dive is to sites along the vertical wall, the exact location of which is determined by the tradewinds and weather. There are many caverns, grottos and sand chutes, especially on the south side. Craig concedes that it is a bit rougher to dive here than from Grand Cayman, but the size and number of fish and the overall pristine condition of Cayman Brac's sites are worth the extra effort. Their three dive boats, two at 40 feet and one 36-footer, give stability and support to divers and their gear.

Divers are encouraged to bring as much dive gear as possible, but full rentals are available at the resort. U/w photography gear is rented by Brac Photographics, a shop just down the road from Tiara Beach. Resort courses as well as open-water and advance courses sanctioned by PADI, NAUI and SSI are available. Repair work is done here, too.

While providing personalized service, including helping guests set up their personal gear, which few services do, Craig allows divers as much freedom as safety allows when they are underwater, as long as they stay within their depth limits.

Between dives, guests explore the beaches and caves of Cayman Brac. There are six bars on the island and guests of Tiara Beach mingle with the guests of other resorts nearby.

Cozumel

Bob Leases

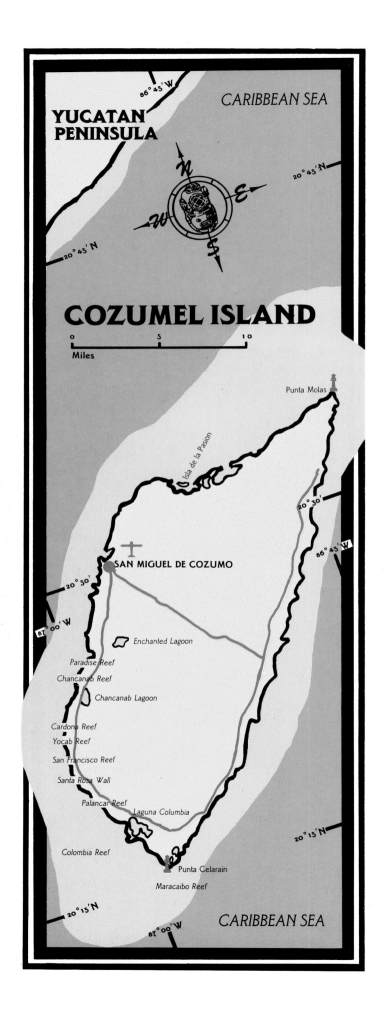

CARIBBEAN SEA

YUCATAN
PENINSULA

86° 45' W

20° 45' N

20° 45' N

COZUMEL ISLAND

0   5   10
Miles

Punta Molas

Isla de la Pasion

20° 30'

86° 45' W

20° 30'

87° 00' W

SAN MIGUEL DE COZUMO

Enchanted Lagoon

Paradise Reef

Chancanab Reef

Chancanab Lagoon

Cardona Reef

Yocab Reef

San Francisco Reef

Santa Rosa Wall

Palancar Reef

Laguna Columbia

20° 15' N

Colombia Reef

Punta Celarain

Maracaibo Reef

20° 15' N

87° 00' W

CARIBBEAN SEA

David McCray

Cozumel

Entry Requirements
   Proof of citizenship for U.S. Citizens
   Passports for all others
Language
   Spanish, English
Airport
   Cozumel Airport
Departure Tax
   US $6
Electricity
   110 volts; 60 cycles—transformers
   available as needed
Size
   300 sq. mi.
Population
   30,000
U.S. Tourist Office
   Mexican Government Tourism Offices
   100 N. Biscayne Blvd.
   Suite 2804
   Miami, FL 33132
   305/371-8037

   Infotur (Travel Agency)
   5th Avenue
   San Miguel, Cozumel
   2-14-51

The island of Cozumel is 12 miles east of the north part of Mexico's Yucatan Peninsula. Cozumel is Mexico's largest island. It has an area of 300 square miles and measures 30 miles long by ten miles wide. Cozumel is less than 600 miles southwest of Miami and 800 miles southeast of Houston.

Thousands of years ago the base of what is now Cozumel was under a shallow sea in which corals lived and died, leaving layers of exoskeletons. The exoskeletons have since become limestone. This limestone is hard and porous and pocked with caves and sink holes. The limestone acts almost as a sponge, holding in rain water so runoff seldom clouds the water around the island. Fresh water springs and swamps help nourish the jungles of the interior of Cozumel, ninety per cent of which is still in its natural, tropical state. The island, being composed of ancient reef, is virtually flat. The highest rock on the island is 45 feet above sea level.

Cozumel's temperatures range from the 70s in mid-winter to the upper 80s and low 90s during the summer. Summer showers are part of the afternoon scene, but sea breezes help make the heat and humidity tolerable. The highest rainfall comes in May and June when about seven inches usually falls, and in September and October, with eight to 11 inches being the norm, depending upon the course of tropical storms. Most hurricanes, though, range farther east.

Cozumel was a religious center for the Mayan Indians. There are many Mayan ruins on the island, mainly temples and shrines, which give evidence of Cozumel being the Mayans' land of the rising sun, a sacred place of fertility and new life. These temples were part of major Mayan settlements and the island, itself, was practically a shrine. Mayans from throughout the empire made pilgrimages to this island called Ah-Cuzamil-Peten, which means "Place of the Swallows."

Cozumel prospered from about 300 A.D. to 1519, the year Cortez landed. He began tearing down temples and built a church somewhere near where the airport is now. The population on Cozumel at that time is estimated at 10,000. Within 50 years it was 300.

Virtually deserted, Cozumel naturally became a haven for pirates who anchored in the deep waters off the protected west coast. In 1848 the island attracted mainland refugees fleeing the aftermath of the War of the Castes. These people successfully established a settlement near the San Francisco Beach area, which was the beginning of Cozumel's modern era.

Tourists began to become aware of it and even Pan Am flew there in the 1920's. The U.S. Army-Air Force built an air base near San Miguel during World War II. That was all the publicity Cozumel needed to become a post-war destination for vacation-starved tourists. In 1970 the population was back up to 10,000. Today it is close to 30,000.

San Miguel is the only real town on the island. Located near the middle of the west coast, it serves as the base for the hotels which line the rock and sand shore to the north and south. San Miguel is coping with the problem and adapting to the challenge of being a small village pressed into becoming the center for a modern resort area. San Miguel and Cozumel retain much of their Mayan/Mexican heritage, though. That heritage combines with the topside jungles and undersea reefs to make Cozumel the dive adventure it is.

Getting There/ Getting Around

Most U.S. flights to Cozumel land after a stop at Cancun, Mexico, a major tourist center and port of entry north of Cozumel. Aeromexico's flights originate in Houston. American Airlines flies in from Dallas-Fort Worth. Continental's flights originate in Houston. Mexicana has service from Miami and United flies out of Chicago.

Some travelers drive from the States to Cancun, then board an Aero Cozumel plane to the island. That drive can take about three days from Houston and a week from California. Others drive to the Playa Del Carmen resort area on the Yucatan mainland opposite Cozumel and take a ferry to the island. Ferries run frequently from the International Pier, two miles south of San Miguel, and Playa Del Carmen, as well as from Cozumel to Cancun. The International Pier is also a cruise ship port.

There are plenty of unmetered taxis, rental cars, jeeps, mopeds and bicycles available on Cozumel. If you want to rent a car or jeep, it is suggested you reserve it from a major agency before you get to Cozumel. Occasionally, vehicles are hard to come by if you wait until you are there to reserve one. At any one time, most of the island's vehicles are vying for room along the ten-mile strip of west coast that runs by the resorts and San Miguel.

A paved road loops around the lower part of the island. There are trails and very bumpy dirt roads off that which give travelers access to many of the ruins and beaches. Driving Cozumel can be about as stimulating as diving Cozumel. Remember—ninety per cent of the island is jungle and sometimes mechanical things don't do well in the mud and the swamps. So be careful, otherwise your vehicle might be added to the list of island ruins.

Topside Attractions

The San Miguel resort area has many restaurants, nightclubs and lounges. The luxury resorts and clubs frequently have

Steve Rosenberg

live entertainment on weekends. A bountiful variety of fresh seafood is served in most restaurants with produce from the mainland. Eating places range from roadside stands and vendors on the beach to plush restaurants serving Mexican and International dinners.

Tourist shops carry some good buys on Mexican-made souvenirs, jewelry and other products, but as always, know what you are looking for and of what the items are made. Keep in mind intelligent buying habits and be aware of U.S. customs restrictions on items you can bring into this country.

The Cozumel resort community is very diver-oriented, but people who fish are comfortable in Cozumel, too. At San Miguel and through many of the resorts, reef-fishing and deep-sea fishing is available. Charter boats range all about the reefs and rocks bordering Cozumel and most of them find good fishing.

Experiencing the tropical jungle and touring Mayan ruins are part of many divers' stay. Some resorts have personnel who conduct tours, both on Cozumel and the mainland. The San Gervacio Ruins on Cozumel are among the most famous now, as they were recently excavated and have been commercialized to a large degree. However, part of the commercialization has made the site more accessible as well as informative. It is approximately a ten-acre site surrounded by deep jungle in the north central part of the island.

Part of your tour may also include a trip to Punta Molas Lighthouse on Cozumel's north tip. There are Mayan ruins and caves throughout this part of Cozumel. The rough dirt road travels along the east coast. The beaches are sandier here than those found on the west as Caribbean waves have pulverized the coral and deposited it as sand along the shore. There are only a few tourist facilities on the east coast, but freedom and wonder come from traveling through jungle and wide open beaches and seeing ancient ruins all in one day. You never know what you will find.

An afternoon trip to the Chancanab Park and Botanical Garden at Chancanab Lagoon a few miles south of San Miguel is a great break from diving, too. There is a saltwater aquarium and restaurant on the beach, as well as 400 identified species of tropical plants. It is a good place to go before heading inland because you can learn a lot about the Cozumel interior here.

Cozumel Diving

One of the greatest appeals of Cozumel diving is the drift diving available along virtually all of the reef wall off the island's west coast. The current *usually* runs south to north, but once in a while it will run north to south. When planning your dive, know what direction it will take you. The current is produced by the Gulf Stream Current which flows between Cozumel and Yucatan. Depending upon weather, time of year, the location, type, and depth of your dive, and other environmental conditions, the current can range from almost non-existent to four knots. So don't get carried away! Always include signaling devices, such as flares *and* whistles, as part of your dive gear whether you are diving from a boat or from shore. The best way to dive Cozumel is to have not only an experienced and competent guide underwater with you as well as an observant, knowledgeable person awaiting your return topside.

The distance of the wall from shore varies from an easy swim from shore, a difficult swim from shore, to an easy boat ride from shore. Most of the dives are done at well-known locales from San Pedro to the south tip of the island.

Caves permeate the reef with added excitement coming from strong currents, sharks, eels, scorpionfish and barracudas, and side trips through tunnels and chimneys. Other caves are more mellow and give intermediate divers a safe introduction to cave diving. These have easy access in and an exit near the surface of the water.

The walls hold every type of Caribbean coral and sponge. The Gulf Stream current feeds the undersea life of Cozumel and observant divers can see how the coral structures and soft corals have been affected by it. The Current, too, feeds the undersea life, providing a constant influx of warm, clear water full of plankton and other microorganisms upon which filter feeders thrive. These currents make night diving a real thrill, because of the current, itself, as well as helping to support a bounty of colorful, feeding polyps, spirulids, and small invertebrates. Where corals and sponges thrive, reef fish are sure to follow, feeding on one another and hiding in the rocks and coral. Directed by the current to follow this food chain, many open-water species are often seen along the wall and in the channel between Cozumel and Yucatan.

Two sections of nearshore reef from the resort strip south of San Miguel are La Ceiba Drop-off and La Villa Blanca Drop-off. The dominant feature of these areas is a steep, sloping wall. The best diving is within 70 feet of the surface. Within these reefs are color gardens frequently dived by novices and as checkout dives for certified divers. Among these are the Paraiso Reefs, nearshore shallow ridges of coral close to many of the same hotels as are La Ceiba and La Villa. The dives are in the 30-foot to 40-foot range and are frequent night dive sites. There are many octopus, eels, lobster and crab throughout the area.

Farther south are vertical drop-off reefs including Santa Rosa, Palancar and Colombia. The currents are predictably strong and have affected the walls more dramatically than the areas to the north. These three sections are located off the southwest coast. Drift dives are the norm here, but within the wall are scores of coral caves, canyons and tunnels which offer many different dives within a relatively small area. There are enormous groupers, manta rays, countless giant sponges and tall trees of black coral. Palancar Reef is the best known and the most heavily dived reef in Cozumel. Now part of the Cozumel Underwater Preserve, this six-mile-long section of reef still ranks as one of the top reef dives in the world.

Between the walls and the Cozumel shore are such dives as Palancar Gardens. These are shallow dives which entice all levels of divers. Palancar Gardens is an area where newly certified divers can begin to learn drift diving. The current here flows over the top of the wall into these shallow areas, carrying divers over gardens of lettuce coral, brain coral, stands of elkhorn, gorgonian and sponges.

Cozumel has a variety of dive services and shops at which divers can get air, boats, guides and equipment. Of course, the more advanced the diver, the greater his freedom and the less he has to depend upon the direction of others. However, beginning and intermediate divers should watch out for themselves and make sure they don't get in over their heads if in the company of more experienced divers. Always dive within your capabilities. If you want to expand them, take an advanced open-water or deep-dive specialty class first, rather than following the bubbles of one of your buddies who is going deeper than *you* should. Cozumel is no place to take chances.

As throughout the Caribbean, Cozumel has many guides and boat captains who are not divemasters, let alone divers. People who dive without the services of a certified divemaster or u/w guide need to be careful of where they go, what the site conditions are, and who is in charge up top.

There is a recompression chamber in San Miguel as well as a hospital, but divers cannot always depend on getting the right treatment at the right time. There are risks diving Cozumel as there are risks anywhere, but being aware of them (anything from a mild brush with fire coral to the bends), can help make you a better diver. The risks as well as the beauty are simply part of diving. Both help tune the senses and make the underwater more alive.

Cozumel Dive Sites

Paraiso Reef North is about a 100-yard-long formation 200 yards offshore from the International Pier. The system is basically three reefs which run parallel to shore 30 feet to 45 feet deep. Divers can easily spend an hour here, day or night, skimming over stands of star and brain coral, sponges and sea fans. Octopus, eels, lobsters and crabs like it, too. Visibility is 100 feet and more.

Divers can dive a **DC-3** right off the La Ceibe Hotel Pier. The wreck was put in 30 feet of water about ten years ago as a prop for a Mexican disaster movie. It's a good check-out dive and popular with beginners.

Chancanab Lagoon is the undersea part of the Chancanab Park and Botanical Gardens. The coral gardens near shore are excellent for night dives and photography. Divers can swim through a tunnel which links the lagoon to shallow, mid and deep water sites on **Chancanab Reef.** About 100 feet down and on the wall are caves only experienced cave divers should try.

San Francisco Reef is a favorite drift dive right off San Francisco Beach. Dived both as a reef dive and a wall dive, it combines shallow and mid-depth reef species with possible sightings of pelagics along the top and face of the wall at depths from 30 to 50 feet. There is 150-foot visibility along the wall.

Santa Rosa Wall is a major reef complex south of the San Francisco Reef and Beach area. The best of the Santa Rosa is at 60 feet to 80 feet. Colonies of sponges literally clog the undercuts and tunnels of the wall. Currents range from moderate to strong. There are a lot of big groupers and eagle rays. The wall can also be taken as a cave dive, as there are many of those here, too. The wall drops almost vertically for a long way.

The **Palancar Reef** complex has quite a variety of sites which, in their totality, are a microcosm not only of the best of Cozumel, but some of the best of the entire Caribbean. **The Gardens** has coral heads and ridges which divers could use their entire vacation exploring and never have to go deeper than 30 or 40 feet. Crevices meander through the rock and some of those have tunnels which lead into the rock. **Big Horseshoe** is part of the El Christo section of Palancar, with El Christo being named for an underwater statue of Christ. Currents constantly feed and clean the Palancar. Sea turtles frequently flap by. Star fish, conch and lobster are often seen in patches of sea grass or on the white sand bottom. Divers go over the **Palancar Wall** to get into the currents which constantly feed and clean this complex. Not every diver is capable of diving the wall here, but it is what most of them aspire to. For here there are caves and tunnels full of sponges, glassy sweepers, barracuda, sharks, groupers, snappers, filefish and eels. Divers never know what will appear from where. The best diving is within 80 feet of the surface.

Another big wall and drop-off is **Colombia Reef.** As mentioned, Colombia is similar in structure to Palancar and Santa Rosa, but is less dived than either of those

Steve Rosenberg

areas. Its sheer wall is covered with black coral, riddled with caves, and patrolled by sharks. Eighty feet is the limit for most dives here, too, but the wall drops off another 3,000. The nearshore Colombia Reef area is an exciting place for a shallow afternoon dive. Beginners can dive it twice a day; experts can finish up there.

Maracaibo Reef is a long boat ride away from most Cozumel resorts. The top of its wall begins in no less than 100 feet of water. The wall has some deep reef coral species and mobile invertebrates which shallower sites do not have. Only deep-diving veterans should even consider this site and should plan ahead for it with a guide or dive service before coming to Cozumel. The current, tiger, hammerhead and mako sharks are the big draws of Maracaibo. Divers can always count on the current coursing through there. The same cannot be said for sharks.

Cozumel Dive Services

BLUE ANGEL'S SCUBA SCHOOL
Service Address:
On the south side of San Miguel
Mailing Address:
280 ATT Cozumel, Quintano Roo, Mexico
Service Telephone:
011-52-987-20913
Reservation Telephone:
Same as above
Hours Service is Open:
8:30 am to 5 pm Seven days a week
Resort Affiliation:
No resort affiliation

Blue Angel's guides divers who stay at several San Miguel resorts. They do an introduction class comparable to a resort course and offer PADI certification. Certified divers who dive with Blue Angel's are required to bring "C" cards as well as referral papers verifying their experience, otherwise they will be asked to go through a safety check and quick re-certification.

Rentals and repairs are available, and they can arrange to have u/w camera gear for those who request it, but divers should request it when making reservations.

The service offers one-tank and two-tank morning and afternoon dives, depending upon the divers and conditions. They try to have a least four divers for a night diving party.

Blue Angel's goes to all the major Cozumel reefs to dive the caves, walls, coral gardens and ridges. Most dives are bottom at about 80 feet. They sometimes go to Maracaibo when a group of experts wants to make the trip. They have one 20-foot dive boat which can hold six divers. Their two instructors enjoy working with small groups and want to keep the school small in order to give personal attention to divers.

*Note—This service is moving closer to the beach to a better location. As a result, its address and phone number may be different than that listed above.

DISCOVER COZUMEL DIVING
Service Address:
Downtown San Miguel on the waterfront
Mailing Address:
P.O. Box 75, Cozumel, Quintana Roo, Mexico
Discover Cozumel Diving USA-90406 Shadows Dr.,
Springfield, OR 97478
Service Telephone:
503/726-2055 (Days) 503/726-8879 (Nights)
Reservation Telephone:
Same as above
Hours Service is Open:
8:30 to noon; 4:30 pm to 8 pm Seven days a week
Resort Affiliation:
No resort affiliation

Divers staying in the San Miguel area can take a bus or taxi from the airport to their hotel. Discover Cozumel Diving is a short walk from many of the resorts along the west beach road.

This service offers resort training and PADI and SSI certification. They have a full rental shop, including u/w photography gear and film processing. They also do repairs.

They have an excellent fleet of five dive boats, ranging from a 35-footer to a 53-footer. Virtually all their dives to the main Cozumel walls are drift dives. They dive Palancar, which is rated among the top three reefs of the world. They dive the caves of Palancar and Colombia. For expert divers they take special day trips aboard one of their largest boats to Maracaibo or Barracuda Reef. Visibility often exceeds 150 feet. Their night dives are boat dives, too, and give divers plenty of opportunities for u/w photography.

Group rates and hotel dive packages are available.

DIVE COZUMEL
Service Address:
On the main west coast road, near the Sol Caribe and La Ceiba Hotels
Mailing Address:
241 AV Melgar, P.O. Box 165, Cozumel, Q.R. Mexico
Service Telephone:
011-5298-72-0145
Reservation Telephone:
800/446-2166
Hours Service is Open:
8 am to 5 pm
Resort Affiliation:
Divers Inn

Rooms:
10

To get to the Divers Inn, guests can buy a ticket at the airport for a bus ride to the resort.

Carlos Sierra, owner and general manager of Dive Cozumel, offers a resort course and PADI certification. They rent all necessary dive and u/w camera equipment. Film processing is available elsewhere on the island. The service also does repairs.

Divers board any of Dive Cozumel's three boats for a two-tank trip which lasts from about 9 am to 3 pm. They dive Palancar, Paradise and Yocab Reefs. They dive Santa Rosa Wall and the caves and tunnels of Palancar. Parties consist of no more than 15 to 20 divers.

Dive Cozumel dives some of the island's best sites as well as giving divers plenty of time to enjoy the sites. The Divers Inn helps guests arrange tours of the Mayan ruins or tour the mainland. Between dives there are beach parties, watersports and shopping in San Miguel.

DIVE PARADISE
Service Address:
On the south edge of San Miguel, near the Barracuda Hotel
Mailing Address:
P.O. Box 222, Cozumel, Q.R., Mexico
Service Telephone:
011-52-987-21007
Reservation Telephone:
206/441-3483
Hours Service is Open:
9 am to 9 pm Seven days a week
Resort Affiliation:
No resort affiliation

Guests staying at any of the south San Miguel resorts have easy access to Dive Paradise. Dive Paradise dive training includes a resort course, PADI and SSI certification, as well as specialty classes in search and recovery, underwater hunting and cave diving. It will soon have deep-compression diving. The service recommends divers bring everything but tanks, weights, belts and backpacks.

The dive packages include a one-tank morning dive and one-tank afternoon dive. Night diving is offered at an extra fee. Dive Paradise keeps its parties to no more than a dozen. They dive everything from the DC-3 wreck just offshore to the El Christo section and caves of Palancar to the Santa Rosa Wall. They also go to Paraiso Reef for beginning divers and for night dives.

Dive Paradise is a popular service for many beach front hotels. They are trained and equipped to service several dive parties at once, but as mentioned, the number of dives in a party is limited to a dozen. They provide good trips as well as good instruction.

Between dives, guests tour such places

as Chancanab Lagoon and Park, go to the beach, or play in San Miguel.

FANTASIA DIVERS
Service Address:
Off Paraiso Reef, seven miles south of the airport
Mailing Address:
100 N. Central Expressway, 1st City Bank, Suite 500, Richardson, TX 75080
Reservation Telephone:
800/621-6831 (U.S.) 214/669-1991 (Texas)
Hours Service is Open:
8 am to 5 pm
Resort Affiliation:
La Ceiba Hotel
Rooms:
113

To get to La Ceiba Hotel, guests can take a taxi or a bus for the seven-mile trip from the airport.

Fantasia Divers offers a resort course and PADI certification. They offer two underwater photography seminars with Nikon, one in September and one in November. Divers can rent any necessary equipment from them, but personal dive gear, including a BC, is recommended.

Dive Fantasia operates at a relaxed pace to give divers plenty of time to enjoy the dives and to relax with a beach lunch in between. They offer a one-tank deep-dive in the morning and a shallower one-tank dive in the afternoon. They have a variety of dive boats for small, medium and large parties.

They dive the sunken DC-3 in front of the hotel, the shallow Paraiso Reefs, Chancanab Lagoon and Palancar Gardens, as well as the tunnels and walls of Palancar and Santa Rosa. Periodically they will do the deep and wild sites off the Colombia Reef, which is about an hour ride from the resort. There is also very good beach entry diving in front of the hotel.

Between and after dives, guests can enjoy a workout in the weight room, tennis, a massage or soak in the resort's hot tub. Fishing, sailing and horseback riding are also available. The hotel will arrange tours of the Mayan ruins or direct you on how to get to some of them yourself.

NEPTUNO DIVERS
Service Address:
South part of downtown San Miguel
Mailing Address:
Rafael Melgar Ave., 11th Ave., Cozumel, Q.R. Mexico
Service Telephone:
011-52-987-21537/21097

Hours Service is Open:
8 am to 5 pm Seven days a week
Resort Affiliation:
No resort affiliation

This fast-growing resort provides dive service and training to San Miguel beach hotels. They provide a shuttle service for guests to their shop. Neptuno Divers does resort training, PADI and NASE certification and underwater search and rescue certification. This full-service operation rents u/w camera gear, has E-6 film processing and repairs equipment. It recently upgraded its tank bank with 300 new tanks.

The two-tank morning trip is a deep-drift dive, then a shallow dive, followed by a shallow afternoon dive. They do a night dive as often as necessary.

Neptuno Divers' boats usually take no more than 12 divers to any one site. They dive the Horseshoe and caves at Palancar, the black coral covered walls at Colombia and a large variety of other sites between nearshore coral gardens and the Cozumel Wall.

Between dives guests have access to the beaches, sites, watersports, shopping and clubs of Cozumel.

SCUBA COZUMEL
Service Address:
Beachfront resort service south of downtown San Miguel
Mailing Address:
Galapago Inn, P.O. Box 289, Cozumel, Q.R. Mexico 77600
Service Telephone:
011-52-987-20627
Reservation Telephone:
800/847-5708
Hours Service is Open:
8 am to 7 pm
Resort Affiliation:
The Galapago Inn
Rooms:
31

The Galapago Inn has been a popular Cozumel beachfront resort for years. The Galapago is part of the resort complex south of San Miguel and serves Galapago Inn guests as well as those staying at other resorts.

Scuba Cozumel is located at the hotel. It teaches a resort dive training course and offers PADI certification. Their dive package includes tanks, weights, belts and backpack. They also rent u/w camera gear.

Most of Scuba Cozumel's diving is done along the prime sites of six-mile-long Palancar reef. They also dive the

Santa Rosa Reef and Wall, where drift dives are done among mountains of coral. Punta Tormentos and Maracaibo Reef are on their dive site menu, too. Night dives happen whenever a boatful of divers want to go.

Scuba Cozumel does one- or two-tank dives in the morning and afternoon. They cover Cozumel with seven dive boats, ranging from four boats over 30 feet to three skiffs for smaller dive parties.

The Galapago Inn was built with the serious diver in mind. The locker area is conveniently located on the resort dock so there is no need for divers to haul equipment back and forth from the resort to the boats. They have an attractive, all-inclusive dive package which includes all diving, food, facilities, and equipment. This is a well-planned, well-operated service.

AQUA SAFARI
Service Address:
On the waterfront, at 5th St. South
Mailing Address:
P.O. Box 41, Cozumel, Q.R. Mexico
Service Telephone:
011-52-987-20661/20101
Reservation Telephone:
800/225-0227 (U.S.) 800/222-1537 (TX)
Hours Service is Open:
7:30 am to 6:30 pm Seven days a week
Resort Affiliation:
No resort affiliation

Bill Horn and Aqua Safari have competently served divers for years on Cozumel. He and his staff have been instrumental in helping develop and protect the Cozumel Underwater Preserve. Aqua Safari serves guests of many hotels on the Cozumel waterfront.

The service offers a resort course off the beach and PADI and NAUI certification. Other than dealing with u/w photography gear, the service can rent and repair just about anything the diver needs.

They do two-tank dives both in the morning and afternoon, with night diving on request. Ninety per cent of all Cozumel diving is drift diving, and their boats take divers to sites along the major walls and follow the divers' bubbles to the pick up point. Two divemasters frequently lead and follow dive parties while on a drift dive. Aqua Safari has two 38-foot boats which hold a maximum of 20 divers.

The service has a friendly and hospitable staff whose top priorities are showing the divers a good time and protecting the reef. You will appreciate their attitude while topside, on the dive boat and underwater.

Jamaica

Jamaica has the topography of a subcontinent. Unique among its Caribbean neighbors, Jamaica was created in the maelstrom of a volcano. As a consequence, the island is composed of sharp angles, steep ravines, rugged peaks, valleys of volcanic soil and other distinctions of character and scenery.

Jamaica, comparable in size to Connecticut, is well-geared toward tourism and agriculture. Montego Bay is the resort capital of the northwest coast. It has the widest selection of hotels, guesthouses, villas and apartments in the Caribbean. Runaway Beach is on the north central coast and has been developed to maintain its natural beauty both on and offshore. Farthest east is Ocho Rios, a beautiful, beachfront complex of many world-renowned resorts. On the northeast coast is Port Antonio, the most secluded and tropical of the island's resort areas. Kingston, the country's capital, dominates the south coast. To the west and inland is the mountain resort area of Mandeville. The western tip of the island has Negril, a modern complex laid out along a seven-mile stretch of white sand beach.

The island is constantly cooled by the northeast Trade Winds, which keep the temperature in the mid-eighties most of the year. The sun shines almost constantly, and when it does rain, it falls usually as brief afternoon showers.

Evidence suggests that Arawak Indians lived on Jamaica for five hundred years before Columbus sited their island in May of 1494. Although he would eventually call the island "...the fairest island that eyes have beheld," there are few indications that Columbus or his men actually landed on that first voyage. Apparently they sailed from the region now called Rio Bueno west along the coast to Montego Bay, then set sail back to Cuba.

He returned later that year, and again sailed along the coast, but it was not until 1503 that he made landfall. Commanding two storm-crippled ships, Columbus and his crew were forced to weigh anchor. They were marooned on Jamaica for over a year until the Governor of Hispaniola, a rival of Columbus, felt he had suffered enough and sent ships to rescue him and his men.

For the next 150 years, Spain began many coastal settlements and explored the interior for metals and jewels, but finding few, Spain paid little heed to Jamaica and when an English force of 5,000 men invaded in 1655, they offered little resistance and conceded the island to England.

Early English settlers planted tobacco, cotton, cocoa and logged indigo, a dyewood. However, piracy helped Port Royal become one of the richest towns in the Americas and certainly the most notorious. Its title as the wickedest city on earth went down with it when most of it sank during the earthquake of 1692.

The eighteenth century saw the reign of King Sugar. Vast acreages of canefields dominated the plains while on hillside slopes palatial residences like Rose Hall near Montego bay were built.

The twin of sugar was slavery. After the extermination of the Indians, Jamaica not only absorbed nearly one million African slaves, but became a huge trans-shipment center for slaves destined for other colonies in the Americas.

In a sense, modern Jamaican society began in 1838 with the abolition of slavery. The newly freed slaves rapidly deserted the plantations and established themselves as free settlers in the hills, whose descendants are regarded as the "backbone" of Jamaica.

As a British colony, Jamaica had three hundred years of stormy political life. Under successive nationalist leaders in the 20th century, the country began moving toward increasing autonomy in the running of national affairs, culminating in full independence in 1962. After a few years of shaky diplomatic relations with the U.S., the situation between the two countries began to improve again in the 1980s and today it is fairly strong.

Jamaica is a member of the British Commonwealth of Nations. The Queen of England is represented locally by the Governor-General. The island's Constitution is based on British legal, religious, educational and political traditions. Jamaica is a parliamentary democracy with an elected House of Representatives and a nominated Upper House—the Senate. The prime minister is the head of government. There is a well-established two-party system and elections are normally held every five years.

Getting There/ Getting Around

Airlines from North America and the Caribbean include: Air Florida, Air Jamaica, American Airlines, Air Canada, Eastern, BWIA, Pan Am, ALM, Cubana, British Airways and Cayman Airways. Jamaica has two international airports: Norman Manley at Kingston and Donald Sangster two miles from Montego Bay, at which most tourists land. Flight times to Sangster International at Montego are: 2½ hours from Atlanta; 1½ hours from Miami; 4 hours from Chicago, 5½ hours from Montreal and 7 hours from San Francisco. Numerous cruise ships call at Kingston, Montego Bay, Ocho Rios and Port Antonio, some on a weekly basis.

Taxis are metered. Taxis and buses run between the airports, seaports, cities and resort areas. A taxi ride from Donald Sangster International to the Montego Bay area is approximately U.S. $5.50.

Interisland travel is also made easy by Trans-Jamaica Airlines, which flies to airports at the major cities including Negril, Montego Bay, Ocho Rios, Port Antonio and the domestic flight airport at Kingston, which is a short taxi ride from Kingston's Norman Manley International.

Avis, Hertz, Martins Jamaica, Budget and many others provide cars for rental in principal resort areas. These agencies deliver cars from major airports as well as from branch offices in major towns. Persons renting cars must be between 25 and 70 years old and have a valid driver's license. Would-be car renters without a credit card must pay a $500 cash deposit at the time of rental. If you plan to stay in Jamaica for any significant length of time and do more than dive and hang around the beach, renting a car can help you enjoy Jamaica and your vacation much more than you would without one. Jamaica has a good system of roads and ample enough gas to provide access to most of the island's points of interest.

Topside Attractions

The major resort areas have all other watersports besides diving, plus golf, tennis, horseback riding, and tours through the local spots. From Montego Bay, a one-day train ride aboard the Governor's Coach into the Jamaican interior is a favorite trek. The train stops at several prominent points along the route. Reservations for the trip can be made at many hotels.

When you are ready to take in some topside attractions, remember that most of Jamaica's more popular beaches are found along the north coast—from broad swaths of pearly white perfection to quiet, private lagoons. Near Montego Bay is, perhaps, Jamaica's most famous beach: Doctor's Cave Beach. Recently it merged with adjacent Cornwall Beach, and the mile-long stretch of sand which fronts the Caribbean Sea makes them an unbeatable combination. There are snack bars and changing rooms there, too.

A trip on the Great River, west of Montego Bay, is another relaxing way to spend the evening. Guides pole canoes upriver to a restaurant for dinner, Jamaican music and other river bank entertainment.

Along the coast from Montego Bay to Port Antonio are many small museums, tours of refurbished plantation homes and historical sites, such as Columbus Park at Discovery Bay, near Runaway Bay. Resorts often sponsor trips to places guests are interested in seeing.

West of Ocho Rios is the famous Dunn's River Falls, a popular rest and photography spot where 600-foot-high waterfalls drop over tiers of rock. A white sand beach and restaurants are nearby. East of Ocho Rios is another guided river tour, this one along the torchlit banks of the White River to a restaurant, bar and Jamaican show.

Along the south coast, spanning the area between Kingston and Spanish Town are several old fortifications, museums, and the Hope Botanical Gardens, which has the most complete display of tropical orchids in the West Indies.

Jamaica Diving

The image of Jamaica diving has been greatly enhanced by the Jamaica Association of Dive Operators (J.A.D.O.). This association strictly abides by a well-thought-out set of rules which does three things: helps assure dives will be safe, exciting and maximize customer satisfaction. All of the dive services listed in this chapter belong to J.A.D.O. Unfortunately, there are a number of beachfront and boat-based operations which are independent operators who are not J.A.D.O. members. Just as you should not exchange American currency for Jamaican with just anyone off the street, you should not buy your air from just anyone off the beach. Even if the resort arranges diving for you, make certain the operator is a J.A.D.O. member! It is much more important to dive only with association members in Jamaica than it is to dive only with dive operator association members in some of the other islands and countries covered in this book.

We made every effort to include every legitimate Jamaican dive operator, but as throughout the Caribbean, dive operators come and go. There is a chance you might have contact with a legitimate operator we do not have listed. If you have doubts about an operator, phone the tourist board or any member listed here and ask if this particular operator is a J.A.D.O. member. You will probably get an answer you can trust. It is important to realize, too, that J.A.D.O. members are all resort-affiliated and are not allowed to provide service to any diver other than those who are guests of their affiliated resort.

Now to the diving. Jamaica has two major areas of prime diving. Generally speaking, they are off the west coast, which is the leeward side of the island, and along the north coast reef, which runs the length of Jamaica, forming a wall between the island and the 3,000-foot-deep Cayman Trench. Summer diving has the best visibility with a range varying from 80 feet to 120 feet. Winter weather can reduce it down to 50 and 60 feet.

At this time, there is very little diving done off the east coast. Prevailing southeast winds make the waters rough. On the south coast there is only minimal tourist facility development and no dive shop operates there anywhere.

Beginning at the west coast seven-mile beach area of Negril, divers will find plenty of good underwater action after a 10 to 20 minute boat ride. Dives through the west coast coral gardens and patch reefs range from 10 feet to 100 feet, with most dives being less than 60 feet down.

Volcanic rocks and coral limestones combine to form mazes of arched tunnels and overhangs. Divers gain access to some of the larger formations by descending crevices slashed into the rock. The walls of these mazes and grottos are deco-rated with branches and plumes of soft corals, knobs of hard corals and the full menu of colorful Caribbean sponges. Schools of silver baitfish flash between the walls, which are also a haven for lobsters, crabs and other common reef life. There is some challenging cave diving here where divers get to explore vertical chimneys and side tunnels coursing off the larger chambers.

The Montego Bay area offers protected shore-entry dives to coral gardens and, incredibly, shore-entry wall dives where the top of the reef wall is a quick kick from north coast sand. Area operators, however, prefer to dive most wall sites from boats. The wall is a solid barrier from Montego east to Ocho Rios, providing many sites which are frequently dived but have yet to be named. This area's characteristics includes fine stands of pillar corals, which are favorite night dive and u/w photography sites because of the color of feeding coral polyps on them and the small reef life which seek shelter there. Generally, though, the reef fish here are a bit smaller and a bit fewer in number than those found on the west coast because they have been pressured harder, but they are returning in force. Divers to the wall, though, get a chance to see jellyfish, barracuda, spadefish, triggerfish, sharks and other pelagics which are usually not seen off Negril.

Another dominant feature associated with Jamaica wall diving is its intricate system of caves which frequently open into the face of the wall and lead through tunnels to coral and sponge covered chambers. Some passageways go way under Jamaica. The wall itself is pocked with mini drop-offs, sand chutes and canyons. These formations greatly add to the hundreds of miles of surface area of rock and coral which protect so much of the life divers see there. Resplendent as this area is with life, texture and mystery it is not well-endowed with diveable shipwrecks. Many which have crashed into the wall have tumbled to depths which exceed what most sport divers should attempt.

Of course, there is a lot of local variety off each beach which gives access to the coral gardens and the walls beyond, but the above description holds pretty much true for the nearshore area between Montego Bay and Ocho Rios. East of Ocho Rios to Port Antonio wind and waves become more of a factor that limit diving, conditions which are amplified along the east coast.

Jamaica Dive Sites
Negril

The Throne Room is a large split in the reef which opens to a sandy area at 70 feet. Caves run off the Throne Room at various places, providing divers with access to inside the reef where squirrelfish and green morays thrive. Octopus and starfish are known to pass through, too.

Rays are often seen along slopes of sea grass growing in the white sand.

King Fish Reef has more tropical fish than any other part of the reef off Negril. It is rife with small, sievelike passageways and undercuts through which yellowtail damselfish, queen angelfish and fairy basslets appear and disappear.

Sands Club Reef has a good reef fish population, too. Some of its coral formations are larger than those of King Fish Reef, making it easier for divers to explore some of the passages. Divers can often be framed by stacks of coral which help make this area good for u/w photography. Large tube and vase sponges are common above which are branches of gorgonians and soft plume corals. Most dives to Sands Club are at 70 feet to 80 feet. There are stands of black coral and lobsters on the ocean floor.

A shallow dive close to the beach is **Coral Gardens**, which has stands of elkhorn and clusters of sponges from 20 feet to 40 feet. It is an excellent night dive with easy access.

Montego Bay

Chalet Reef offers many types of strong, shallow water coral and reef fishes. Depths here go to about 35 feet, with clumps of pink, lavender and purple sponges becoming prominant at about 20 feet. This is a colorful dive for divers and the 60-foot visibility is more than ample to see what is around in this shallow site.

Canyon 1 features a terrain of canyons and archways with barrel sponges, black coral, soldierfish, fairy basslets, drums, grunts and spider crabs. Depths are to 80 feet with visibility at about 70 feet. This dive is a favorite challenge for divers familiar to Montego Bay and highly recommended. **Canyon 2** has much the same depth, visibility and marine life as Canyon and Chimney, but also has small passages running out to the exterior wall.

Arena is an advanced boat dive to about 70 feet. There is a large, white sand plot surrounded by coral walls containing a network of caves with two openings to the outer wall. Marine life includes tube sponges, gorgonians, sheet corals, crabs and black coral. It is also a fair bet to come here for a look at an eagle ray or a sea turtle.

Duppy's Hole is a fun cave and chimney dive. Beginning out along the wall, divers enter Duppy's Hole at 80 feet, then work up the chimney to about 30 feet, to finish the dive off in the shallows. There are occasional nurse sharks and barracudas here.

Airport Reef, so named because of its close offshore proximity to Sangster International, is, nevertheless, a good dive which offers both deep and shallow diving. Visibility is often in the 80-foot range. There are schools of sergeant majors, parrotfish and yellowtails.

The Wall consists of a steep drop-off beginning at 30 feet down to several thou-

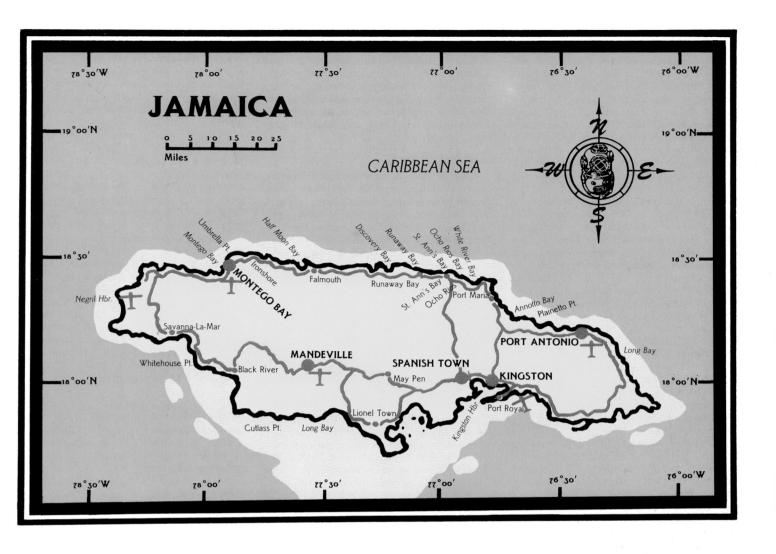

JAMAICA

CARIBBEAN SEA

Jamaica

Entry Requirements
U.S. & Canadian citizens need proof of citizenship and an onward or return ticket. Others need passports

Language
English

Airlines
Air Jamaica, BWIA, American Airlines, Pan Am, Air Canada, Eastern and Air Florida

Airports
Donald Sangster International, 2 miles from Montego Bay
Norman Manley International, 13 mi. from Kingston

Departure Tax
JA $20 (approx. U.S. $3.50)

Electricity
110 volts, 50 cycles. Some hotels use 220 volts only; transformers available

Size
4,411 sq. mi.

Population
2.1 million

Other:
The Jamaica dollar is the only legal tender in the island. Visitors must convert their currencies to Jamaican dollars at commercial banks or the exchange bureau operated by the Bank of Jamaica at the airport, cruise ship piers and at most hotels.

sand. Dives to it seldom exceed 90 feet. Tunnels are bored into the coral and sponge covered wall. Plumes of soft corals, some hydroids, and stands of black coral are found. Sharks, a few small schools of barracuda, and trumpetfish are common.

The Widow Makers Cave is often taken as part of a two-tank dive. This wall dive starts with a tunnel at 90 feet that bores into the reef wall. Other passageways and crevices exist here, allowing divers a chance to see everything from invertebrates, to small reef fish to pelagics.

A long-time favorite shore dive which has been developed over the years to get fish used to divers is called, among other names, **The Feeding Station**. Just diving through the channels in the reef down to 70 feet is exciting, but it's a kick to feed the fish, too, which include angelfish, yellowtails, parrotfish and sergeant majors. It is also a good place for u/w photography.

Giant Pillar Coral Reef is in 25 feet of water. Some of the largest pillar coral in the Caribbean can be seen here, which measure at least nine feet high. Other corals, reef fish and some sponges thrive.

Sponge Plunge is an advanced boat dive with depths of 85 feet and visibility of 50 feet to 80 feet. Divers find one of the Caribbean's widest variety of sponges here. Other marine life includes deepwater gorgonian, black coral and red banded coral shrimp. Along the rock ledges and overhangs are fairy and black basslets.

Runaway Bay

The Runaway Bay area has several protected reef formations which hold scores of dive sites. Among the best of them are **Silver Spray Reef**, a nice, shallow reef dive with excellent ambient light where sunlight splays off on coral boulders, creating ever-changing conditions for macro photography. Coral gardens with brain coral, star coral and some finger coral with sponges create a reef fish habitat.

Shipwreck Reef has a sunken freighter which has been down there for 40 years. This is a shallow reef with many caverns and gulleys traversing through it. It is a good place for maximum bottom time.

One of Jamaica's best wall dives is called **The Canyon**. The Canyon features a geographically unique double wall that begins at 35 feet on top down to about 150 feet. Divers swim between the walls where there may be nurse sharks, barracuda, trumpetfish, and porcupinefish. The walls are festooned with sponges, plume gorgonians and hard corals.

Ricky's Reef is an extensive reef system part of the main Jamaican wall. The most thrilling of the dive starts at 70 feet and drops down into the trench. Enormous purple tube sponges and vase sponges adorn the walls. Thickets of soft corals are a haven for brittle stars, bluehead wrasse, and chromis. The colors on the wall and the glory of being suspended over the

trench provide the diver with a wonderful experience.

Runaway Bay Caves is a chain of caves about a 20-minute boat ride west of Runaway Bay. At 100 feet, colonies of blue vase sponges cling to the reef wall. Inside the caves schools of yellowtail snappers, octopus, spotted eels and blue chromis can be found.

Ocho Rios

Devil's Reef is an excellent dive over the top of a plateau 70 feet down. Any number of large reef fish and pelagics may be seen, including rays, sharks, Atlantic spadefish and barracudas. The plateau slopes down to about 190 feet, with coral heads and undercuts being found along part of the terraces.

Dickies Reef is a popular nearshore dive from 20 feet to 60 feet. The shallow waters, especially, give ample opportunity for natural light photography. A lot of invertebrates can be found in the small coral beds and make good subjects.

Three Stones Ledge is a dive where the wall starts at 40 feet and plunges into the Cayman Trench. It is full of chimneys, crevices and gulleys.

Top of the Mountain is a 30-foot-tall pinnacle of coral covered with soft gorgonians, black coral and orange sponges. The base sits in about ninety feet of water on the wall that then plunges down in the trench. Ten feet above the floor is a cave that opens into the pinnacle.

Jamaica Dive Services

CARIBBEAN AMUSEMENT COMPANY
Service Address:
    Between Ocho Rios and Montego Bay, in Falmouth
Mailing Address:
    Trelawny Beach Hotel, Falmouth, Jamaica
Service Telephone:
    809/954-2450 ext. 160
Reservation Telephone:
    Same as above
Hours Service is Open:
    8:30 am to 4 pm Seven days a week
Resort Affiliation:
    Trelawny Beach Hotel
Rooms:
    350

The Caribbean Amusement Company, formerly known as Tojo Watersports, has been providing dive services to Trelawny guests for years. The resort will arrange transfers for guests who land at Montego Bay's Sangster Airport.

Steve McClure and John Wright jointly own this operation and offer a resort training course three times a week, which is free when guests buy a dive package. They provide Canadian open-water certification under the ACUC system. Dive

gear is included with the package, but no u/w photography gear is available.

Their three dive boats range from 20 feet to 30 feet and normally carry no more than ten divers at any one time. They will dive twice a day and offer occasional night dives, but only one dive per day is included in the dive package.

They dive a lot of caves here and go to a different site each day. Big Head is a 60-foot cave dive heavy with tropical fish, some lobster and sponges, sea fans and hydrocoral covering the walls and floor. Split Rock is an intriguing cave dive from 30 feet to 50 feet down. Night dives will include some nearshore coral gardens with an abundance of lobsters, urchins, feeding coral polyps and reef fish.

Trelawny is a self-contained beachfront resort 23 miles from Montego (Mo) Bay. There is a lot of natural beauty in the rivers and mountains here. Watersports are also available from Caribbean Amusement Company, and are part of the service package. Guided glass bottom boat trips, islands tours, tennis, entertainment and bus transportation into Mo Bay are available from the resort.

NEGRIL SCUBA CENTRE
Service Address:
    On the western tip of Jamaica at Negril Beach
Mailing Address:
    Negril Post Office, Negril, Jamaica
Service Telephone:
    809/947-4323
Reservation Telephone:
    Same as above
Hours Service is Open:
    9 am to 5 pm Seven days a week
Resort Affiliation:
    Negril Beach Club
Rooms:
    100
Cottages/Villas:
    14 time sharing condos

Guests of Negril Beach Club take a bus, taxi, rent a car, or a Trans-Jamaica flight to cover the 50 miles between Negril Airport and Sangster Airport.

Divers of the Negril Scuba Centre get plenty of competent, individual attention. Owned by Karen McCarthy, this service prides itself on being professional, safety-conscious and fun. A resort course is offered, MDEA (Multi-national Divers Educational Association) certification has been offered for some years and PADI sanctioned training is now available. All rentals are available including camera equipment. Divers who bring everything but a weight belt and tank get a $5 discount per dive.

The Scuba Centre does a deep morning dive, a reef dive in the afternoon and night dives on request. They dive from two small dive boats and a 40-foot catamaran which holds 20 to 25 divers.

Their favorite sites include The Throne

Margo Nelson

Room, Sands Club Reef, Bay Fish Reef and King Fish Reef. Most of their dives are between 70 feet and 80 feet. Lobsters, octopus, rays and reef tropicals abound. Many good sites are directly out from the shop about a half-mile away.

Between dives guests can sail, go deep-sea fishing or horseback riding, play tennis, or get an all over tan. The Negril area itself is a seven-mile stretch of white sand and relatively few resorts. It provides the perfect setting for every pleasure.

POSEIDON NEMROD DIVERS

Service Address:
Two locations: At Chalet Caribe, 6 mi. west of Mo Bay
At Farguerite Restaurant in Mo Bay

Mailing Address:
P.O. Box 152 Reading, St. James, Jamaica, W.I.

Service Telephone:
809/952-3624; for both services

Reservation Telephone:
Same as above

Hours Service is Open:
8 am to 4 pm Seven days a week

Resort Affiliation:
Chalet Caribe Hotel

Rooms:
28

Poseidon Nemrod Divers has been owned and operated for years by Theo and Hannie Smit. Their main shop is located at the Chalet Caribe on the coast road to Negril, six miles west of Mo Bay. This service handles the reservations for both shops. The Chalet Caribe shop does only shore-entry dive. The Farguerite shop does all boat diving from the Mo Bay Beach.

Poseidon offers a resort course and full certification under the PADI, ACUC and MDEA systems. They are beginning to concentrate more on specialty classes in underwater photography and video, too. Full rentals, including u/w photo gear, are available, but E-6 developing is not yet here. Most of their repairs are limited to Sherwood equipment.

The service concentrates on diving in the morning here because the wind can kick up a little bit in the afternoon. They offer a one-tank wall dive at 9 am and a shallow reef dive at noon. Night diving is on request.

Poseidon dives Airport Reef and Point Reef. They also do The Window, an intriguing coral opening into the wall via a tunnel which bores into the reef. Other favorites are Canyon 1 and Canyon 2, Duppy's Hole and Widow Maker's Cave. Theo and Hannie established the Fish Feeding Station mentioned earlier, which is so popular with u/w photographers and novices.

Between dives, many guests of Chalet Caribe explore the Jamaica countryside. There are guided raft trips up the nearby rivers and trips to the falls at Ocho Rios. Watersports and golf are also available.

SEA & DIVE JAMAICA
Service Address:
In Ocho Rios
Mailing Address:
Arawak P.O., St. Ann, Jamaica, W.I.
Service Telephone:
809/972-2162
Reservation Telephone:
Hotel Phone - 809/972-2318
Hours Service is Open:
8 am to 5 pm Seven days a week
Resort Affiliation:
Arawak Inn
Rooms:
17

The most convenient way to get to the Arawak Inn is to take a Trans-Jamaica flight from Montego Bay to Ocho Rios. For guests who have a hotel package, a shuttle is provided for them from the airport. Sea & Dive Jamaica also has concessions located on the properties of Shaw Park Beach Hotel and Couples Resort, two beachfront resorts on opposite sides of Ocho Rios.

Sea & Dive Jamaica, owned and operated by Mike Drakulich, has been operating in Jamaica longer than any other service. One of the founders of the J.A.D.O., Mike has long had a solid commitment to Jamaica and to the people who come here to dive. A resort training course in addition to PADI, NASDS and ACUC certification are offered. They offer two types of basic dive packages, with price based upon how much personal gear divers bring. They rent u/w camera gear and do some repairs.

In addition to a shallow training dive every morning, Sea & Dive offers two-tank boat dives daily, and night diving twice a week. They dive the plateau and deep terraces of Devil's Reef, the chimneys and crevices of Three Stones Ledge on the wall of the Cayman Trench, and at the time of writing, plan to sink a 187-foot troller to give divers a shipwreck off their coast. The coral pinnacle known as Top of the Mountain is also a good site which holds gorgonians, tube sponges, orange sponges and encrusting sponges and corals. All of these sites appeal to experienced divers.

They have four boats including two 22-footers which give quick access to sites for small dive parties and a 41-foot custom dive boat for groups of up to 25.

Guests who stay at any of the three resorts with which Sea & Dive Jamaica operates can enjoy glass-bottom boat tours, skiing, windsurfing, other watersports and sunset cruises three times a week. A trip to Dunn River Falls is sponsored by the resort, too. "Illusions" is a popular disco at the Arawak and "Silks" is the spot at the Shaw Park Hotel.

SEAWORLD RESORTS, LTD.
Service Address:
4 miles from Mo Bay; 5 minutes from airport
Mailing Address:
Cariblue Beach Hotel, Montego Bay, Jamaica, W.I.
Service Telephone:
809/953-2180
Reservation Telephone:
Same as above
Hours Service is Open:
8 am to 5 pm Seven days a week
Resort Affiliation:
Cariblue Beach Hotel
Rooms:
24

Roy Watkin manages this service, conveniently located on the north coast with easy access to much of the best Jamaica offers. The resort provides a free shuttle service for its guests who land at Sangster Airport.

This Seaworld Resorts service offers a resort training course, as well as PADI and NAUI open water certification. Experienced divers should bring their personal dive gear, "C" card and log book. Their full rental shop includes u/w photography equipment.

This service has two dive boats, a 28-footer and 32-footer. The usual number in a dive party ranges from ten to 15. Divers have their choice of diving any of the two-tank dives the boats go to daily. Some of the more popular sites are the exquisite coral formations of Seaworld Reef, the swim-through tunnels at Chub Reef, and Green Hill Reef, which is a favorite 60-foot dive. The Widow Maker's cave at 90 feet and many unnamed sites along the north wall are within a 15-minute boat ride from the dock. All common Caribbean reef fish are represented here, but not in large schools. The instructors are discovering and exploring new sites which will soon be offered to guests. Night diving is on request.

The Cariblue Beach Hotel is close to golf, tennis and the restaurants and shopping of Montego Bay. Roy Watkins also conducts tours all over the island as part of his Two Dining Tours service. The resort has two deep sea fishing boats, offers an all-day yacht cruise to Negril including food, drinks and music, and a dinner cruise aboard a Chris Craft Commander.

SUNDIVERS
Service Address:
Runaway Bay is 45 mi east of Mo Bay; 18 mi west of Ocho Rios
Mailing Address:
P.O. Box 212, Runaway Bay, Jamaica
Service Telephone:
809/973-2346
Reservation Telephone:
809/973-3507
Hours Service is Open:
7:30 am to 4:30 pm Seven days a week
Resort Affiliation:
Club Caribbean
Cottages/Villas:
116 cottages

Guests of Club Caribbean are picked up by a resort shuttle from the airport, which is included as part of the hotel package. Sundivers and Club Caribbean combine to create the only PADI 5 Star facility on Jamaica.

In addition to resort training, Sundivers offers PADI, ACUC and CMAS certification. It also offers speciality classes in deep diving, night diving, u/w photography, u/w navigator, research diver and wreck diver. They recommend divers bring only their mask, fins and snorkel; all other gear is included in the dive packages. They have a complete u/w video lab, do E-6 film processing, and repair some types of dive equipment.

Sundivers offers a two-tank morning dive and a one-tank afternoon dive, with night diving on request. Divers motor out to the reefs and walls aboard any of their several inflatables, which range from 17- to 26-footers. Their five full-time instructors take divers to over 20 sites which are a ten- to 30-minute boat ride away. They dive the double walls of The Canyon, a wall site called Spanish Anchor, Pear Tree Bottom, revered for its tunnels which run through thick walls of coral, and Shipwreck Reef. These sites have reef fish common to Jamaica and a profusion of sponges which surpass the color and variety to be found in many other places.

The hotel, itself, has a full entertainment package including reggae music, dancing, horseback riding and plantation tours. Many guests visit Dunn's River Falls, Runaway Caves and the world's largest reef ecology lab called Discovery Bay Marineland. It is part of the University of the West Indies, and is seven miles west of the resort.

Netherland Antilles

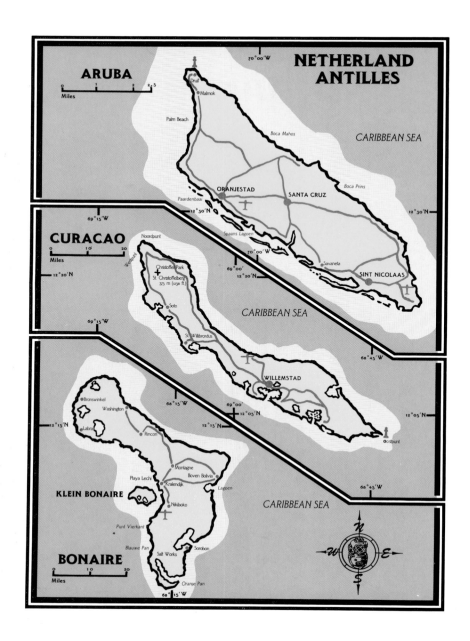

Netherland Antilles

Entry Requirements
Valid passport with an onward or return ticket to a destination outside of the Netherland Antilles

Language
Dutch English & Spanish are also widely spoken. Local language is Papiamento.

Airlines
ALM, Eastern and American

Airports
Queen Beatrix on Aruba
Flamingo on Bonaire
Curacao International on Curacao

Size
Aruba: 70 sq. mi.
Bonaire: 122 sq. mi.
Curacao: 210 sq. mi.

Population
Aruba: 67,000
Bonaire: 9,700
Curacao: 132,000

U.S. Tourist Offices:
Aruba Tourist Bureau
399 NE 15th St.
Miami, FL 33132
305/358-6360
800/327-8226

Bonaire Tourist Office
1466 Broadway, #903
New York, New York 10036
212/869-2004

Curacao Tourist Board
330 Biscayne Blvd. #806
Miami, FL 33132
305/374-5811

Aruba, Bonaire and Curacao are the ABC islands of the Netherland Antilles. The ABC islands, which are off the northwest coast of Venezuela, are one of the two groups of Caribbean Islands which comprise the Netherland Antilles. The other group consists of three smaller islands: Saba, St. Eustatius and the southern part of St. Maarten, all in the eastern Caribbean. The six islands of the Netherlands Antilles are governed as an equal partner with the constitutional monarchy of the Netherlands. The Queen is represented by the Governor, with other appointed and elected officials providing legislative direction.

As a group, the ABC islands were bounced between colonial powers during the 15th and 16th centuries. The Spanish, British and Dutch all were contenders for these islands. Curacao came under Dutch control when they occupied it as a maritime base during their war with Spain in 1634. Soon Dutch colonists came and settled on Bonaire and Aruba. In the 1700s Curacao was settled by Portuguese Jews and other religious minorities escaping persecution in Europe, but the islands remained in Dutch control. Britain took them over in 1800 during the Napoleonic Wars, but the Dutch returned in 1816 and the islands were then recognized by other European powers as part of the Dutch Empire.

The government subsidized salt production, farming, and ranching, three industries which did gain a foothold on these flat, arid, rocky islands. With the abolition of slavery in the Dutch Empire in 1863, these operations turned out to be unprofitable. The economy of the ABCs floundered until 1924 when oil was discovered in Aruba and later in Curacao. People from Bonaire migrated to the other two islands to work.

After World War II business and military men saw the Caribbean's potential for tourism. People came back to Bonaire as industry came to it, and Bonaire began to become a paradise retreat. Since 1951 the oil industry, salt producers and tourism have made steady advances throughout the ABCs. They have worked together to maintain a viable economy and an aesthetic environment. Duty-free shopping and gambling are available on all three islands.

Aruba is known more for its fringe of white sand beaches, resorts and casinos than for diving. The shore is partly protected, however, by reefs which have some good dive sites. It is the most westerly of the ABCs, and lies 15 miles north of Venezuela. Tourism and one of the largest oil refineries in the world keep the economy thriving. All that remains of the Arawak Indians who lived here when the Spaniards came in the 1500s are hieroglyphics painted on the granite surfaces of caves on the wild, windward side of the island.

Curacao, the middle island, is 35 miles north of Venezuela. As the seat of the Dutch ABC islands' government, Curacao has more people, better air service and more industry than Aruba and Bonaire. Its capital, Willemstad, has more of an Old World sophistication and better shopping than Aruba and Bonaire.

Tourism has become nearly as important to Curacao as oil refining. Curacao and the port of Willemstad attract more than a quarter of a million cruise ship passengers a year in addition to business people and other tourists.

Bonaire, 50 miles north of Venezuela and 40 miles east of Curacao, is the easternmost of the ABCs. Its history and geology combine to make this island the most appealing to the dive traveler. Bonaire is as arid and barren above water as it is rich with life below.

Bonaire has four basic geographic distinctions. The northeast coast is the rugged windward side; its waters are buffeted by incoming trade winds. The leeward coast lies within a bay that makes up most of the east side of the island. In the most protected part of the bay, and behind the uninhabited island of Kelin Bonaire, is Kralendijk, the island capital.

White sand beaches line the shore north and south of Kralendijk. The northern interior of the island is hilly and dry. The southern half of the island is a flat desert. Salt pans, where sea water is evaporated to yield its salt, share a border with the Pekel Meer Flamingo Sanctuary.

The ABCs are south of the major hurricane belt and they receive only about 20 to 22 inches of rain a year. October and November are the most likely months to bring violent storms. Thorny brush, cacti and agaves in the lowlands and deserts are periodically broken by dry forests which grow on the hills. The islands are close to the equator, so the temperature remains around 80° to 85°F all year, which is tempered by ocean currents and constant trade winds.

Getting There/Getting Around

From the United States, ALM, American and Eastern Airlines are the most prominent carriers to the ABCs. ALM is the major carrier for interisland travel. There are international airports on all three islands: Queen Beatrix near Oranjestad, Aruba; Flamingo Airport near Kralendijk, Bonaire; and Curacao International Airport on Curacao.

All taxis must be registered and are designated by the TX on the license plates. They are not metered, but there are standard prices listed on tariff sheets available in the cabs or from your resort. You can check these before negotiating. Buses and rental cars are available at all airports, major cities and resort areas.

Topside Attractions
Aruba

Oranjestad is the only sizable population center on Aruba. There are shopping areas and some interesting sections of town where buildings, blending Dutch and Spanish styles, retain an Old World atmosphere. The hotels offer restaurants, gambling and night club shows.

The 70 square miles of Aruba are easy to tour. For those who want to experience the more open, rugged and windswept northeast coast, The Natural Bridge near Andicuri is a popular spot at which to stop. There are also caves with Indian drawings and caves, such as those at Arikok, in the National Park.

The prime beach and resort area is north of Oranjestad in the Palm Beach area on the sheltered northwest coast. Offshore is Arashi Underwater Park. Just inland and north of Oranjestad is Bubali Bird Sanctuary.

Bonaire

Visitors can take in most of Bonaire's cultural and historical offerings in a day. Kralendijk, the well-kept capital city of the island, is worth a tour and offers duty-free shopping.

There are scheduled bus tours, as well as self-guided ones, to the north and south parts of the island. Each of the bus tours takes about two hours and can be arranged from the resorts.

Wildlife and a natural setting are valued on Bonaire. To protect the endangered flamingoes, there are two flamingo sanctuaries on this 122-square-mile island: Pekel Meer on the southern tip, adjacent to the Solar Salt Works, and Goto Meer on the northwest. Also to the north is 13,500 acre Washington/Slagbaai National Park. Virtually the entire coast line of Bonaire and Klein Bonaire is included in the Bonaire Marine Park. Lectures and slide presentations about the park are presented at the Flamingo Beach and Bonaire Beach Hotels.

The island's hotels are the center of most entertainment. During the day there is skiing, sailing, deep-sea fishing and tennis. At night, the night clubs, casinos and lounges help get guests ready for another day.

Curacao

As do all the Netherland Antilles, 210-square-mile Curacao has a distinct Dutch atmosphere. Dutch food and architecture complement one another during sight-seeing and shopping trips through the free-port city of Willemstad. An added plus of Curacao is that in and around Willemstad are four gambling casinos. Curacao has 38 beaches, the best of which are along the southwest end of the island, where the major resort and business area is.

A recent addition to the capital of Willemstad is the Seaquarium, located near the Princess Beach Hotel. This 40,000-square-foot attraction is filled with tropical fish, anemones, sponges, starfish, coral and sharks. The park's restaurant patio overlooks Curacao's Underwater Park.

Island tours are frequently part of hotel packages and include trips to such places as the 4,500-acre Christoffel National Park which is the protected home of many indigenous plants and animals. Hiking trails and roads take visitors to the park interior where Arawak Indian drawings and caves offer a flashback into history.

Dive travelers should remember that many of Curacao's resorts cater to people on business rather than on vacation. Curacao is worth experiencing, though, and since it lies so close to Bonaire, it is easily available to people who want to dive by day in Bonaire, but play by night in Curacao.

ABC Diving

Aruba

Most of Aruba's diving takes place off its west coast. There are shipwrecks and reefs loaded with tropical fish and corals. The southern coast also has some fine diving centered around the Golden Island Reef.

Bonaire

For ease, convenience and an abundance of dive sites with good year-round visibility, few places compare with Bonaire. Bonaire's water, unstirred by industry or storms, has by far the best visibility of the ABCs. The diving is ideal for novice and expert alike. There are many high-quality shore dives, though getting down to the beach from some of the bluffs is sometimes harder than the dive.

Strict fishery policies protect Bonaire's marine life. Virtually all reef species in the southern Caribbean Sea can be found off Bonaire, so these calm, clear waters are favored by macro photographers for the wealth of small invertebrates and reef fishes in the fringing coral reefs.

Most of the reefs of Bonaire's leeward side slope away from the island, so these are not true walls, but rather steep drop-offs diversely covered with volcanic rocks, sand chutes and ledges, vase, basket and rope sponges and colonies of coral. Depths beyond the reef frequently go to hundreds of feet. Well-established coral gardens run along most of the perimeter of the island, with pillar coral, gorgonians, black coral trees and sponges covering the volcanic base. Reef terraces and limestone outcroppings are extensive and provide a haven for all kinds of marine life.

Curacao

At least 20 of Curacao's beaches provide easy access to offshore reefs, caves in volcanic rock and coral grottoes. Good diving often begins in 20 feet of water where sand and coral make a bright backdrop for schooling tropical fish. In places, the reef slopes or drops in terraces to a rock bottom several hundred feet deep. At other sites, there are wall dives beginning in water as shallow as 35 feet.

Some of the most popular shore entry sites are done from beaches fringing the Curacao Underwater Park on the south coast. Divers should be cautious of the large number of boats which operate from the more popular beaches when they make beach-entry dives. In addition, there are 20 mooring buoys in the park at which boats tie to dive sites from Princess Beach down the shore south and east to East Point.

ABC Dive Sites
Aruba

EAGLE PIER is the remnants of an oil rig less than half a mile at sea and south of Oranjestad. Its pilings are being covered with encrusting corals and are anchored in about 50 feet of water.

THE WRECK OF THE ANTILIA is a popular shipwreck dive. The Antilia is a 250-foot long German freighter which went down in World War II. Now in about 60 feet of water, it attracts schools of tropicals including angelfish, snappers, basslets and sometimes barracuda.

THE PEDERNALES is another wreck just offshore from Oranjestad in 20 to 25 feet of calm water, making it a fine site for most divers and many small tropicals, including schools of chromis.

Golden Island Reef, being off the south coast, has some currents and clearer water, making it more prolific for sponges and coral which grow larger, faster and more colorfully than they do in sites off the west coast. At 40 to 60 feet, formations have been scoured into the reef and are filled with tropical fish.

Kuiperi Reef is an area of patch corals among coral-encrusted volcanic rocks. Challenging to novice and experienced divers, it has sites ranging from 30 feet to over 100 feet.

Bonaire

The Sampler is a reef off of Klein Bonaire. It starts in 15 to 20 feet as a channel. Divers swim through and gradually descend to a drop-off of 200 to 300 feet. Called The Sampler because it has a little bit of everything, it is best known for its moray eels, which guides frequently feed by hand.

The City of Angels, a reef known for its angelfish, is from 30 to 60 feet deep. Barracudas are sometimes seen hovering next to the rock and coral. This is a double reef formation with a sand slide at the bottom of the first reef, which gives way to a second drop-off. That's where the big rays and other large fish are seen.

HILMA HOOKER is a 240-foot freighter which sank in 1984. Once a drug runners' boat, the Hilma Hooker began to sink when police boarded her and began removing drugs from the walls. She sprang a leak and went down. It is turning into a nice dive site for divers new to wreck-diving and photography. She rests on her side on a slope angling from 60 to 90 feet down.

Eebo's Special begins as a shallow reef perfect for snorkelers as well as divers. Located just off the north side of Klein Bonaire, it gradually slopes toward deep, open water. Two small caves go back into reef.

Garden of Eels is at the base of a reef where there are so many eels they look like a field of waving grass. The eels pull down to their holes by the thousands as divers approach, then come up again as soon as the swimming silhouettes pass.

Carl's Hill is a sheer wall starting in shallow water. The top of the wall and its upper face give beginners a chance to safely explore picturesque coral and reef formations associated with a wall dive. The wall itself plunges down deeper than any sport diver should go.

THE STACE is an old tug boat lying on its side in 60 feet of water. The site has good visibility, making it nice for u/w photography. Angelfish, grouper and

other tropicals have started to make it home.

Karpata Island, off the north coast, is one of the prettiest and most popular dives around. In the shallows are nudibranchs and flamingo tongues feeding on sea fans. Ravines and channels are cut through the reef to a drop-off of unknown depths. This is a very pretty dive. Near the Karpata anchorage are chains, anchors and other remnants from the plantation era.

A Thousand Steps is a popular night dive site, named for the steps which lead down the steep bluff to the beach. This is an excellent site full of multi-hued sponges and coral to depths exceeding 100 feet.

Devil's Garden is off the southern point, an area which can have rugged waves and a strong current. But it's a fascinating area topside and below. Soft corals and sea fans lead the way to a drop-off of coral, sponges, and cracks in the reef. Larger fish cruise the water above the deep.

The Rock Pile, named for a pile of rock on the shore which helps guides find the site, is a dramatic steep drop-off with coral. Divers explore the formations along the face of the drop-off then come back up to the shallows which have star corals, elkhorn, sea fans and gorgonians.

Curacao

Curacao has both true wall dives and steep, sloping drop-offs. **Gary's Wall,** for example, is a true wall which starts at about 25 feet, then plunges for another 250 feet. Soft and encrusting corals grow on the sides of the wall and in cracks of the reef, through which divers can swim under and between coral arches and many different colors of sponges. There are some small caves here, too, with squirrelfish, jacks, angelfish and groupers.

Roberts Reef is a shallow coral garden with brain coral, staghorn, star coral, pinnacle coral and others in about 20 to 30 feet of water.

THE SUPERIOR PRODUCER is a 150-foot-long ship 110 feet down. It sits perfectly straight up in the water, looking as if someone drove it down and parked it. One of the Caribbean's better explorable wrecks, it has been there since about 1977 and is getting a nice growth of encrusting coral on its superstructure.

North Coast Shelf slopes out into open water from an area usually characterized by rough seas, but veterans like to come here for an all-day dive trip. The shelf begins about 15 feet down. It very gradually slopes for about a quarter of a mile to 30 feet. There the slope comes to the lip of the reef and spills over to a several thousand foot drop-off.

South Coast has a topography comparable to the North Coast. The water can be choppy, but this area is usually more calm and better protected from the wind. The visibility is better here, too, and can be up to 100 feet. Sites to the South Coast Slope are accessible from the southern beaches off Curacao's Underwater Park.

Aruba Dive Service

DE PALM WATER SPORTS
Service Address:
   West side of Aruba, near Oranjestad
Mailing Address:
   L.G. Smith Blvd., 142, P.O. Box 656, Oranjestad, Aruba, N.A.
Service Telephone:
   011-297-8-24400 or 011-297-8-24545
Reservation Telephone:
   Same as above

Steve Rosenberg

Hours Service is Open:
8:30 am to 5 pm Closed Sunday
Resort Affiliation:
No resort affiliation

De Palm Water Sports has been in business on Aruba since 1959 and serves guests of most of the resorts and hotels in Oranjestad and Palm Beach resort area.

De Palm Water Sports offers a resort course, but no certification. Certified divers who want to dive with them and rent gear must bring a "C" card. Divers should bring everything except tanks and weight belts. They have a limited number of u/w camera gear, which should be reserved in advance. Film processing is available in Oranjestad.

In the morning they frequently dive the Pedernales Wreck, which is right in front of the dive service office. In the afternoon they dive the 240-foot-long wreck of the Antilia. They do two-tank wall dives to the south coast to places along the Golden Island Reef Area or to Kuiperi Reef. Their three dive boats can hold from 15 to 30 divers, thereby avoiding having to mix novice divers with more experienced ones.

Between dives there is sailing, island tours, horseback riding and deep sea fishing.

Bonaire Dive Services

DIVE BONAIRE
Service Address:
Seven minutes south of Kralendijk, at the Flamingo Beach
Mailing Address:
Divi Hotels, Marine Sports Division, Peter Hughes, 2401 N.W. 34th, Miami, FL 33143
Reservation Telephone:
800/367-3484
Hours Service is Open:
8 am - 12 pm; 1 pm - 5 pm Seven days a week

Resort Affiliation:
Flamingo Beach Hotel
Rooms:
150
Cottages/Villas:
40 time-share apartments

Dana Bied manages this Peter Hughes operation at the Flamingo Beach Hotel. The service actually has two locations; one to accommodate the main body of the resort and the other that dives with people staying at the new time-share apartments. Both locations are on the hotel premises and guests can dive with either one. The resort provides a shuttle service for its guest from the airport.

The service has a resort course, PADI open-water and advanced open-water certification and night dive certification. They rent all scuba gear including u/w camera and video equipment. A complete u/w photography lab is on the hotel premises.

Their nine-boat dive fleet goes to a large variety of Bonaire sites daily. They never take more than one boat to a site and dive parties usually range from 16 to 24 people. Their morning and afternoon dives are one-tank dives. They do a one-tank night dive every night from the beach as well as from a boat.

They dive The Sampler off Klein Bonaire, The City of Angels and do a lot of night diving and u/w photography off the Town Pier. They go north to dive sites off the Washington/Slagbaai National Park such as Playa Funchi, Boca Slagbaai and Playa Frans. Dana reminded us that all reef around Bonaire is part of an underwater preserve so nothing can be taken from the sea. This restriction is very strictly enforced. Violators can get a $5,000 fine and time in jail.

The Flamingo Beach Hotel is a 4 Star Hotel. It has a large, fresh water pool, outdoor jacuzzi. The first barefoot casino in the world is at the hotel. They also arrange sightseeing tours, afternoon and sunset sailing, picnics to Klein Bonaire,

wind surfing, deep-sea fishing and water skiing.

BONAIRE SCUBA CENTER
Service Address:
One mile north of Kralendijk
Mailing Address:
P.O. Box 775, Oregon, New Jersey 08879
Service Telephone:
201/566-8866
Reservation Telephone:
800/526-2370
Hours Service is Open:
8:30 to 5:30 Seven days a week
Resort Affiliation:
Hotel Bonaire
Rooms:
125

The Bonaire Scuba Center, managed by Al Catalfumo and Eddy Statio, is on the property of the Hotel Bonaire, the island's largest hotel and casino. A transfer from the airport to the resort is included in dive packages.

The Bonaire Scuba Center offers a resort course, PADI, YMCA and occasionally SSI certification. Their shop includes a complete line of rental equipment, camera equipment and E-6 film processing.

They get to the dive sites via one of the three flattops, or a truck which takes divers overland to one of the prime beach entry sites. They are the only service that still does that. Dive parties range from 12 to 20 divers.

They dive many of the Klein Bonaire sites from 20 to 120 feet. Popular dives include Eebo's Special, Front Porch Reef right by the shop, Garden of Eels, and Angel City. They also dive some of the more distant sites such as Carl's Hill and around Karpata Island. With super experienced divers they may go to the east coast and dive, but the conditions there are always rugged.

Between dives they do the North and South Island Tours. The resort offers wind surfing, water skiing and there are sunset cruises aboard the sailboat, Lady Joma.

Bonaire Scuba Center is extremely proud of their guides. They are all Bonairian and very, very confident. They offer diving for the beginner as well as the professional and will assist divers with doing shore dives on their own. The resort and island, themselves, offer plenty of action for non-divers.

BUDDY'S DIVE RESORT
Service Address:
2 miles north of Kralendijk
Mailing Address:

P.O. Box 231, Bonarie, N.A.
Service Telephone:
  011-599-78065 or 011-599-78647
Hours Service is Open:
  8:30 am to 6:30 pm
Resort Affiliation:
  Buddy's Resort
Cottages/Villas:
  8 bungalows

For guests who request it, a staff member from Buddy's will pick them up at the airport and bring them to the resort.

Owned and operated by Joop and Yvonne Rauwars, Buddy's is a small resort which offers a resort course and PADI certification. As Joop is the only diver, there are no more than ten divers to a party, with six being the average. Rental equipment is available as are a couple of u/w cameras.

Most of the divers who come here are certified and often dive in small, independent groups. Joop has a 23-foot dive boat for boat dives whenever people want to get together. A marine biologist accompanies divers on many of the trips to help explain the reef and the life found there. Joop also guides night dives.

Guests to this resort go to A Thousand Steps and sites all along Klein Bonaire to the southern tip of Bonaire where there is a deep double reef and some of the larger fish in the area. They also dive a few wrecks including the Hilma Hooker.

The personalized service available from this resort is a reason why many of its guests like to return here to dive. Between dives there are ferry trips to Klein Bonaire, water sports and island tours.

CARIB INN
Service Address:
  A ten minute walk south from Kralendijk
Mailing Address:
  P.O. Box 68, Bonarie, N.A.
Service Telephone:
  011-599-78819
Reservation Telephone:
  Same as above
Hours Service is Open:
  8 am to 12 pm; 1 pm to 5 pm Seven days a week
Resort Affiliation:
  Carib Inn
Rooms:
  10
Cottages/Villas:
  seaside bungalow and apartments

Bruce Bowker, the builder, owner, manager and dive master of the Carib Inn, runs this small, very personal, diver-dedicated resort. Bruce is highly regarded by his customers, many of whom come back to the Carib Inn whenever they can. One reason they do is because Bruce has charted sites to which other services do not go.

Divers should bring their personal gear, but all equipment is available for those who need it. Though the Carib Inn does not have u/w cameras, they are available next door at the Flamingo Beach Hotel.

Bruce does a one-tank dive in the morning and afternoon. Night diving is available from shore any night and a couple of times a week from a boat when at least six divers want to go.

Among Bruce's favorite dives are The English Gardens, a beautiful drop-off alive with soft corals; The Invisibles, which are two coral-covered islands separated from one another by a channel of sand; The Devil's Garden, off the southern tip of the island; and Sponges, a site jam-packed with every sponge available off of Bonaire. The average number of divers in a party is six and they dive from one of Bruce's two 24½-foot Privateers.

Bruce does not offer any other watersports simply because that would take him away from diving. At night, many of the guests try their luck at one of the island's casinos, one of which is at the Flamingo Beach.

CAPT'N DON'S HABITAT
Service Address:
  On a seaside bluff, one mile from Kralendijk
Mailing Address:
  P.O. Box 237, Waitsfield, Vermont 05673
Service Telephone:
  011-599-78290
Reservation Telephone:

Susan Speck

802/496-5067
Hours Service is Open:
24 hrs.; Seven days a week
Resort Affiliation:
Capt'n Don's Habitat
Cottages/Villas:
54 beachside units; more under construction

Guests to Capt'n Don's are picked up by a taxi at the airport, the cost of which is included in the dive package. Captain Don Stewart built this dive resort, which has since earned the title of a PADI 5 Star training facility.

Besides offering a resort course and PADI certification, this service offers classes in u/w photography, deep diver, night diver and all other PADI specialty courses. Another offering is the Touch the Sea underwater tours, conducted by Dee Scarr. This is a course where Dee dives with two to four divers and teaches them to interact with the marine life and do such things as feed eels and pick up urchins.

All rental gear is available, including u/w cameras and E-6 film processing. Capt'n Don's even does some camera repair work.

This service does a one-tank dive in the morning and afternoon. Dive parties are limited to 12 divers on a boat. All night diving is done either at Lamachaca, which is one of the larger marine park dive sites and right off the beach of the resort, or off the Town Pier. The dive boat fleet consists of four flat tops.

Capt'n Don's Habitat is a totally diver-oriented facility. Capt'n Don, himself, was one of the first pioneers of Bonaire diving. He has discovered many of the dive sites and continues to be instrumental in developing better ways to provide service as well as to protect Bonaire's marine park.

Curacao Dive Services

DIVE CURACAO WATER SPORTS
Service Address:
South of Willemstad
Mailing Address:
Martin Luther King Blvd.,
Willemstad, Curacao, N.A.
Service Telephone:
212/840-6636 or 011-599-96-14944
ext. 20
Reservation Telephone:
800/223-9815
Hours Service is Open:
8 am to 5 pm Seven days a week
Resort Affiliation:

Princess Beach Hotel
Rooms:
140

Customers of Dive Curacao Water Sports will be picked up at the airport by a taxi and brought to the Princess Beach Hotel.

This dive operation offers a resort course, PADI certification and advanced open-water certification. All essential scuba gear is available to rent, but u/w cameras are not.

Dive Curacao Water Sports does one- and two-tank dives in the morning and afternoon and night diving on request. Most of their dives are on the Princess Beach Wall, to such sites as Oswaldos Drop-off which is a short boat ride away. They also dive Car Pile, which is a veritable underwater junk yard of coral encrusted cars. There are some good shipwrecks nearby, too, including the Superior Producer, 100 feet down, and the Tow Boat shipwreck in Curacao Underwater Park. The service has three dive boats, one with a 30-diver capacity and two which can handle up to ten divers.

DIVE PISCADERA WATER SPORTS
Service Address:
Piscadero Bay, south side of island,
5 minutes from Willemstad
Mailing Address:
Curacao Caribbean Hotel and Casino,
Willemstad
Service Telephone:
011-599-96-25905
Reservation Telephone:
Same as above
Hours Service is Open:
8 am to 5 pm Seven days a week
Resort Affiliation:
Curacao Caribbean Hotel and Casino
Rooms:
230

Dive Piscadera Water Sports caters to all levels of diver. New divers have the choice of taking a resort course or becoming certified under either the PADI or NAUI system. Certified divers should bring their personal gear, but new rental gear is available for those who need it. They have no u/w cameras, but those who take u/w pictures can have their film processed overnight in Willemstad.

The service offers one- and two-tank morning and afternoon dives, depending upon what the dive party wants. Dive Curacao Watersports has four dive boats and the average number in a dive party ranges from between six and twelve.

Among the more popular coral garden and reef sites include Blue Beach and Roberts Reef, two sites with large brain coral and massive stands of stag horn. Gary's Wall is a wall dive that starts at 25 feet then drops off for a couple of hundred. They also dive the wreck of the Superior Producer. Manta rays frequent the area and divers can also sometimes catch sight of a school of dolphins.

Between dives there is deep-sea fishing, water skiing, horseback riding and sailboat cruises to some of the more remote sections of the island. The nightlife is centered around the casinos and discotheques.

The resort offers very cosmopolitan service. Between them, staff members speak six different languages: French, German, Chinese, Dutch, English and Italian.

MASTER DIVE, INC.
Service Address:
Two locations:
one in Willemstad; another at the
Coral Cliff Hotel at Santa Marta Bay
Mailing Address:
Fokkerweg 13, Willemstad, Curacao,
N.A.
Service Telephone:
011-599-9-54312
Hours Service is Open:
8 am to 5 pm Seven days a week
Resort Affiliation:
Coral Cliff Hotel
Rooms:
35

The resort will arrange to have a shuttle pick up its guests at Curacao Airport if arrangements are made to do so ahead of time.

Master Dive, Inc., offers a resort course and all certifications up to dive master. All equipment is available from the service, including a limited supply of u/w camera gear. Film processing and equipment repair are also available.

Most of the diving is done within Curacao National Park to sites which include coral gardens, double reefs and walls, and may be either one- or two-tank dives. There are good stands of sea fans, brain coral, black coral and many different types of sponges throughout the park. Master Dive also goes to the Tow Boat shipwreck and the Superior Producer. They have two dive boats, a 12-footer for quick trips to the reef, and a 26-footer which can carry up to ten divers.

Master Dive has been operating on Curacao since 1970 and has built its reputation on giving personalized service. Between dives guests can wind surf, sail or cruise to other parts of the island. Casinos, nightclubs and shopping are available nearby.

Puerto Rico

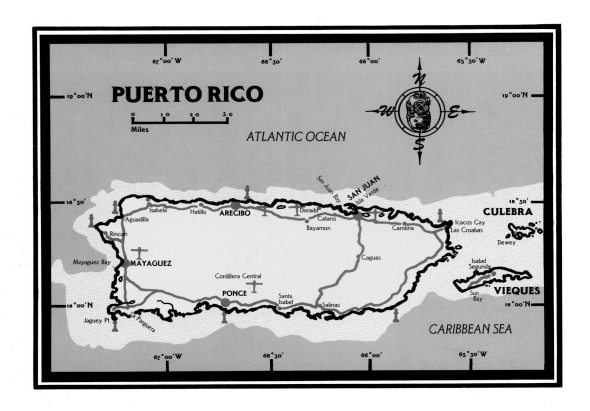

Puerto Rico

Entry Requirements

U.S., Canadian and British citizens require an onward or return ticket and proof of citizenship. Others require a passport.

Language

English & Spanish

Airlines

American, Eastern, ALM, Pan Am, BWIA

Airports

Luis Munoz Marin International

Isla Grande Airport

Departure Tax

$5

Electricity

220-230 volts; 60 cycles

Size

35 miles x 100 miles

Population

3.2 million

Tourist Offices

Puerto Rico Tourism Company
Old San Juan Station
Box 3072
San Juan, Puerto Rico 00903
809/724-7171

Puerto Rico Tourism Company
1290 Avenue of the Americas
New York, NY 10019
212/541-6630

Puerto Rico, smallest and easternmost of the Greater Antilles, lies between the Atlantic Ocean and Caribbean Sea. It is 1,040 miles from Miami and 1,622 miles southeast of New York.

The central mountain range of Puerto Rico rises over 4,000 feet, to the highest point of 4,389 feet at Cerro La Funta. Peaks and shoulders extend the length of the island, but low coastal plains encircle them. Valleys plunge into areas of moist vegetation bordered by the rough Atlantic Ocean to the north, and into semi-arid Caribbean regions of the south. Also to the north, porous limestone has dissolved into many sinkholes and caves. Fruits and flowers grow abundantly, and several national parks have been designated on the island to protect the prime landscape.

The Taino Indians, one of many Arawak Tribes in the Caribbean, lived on Puerto Rico and called it Boriquen. Columbus came here during his second voyage to the New World, and landed on November 19, 1493. In 1508 Juan Ponce de Leon, Puerto Rico's first governor, came to the island and founded the first Spanish settlement, Caparra. For health and strategic reasons the settlement was moved in 1521 to what is now Old San Juan.

During the 17th and 18th centuries, Puerto Rico was attacked by the French, English and Dutch who tried to wrest the island from Spanish control. During that time, the native Indian culture was destroyed, and slaves and settlers were brought to work the island's ranches, farms and plantations. Spain held on to the island and by the end of the 19th century Puerto Rico had succeeded in maturing socially, economically and politically to grow beyond the military fortress role it had played in the past.

Following the Spanish-American War in 1898, Spain ceded the island to the United States. Puerto Ricans became U.S. citizens in 1917 and adopted Commonwealth status in 1952. The governor and other representatives are elected by popular vote.

Because Puerto Rico has a strong Spanish heritage, clothing tends to be more formal here in the evenings than on other islands. Shorts or sportswear should not be worn in church or public buildings, or while shopping.

The temperature averages between 75°F and 85°F most of the year. The wettest months are September through November; the driest are February and March. The northern part of the island, especially the northeast region of the El Yunque rain forest, gets the most rain.

Getting There/ Getting Around

Most major airlines servicing the Caribbean, Central and South America, the United States and Europe offer direct flights from metropolitan areas to the Luis Munoz Marin International Airport near San Juan. Some charter service and small planes flying to adjacent islands leave from the Isla Grande Airport.

All authorized cabs are metered. The 15-minute ride from the airport to San Juan costs about $10. There are also limousines and buses which carry passengers from the airport to various hotels. Ferries from San Juan Bay run continuously between San Juan Bay, the city of Fajardo on the east coast and the islands of Culebra and Vieques. There is also service from San Juan Bay to Crown Bay in St. Thomas, USVI.

Major and minor car rental agencies abound in Puerto Rico. Reservations for them should be in advance. Cars can be picked up at the airport, in San Juan and most other cities and tourist areas.

Topside Attractions

Puerto Rico is loaded with sport opportunities. Major hotels have one, or a combination of sports, such as tennis, golf and horseback riding. Public golf courses are at the Berwind Country Club in Rio Grande. The Puerto Rico Tourism Company has an 18-hole golf course in Aguadilla, a city on the west coast. There are public tennis courts in all the major cities.

Deep-sea fishing is excellent. More than 30 world records have been broken in Puerto Rican waters where blue and white marlin, sailfish, wahoo, allison, tuna and tarpon present an exciting challenge. Sport fishing boats are available through many of the hotels and marinas.

Sightseeing on Puerto Rico should include a trip to Old San Juan, the oldest city under the U.S. flag. A foot tour is the best way to see the historic section with its formidable forts and city walls.

If you like a more rustic setting, Puerto Rico's forest reserves are easily accessible and recommended to visitors. The wild areas are filled with a profusion of waterfalls, native tropical plants and birds. It is best to get directions from the ranger station nearest you for specifics.

A fine example of the Puerto Rican countryside can be enjoyed via a series of beaches that face the open oceans. Since the world surfing championship in 1968, its half-dozen reef-lined Atlantic beaches have become a winter mecca for skilled surfers. Endangered humpback whales can be seen close to the coast at Rincon in winter, spouting water and flicking tails as they cruise the Caribbean.

One of the more enchanting attractions for those who do an extended tour of the island is Phosphorescent Bay near the south coast city of Parguera. Microscopic organisms light up the night with their luminescence when disturbed by any movement in the water. This fragile, evanescent vision can best be seen on dark, moonless nights. It is a phenomenon rarely found, and then only on protected shorelines in tropical waters. Boats leave La Parguera for the one-hour trip to the bay in the evening.

Culebra is an island halfway between Puerto Rico and St. Thomas, USVI and is little known to outside visitors. White sand beaches, particularly Flamenco Beach, clear waters, and outstanding coral reefs appeal to more visitors immediately. Twenty-three offshore islands and four tracts of Culebra land make up the Culebra National Wildlife Refuge, established by President Teddy Roosevelt in 1909. Small planes fly to Culebra from Isla Grande Airport, and ferries leave from Fajardo for the island.

Vieques Island is a major resort island six miles east of Puerto Rico. Planes and ferries from the mainland go there, too, and some of the dive services plan boat trips to the island and its surrounding reef.

Puerto Rico Diving

Puerto Rico is relatively untapped by scuba divers from outside of the island. Many small shops cater just to the local residents, but a handful conduct dives for the resorts in San Juan and Fajardo.

Coral reefs protect much of Puerto Rico's coastline. Some of the reefs feature walls which plunge several hundred feet; others slope as deep as 90 feet to sand and grass bottoms. Small coral islands and cays abound. These greatly increase the amount of virgin reefs to explore, and the topside seclusion you can enjoy after a dive. Within the reef are terraces of coral and archways of rock in which lobster octopus, starfish, and many species of conch abound.

Puerto Rico can entice divers of all skill levels. The large amount of shallow and deep coral formations offer both protected bays in which to dive as well as current dives. These same reefs, which provide a home to morays, grouper, barracuda and crawfish, have helped provide other habitats for these creatures by destroying many ships which now lie beneath the waves. On the average, visibility ranges from 50 to 150 feet.

Predominant winds on the east side of Puerto Rico can make boat anchoring and diving tricky, but there are some good sites there, including excellent current dives. There are also places off the west and north coasts which, when the surf comes up, pull currents through coral passages.

Puerto Rico Dive Sites

The coral gardens around **Icacos Island** are sheltered from the Atlantic by protective reefs. The reefs are a good place for beginning divers and u/w photographers. Only three miles from Puerto Rico, the waters inside the reef are no more than 30 feet deep and are colored with coral and sponges.

Paliminos Island and **Paliminitos Island** are two islands three miles southeast of Icacos. There are coral grottos which are popular with u/w photographers. Currents have helped carve deep canyons in the reef.

Margo Nelson

The best sites of **Vieques Island** are off its southwest beaches. This area has the calmest, clearest water. Beds of turtle grass and mounds of coral are a site for rays, small tropical fish and conch.

Culebra Island has **Flamenco Wall**, a powerful wall dive of coral crevices and sand chutes decorated with dangling rope sponges, orange and lavendar sponges, gorgonians and hard coral. The crevices might have grouper, barracuda, trumpet fish, angels or morays. Above the wall are nice coral formations, star fish and lobster.

Bohardo Island has dive sites as pure as any you will find in the Caribbean, with the advantage of not being crowded. Divers can expect to see almost anything along its reefs. Nearshore sites range from 20 to 40 feet. A sloping and terraced bottom of sand and coral leads to deep sites ranging from 80 to 150 feet. Rays, dolphins, sharks, sea turtles and barracuda have been seen there.

Puerto Rico Dive Services

Caribe Aquatic Adventures
Service Address:
    Beachfront hotel service in San Juan, north coast
Mailing Address:
    Caribe Hilton Hotel, P.O. Box 1872, San Juan, PR 00903
Service Telephone:
    809/721-0303 ext 447 or ext 627
Reservation Telephone:
    Same as above
Hours Service is Open:
    8 am to 5 pm
Resort Affiliation:
    Caribe Hilton Hotel
Rooms:
    900

Guests of the Caribe Hilton and Caribe Aquatic Adventures land at Munoz Marin International Airport and take a 15-minute cab ride to the hotel.

Caribe Aquatic Adventures offers a resort course, PADI and NAUI certification, advanced open-water, diver rescue and a scuba diving camp for kids.

They have a full rental shop for guests as well as for anyone else who dives with them. They have u/w photography equipment and do equipment repairs.

They offer four one-tank dives daily and night-diving on request. Dive parties are limited to ten divers on either of their two boats. They have two reefs in front of the hotel which they dive. The first one is a good training site in 15 to 20 feet of water. The outer reef goes to about 30 feet and has a lot of overhangs, caves and coral. One site is the Figure Eight, a winding coral formation with many small overhangs with sponges, coral, and parrot fish and shellfish. Also in front of the hotel is The Horseshoe, a nice cave with larger overhangs. They have special all-day trips such as a dive and sail trip to sites around Icacos Island.

Between dives guests relax on the beach, tour San Juan or other parts of the island such as the Bacardi Rum factory and America's only tropical rain forest national park.

Caribbean School of Aquatic, Inc.
Service Address:
    On Concado Beach; across from San Juan
Mailing Address:
    La Concha Hotel, Ashford Aven. Concado, PR 00905
Service Telephone:
    809/723-4740 Evenings call 809/728-6606
Hours Service is Open:
    8 am to 5 pm
Resort Affiliation:
    La Concha Hotel
Rooms:
    400

The Caribbean School of Aquatics began to fully establish itself during the 1985-86 season. It is a dive service for both the Concado area and Fajardo, a resort village on the east coast where the School also has a boat docked. The service offers a resort course and PADI and NAUI certification. The rental shop is growing, but there was no u/w camera equipment at the time of writing.

During the height of the season they dive every day and three times a week in the off-season. Weather permitting, they do night dives on request. They have three boats and do the majority of their diving off Palomino Island.

Carlos Dive Shop (3)
Service Address:
    At the Marina Puerto Chico, in Fajardo Marina
Mailing Address:
    Puerto Chico, Carretera al Conquistador, Fajardo, PR 00740
Service Telephone:
    809/863-3000
Reservation Telephone:
    Same as above
Resort Affiliation:
    No resort affiliation

Carlos Florez has been teaching diving

in the Caribbean since 1958. His dive shop is located at the Marina Puerto Chico, near Fajardo, where gear can be rented, classes are taught and trips are planned.

He has three boats which cruise the sea east of Puerto Rico to the small coral cays and the major islands. He offers custom-tailored diving and can handle small and large parties with equal ease.

Most Fajardo area hotels can arrange diving for their guests with Carlos.

Trident Water Sports
Service Address:
  A Condado beachfront resort service
Mailing Address:
  999 Ashford Ave., San Juan, PR 00907
Service Telephone:
  809/721-1000 ext 1592 or ext 1361
Reservation Telephone:
  Same as above
Hours Service is Open:
  8 am to 6 pm Seven days a week
Resort Affiliation:
  Condado Plaza Hotel and Casino
Rooms:
  587

The Condado Plaza Hotel and Casino is about a 20-minute ride from the Marin International Airport. Trident Water Sports is a new and growing operation. They offer a resort cruise, PADI certification, and rent all basic scuba gear. Trident does both one- and two-tank dives in the morning and afternoon, and night diving on request.

Some of their training sites and novice dive sites center around the shallow reefs just off the beach. As built up as this beach area is, though, it has not been heavily dived and there are a lot of fish and coral. The Cerro Gordo reef, which goes down to 25 feet, is one area to which they go. Visibility may be around 40 feet. There are some small caves, crevices and overhangs. Many of these places can be snorkeled to from the beach.

Trident also cruises to sites off the islands of Icacos, Palominiotos Culebra, as well as to the smaller islands of Bohardo, Grouper Cay, Luis Pena and Tamarindo, which are areas of truly virgin sites. Though boats may have to cut through rough water to get there, there are shallow and deep dives in calm, clear water where dolphins, rays, barracuda, sharks, starfish and lobsters are seen.

So, diving with Trident Water Sports gives people a chance to have the amenities of San Juan nearby, tour a good part of Puerto Rico, while providing boat and shore dives at dive sites just now being charted and explored.

Margo Nelson

WE DON'T TURN OUT RUBBER STAMP DIVERS

CERTIFIED

Every diver is an individual with different needs. NAUI instructors help each diver improve his skills to meet those needs. We offer higher standards, not overstandardization. Instead of the quantity of divers certified, NAUI instructors work to develop quality divers. Experience has taught us that a diver taught right, the first time, feels happy, confident and comfortable in the water. Assembly line instruction only creates diver dropout. Don't be fooled by rubber stamp dive training. Turn to NAUI for a lifetime of diving fun and adventure.

NAUI
National
Association Of
® Underwater Instructors

YOU GET MORE OUT OF DIVING
BECAUSE WE PUT MORE IN.

Send me the facts on "How not to be a rubber stamp ☐ Diver ☐ Diving Instructor ☐ Dive Store."
Name _____ Tel. _____
Address _____
City _____ State _____ Zip _____
Send me the name of my nearest NAUI Pro Facility.
HEADQUARTERS: 4650 Arrow Highway, Suite F-1, P.O. Box 14650, Montclair, CA 91763. (714) 621-5801.

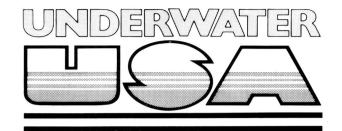

UNDERWATER USA

Don't miss a single issue of America's first newspaper for divers.

For the seasoned veteran or the novice, UNDERWATER USA provides current and interesting facts each month about dive spots from across the United States and throughout the Carribean. In each issue you will be informed about the latest in dive medicine and marine science, equipment news and what's happening in the dive industry, and more.

Call to subscribe.

1-800-228-DIVE

Roatan and the
Bay Islands

Margo Nelson

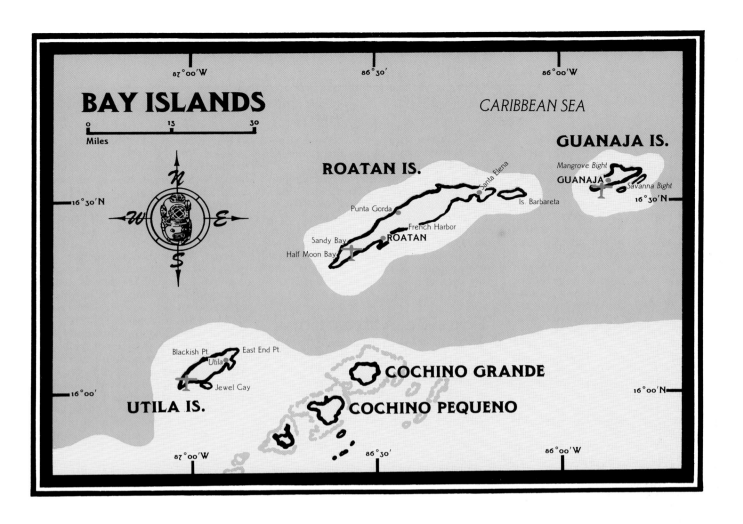

Roatan and the Bay Islands (Honduras)

Entry Requirements
Passport for all visitors, plus an onward or return ticket

Language
Spanish; English

Airports
Villeda Morales in San Pedro Sula
Goloson in La Ceiba

Departure Tax
U.S. $5

Electricity
220 volts; 60 cycles
110 volts; 60 cycles

Population
Honduras: 4,276,000
Bay Islands: 15,000

U.S. Tourist Office
Honduras Information Service
501 Fifth Avenue
Suite 1611
New York, NY 10017
212/490-0766
212/683-2136

The Bay Islands range between 30 to 70 miles off the north coast of Honduras, Central America. Territorially part of Honduras, the Bay Islands consists of Roatan, the largest at 32 miles by two miles, Guanaja, Morat, Barbareta, Utila, Cayos Cochinos and hundreds of smallers cays, many of which are uninhabited. Roatan is approximately 875 miles south-southwest of Miami.

Roatan and the other major islands are covered with lush, tropical vegetation. They look much as they did when Columbus landed on Guanaja in 1502. The islands are part of the upper peaks of a mountain range which extends from Honduras. The islands themselves are rugged and steep with deep offshore trenches and channels. Observing these, Columbus named the area Honduras, which is Spanish for depths, and claimed the islands for Spain.

Spanish influence was never extremely strong on the Bay Islands. Consequently, Henry Morgan and other plunderers moved in to the protected waters around the Bay Islands to strike at Spanish ships carrying gold and silver mined from the Honduras mainland. The pirates of Roatan indirectly established the islands' ties to England. After the pirates' demise, English settlements sprang up on the islands and the Bay Islands eventually became a British Crown Colony in 1852. The islands were ceded to Honduras in 1861, but many people have migrated here from the Cayman Islands in the past one hundred years and have helped to maintain the European heritage. Today, most Bay Islanders speak English as well as Spanish.

Summer temperatures for the Bay Islands and the Honduran mainland range from a humid 80° to 100° F. Inland temperatures in the highlands seldom get over 80°. September through December is the rainy season with only light, occasional showers falling the rest of the year.

Honduras is a democracy with an elected president. The government is stable, popular and friendly to the United States. The population of the Bay Islands is approximately 15,000.

Getting There/ Getting Around

TAN/SASHA is the national airline of Honduras and the only airline which goes there. TAN/SASHA flies out of Miami seven days a week, out of Houston Tuesday, Thursday, Saturday and Sunday, and out of New Orleans on Monday, Wednesday, Friday and Sunday. Most resorts have dive packages which include transportation from each of these cities. Flights may or may not be direct from the States to Honduras.

Planes land at La Ceiba Airport or San Pedro Sula Airport in Honduras. From there, a commuter flight will take you to the airfield closest to your resort. If it is not possible to continue from the mainland to your resort due to darkness, TAN/SASHA will pay the hotel, dinner and transportation costs of passengers who stay the night at La Ceiba or San Pedro Sula.

Topside Attractions

Most activities on the Bay Islands center around the resorts. Each has a little something different to offer its guests by way of entertainment and amusements. For the explorer there is a lot of boat traffic between the islands which will take passengers to villages on the major islands. There are virtually no roads on the islands. All travel is done on foot and by boat.

Ruins from the Mayan Empire dot the Honduran mainland. Resorts sometime sponsor tours to such places as Copan, once a major Mayan city and now a prime attraction to photographers.

Bay Islands Diving

There are 65 known species of coral in the Caribbean. A research team from the University of Southern Florida found 63 species off the coast of Roatan. This representation shows just how much diving diversity is packed around the Bay Islands.

Virtually each of the Bay Islands is surrounded by a barrier reef which protects nearshore gardens of coral, tropical fishes, and shallow water sponges. Conch, lobster, sea stars, brittle stars and hosts of other mobile and sessile invertebrates populate the waters. The barrier reefs drop vertically as much as 150 feet to the rims of deep trenches thousands of feet deep. In some places the top of the wall starts 15 feet deep; in most places the top is no deeper than 40 feet. There is excellent drift diving along the face of the walls, allowing experienced divers to cruise effortlessly through the water over deep blue depths. In other places, where the wall is shallow and the current is nil, new divers can safely begin to experience what wall diving can be.

The Caribbean Current courses through the Bay Islands as it flows along the coast of Central America. The currents it generates have cut countless canyons through the barrier reef. Some of these canyons are wall dives in themselves, with vertical sides plunging as deep as 100 feet. The canyons can be pocked with sand chutes and coral archways. Other places have caves and tunnels large enough to drive a truck through. These are formations through which lava flowed as the mountains which are now the Bay Islands were formed.

Some veteran divers of the Bay Islands prefer diving around and through the massive rock pinnacles more than any other type of diving. Pinnacles are encrusted with corals, painted with sponges and bored with crevices and caves, making the pinnacles virtually worlds of their own. Groves of black coral, beds of lettuce coral, and ledges full of vase and basket sponges provide a never ending source of action as divers witness the vitality and totality of the sea.

Some divers choose the Bay Islands to get their wreck diving training, and there are ample wreck sites from which to choose. There are 13 ships just in the entrance of Port Royal Harbour, Roatan, alone. Henry Morgan sank them there when he was plundering Spanish gold in order to prevent vengeful Spanish warships from coming into his home port and blasting him.

The Bay Island dive resorts carefully regulate spear fishing and shell collecting from their shores. It's a thrill when guests capture conch and lobster, or spear a snapper and bring it up for supper, but guides do not allow rampant shell collecting or spearing just for a good time or a souvenir photo.

The Bay Islands are for people who appreciate and enjoy remote pleasure. There are no phones on the islands. Most of the contact with the outside is by radio. But though at high tide water may be lapping at your porch, the dive resorts of Roatan, Guanaja, Cayos Cochinos and Barbareta, are built, equipped and powered to ensure a quality and comfortable vacation. All things considered, it is amazing that the Bay Islands and all they have to offer are less than a day's flight away from the States—usually.

Roatan Dive Sites

Coco View Wall is a vertical precipice which starts at the surface of the water. The wall is located in front of the Coco View Resort. Divers can swim to the site from shore, following one of the surge channels for about a quarter of a mile to the lip of the wall. A reverse ledge directs divers down into crevices covered with sponges, pillar coral and soft corals. Schools of tropical fish abound. At 110 feet a sand spill gives divers a visual reference as to how deep they are.

THE WRECK OF THE PRINCE ALBERT is a 140-foot tanker which sank in 1983 about 225 feet from shore. It is an easy beach dive and is used for wreck-dive certifications and coral identification.

Mary's Place is a giant volcanic crevice in the reef fractured in several different directions by ancient hurricanes. It can be taken as either a wall dive or reef dive. The wall here starts at 15 feet. Divers can explore it down to 110 feet where there is an eight-foot-wide tunnel going into and up through the wall. At about 50 feet divers can split off to a side chute and exit out of the reef. The tunnels and wall here have one of the most diverse collections of corals, sponges and fishes as anywhere in the Caribbean.

West End Reef, just off the West End Beach, is a popular all-day dive site for all levels of divers. Good beach-entry diving can be found along this sloping reef, from 20 feet to the drop-off down to 125 feet.

Hole-in-the-Wall is a swim-through tunnel in the top of the reef and exits on the wall at about 140 feet. This site also includes deep canyons which cut as deep as 300 feet into the rocky base of Roatan. Coral arches span walls of rock crevices populated with angelfish, Spanish Hog Fish, barracudas and grunts.

The Outhouse Wall is an inward slanting wall of rock and coral ledges, caves and tunnels. This site also has three massive 60- to 70-foot tall coral heads. Lobster, rays, tarpon and barracuda are common sights.

The Bear's Den is a massive coral reef with a swiss-cheese complex of caves. The crevice runs through stands of coral and sponges with depths from 20 to 70 feet. In addition to schools of reef fish, there are spider crabs, sea stars and rays.

THE GWENDOLYN is a sunken, 120-foot wooden freighter and is at least a 25-minute boat ride from Port Royal Harbour. Experienced divers have to ask for this site because it is a long way out.

Cayos Cochinos

Near the south end of Roatan is the small island of Cayos Cochinos Grande. Indicative of the island's most diveable coral formations is **Honeycomb Reef**. Pocked with large caverns in shallow water, this reef is a fun dive for all levels of divers. Every 10 feet to 15 feet of reef seems to have a cave or tunnel drilled through the reef. Most exit at the surface of the water.

Fifteen minutes out from Cayos Cochinos Grande are **The Banks**. The top of the wall of this vertical drop is at 35 feet. Visibility can exceed 150 feet, which helps divers spot its legendary eight-foot-tall trees of black coral.

Barbareta Dive Sites

Morat Reef is a shallow, flat reef that introduces beginners to the intracies of coral gardens. Shellfish and small reef fish cruise around brain coral, star coral and sponge colonies.

Pigeon King Reef is a spectacular wall dive with eight- to ten-foot sponges on a wall that drops off to over 2,000 feet. Sharks and open-water fish sometimes swirl within view when visibility is around 150 feet. Channels and crevices are cut into the reef in which everything from schools of baitfish to nurse sharks may be found.

Half Moon Bay is a protected cove with a massive 40-foot-tall, 100-foot-wide coral head right in the middle of it. Beginners and advance divers love to ease around it. So do lobsters. Half Moon Bay Beach is on Barbareta Island and is one of the most treasured beaches of the Bay Islands.

Guanaja Dive Sites

The sites off Guanaja are as varied and colorful as they are throughout the Bay Islands. One of the good things about

Steve Rosenberg

Guanaja is that beginners can safely dive some very exotic sites here without getting into deep water or currents.

The Cut is a 10-foot to 50-foot canyon in the reef. Caves there have squirrelfish, basslets, hydrocorals and sponges. **Wonderful Reef** is of the same mold as The Cut. It slopes a little deeper though, approximately to 70 feet, but has virtually no current with which novices must deal.

Black Rock is a ten- to 50-foot-deep cave dive. The area is riddled with canyons and caves. The entrances to these openings seemingly hide behind stands and archways of corals. New caves have been found when sharp-eyed divers see fish seemingly disappear into a solid wall.

Roatan Dive Services

ANTHONY'S KEY RESORT
Service Address:
At Sandy Bay, on the north shore of Roatan
Mailing Address:
1385 Coral Way, Suite 302, Miami, FL 33145
Service Telephone:
305/858-3483
Reservation Telephone:
800/227-3483 or 800/343-3483
Hours Service is Open:
8 am to 5 pm Seven days a week
Resort Affiliation:
Anthony's Key Resort
Cottages/Villas:
44 bungalows

Wes Wright

Guests of Anthony's Key will be picked up at the Roatan airfield and taken to Anthony's Key Resort, the largest dive resort in the Bay Islands.

Anthony's Key offers a resort course, PADI open-water and PADI advanced open-water certification. All dive equipment is available to rent, most of which is included in the dive package. In addition they have strobe lights, u/w cameras, lenses and E-6 film processing.

This service does two one-tank dives in the morning and a one-tank afternoon dive. Night diving is offered twice a week.

The largest of their five boats can comfortably accommodate 20 divers, but they usually take no more than ten divers in a boat at a time. Many sites are within a ten-minute boat ride from the dock, but they will go to special sites farther away for those who request them.

Among their best loved sites are West End Beach where they do an all-day trip that includes a morning dive, picnic on the beach, followed by an afternoon dive and beach party. This is a great place for all divers and u/w photographers as it includes everything from 20-foot-deep coral gardens to a 125-foot drop-off with a wall loaded with black coral, soft corals and sponges.

Other specialties include a host of wall and drift dives. They dive the Hole-in-the-Wall, the caves of the Bear's Den, the Wreck of the Gwendolyn and ever-popular Peter's Place, a veritable photography studio of coral ranging in depth from ten to 100 feet.

THE REEF HOUSE
Service Address:
On Oakridge Cay, in Oak Ridge Harbor, Roatan
Mailing Address:
P.O. Box 640399, Kenner, LA 70024
Service Telephone:
504/467-2949
Reservation Telephone:
800/341-1950 ext. 73
Hours Service is Open:
8 am to 5 pm Seven days a week
Resort Affiliation:
The Reef House
Rooms:
14
Cottages/Villas:
3

Guests of the Reef House land at the Roatan Island airfield where a resort staff member will take you to the resort. Oak Ridge Cay, on which the Reef House is located is just a skip across the water from Roatan. It gets its name from literally being built on a reef.

The resort offers a resort course and PADI certification. Rentals and repairs are available, but u/w photographers need to bring all their gear and film.

The Reef House has access to excellent dives via the shore or by way of their 37-foot dive boat. There is a 400-foot drop-off right in front of the resort which divers swim to by going through a 100-foot-long channel in the reef which leads to the top of the wall. They do both one- and two-tank dives in the morning and afternoon, with occasional night diving.

Their dives encompass a host of reef sites, with caverns and crevices cracked through the reef, each offering something unique. Mary's Place, for example, a series of gaping reef cracks and sponge-filled crevices, is considered by many the best dive off of Roatan. They also dive Crab Wall and The Sponge Garden both down to 60 to 70 feet. Each of these sites is appropriately named by the dominant life seen there. Many sites off Roatan's south coast are dived, including caves from 40 to 120 feet and the shipwrecks of Port Royal Harbour. The Reef House goes to a couple of more recently sunk wrecks, including a 50-year-old freighter down in 40 to 60 feet, which is a dive for most any diver.

The pool of the Reef House Resort was put right in the reef. Divers and snorkelers can simply put their gear on in it. The resort is near Oakridge Village, which even brings a little bright nightlife to this small island. Other activities include shell collecting, horseback riding on Roatan, deep-sea fishing, and trips to nearby Port Royal and French Harbor.

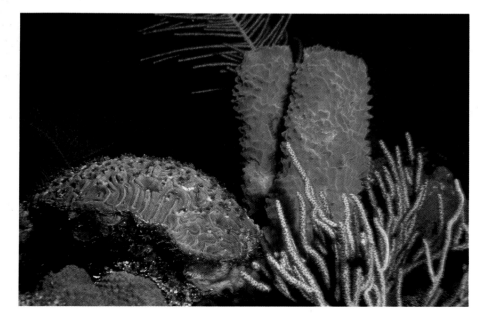

Steve Rosenberg

COCO VIEW RESORT
Service Address:
   East of Old French Harbor, south
   shore of Roatan
Mailing Address:
   P.O. Box 877, San Antonio, FL 34266
Service Telephone:
   904/588-4131
Reservation Telephone:
   800/282-8932
Hours Service is Open:
   24 hrs a day. Seven days a week
Resort Affiliation:
   CoCo View Resort
Rooms:
   16
Cottages/Villas:
   2 beach houses

CoCo View Resort picks up its guests at the Roatan airfield and boats them to the beachfront resort on a peninsula on the south shore of Roatan.

CoCo View considers itself a hard-core dive facility. They do a resort training course, SSI certification, and instructor certification. They also do specialty courses in u/w photography, marine biology and underwater archeology, which are popular with university students and faculty. Divers should bring personal dive gear. A small amount of u/w photography gear is available. If you want it, ask for it ahead of time. The resort also does film processing and equipment repair.

Mornings begin with a pre-dive briefing over coffee. Dives start after breakfast. They normally do two one-tank dives a day, specializing in unlimited shore entry diving to coral gardens, tunnels, surge channels and sites along the CoCo View Wall. Within a quarter mile of shore, the wall drops off to 200 feet.

CoCo View also does a lot of boat diving to sites such as Mary's Place and to shipwrecks. They dive the Prince Albert, a wreck about 225 feet from their club house door. They have a 37-foot custom-built dive boat and are in the process of building another.

In addition to its dive boats, CoCo View has a 44-foot motor/sail live-aboard, virtually a floating resort. Dive trips can last for a week, or guests can choose a surf or turf package and spend three days on the boat and four days at the resort.

Between dives there is fishing, windsurfing and canoeing at the resort.

ROATAN LODGE
Service Address:
   On Roatan's southeast coast; just east of Port Royal
Mailing Address:
   2616 S.W. Parkway, Wichita Falls, TX 76308
Service Telephone:
   817/322-4662
Reservation Telephone:
   800/523-6431
Hours Service is Open:
   Whenever the customers need
Resort Affiliation:
   Roatan Lodge
Cottages/Villas:
   6

The Roatan Lodge has six widely-spaced bungalows which sit on the hill overlooking the harbor. This a small, but complete dive resort. Its deep, protected anchorage is favored by sailors who come to the lodge for diving and dining and add to the zest of the resort. Guests who arrive by air are picked up by car at the Roatan airfield and taken to Oakridge

harbor. A resort boat takes guests from there to the lodge. Small charter and private aircraft can also land at the airstrip near the resort.

A resort course, as well as PADI, NAUI, SSI and YMCA certification are offered. Divers should bring their basic gear, including u/w cameras.

The resort follows no pre-arranged schedule and works with guests to dive whenever they want. There are good shore-entry dives and excellent sites in Port Royal Harbor. They dive some of the wrecks Henry Morgan put down at its entrance.

Catering to all levels of diver, Roatans' Lodge's instructors take divers anywhere from the shallows of Morat Reef to wall and drift dives over the Barbareta Wall to their south. They have one 38-foot dive boat that easily handles 20 divers from which divers dive surge channels, tunnels, caves, coral gardens, shipwrecks and the Barbareta.

The center of activity is the main lodge and patio overlooking the harbor, but there are beach parties, dancing and boating to other cays. Sailing and horseback riding are available.

BARBARETA
Service Address:
   On Barbareta Islands; 2 miles east of Roatan
Mailing Address:
   2616 S.W. Parkway, Wichita Falls, TX 76308
Service Telephone:
   817/322-4662
Reservation Telephone:
   800/523-6431
Hours Service is Open:
   9 am to 6 pm Mon–Sat

Resort Affiliation:
   Barbareta Resort
Cottages/Villas:
   12

Barbareta is a 3.5 mile by one-mile-long island between Roatan and Guanaja. Guests of Barbareta Resort are flown by a charter aircraft from La Ceiba, Honduras to the island's grass airfield. The flight takes about 30 minutes.

Barbareta Resort offers a resort course plus PADI, NAUI, YMCA, SSI and NASDS certification. Divers should bring as much of their equipment as possible, but equipment is available for those who have none. They also rent u/w camera gear and do E-6 film processing.

Most dives are one-tank. The resort follows no set schedule, so divers can dive pretty much where and when they want, including night diving virtually any night.

Their dive boat fleet includes a 12-foot and 26-foot Zodiac, a 22-foot Maco and, for larger groups, a 42-foot dive boat. They dive Morat Reef, Pigeon King Reef Drop-off, Barbareta Wall off Roatan and the shipwrecks in Port Royal. The coral head in the middle of Half Moon Bay is a favorite spot for beach entry dives and resort training. Carolina Canyon is another popular dive. Coral hangs so thickly from the walls it is like an underwater jungle.

Barbareta is a privately owned island with no one living on it full-time other than the managers. You can be as wild or relaxed as you want. Nudist groups like that in a resort. Guests are even allowed to spear or collect a very limited number of fish, lobster and conch to eat.

Between dives there is horseback riding, fishing, windsurfing, parasailing, hobie cats and volleyball. But the number-one attraction here are the Mayan Ruins. Mayan Indian potters used to come to Barbareta to make their pottery which was then shipped all over their empire. Some pieces of pottery are still found.

The island is a true jungle and dive adventure. There are iguanas, alligators, boa constrictors and tropical birds. It's a place to go where you can walk the beach and not see a beer can, footprint or fire pit.

BAYMAN BAY CLUB
Service Address:
   Northwest shore of Guanaja Island
Mailing Address:
   1, Isle of Venice, #206, Ft. Lauderdale, FL 33301
Service Telephone:
   809/524-1823; or 305/525-8413
Reservation Telephone:

Same as above
Hours Service is Open:
   24 hrs. Seven days a week
Resort Affiliation:
   Bayman Bay Club
Cottages/Villas:
   12

Guests of the Bayman Bay Club land on Roatan where a resort boat will pick them up and take them to Guanaja, which is a 15-minute boat ride east of Roatan.

The resort caters to certified divers and offers no certification. Divers should bring all personal gear except tanks and weightbelt.

The resort does two boat dives a day, both of which are one-tank dives. Night diving is available off the docks and, when conditions permit, they will take one of their two dive boats to a night dive site. Most boat dives are between a ten- to 25-minute ride from the dock.

They dive The Cut, which is a cut in the barrier reef with caves and a lot of fish. Interesting for novice as well as advanced divers, it goes from ten to 50 feet deep. They also go to Pinnacle Wall and Wonderful Reef, two more sites that appeal to all divers. An advanced dive is Famous Drop. It is a wall that begins about eight feet down and plunges to 180 feet. There are many different coral formations to explore throughout the reef and in the face of the wall. They dive the canyons and caves of Black Rock and several nearby shipwrecks.

The bungalows and main lodge of this secluded resort are built on a hill overlooking a beach of white sand and aqua water. Between dives there is swimming, beachcombing, eating and drinking. One afternoon a week, they hike back to a 40-foot waterfall, probably the only one in the Bay Islands, and give guests a feel for the jungle interior.

CAYOS DEL SOL
Service Address:
   On Cayos Cochinos Grande, 20 miles so. of Roatan
Mailing Address:
   1714 Washington St., Waukegan, IL 60085
Service Telephone:
   800/336-7717 or 512/444-4946
Reservation Telephone:
   Same as above
Hours Service is Open:
   Whenever people want to dive—Seven days a week
Resort Affiliation:
   Cayos Del Sol Resort
Rooms:
   23

Divers will find Cayos Del Sol fun and thrilling. Cayos Cochinos Grande, on

which the service resort is located, is the largest of a group of very small cays known as the Cayos Cochinos—Hog Islands. The resort staff, and a handful of others are the only people there; less than 20 live there year round. After arriving in Honduras guests stay overnight at La Ceiba and leave for Cayos Cochinos the next day. For groups of two or three the resort will fly them from Honduras to their island in a small plane. The resort picks up larger groups in one of their boats and has a boat party for those who are coming and those who are leaving. Guests should have only 30 to 40 pounds of luggage. The islands are about 25 miles northeast of La Ceiba.

Bill Atwood, owner of Cayos Del Sol, offers a resort course and PADI certification. The rental shop is stocked with new gear and will soon have an entire Sony u/w video system. Divers should bring their personal dive gear.

Their diving is flexible, but it usually consists of a two-tank morning and one-tank afternoon dive. They comfortably carry up to 18 divers on their 45-foot boat and 12 divers on their 32-footer. They night dive any time you want.

Good examples of the type of diving they do include the big caverns of Honeycomb Reef and the sheer wall of The Banks. They have excellent nearshore snorkeling and novices sites, where 20 feet to 30 feet depths hold coral gardens, sponges and fish. Their instructors are exploring various wreck sites. They have a few offshore anchors and are closing in on finding some good diveable wrecks.

Cayos Cochinos is a very pristine island, and home to many native plants, birds and animals. The resort has windsurfing and guests frequently go to one of the dozen smaller cays around the island for private tanning or a picnic.

PIRATES' DEN
Service Address:
   On the north shore of Roatan, to the east of Sandy Bay
   Roatan, Bay Islands, Honduras
Hours Service is Open:
   As needed by guests
Rooms:
   24

The Pirates' Den is a small, but full-service dive resort. At this time, there is no stateside phone or address at which they may be contacted. Inquiries can simply be directed to Pirates' Den, Roatan, Bay Islands, Honduras.

This service is located about 100 yards east of Anthony's Key Resort on the north shore of Roatan. It specializes in diving the coral gardens inside the north shore barrier as well as dives along the walls.

The SSI Specialty Diver Program

STRESS/RESCUE • BOAT DIVING • NAVAGATION • UNDERWATER PHOTOGRAPHY
SPEARFISHING • DEEP DIVING • LIMITED VISIBILITY
WRECK DIVING • EQUIPMENT

U.S. Virgin Islands

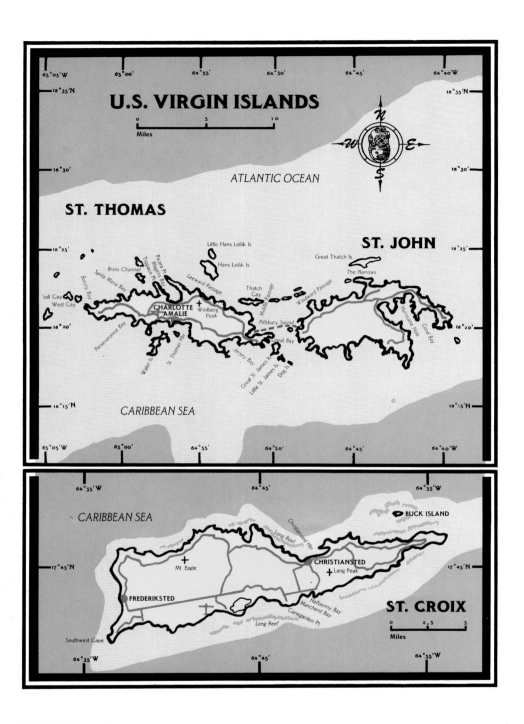

U.S. Virgin Islands

Entry Requirements
    U.S. & Canadian citizens need proof of citizenship. Others need passport and onward ticket

Language
    English

Airports
    Cyril King on St. Thomas
    Alexander Hamilton on St. Croix

Departure Tax
    $3

Electricity
    110/220 volt; 60 cycles

Size
    St. Thomas: 28 sq. mi.
    St. John: 20 sq. mi.
    St. Croix: 84 sq. mi.

Population
    St. Thomas: 46,630
    St. John: 2,570
    St. Croix: 53,210

Tourist Offices
    U.S.V.I. Division of Tourism
    P.O. Box 1692
    Charlotte Amalie
    St. Thomas, U.S.V.I. 00801
    7-74-13-31

    U.S.V.I. Tourist Office
    7270 N.W. 12 Street
    Suite 620
    Miami, FL 33126
    304/591-2070

The U.S. Virgin Islands are about 1,100 east-southeast of Miami. Located in the north arc of the Lesser Antilles, the USVI are comprised of three main islands: St. Thomas, St. John and St. Croix, and another 50 small islands and cays.

The group is considered to be among the driest of the Caribbean islands even though they look green and verdant. They are rugged and hilly, with only St. Croix having an appreciable amount of land suitable for farming and pastureland.

St. Croix, at 84 square miles, is the largest island and lies entirely in the Caribbean Sea. It holds nearly two-thirds of the territory's land area. Croix is pronounced Croy, and its residents are CROO-shuns, spelled either Crucian or Cruzan.

Forty miles to the north are the other two main islands: St. Thomas and St. John. They lie between the Atlantic Ocean and the Caribbean. Both are more mountainous than St. Croix. The most cosmopolitan of the Virgins is St. Thomas. At 28 square miles, its capital city is Charlotte Amalie.

Two-thirds of St. John's 20 square miles is dedicated to the Virgin Islands National Park with a visitor center at Cruz Bay. The park is highly valued by the Park Service as well as visitors. It includes two prime snorkel trails, which are good for identifying common shallow reef life.

Christopher Columbus came to the Virgin Islands during his second voyage to the New World while sailing through the Antilles for Hispaniola. He sighted the island natives called "Ay Ay" on November 13, 1493, and dubbed the island Santa Cruz. (The island's current name is St. Croix, which is French for Holy Cross.) Columbus then anchored off Salt River, hoping to obtain fresh water, but his landing party was greeted with Carib arrows.

Turning north, the fleet explored the islands on the far horizon, including Anegada and Virgin Gorda, the easternmost of what are now the British Virgins. Columbus sailed through the Sir Francis Drake Channel and charted its islands, then went on to St. Thomas and St. John. He was so awestricken by the countless beautiful islands that he named the area in honor of St. Ursula and her legendary 11,000 martyred virgins. He did not stop on any of the islands but sailed on to Puerto Rico and landed there on November 22.

Though Spain claimed most of the Caribbean islands through Columbus' explorations, she made little effort to colonize the smaller ones. By the early 1600s England and Holland were contending for the Virgin Islands. On St. Croix the English governor was killed. His settlers retaliated by killing the Dutch settlers' governor. The Dutch withdrew in 1645, but soon occupied the then uninhabited island of St. Thomas. They took over St. John in 1684. Meanwhile, French interests had bought St. Croix from Spain, but turned it over to the Knights of Malta in 1653. Later the French gained possession again, only to sell the island to the Dutch in 1733, who coveted St. Croix for cotton, rum and sugar production.

Slavery, upon which the large plantations depended, could not and did not continue. With the abolition of slavery in the Dutch West Indies in 1848 and the ensuing demise of sugar and cotton, Dutch prosperity on the islands waned. Despite their best efforts, the colonies could not overcome the hurricanes, earthquakes, epidemics and labor riots of the last third of the 19th century.

American efforts to buy the Virgin Islands did not succeed until World War I when the U.S. was worried about German U-boats blocking the Panama Canal. The Dutch sold them to the States in March of 1917. Terms of the treaty included that the islands retain their free-port status, a condition which is still in effect.

Danish influence in the USVI is still felt and is evidenced by city names like Christiansted and Frederiksted. A new prosperity based on tourism has surfaced and, largely because of immigration, the population has more than tripled since 1960.

The USVI are an unincorporated territory of the United States with a non-voting delegate to the House of Representatives. The Virgin Islands have a governor who is elected every four years and 15 local representatives elected to two-year terms. All persons born in the USVI are United States citizens.

Getting There/ Getting Around

Many major carriers fly into the USVI from Central America, South America, the Caribbean Islands and North America. The USVI have international airports on St. Thomas and St. Croix with most flights from the U.S. mainland landing first on St. Thomas then on to St. Croix.

American Airlines is the major carrier for the northeastern U.S. Delta Airlines has flights from Los Angeles, and major cities in the Midwest and South. Eastern Airlines flies out of Los Angeles, Chicago, St. Louis, and the major cities on the eastern seaboard. Pan American provides service from New York, Miami and from islands to the south. Other carriers provide service as well.

Interisland service is provided by Aero Virgin Islands, Crown Air, Virgin Air, V.I. Seaplane Shuttle, Arrow Air, and LIAT.

All major cruiselines operate year-round Caribbean cruises from Miami, San Juan and other eastern ports to St. Thomas/St. Croix and return.

Taxis are unmetered, but usual rates are often posted. You can get to many resorts and places of interest from the airports for well under $10, but agree upon a price first.

Major U.S. car rental agencies have cars available at the airports and they are expensive. Resorts can help you with arranging transportation and island tours.

The islands of St. John and St. Thomas are separated by two-mile-wide Pillsbury Sound. Beginning at 6:30 am, ferries make the crossing every hour from Red Hook Dock on St. Thomas to Cruz Bay, St. John. The trip takes less than 30 minutes. Passengers can also board a ferry or sea plane at Charlotte Amalie, St. Thomas and ride to St. John.

Topside Attractions
St. Thomas

Charlotte Amalie, port city of St. Thomas and capital of the U.S. Virgin Islands, rises in a series of terraces up the sides of three hills called Denmark, Synagogue and Government. These hills overlook the city's deep-water harbor, which is one of the busiest cruise ship ports in the Caribbean.

On the historical side, Charlotte Amalie holds more century-old buildings than any town of equal size in the United States. The buildings themselves are a national treasure. Uncovered when hundreds of years' worth of grime were chipped away were the artful brick and stoneworks set by Danish masons in the 1700s, floors of Spanish marble and Italian tile, soaring Spanish arches and ornate French balconies.

Charlotte Amalie has been a free port since the 1700s when the islands were a Danish possession. The free-port status and large number of visitors combine to make this city one of the greatest allures of those born to shop. There are many shops, with products ranging from poor to excellent, selling wares from around the world.

A walking tour of the town is the best way to get to know it. The following are some of the more popular places visitors like to see:

Steve Rosenberg

Government House, which is impressive from the outside because of its wrought-iron railings and red-tile roof, is best viewed from the small park across the road, or from Bluebeard's Castle, where its roof and national flags set it apart from surrounding buildings.

Virgin Islands Museum is housed in the 300-hundred-year-old Fort Christian. This unpretentious museum has more history than artifacts. There is a small collection of Arawak and Carib Indian relics and a display depicting the history of the islands.

Hotel 1829 was built in that year by a French sea captain named Lavalette. This old mansion has been turned into a guest house. Its courtyard is a popular lunch spot.

Crown House is an 18th-century mansion at the top of Government Hill. The street of 99 steps leads you between Hotel 1829 and Government House. Inside, there are hand-carved furnishings from the West Indies and Chinese tapestries.

Blackbear's Castle was known originally as Fort Skytsborg. There are only remnants left of the 17th-century fortifications.

Market Square on the west end of Main Street was the site of one of the busiest slave markets in the 18th century. It is now roofed and houses booths for people selling local produce.

The Jewish Synagogue at the top of Synagogue Hill is the second oldest synagogue in the western hemisphere. Built in 1833, it overlooks the town like a venerable rabbi.

To see the rest of the island and kick back with a drink and a meal, you will need a taxi or a rental car. Adequate, but narrow, mountainous roads take you to the sites and vistas overlooking the ocean and island. Places such as Frenchtown,

on the western shore of Charlotte Amalie Harbor, offer a better selection of food and restaurants than you will find in many other places.

Two other topside attractions worth mentioning are Coral World and the 175-acre College of the Virgin Islands. Coral World is one Coki Point on the northeast coast. It has an underwater observation tower and marine park open to the sea. Aquariums that contain many types of sea life are housed in geodesic domes within the complex, where you will also find a museum restaurant and gift shops. Adjacent to Coral World is the very popular Coki Beach. From there you can look north across the water and see Thatch Cay and some of the green mountains of St. John to the east.

St. John

Ferries from St. Thomas dock at Cruz Bay, a small St. Johnian town where you can pick up supplies, rent a jeep, and get park information from the Visitor Center of the Virgin Islands National Park. There are two main roads which, in a roundabout way, take you to many of the protected bays and public beaches around St. John and also get you to trailheads in the national park. Most of the accommodations are at Cruz Bay and there is camping in designated places on the island.

Scuba diving, going to the park and viewing historical sites, such as the Arawak Indian petroglyphs and the museums at Cruz Bay and Cinnamon Bay, are the main reasons for going to St. John.

St. Croix

Largest of the U.S. Virgin Islands, St. Croix is 23 miles long and six miles at its widest point. From the rain forests in the west to its eastern desert, it has the most varied climate and terrain in the Virgin Islands. Heavily farmed in the years prior to emancipation, the island still shows the outline of pastures and sugarcane fields of the plantations.

The island has two major towns: Christiansted, which has the older original buildings, and Frederiksted. Much of the early architecture of Frederiksted was washed away by a tidal wave in 1867 or destroyed by fire during the labor riots of 1878. The city was rebuilt in the Victorian style and is totally different from the early Danish.

Topside attractions are farther apart on St. Croix than on St. John or St. Thomas, so it is advisable to take a taxi or rent a car to go sightseeing.

The city of Christiansted was established on the north coast by the Danes in 1733. The town has a Danish look but an

American flavor. The waterfront and town square are national historic sites, so they are well kept. The red-roofed buildings of the port area are maintained well and the small shops under the breezy, open arcades make it a popular place to shop.

Fort Christianvaern was built over the ruins of a French fort. Inside, furnishings are sparse, but you can explore the dungeons and read of battles fought, or you can take a short course on how to load and fire the old cannons.

Northeast of Christiansted is Buck Island Reef National Monument, the only U.S. underwater national monument. There are trails for snorkeling as well as beaches and picnic tables. The reef and island can easily be reached by guide boats available at Christiansted.

A good spot to see a restored sugar plantation and become familiar with island flowers, Indian crops and other plants is at the St. George Village Botanical Gardens. The house is representative of the plantation mansions of the era.

In the west coast town of Frederiksted is Fort Frederik, a recently restored site with quite a history. The fort lays claim to having been the spot where the 13-starred American Flag was first saluted by a foreign power in 1776. It is also where the declaration of emancipation of the slaves of the Danish West Indies was read on July 3, 1848.

While you are in Frederiksted, stop at the Cruzan Rum Pavilion for a tour of how rum is produced and a taste of the product.

USVI Diving

The U.S. Virgin Islands are in character with the rest of the geology of the area. They are coral-based islands which rise from warm, shallow water. Most of the dives feature coral gardens and reefs which slope rather than plunge, to depths usually no more than 90 feet. There are also quite a few coral tunnels and caves, which were formed by karstic action, commonly beginning at 50 feet.

Gliding through the water, divers and snorkelers can see sponges, sea fans, coral gardens and undersea grasslands which hold fish and turtles. Crevices of the reefs hide lobsters, crabs, many eels and urchins. Fish also congregate about the shipwrecks, perhaps best represented by the RMS Rhone, lying in 30 feet to 80 feet of water in British Virgin Island territory. About the only thing these islands lack is deep wall diving such as that found along barrier reefs. There are some drop-offs, though. The two best sites are off the north shore of St. Croix and six

miles out from the south shore of St. John, which is also a good site for current diving.

The Virgin Island's attraction to the seasoned diver may well center around live-aboard boat diving, or anchorages for yachts around secluded cays. This option certainly adds to your range of dive sites. Some dive service guides will meet you at an anchorage of your choice and guide you through the underwater sites. This way you have a chance to get into the deeper, open water where the visibility is better than in the shallow sea between the islands and cays. With a charter boat, good, secluded diving can almost always be found.

The Virgin Islands National Park on St. John includes most of the island's reef. The park is off-limits to scuba, but snorkelers can swim along the underwater trails. Good diving can be found near St. John's outlyings cays and in the Cruz Bay area off the west to southwest end of the island.

As a heavy tourist traffic area, the U.S. Virgin Islands are tame by many explorers' standards; however, their topside amenities are what attract people to them. They rank among the best places for novice divers, which appeals both to resort guests as well as to cruise ship passengers who are in port to tour, shop and dive. Many cruise ships stop at Charlotte Amalie for passengers to do all three.

USVI Dive Sites

St. Thomas Dive Sites

The **Cow and Calf** is one of the most popular dives in the USVI. Located off the south end of St. Thomas it is a system of swim-through caves and archways ranging in depth from 15 feet to 50 feet. It has excellent visibility and natural light. U/w photos can be taken of some of the shallower corals and sponges. Reef sharks are also residents here.

Frenchcap Cay is five miles south of St. Thomas. It has several excellent sites along its fringe of reef. One site includes diving down to the **Cathedral**, a large cave on its north end with the entrance enveloped by a thick stand of elkhorn coral. Inside, there are squirrelfish, wrasses and cave-loving coral such as pink hydrocoral. Around Frenchcap are other systems of canyons and tunnels. On its west side is a mini drop-off dive to about 90 feet which rays, barracuda and trumpetfish frequent. **Frenchcap Cay Pinnacle** is another Frenchcap Cay site most often dived from 30 feet to 90 feet. It includes a 50-foot-long peak of rock cov-

ered with hard corals and sponges. Visibility approaches 150 feet, so divers can see horse-eye jacks, eagle rays, sergeant majors and yellowtails.

Coki Beach and Coki Point are two excellent sites for snorkelers and novice divers. It is a marine biology area, located off the northeast coast near Coral World. The site is filled with tropicals from 15 feet to 30 feet down, including sergeant majors, queen angelfish, chromis and arrow crab. There are short coral heads along its sloping bottom that hold anemones and urchins.

Thatch Cay, a stone's-throw away from Coki Point, is representative of the diversity found around the smaller cays of the Virgin Islands. Small caves are bored into the reef, as well as coral crevices which hold small eels, brown chromis and many types of sponges, inculding tube and barrel sponges. Sometimes a mild ocean current can be felt, especially if you are diving between Thatch Cay and Coki Point. At such times you can see how gorgonians, especially the sea fans, grow perpendicular to the current in order to more efficiently feed on the plankton. Thatch Cay is also laced with caves and coral chimneys. One underwater tunnel winds completely through Thatch Cay from its northwest to its south side. Pink and purple sponges abound and many small reef fish, such as angelfish and yellowtail damselfish inhabit the caves.

One shipwreck in this area is the **GENERAL ROGERS**, a U.S. Coast Guard cutter off the northeast coast of St. Thomas. It rests upright about 60 feet deep and is a favorite haven for both fish and diver.

Fortuna Beach on the west end has good beach–entry diving, though boats dive sites farther out along the reefs. Coral gardens range from 15 feet to 30 feet of water. Here there are brain coral, some elkhorn and star corals and schools of yellowtail snappers. Beginning at about 20 feet, there are small tube sponges and clumps of a variety of other sponges. This is a very protected site, making it excellent for u/w photography and night diving for people new to those aspects of the sport.

Many divers of St. Thomas dive two of the best-known wrecks in the Caribbean: **THE WRECK OF THE RHONE**, which is in the British Virgin Islands territory and dived by most services from both the BVIs and the USVIs, and the **CARTANSER SENIOR**, a steel-hulled freighter which was intentionally sunk several years ago. The 190-foot-long Cartanser Senior lies upright in 40 feet of water near Buck Island. Many common reef fish abound. It is a favorite spot for underwa-

ter photography as well as learning to wreck dive. The **RHONE**, a combination sailing/steam engine ship, sunk in a storm in 1867 after crashing into the reef off of Salt Island. Large sections of this ship lie from 30 feet to the ledge 80 feet below. It is an exciting dive with very good visibility. Not only is the ship full of coral and fish, but rays, barracuda and occasional sharks also pass by.

St. John

Tarpon Alley consists of fissures winding through coral banks, creating channels for schools of tarpon and hiding places for small baitfish. Depths vary from 45 feet to 55 feet. Several species of gorgonians and hydrocorals grow along the walls.

Mingo Cay and Grass Cay are two small cays in Pillsbury Sound, the channel which runs between St. John and St. Thomas. On the south side of Mingo is a small wooden boat lying amid the coral at 45 feet. Covered with about a 15-year-growth of coral, some divers find this wreck to be more fun than some of the larger ones nearby. The Grass Cay area is also frequently dived from St. Thomas. It has some dark canyons and rock arches amid large boulders, brain coral and stands of elkhorn. The coral floor at 70 feet also holds many sponges and small crevices for shellfish.

Carvel rock is dotted with large, coral encrusted volcanic rocks. Several long canyons are nearby with schools of tarpon cruising in and around them. Rays lie in spots of sand 40 feet down. Sharp-eyed divers might also see a porcupinefish which feed on sea urchins found here.

Lavongo Cay has spots good for snorkelers and divers. Corals begin at 15 feet and blend into a colorful coral and sponge community to depths reaching 60 feet. Brittle stars are often found near and on the tube and vase sponges. There are a lot of reef fish hovering around the coral and rock. Morays are hidden back in the crevices near the bottom.

Congo Cay has a large population of shellfish in addition to many small reef fish. There are shrimp and arrow crabs as well as barracuda and occasional shark. These bigger fish cruise through Pillsbury Sound.

Fishbowl is an intermediate depth dive of coral tunnels with schools of yellowtail snapper, angelfish and grunts. It, too, is between St. John and St. Thomas and attracts pelagics which are attracted to the reef fish which feed on plankton brought in by tidal currents. In other words, the fish life here is a miniature food chain.

St. Croix Dive Sites

To the north of St. Croix are several wall dive sites along a vertical reef. The top of the wall begins at 25 feet in some places and drops anywhere from 100 feet to 2,000 feet. Some such sites begin as close as 150 yards offshore from Cane Bay Beach. **North Star Wall**, for example, takes a 90° plunge. Its wall is laced with plume gorgonians, sea fans, and black coral. At 60 feet is a cave bored into the face of the wall.

Salt River Drop-off, which is east of North Star but part of the same general formation, includes a major canyon which cuts into the wall. The wall starts at 25 feet and drops straight down for about another 1,000 feet. Sometimes there are hammerhead and other reef sharks here. There are also a lot of turtles cruising through the shallower depths and trumpetfish hovering against the walls of the canyons.

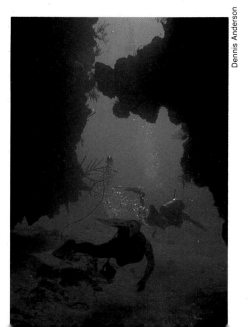

Dennis Anderson

Cane Bay Garden is a coral garden 25 feet to 50 feet deep. Located just off the north shore, the bottom of Cane Bay Garden is full of brain corals and star corals with stands of gorgonian and elkhorn and colonies of sponges upon them. Encrusted corals have covered some Danish anchors which have lain on the bottom for over 200 years. There are schools of blue wrasse, blue chromis and yellowtail snapper, too.

Frederiksted Pier is a surprisingly good pier dive, replete with its famous herd of seahorses. Located in the Frederiksted Harbor, this easy dive starts at 15 feet and goes to about 45 feet. Divers find old, sponge-encrusted propellers and pilings. Though the water at times is murky, it can also approach 80 feet and is a popular night dive when the colors of the feeding polyps of coral come out as do spirulid worms and feather-dusters.

There is a new wreck off Butler Bay on the west side of St. Croix. It is the 177-foot freighter **ROSA MARIA**, which sunk in 1986. Though it capsized and killed two people when it was towed to Butler to be sunk, the ship turned upright and now rests that way on the bottom and intact.

The Suffolk Maid is a 133-foot freighter which broke loose from its mooring during a 1984 storm and went aground. After its superstructure was stripped, it, too, was towed to Butler and sunk in about 45 feet of water.

There are some good dives east of St. Croix which some boats go to while traveling between the U.S. and British Virgin Islands. These **East End** sites include areas near Buck Island Reef National Monument. East End dives are open-water sites frequented by large sea turtles, occasional colonies of conch, schools of tarpon, barracuda, eels and large eagle rays.

St. Thomas Island Dive Services

AQUANAUTICS INTERNATIONAL
Service Address:
Located at the Consolidated Autoparts Bldg. in Charlotte Amalie
Mailing Address:
P.O. Box 4293 St. Thomas, USVI 00801
Service Telephone:
809/776-4218
Reservation Telephone:
Same as above
Hours Service is Open:
M-F 8:30-5:30; Sat 8:30-4; Sun 9-12
Resort Affiliation:
No resort affiliation

In addition to the shop listed above,

Aquanautics International has a reservation counter in the Quick Pic Shop in downtown Charlotte Amalie and in the Haven Site Mall Quick Pic Shop. They offer a resort course and NAUI open-water certification. Divers need not bring anything to dive, which is great for cruise ship passengers, unless they have a mask and snorkel available. Aquanautics rents, sells and services dive equipment.

They offer both one- and two-tank boat dives to sites which accommodate customer desire and skill level. However, they do no night diving. Their sites include Frenchcap Cay Pinnacle and dives out from Morningstar Beach and Bolong Bay, both east of Charlotte Amalie.

AQUA ACTION
Service Address:
Near Compass Point on the extreme east coast
Mailing Address:
P.O. Box 12138, St. Thomas, USVI 00801
Service Telephone:
809/775-6285
Reservation Telephone:
Same as above
Hours Service is Open:
8:30 am to 4:30 pm Seven days a week
Resort Affiliation:
Secret Harbor Hotel
Rooms:
50

Secret Harbor Hotel's Aqua Action dive service is a ten-mile taxi ride from the airport. Divers who bring personal gear receive a discount, but everything needed to dive is available at the shop. They may expand their u/w photography services soon, but right now only CNC 110 cameras are available. Repairs are pretty much limited to Scuba Pro gear.

Russell Coffin, who owns Aqua Action, offers a resort course as well as PADI, NAUI and SSI open water certification.

They offer one- and two-tank boat dives twice a day and night diving on request. They dive caves at sites such as Cow and Calf and The Cartanser Senior shipwreck. Frenchman's Reef, located off of Morning Star Beach, has two sunken WWII barges at 35 feet and is one of Aqua Action's popular photography spots. They also dive the patch and fringe reefs around Great St. James and Little St. James cays, which are east of Compass Point, and Frenchman's Cap Cay drop-off down to 90 feet where there are octopus, squid and parrotfish.

Aqua Action's 30-foot dive boat has room for 12 divers, but most parties are limited to six. The resort, itself, is in a quiet location, with the bustle of Charlotte Amalie nearby for those who want it. Aqua Action is one of the few dive shops that has a beach location and since they keep their dive parties small, novices get good personal attention. Secret Harbor Resort also staffs a complete watersports center.

CARIBBEAN DIVERS
Service Address:
At Red Hook, near the dock
Mailing Address:
Red Hook, St. Thomas, USVI 00802
Service Telephone:
809/775-6384
Reservation Telephone:
Same as above
Hours Service is Open:
8:30 am to 5:30 pm Seven days a week
Resort Affiliation:
No resort affiliation

Caribbean Divers is a one-man operation owned by Dave Fredebaudh. Full rentals are available, as well as 110 and 35 mm cameras. Morning and afternoon one-tank dives are offered, with two-tank dives and night diving available for certified divers. Dave offers a resort course as well as PADI and SSI certification.

Dave will take two to six divers on his 24-foot boat to many of the sites around St. Thomas and St. John, as well as to the Rhone in the BVIs. Some of his favorite reef dives are to Lavongo Cay, Great and Little St. James cays and Carvel Rock where there are gardens of elkhorn, brain and star corals, stands of fire coral and sea fans and ledges full of sponges.

Dave prides himself on the personal attention he gives, which contributes to diver safety and an overall good time.

CHRIS SAWYER'S DIVING CENTER
Service Address:
At the Compass Point Marina
Mailing Address:
41-6-1 Estate Frydenhoj, St. Thomas
Service Telephone:
809/775-7320
Reservation Telephone:
Same as above
Hours Service is Open:
9 am to 5 pm
Resort Affiliation:
No resort affiliation

This is one of two Chris Sawyer operations on St. Thomas. Located at Compass Point on the southwest coast, Chris serves guests from nearby resorts. A resort course as well as PADI and NAUI certification are offered.

All equipment is supplied here, including u/w photography gear which probably will be supplemented with photogra-

phy classes beginning in the 86–87 season. They do limited repairs on personal gear.

Chris caters to small dive groups. Even though his 42-foot dive boat is registered to carry 12 divers, dive parties are limited to eight. They dive in groups of four with an instructor for each group. Parties go throughout the St. Thomas-St. John area to such sites as Congo Cay, an exquisite dive which can thrill novice and experienced divers throughout its 20-foot to 90-foot-depth range. This site has terrific marine life including eagle rays, eels, barracuda and schools of bluehead wrasse. They also dive The Rhone and Big and Little Tobago, all three of which are in the British Virgin Islands. Chris will take divers to the tunnels and caves of Thatch Cay, Cow and Calf and Big Tunnels.

The small groups this service limits itself to enables divers to get a lot of personal service and hassle-free diving. The rental equipment is top-of-the-line gear which helps to make this the safe operation it is.

CHRIS SAWYER DIVE CENTER
Service Address:
On Coki Beach by Water Bay
Mailing Address:
Box 8267 c/o Virgin Grand Beach Hotel, St. Thomas 00801
Service Telephone:
809/775-1510, ext. 100 or 101
Reservation Telephone:
Same as above
Hours Service is Open:
8:30 am to 5:30 pm
Resort Affiliation:
Virgin Grand Beach Hotel
Rooms:
333

Located in the luxury class Virgin Grand Beach Hotel, right on Coki Beach on the northeast shore, this is the second of Chris Sawyer's dive operations. Service is comparable to that mentioned in the preceeding description, with the addition of the amenities of the hotel added, including all other watersports. Please refer to the other description for details.

The service is located approximately seven miles from Charlotte Amalie and nine miles from the airport. Shuttles will be provided for larger groups arriving at the airport if arrangements are made in advance.

JOE VOGEL DIVING COMPANY
Service Address:
On Mandahl Rd. (Rt. 42), near Mahogany Run Golf Course
Mailing Address:
P.O. Box 7322, St. Thomas, USVI 00801

Steve Rosenberg

Service Telephone:
809/775-7320
Reservation Telephone:
Same as above
Hours Service is Open:
9 am to 5 pm Mon–Sat
Resort Affiliation:
No resort affiliation

Located just a short trip from Mandahl Beach, Joe Vogel has been diving for over 25 years off St. Thomas. He and his wife, Debby, specialize in training new divers as well as giving private and semi-private classes in u/w photography. Their combined safety and performance records are outstanding and have been written up in several guide books and dive publications. Joe is an ex-Navy Seal and a contributing founder of NAUI. In addition to offering a five-hour resort-training course, the Vogels offer NAUI certification. This service is unique on St. Thomas in that it does only beach-entry dives and provides transportation to the entry sites after picking up customers at their resorts. Dive equipment, including camera rentals and film, is available.

The Vogels will take divers to practically any beach on St. Thomas. Their favorites are off Coki Beach to dive the reefs and ledges there, and to Fortuna Bay on the southwest coast, where there is a good variety of sponges and corals. They do a sunrise dive six days a week, including one to a 4-prop Constallation, an airplane on the reef in 40 feet of water. They also offer an afternoon dive and an afternoon resort course on alternating days of the week, as well as night dives on Tuesday,

Thursday and Saturday.

SAPPHIRE WATERSPORTS
Service Address:
  3 mi. east of Charlotte Amalie
Mailing Address:
  P.O. Box 2432, St. Thomas, USVI 00801
Service Telephone:
  809/775-6755
Reservation Telephone:
  Same as above
Hours Service is Open:
  8 am to 5 pm Seven days a week
Resort Affiliation:
  Sapphire Hotel
Rooms:
  18
Cottages/Villas:
  12 condos

Managed by Fred Williams, Sapphire Watersports dives many sites from Frenchcap Cay and The Cow and Calf on the south side of St. Thomas to the coral encrusted volcanic tunnels of Dog Rocks to the east, as well as the minor cays between St. Thomas and St. John.

This full-service shop has a resort course, PADI certification and rentals, including some u/w photography gear. Repairs on personal gear, though, is limited.

They do a two-tank morning dive, an afternoon dive and night diving two or three times a week, depending on how many requests they get. Their dive boats are a 20-footer, 32-footer and a 42-footer. Besides cave-diving at The Cow and Calf, they also do the caves off Thatch Cay and The Tunnels as well as The Cartanser Senior, General Rogers and the Rhone shipwrecks. Divers also encounter pelagics, rays and barracudas when at Fishbowl, a mid-depth, quasi-open water dive between St. Thomas and St. John.

Fred and his staff are easy to get along with and enjoy diving what the divers want. At the resort itself a complete line of watersports and tennis are available.

SEA ADVENTURES
Service Address:
  South shore at Charlotte Amalie Harbor
Mailing Address:
  P.O. Box 931, St. Thomas, USVI 00801
Service Telephone:
  809/774-9652
Reservation Telephone:
  800/524-2096
Hours Service is Open:
  7:30 am to 9 pm Seven days a week
Resort Affiliation:
  Frenchman's Reef Hotel & The Windward Passage Hotel
Rooms:
  520   147

Sea Adventures is a full watersport facility serving guests of the islands' largest hotel, The Frenchman's Reef on Morningstar Beach, and the Windward Passage, which is in downtown Charlotte Amalie. This is a major service providing a resort course as well as open-water training under PADI, NAUI and SSI. Resort courses are offered both in the morning and the afternoon. They have full rentals available, but very limited camera equipment which may be upgraded soon.

Divers board either of their three boats for one- or two-tank dives in the morning and afternoon. Parties range from six to 30 divers. Night dives are done on request.

Some of their prime reef dives are The Cow and Calf caves and Andres Reef, a 45-foot dive full of shellfish, including conch tucked away in tufts of seagrass and schooling fish. They also boat beyond Frenchcap Cay and the Sail Rock to dive their coral rock pinnacles down to 90 feet, and the Capella Cliff drop-off down to 85 feet. Their wreck-dives include the Cartanser Senior and a weekly trip to the Rhone.

In addition to diving, Sea Adventures is a full watersport facility; everything you need for fishing and boating is available from them. They offer sunset cruises and topside island tours where people can learn about places they want to explore further on their own, including shops, beaches, restaurants and lounges.

ST. THOMAS DIVING CLUB
Service Address:
  Located in the Bolongo Bay Beach Hotel at Bolongo Bay, 3 mi. southeast of Charlotte Amalie
Mailing Address:
  P.O. Box 4976, St. Thomas, USVI 00801
Service Telephone:
  809/775-1800 ext. 185
Reservation Telephone:
  Same as above
Hours Service is Open:
  8:30 am to 4:30 pm Seven days a week
Resort Affiliation:
  Bolongo Beach and Tennis Club Hotel; Lime Tree Beach Hotel; Watergate Villas; Villa Olga

The St. Thomas Diving Club is rated as a 5 Star PADI facility. They offer not only resort courses, but PADI certification and instructor training as well as specialty training in u/w photography, wreck diving, deep diving, night diving, underwater hunter and collector training, and a research dive specialty for qualified people who arrange it in advance.

Now solely located in the Bolongo Bay Beach Club Hotel, the St. Thomas Diving Club also had to shop in the Villa Olga dive resort until 1985. However, they still are the service center for that waterfront resort, as well as for the other hotels listed above. They have a full rental shop with u/w photo equipment, plus repair service.

From their boats they do a two-tank morning dive and a one-tank afternoon dive in addition to morning and afternoon beach-entry dives. Night diving is available twice a week.

Their sites include the coral reefs and pinnacles ranging in depth from 20 feet to 80 feet. They dive Andres Reef, an 80-foot dive which is comparable to a mini-wall, and The Cow and Calf where they often see sharks. They also dive Little Buck Island, which can be seen from Bolongo Beach, and Little St. James Island to the east. They also dive the usual shipwrecks. Instructors are continually diving and exploring new sites which have not

David McCray

yet been named.

Other watersports and most of what St. Thomas offers is available from each resort this club serves.

VIRGIN ISLAND DIVING SCHOOL
Service Address:
  Charlotte Amalie
Mailing Address:
  P.O. Box 9707, St. Thomas, USVI 00801
Service Telephone:
  809/774-8687
Reservation Telephone:
  Same as above
Hours Service is Open:
  7 am to 5 pm Tues–Sat; Mondays during main season
Resort Affiliation:
  No resort affiliation

Virgin Island Diving School has been operating here for 14 years. For people coming in on a cruise ship, they offer shuttle service.

They dive with all levels of diver, but specialize in giving undersea adventure to people who have never had tanks on before. In addition to their resort course, PADI, NAUI, and SSI certification is available. They also do advanced open-water training, instructor certification, dive-master training, rescue training and will possibly soon expand to u/w photography classes.

They rent all dive equipment most people need, but recommend divers bring a mask, fins, snorkel and gloves. Repair service is available.

They offer two morning and two afternoon boat-dives a day, plus night diving on request. Boat dives are limited to six divers to a party.

For people new to diving, the school recommends the Coki Beach area, Fortuna Beach and Hull Bay where you will see lobsters, conch, sergeant majors and schools of grunts, yellowtail snappers and chromis. The deeper reefs have barracuda, horse-eye jacks and rays among beds and heads of hard corals.

They dive several shipwrecks including the Constellation airplane wreck off Fortuna Beach and vertical reefs off Water Island and Dog Island.

St. John Dive Services

CRUZ BAY WATERSPORTS
Service Address:
  In Cruz Bay, west end of St. John
Mailing Address:
  P.O. Box 252, St. John, USVI 00830
Service Telephone:
  809/776-6234
Reservation Telephone:
  Same as above
Hours Service is Open:
  8:30 am to 5:30 pm Seven days a week
Resort Affiliation:
  No resort affiliation

Marcus Johnston owns Cruz Bay Watersports, which is a short walk from the Cruz Bay dock where ferries arrive from St. Thomas every hour. He and his staff provide resort training, open-water PADI certification, which takes three days, and rescue and dive-master courses. Marcus suggests divers bring any personal gear they can, but his service has whatever the diver needs. They do have u/w photography cameras, but do no film processing. Repairs are limited to Sherwood gear.

They do a two-tank morning dive to some of the deeper areas off St. John, such as the South Drop-off six miles offshore. They also offer a one-tank afternoon dive to Carvel Rock, Grass Cay, Fish Bowl, The Cow and Calf and Tarpon Alley off the southwest side of St. John. At these sites are a variety of gorgonians, pillar corals, anemones and shellfish on the coral ledges and pelagics beginning in about 45 feet of water.

They do night dives and wreck-dives on request, including the Cartanser Senior, General Rogers and The Rhone.

Marcus has three dive boats including a 40-foot custom-built dive boat with room enough for 20 divers and their gear. But he said there is no minimum number of divers he will take and he's ready to dive every day of the year.

CINNAMON BAY WATERSPORTS CENTER
Service Address:
  5 miles from Cruz Bay, on the north coast
Mailing Address:
  P.O. Box 720, Cruz Bay, St. John, USVI 00830
Service Telephone:
  809/776-6330 & 776-6458
Reservation Telephone:
  800/223-7637
Hours Service is Open:
  8 am to 5 pm Seven days a week
Resort Affiliation:
  Caneel Bay Resort
Rooms:
  158

Cinnamon Bay Watersports Center is part of the Caneel Bay Resort, a waterfront facility on the largest beach on St.

Steve Rosenberg

John, Caneel Beach. This general area is also adjacent to the north shore camping facilities for visitors to the St. John and the Virgin Island National Park. Guests take a taxi or rent a car from Cruz Bay to get to here.

Jeff Strychalski manages Cinnamon Bay Watersports and offers a resort course and open-water PADI certification. Dive packages are available which include all necessary dive equipment, but it is recommended divers bring a regulator, snorkel and mask, if possible. The service also rents u/w photo gear with film processing being available elsewhere on the island. They do one- and two-tank dives in the morning and afternoon. Night dives are conducted only on Wednesdays.

Cinnamon Bay has a 42-foot dive boat which will hold over 40 people, but they take out no more than 15 divers at a time. Their onboard compressor eliminates the need for divers to lug tanks back and forth for air fills. They boat to sites north, west and south of St. John to Carvel Rock, Fishbowl, The Cow and Calf, Grass Cay and various shipwrecks. They also do an all-day trip to dive the Rhone in the BVIs.

Besides having access to the largest beach on St. John, guests here frequently hike through the park trails or participate in some of the many park education programs.

ST. JOHN WATERSPORTS, INC.
Service Address:
Three minute walk from Cruz Bay ferry landing
Mailing Address:
P.O. Box 70, Cruz Bay, St. John 00830
Service Telephone:
809/776-6256
Hours Service is Open:
8:30 am to 6 pm M–F; 8:30 am to 5 pm Sat & Sun
Resort Affiliation:
No resort affiliation

St. John Watersports serves guests of Cruz Bay area resorts as well as people coming to the island just for the day. They offer a resort-training course and PADI certification, usually in the afternoon. They rent all snorkeling and scuba gear, but recommend divers bring personal dive gear.

St. John Watersports does a two-tank morning and offers both a resort dive and a one-tank boat dive in the afternoon. Night diving is held on request.

They dive the coral gardens, canyons, tunnels and caves around St. John and the cays in between St. John and St. Thomas, such as Little St. James and Dog Rocks. Most dives are between 40 feet and 60 feet, which are the depths of the caves, reef fish and some of the smaller pelagics. They take groups of usually no more than six divers aboard their 23-foot dive boat, which helps them get loaded and to the sites quickly. Owners Stu and Paula Brown keep the operation small in order to accommodate the services' schedule around the customers.

The service has other watersports available, including day sailing and a full-line sports clothing shop.

UNDERWATER SAFARI
Service Address:
Charlotte Amalie
Mailing Address:
P.O. Box 8469
Service Telephone:
809/774-1350
Reservation Telephone:
Same as above
Hours Service is Open:
8 am to 5 pm Mon–Sat; 8 to 4 Sundays
Resort Affiliation:
No resort affiliation

Underwater Safari is a retail shop and books divers with dive services, depending upon the needs of divers and where they will be staying while in the islands. Underwater Safari has probably the largest selection and greatest inventory of any shop or service in the islands. Underwater Safari also rents dive equipment, incluidng u/w cameras. Limited equipment repair is available.

Manager Mark Barnett stated he was in the process of redoing the shop and hoped to soon have a dive boat ready for action to take divers into the water, as well as continue to be a retail outlet.

St. Croix Dive Services

CRUZAN DIVERS, INC.
Service Address:
In Frederiksted, on the west coast
Mailing Address:
12 Strand Street, Frederiksted, St. Croix, USVI 00804
Service Telephone:
809/772-3701
Reservation Telephone:
Same as above
Hours Service is Open:
Summer: 9–5 M–F; 9–4 Sat/Sun; Winter 8–5 M–F; 8–4 Sat/Sun
Resort Affiliation:
Royal Dane
Rooms:
21

Guests of the Royal Dane land at Alexander Hamilton Airport and will be picked up by the resort if prior arrangements have been made. Cruzan Divers accommodate all skill levels of diver and teach a resort course as well as offer NAUI certification. They offer full rental and repair service.

All diving is tailored to what the customer wants. For instance, if you want a one-tank morning dive or a two-tank night dive, it is no problem having Cruzan set it up for you.

They have two dive boats: a 23-footer with a six-diver capacity and a 42-foot Lindsey for as many as 26 divers. They dive to sites all along the reef which parallels the entire west coast. It begins at 30 feet, then slopes to 90 feet to 110 feet. Off the north coast they dive North Star and Cane Bay. Both start at 45 feet and drop for 1,000 feet and more. There, divers find turtles, angelfish, triggerfish and trumpetfish. They also dive Salt River Drop-off.

Just off the west coast's Butler Bay are three wrecks: the Rose Maira, Suffolk Maid and the North Wind, which was a tug boat sunk for a movie prop at 45 feet. They also dive Frederiksted Pier.

Frederiksted is one of St. Croix's two main towns and is the quieter of the two. Nightlife centers around the city's restaurants and two bars. Outside of town horseback riding, fishing and other watersports are available.

CARIBBEAN SEA ADVENTURES
Service Address:
On the Christiansted Wharf
Mailing Address:
P.O. Box 3015, St. Croix, USVI 00820
Service Telephone:
809/773-6011
Reservation Telephone:
Same as above
Hours Service is Open:
8 am to 5 pm
Resort Affiliation:
Buccaneer Hotel - Grapetree Beach - King Christian
Rooms:
150   70   50

Caribbean Sea Adventures has operated a watersports facility longer than any on St. Croix: 16 years. They have centers in both the Buccaneer and Grapetree Beach hotels. For groups of ten or more they will provide a shuttle service from Alexander Hamilton Airport; smaller groups need to take a taxi.

Caribbean Sea Adventures offers a resort course, PADI, NAUI, SSI and NASDS certification as well as periodic underwater photography courses. They rent all gear, including u/w cameras, and do equipment repair. Guests are advised to bring personal dive gear, however.

They have a two-tank morning dive and a single-tank afternoon dive, with night diving on request. Caribbean Sea Adventures keeps the diving fresh by going to over fifty different dive sites. They have two 40-foot flattops, and, for smaller parties, a 27-foot Lindsey and a 20-foot Seaspray.

They dive the reefs and wall out from Caine Bay and Salt River, where there are black corals, hard corals, plumes of gorgonians, sea fans and sponges growing on and in the formations. They are the only dive operation allowed to scuba dive at Buck Island National Monument.

Owner Larry Angus and his staff provide friendly, competent service. Charter boats, deep-sea fishing and most other watersports are available from his center. The entertainment and the sites of St. Croix are easily accessible for guests of Christiansted's resorts.

DIVE EXPERIENCE, INC.
Service Address:
On the Christiansted waterfront with the Comanche Hotel
Mailing Address:
P.O. Box 4254 Christiansted, St. Croix, USVI 00820
Service Telephone:
809/773-3307
Reservation Telephone:
Same as above
Hours Service is Open:
8:30 am to 5 pm Mon–Sat; 8:30 to 4 pm on Sunday
Resort Affiliation:
Comanche Hotel; Tamarind Reef Beach Club
Rooms:
46
Cottages/Villas:
- 16

Dive Experience, Inc., already a complete dive service, is an expanding facility. In August 1986, they became a PADI 5 Star training facility. They now offer a resort-course, PADI certification and specialty training in wreck diving, u/w photography and video, night diving and deep diving, as well as NAUI certification. Shuttles are available at the airport for large groups, but most others ride the ten miles to Christiansted in a taxi.

Dive Experience keeps its gear upgraded with new, top-of-the-line equipment. Divers really don't need to bring anything other than a light wetsuit and regulator. The service also rents CNC 110 cameras and repairs just about any piece of dive equipment.

Dive Experience has a 30-foot dive boat and a new, 40-foot custom-built boat. An instructor will take as few as two divers and cruise to sites along the north drop-offs and reefs including The Stacks, Rough Stop Twist, Cane Bay and North Star. They dive many of the nearby wrecks, plus do an all-day dive trip to the Rhone once a month. They also dive the south side of Christiansted, which is very seldom done by other services. Common life along the drop-offs include hammerhead sharks, tarpons, eels, lobster and a host of colorful tropical reef fish. They will take snorkelers to Buck Island monument via their glass-bottom boat. Michelle Pugh, owner of Dive Experience, recommends the Buck Island trip to St. Croix visitors.

Off the beach there is excellent windsurfing and sailing. Christiansted, itself, has several good restaurants and bars with live entertainment.

SEA SHADOWS
Service Address:
On Cane Bay's King's Wharf
Mailing Address:
P.O. Box 505, Cane Bay, St. Croix, USVI 00820
Service Telephone:
809/778-3850
Reservation Telephone:
Same as above
Hours Service is Open:
9 am to 5 pm Seven days a week
Resort Affiliation:
No resort affiliation

Sea Shadows gives divers access to the prime dive spots off the north shore. They offer not only a resort course, but every specialty course there is: search and recovery, equipment specialist, underwater hunter, night diver, deep diver, and reef life. Divers can be certified under either the PADI or NAUI system.

They recommend divers bring personal dive gear such as mask, snorkel and fins. They rent equipment, including u/w cameras. Sea Shadows also repairs equipment.

They will do a one-tank morning dive and a two-tank afternoon dive, unless divers want to do two two-tank dives back to back. They will night dive any time they have two people.

They do mostly beach dives but charter a dive boat twice a week to take people on a two-tank dive to the Salt River Drop-off and other sites out from the coast. Then there is the Puerto Rican trench, which gives divers the chance to dive a drop-off from the beach. For wreck dives for novices, Sea Shadows recommends the recently sunk ships in Butler Bay. They dive other wrecks as well, including a boat dive to one 110 feet deep. Throughout their sites garden eels, turtles, schools of spadefish, yellowtail snappers and angelfish abound.

Sea Shadows, in operation for about four years, also offers topside tours around St. Croix. To give the type of personal service they like to give, they keep classes, dive parties and tour groups small.

VIRGIN ISLAND DIVERS, LTD.
Service Address:
In Christiansted, overlooking the harbor
Mailing Address:
Pam Am Pavilion, Christiansted, St. Croix USVI 00820
Service Telephone:
809/773-6045
Reservation Telephone:
Same as above
Hours Service is Open:
8:30 to 5 Mon–Sat; Seven days a week in winter
Resort Affiliation:
Hotel Caravelle
Rooms:
50

Kathleen and Jimmy Antione, owners of Virgin Island Divers, continuously try to improve and expand their service. At the moment they offer a resort course and PADI certification. Soon NAUI certification will be part of their program. They also offer u/w photography and video training.

They offer full rental, including u/w cameras, and repairs, but advise divers to bring any gear with which they are comfortable and be prepared with towels, food and drinks when on one of their longer boat dive trips. They do two-tank morning dives and full-day boat trips in a relaxed and friendly way. Night diving is available on request. Frederiksted Pier is popular for that.

They have one dive boat and were in the process of getting another one at the time of writing. They dive the drop-offs off the north and east shore, including Summary Bay, Salt River, Cane Bay and North Star. They also dive the recent shipwrecks at the bottom of Butler Bay and the Hydro Lab.

The staff try to help guests have the best vacation possible. In addition to diverse diving, this includes taking charter boat trips, golfing (there are two courses on the island), sailing, touring Buck Island, or having a beach barbecue. They can also tip you off as to where to find good deals in the duty-free shops on the island.

The British Virgin Islands

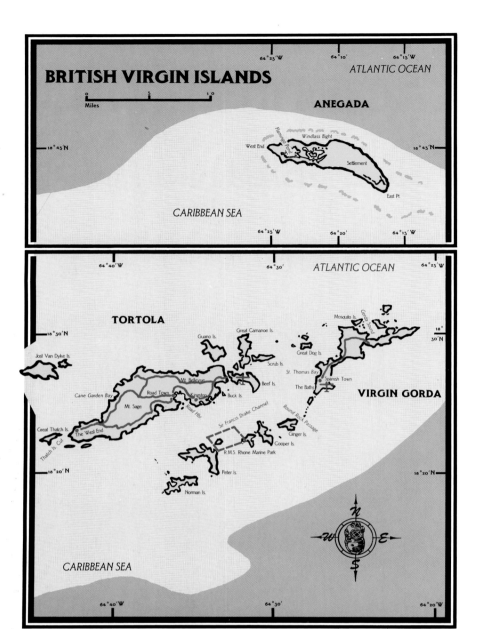

British Virgin Islands

Entry Requirements

    Proof of Citizenship for USA & Canadian citizens. Passports for all others. Onward or return ticket for all

Language

    English

Airlines

    Air BVI, Crown Air, Coral Air, LIAT, British Caribbean, Eastern

Airports

    Beef Island Airport

    Virgin Gorda Airport

Departure Taxes

    U.S. $5 Air; $3 Sea

Electricity

    110 volts; 60 cycles

Size

    59 sq. mi.

Population

    12,500

BVI Tourist Office

    BVI Tourist Board

    Box 134

    Road Town, Tortola, BVI

    809/494-3134/3489

    BVI Tourist Board

    370 Lexington Avenue, Suite 412

    New York, NY 10017

    212/696-0400

The British Virgin Islands lie 60 miles east of Puerto Rico and about 1,100 miles southeast of Miami. Virgin Gorda and Tortola are the main islands of this British Crown Colony, which is composed of approximately 50 small islands and cays. Most of the islands are tightly grouped around the Sir Francis Drake Channel. The islands are volcanic in origin, with the exception of Anegada, a coral atoll sitting alone on the outer fringe of the arc of the Lesser Antilles, nine miles north of Virgin Gorda.

Columbus sailed through the area in 1493 and claimed the islands for Spain. The islands remained in Spain's hands for over 100 years until the ships of Sir Francis Drake nominally put them under English control. It took England almost 80 years to solidly establish its claim to the islands, having to battle the Spanish, Dutch, and other colonial powers for them. When English settlers began arriving in substantial numbers in the 1700s the British Navy protected them from pirates and other harassment as part of its effort to keep the shipping lanes open. The islands were governed as part of Britain's Leeward Islands and became a Crown Colony in 1971. The colony now has limited self-rule. The Queen-appointed Governor, Prime Minister and four other members compose the Executive Council. The Legislature consists of seven popularly elected members and four appointed members.

The islands are a blend of rocks and mountains, moist valleys, arid hills and white sand beaches. Differences in rainfall, soil and exposure have created a wide variety of vegetation. Some land which was cleared for the plantations years ago is dotted with cactus, loblolly, frangipani and wild tamarind. In the valleys are tropical fruits and flowers including bananas, mangoes, bougainvillea and hibiscus. Palms and mangroves grow near some of the beaches.

The island of Tortola has all the topside diversity found throughout the British Virgin Islands—everything from secluded north coast beaches to 1,780-foot Mount Sage. Road Town, the islands' capital, has 4,000 of Tortola's 9,000 people. It lies near the center of Tortola's protected south coast and looks out over the Sir Francis Drake Channel. Off the east coast of Tortola is Beef Island. Beef Island is the site of the main British Virgin Islands Airport. The two are connected by the 300-foot-long Queen Elizabeth Bridge.

About two miles east by northeast of Beef Island is Virgin Gorda. On its north are mountains which rise as high as 1,300 feet. These give way to the rock flats on the south. Virgin Gorda has a population of 1,000, most of whom live in Spanish Town. Spanish Town has a marina which is popular with boaters and the town, itself, provides visitors access to island beaches and other sites. The island also has a 3,000-foot runway.

The islands have a subtropical climate. Trade winds and warm water help keep the islands' temperature within 75° to 85° in winter and 80° to 90° in summer.

Getting There/ Getting Around

Most travelers to the British Virgin Islands land at Beef Island Airport, usually after a stopover in San Juan, Puerto Rico or St. Thomas in the US Virgin Islands. British Caribbean is a new airline which is enjoying growing popularity and support. Other carriers are Air BVI, Crown Air, Coral Air, LIAT and Eastern Airlines.

Most of the accommodations are on Tortola. A taxi ride from the airport to the resorts usually costs around $12 to $15, depending upon what you and the driver agree. Ferries are the most common way of interisland travel. Ferries leave the CSY Dock, just east of Road Town, for Peter Island, Virgin Gorda, Anegada, and points in the US Virgin Islands. Charter boats are available, too.

The roads of Tortola definitely do not go straight as the crow flies. For travelers who want to rent a car to tour the hairpins of Tortola, rentals are available in Road Town. Rentals are also available on Virgin Gorda. Some resorts rent mopeds and bikes or can arrange them for you.

Topside Attractions

The British Virgin Islands are best known for sailing, and island hideaways on some of the less populated cays are favored by yachtsmen. But the BVIs are also a good place to learn to sail. Their protected waters and dependable breezes entice many landlubbers to take to the sea. Road Town is the largest bareboat yacht chartering center in the Caribbean. As such, it sometimes reaches a bustling level foreign to the rest of these islands. The Offshore Sailing School and Boardsailing BVI, located on Tortola and Beef Island respectively, are two schools visitors may contact to learn to futher explore the Caribbean Islands on their own.

There are a few dozen shops in Road Town, and some of the resorts nearby offer local entertainment. As the area gets more prominent, visitors will be able to see and hear better-known entertainers.

Tours are offered on the island. They go to such places as Cane Garden Bay on the north coast and to Mount Sage, a national park established to protect some of the native trees and other vegetation of Tortola. There is also a mountaintop restaurant at Sky World where patrons get a 360° view of the Caribbean and can often see Puerto Rico and St. Croix.

Virgin Gorda is best known for its beaches where privacy and a view of the surrounding cays can be enjoyed. Virgin Gorda also has "The Baths," a unique rock formation with dimly-lit sea caves. For those who like to explore the land, a hike up 1,370-foot Gorda Peak is an interesting nature walk.

British Virgin Islands Diving

While the British Virgin Islands have no wall dive per se, it does have a great variety of diving and many types of diving situations. Ones which may have the most interest to divers are the caves and shipwrecks. There are many caves here. They are not cavernous ones such as those associated with blue holes and collapsing formations of coral. Rather, the British Virgin Islands caves go for distance, and have some of the longest tunnels in the Caribbean. It is possible to navigate through these as far as 300 to 450 feet. Many of these caves are from lava tubes. As lava poured from the earth, the outer lava cooled, but the inner lava flowed out, creating these long tunnels now full of tropical marine life.

The history and the natural history have combined to litter the floor with shipwrecks. Over 300 known wrecks are along Horseshoe Reef, north of Anegada. Horseshoe is the third largest barrier reef in the western hemisphere. After several centuries underwater, many of these have become so encrusted with coral, divers can barely see their outline on the reef. Others, such as the Rhone and Chikuzen are easy and interesting to dive for most levels of diver and have become synonymous with British Virgin Island diving.

New sites throughout the reefs are constantly being discovered and explored. Some operations will take a small boat of divers with the intention of diving truly virgin sites, sites which no one has probably ever dived before. Pinnacle diving and diving around submerged mountains of rock and coral are prominent undersea features. Wherever there are mountains there are valleys, and the sides of those in the British Virgin Islands are painted with sponges, encrusting corals and soft corals, and populated by lobsters, batfish, drums, triggerfish, southern rays and eagle rays. Hundreds of copper sweepers school beneath rock ledges. Divers can see schools of tuna, tarpon and dolphins flash as they go through island passages to the open Atlantic.

The BVI Dive Operators Association is an active group of professionals to which most of the dive services here belong. The operators are aware of how important safety and conservation are to their businesses. They were instrumental in establishing the British Virgin Islands Underwater National Park, which encompasses much of the islands' best diving and fish habitat. They meet once a month to work on projects aimed at keeping the marine environment healthy. They have done such things as installing moorings at the national park site of the Wreck of the Rhone so boats can tie to them, rather than dropping anchor of top of the coral. They cooperate among themselves to provide safe service and keep up on dive trends and advancements. They compete among themselves to expand their knowledge of the waters to give visitors an ever-growing choice of diving.

Dive Sites

Blonde Rock is between Peter Island and Salt Island in the middle of the Salt Passage. It has two enormous 50-foot-tall rock pinnacles encrusted with sponges and coral. Divers explore their base 65 feet down and can swim through crevices full of fish, lobsters and crabs. Sponges dangle from rock overhangs. All along the pinnacles, which reaches within ten feet of the surface, are other gullies and small caves to swim in. Sharks are frequent visitors, too, and help make this a great u/w photography site. This is one of the best sites around.

Black Barrel Rock Point is another magnificent rock pinnacle usually patrolled by large schools of barracuda. In calm water divers can sometimes see these silver fish being freed of parasites by cleaner fish. This site is also in a route frequented by schools of tuna, tarpon and dolphin.

Alice in Wonderland, named for the giant mushroom coral reminiscent of where the caterpillar in the book *Alice in Wonderland* set smoking his pipe. This site is off Ginger Island. At depths which range from 20 feet to 100 feet, it can be taken as either a shallow or deep dive. Reef fish abound through stands of shingle coral, star coral and pillar coral.

The Green Giant Bellybutton is off the southside of Ginger Island. Its name is derived from the huge round brain coral with a little hole in it that looks like a navel. Big mushroom coral heads abound at 60 feet on this site's sandy plateau. The plateau gently slopes down to 100 feet. This area attracts large fish, including nurse sharks and groupers. Divers frequently swim with sea turtles, rays, octopus, eels and drums here, too.

The many crevices and coral archways within the two big valleys of **Painted Walls** have red, purple, bright yellow and orange sponges which create a living undersea mural. Near Dead Chest Island, this is a super u/w photography site when the water is calm. Depths vary from 30 feet to 50 feet.

THE RHONE went down in a hurricane in 1867. The bow of the ship lies in 80 feet of water and its crow's nest sits intact upon the mast. Lots of fish are nearby, including two, 200-pound-groupers. The boilers and superstructure are beautifully encrusted with all kinds of coral. Some claim The Rhone crabs are bigger than any Alaska King Crab that has ever lived.

Carrot Shoal is between Peter and Norman island. Carrot Rock, a pinnacle of stone and coral, sticks out of the water marking the site. At 60 feet is a sandy area where going into the formation are swim-through tunnels. This site is in the open sea, so divers see a lot of large fish and pelagics.

The Ledge of Brewers' Bay is a mini-wall that starts at 25 feet with a sheer wall, then drops down to 75 feet. Throughout this area are spotted eagle rays and sting rays. Located on the north side of Tortola, it is an area which can only be dived during the summer when the winds are predominantly from the

David McCray

east and southeast, but if you want to see big fish such as bull sharks, this is the place.

In the channel three-quarters of a mile south of Norman Island are the **Santa Monica Rocks**. This site has excellent visibility, frequently exceeding 100 feet. Its two pinnacles rise from 80 feet deep to within 15 feet of the surface. This is a rugged area of currents, caves and tunnels. There is a large school of resident barracuda and hosts of reef fish and sponges.

The **WRECK OF THE CHIKUZEN** is a Japanese refrigeration vessel that drifted up from Santa Monica and came to rest six miles north of Beef Island. This 130-foot-long ship is upright and completely intact. It rests in 80 feet of water where reef fish, rays and coral are keeping it company.

Indian Rocks is a great site for new divers. Four rocks stick above the surface off of Pelican Island. Divers swim through a 30- to 50-foot-deep gully, but basically circle around the pinnacles and over coral gardens. This site is not quite as colorful as it used to be since a couple of hurricanes passed through.

Black Bluff is a virgin reef to the southeast side of Virgin Gorda. Giant stands of mushroom coral are riddled with swim-through tunnels and caves.

Blinders has been called an underwater version of the Flintstones and the town of Bedrock. There are massive piles of granite boulders divers can swim among as well as coral archways and tunnels.

British Virgin Islands Dive Services

AQUATIC CENTRES
Service Address:
Two locations - East Road Town; West Road Town
Mailing Address:
P.O. Box 108, Road Town, Tortola, B.V.I.
Service Telephone:
809/428-5859
Reservation Telephone:
800/345-6296
Hours Service is Open:
8 am to 6 pm Seven days a week
Resort Affiliation:
Prospect Reef Resort; Treasure Isle Hotel
Rooms:
130   40

Aquatic Centres is a PADI training facility offering PADI certification, resort training, and u/w photography and video classes. They rent and repair all dive and camera equipment and have E-6 film processing. By way of personal gear, however, Manager Derryln Churchwell recommends divers bring at least their own face mask. They have dive shops in both of the resorts mentioned above. Guests usually take a taxi from the Beef Island Airport.

Aquatic Centres offers a two-tank morning dive and one-tank afternoon dive. They night dive on Wednesdays or Thursdays to a variety of sites, everything from Angelfish Reef to the Wreck of the Rhone.

Most dives are in the Sir Francis Drake Channel. There are many different reef sites there and the best dives are within 65 feet. They dive Blonde Rock, Painted Walls, the rock pinnacle of Dry Rocks East between Cooper and Salt Islands and Carrot Shoal, one of Derryln's favorite dives.

This service has two boats, a 30-footer and a 35-footer, and plans to add another boat soon. To keep parties small, both boats have a ten-diver capacity. The instructors are very knowledgeable about local marine life and give a slide show on it once a week.

Between dives, many people enjoy fishing, sailing, or going to the beaches which fringe Tortola. Tours to the north side of the island to places such as Cane Garden Bay are popular.

BLUE WATER DIVERS
Service Address:
At Nanny Cay, on Tortola's SW coast between Road Town and West End
Mailing Address:
P.O. Box 437, Road Town, Tortola, BVI
Service Telephone:
809/494-2847
Reservation Telephone:
Same as above
Hours Service is Open:
8 am to 5 pm Seven days a week
Resort Affiliation:
No resort affiliation

Resorts dot the secluded southwest beaches of Tortola, many of which are between a 15- and 20-minute drive from Road Town. Dive travelers who stay at the Sugar Mill, Sebastian's, Flying Cloud or The Windjammer will usually be served by Blue Water Divers. Guests normally get to their resort by taxi, but Blue Water Divers will supply an airport shuttle for large diver groups.

Louis Prezelin

Blue Water offers a resort course and PADI certification. They are a full rental and repair service, including u/w camera equipment, but have no film processing. They even take u/w video pictures for divers who want a souvenir film of their trip.

Divers board either a 30-foot Lindsey or 30-foot flattop for two-tank dives which span sites lying in the Sir Francis Drake Channel from Norman to Mosquito Island to the mini-wall north of Tortola near Brewer's Bay. Santa Monica Rocks is a favorite site of Blue Waters. It is south of Norman Island and just one of many of the area's pinnacle and cave dives. They dive some off Jost Van Dyke, but prefer to go farther east to Green Cay, which has a fabulous cut on its back side full of big fish. Other sites include the Chikuzen, the Rhone, Alice in Wonderland and Painted Walls. Night diving is on request.

This service is part of a very relaxed prime beach area. Between dives, guests frequently rent a car to explore the island. There is also windsurfing and sailing, which Keith Royle or other members of the staff, will help arrange for you.

UNDERWATER SAFARIS
Service Address:
On the "On the Moorings" Dock, Road Town
Mailing Address:
P.O. Box 139, Road Town, Tortola, BVI
Service Telephone:
809/494-3235
Reservation Telephone:
800/535-7289
Hours Service is Open:
8 am to 5 pm Seven days a week

Resort Affiliation:
Moorings Mariner Inn
Rooms:
80

Underwater Safaris, which combines diving with crew and bare-boat charter services, is the newest and largest operator in the British Virgin Islands. They provide many watersport services to guests staying in the Road Town area. For guests staying at the Mariner Inn, taxi service is provided from the airport as part of the dive package.

This is an excellent, full-service center with new and well-maintained Sherwood, Tabata and Sea Quest gear. Their larger boats are fully equipped as well, and are considered to be floating dive shops. This PADI facility offers resort courses, PADI open-water certification, advanced open-water, rescue diver, assistant instructor and dive master certification. In addition to renting and repairing many types of equipment, the shop also has Nikon 5, CNC 35 and 110 cameras.

Underwater Safaris's three dive boats range to over 35 sites between Norman Island to the south and Ginger Island and Camanoe Island to the east and northeast. They do a two-tank morning dive and one-tank afternoon dive. For a minimum of four divers, night diving is on request and is included in the dive package.

Their favorite sites around Norman Island include Spy Glass Wall and The Indians. They dive the Rhone day or night. This is a favorite place where instructors take souvenir video tapes of the divers. They dive Black Barrel Rock Point on the open ocean side of Cooper Island, Alice in Wonderland, and The Green Giant Bellybutton. Other prime targets are Green Cay, Great Camanoe, and the reefs and pinnacles off Little Camanoe British Virgin Islands and Guana Islands.

Between dives guests waterski, windsurf, parasail or go day sailing. The resort has tennis courts and an aerobic center. Shopping and other amenities are available in Road Town. Some visitors will taken the 45-minute ferry boat ride to St. Thomas.

Among the features this service offers are rendevous tours, where one of its dive boats will meet a charter boat or private boat at a pre-selected anchorage and take the people diving. Large groups may choose to rent a boat from Underwater Safaris. The boat's skipper will take them to anchorages throughout the islands, teaching those who want to learn to sail.

They can stay at a different island each night and dive wherever they want.

Virgin Gorda Dive Services

DIVE BVI, LTD.
Service Address:
Virgin Gorda Yacht Harbour on SW coast, in St. Thomas Bay
Mailing Address:
P.O. Box 1040, Virgin Gorda Yacht Harbour, Virgin Gorda, BVI
Service Telephone:
809/495-5513
Reservation Telephone:
800/387-4964
Hours Service is Open:
8:30 am to 5 pm Mon–Sat; by arrangement on Sunday
Resort Affiliation:
Leverick Bay Resort
Cottages/Villas:
8 condos; several villas

Dive BVI, Ltd. has a full-service resort at its Yacht Harbour location as well as a small facility at Leverick Bay, on the north coast. Guests either take a ferry to the island from Tortola, or, after a brief stop at Beef Island Airport, continue on to Virgin Gorda Airport where taxis are available.

Dive BVI is a PADI facility offering a resort course, open water, advanced open water, dive master, and rescue certification. Rental equipment is included in the dive packages. U/w camera equipment is available. Overnight film processing is available at a nearby lab.

Plans call for Dive BVI to supplement its 38-foot dive boat with a new, larger boat in the near future. The number of divers in a boat will continue to be 12 or less. The service begins a two-tank morning dive at 9 am, followed by a one-tank shallow dive in the afternoon. Night diving should be requested ahead of time.

The instructors and guides at Dive BVI take divers to the pinnacles at Toe Rock and the long caves off Guana Island. Other favorites are The Blinders, the reefs of Scrub Island and Black Bluff, and the 100-foot depths of Alice in Wonderland. Tuna, eagle rays, southern rays, lobsters, crabs, drums, grunts and angelfish are a few of the very abundant fish in these areas. Wreck diving includes trips to the Rhone and the Chikuzen. Dive parties frequently go exploring to find and charter new sites.

The service prides itself on quality rather than quantity. They purposely keep the dive parties small and never mix certified divers with new divers.

Virgin Gorda is for relaxing. Between-dive activities include a trip to The Baths, or wandering along any of the island's 20 beaches. There is a new restaurant and disco at the Little Dicks Hotel and Restaurant, and a local band is always playing somewhere on the island. Shoppers can take a ferry to Road Town or to St. Thomas in the US Virgin Islands.

KILBRIDES UNDERWATER TOURS
Service Address:
North Sound, Virgin Gorda
Mailing Address:
P.O. Box 40, Saba Rock, Virgin Gorda, BVI
Service Telephone:
809/494-2746
Reservation Telephone:
Same as above
Hours Service is Open:
8 am to 5 pm Seven days a week
Resort Affiliation:
No resort affiliation

Kilbrides Underwater Tours conducts resort courses and dive trips for guests staying at the Bitter End, Greg's Anchorage and Biras Creek Resort. PADI and NAUI certification are available as are specialty classes in u/w photography and video. They rent all necessary scuba gear and, as they have recently expanded into u/w photography and video, will be increasing their selection in that equipment area, as well. Repair service on personal equipment is not available.

Kilbrides does a two-tank morning tour, with divers returning around 1 pm to 2 pm. They night dive on request. They are the only operation which regularly dives Anegada's Horseshoe Reef, which has some excellent wreck-diving. They take an all day trip there, dive a couple of wrecks in the morning, take a lunch break, then go underwater again.

They dive a dozen sites in the Dog Islands, which have arches, canyons and ledges of stone. Whereas the other dive operations concentrate on sites west of Virgin Gorda, Kilbrides emphasizes diving to the east, thereby exploring sites few others see. They do dive the Rhone twice a week, however, and the Chikuzen.

The Kilbrides are the only family in the world with three generations of dive instructors right now. They have been among the pioneers of BVI diving and remain on the frontier by expanding their service, promoting the islands, and continuing to explore new sites.

Caribbean Live-Aboards

Belize Live-Aboard Dive Boats

Isla Mia 75'

c/o See & Sea Travel
50 Francisco Street, Suite 205
San Francisco, CA 94133
(415) 771-0077
(800) 348-9778

On a Saturday evening, the Isla Mia will take 8 to 16 divers to Lighthouse Reef for one week of diving.

La Strega 85'

Hugh Parkey
P.O. Box 673
Belize City, Belize, C.A.
011-501-3108

U.S. contact:
Poseidon Venture Tours
359 San Miguel Drive
Newport Beach, CA 92660
(714) 744-5373
(800) 854-9334

"La Strega carries divers to the Turneffe Islands, Lighthouse Reef and Glover's Reef."

Princess 40'

Princess Charters
P.O. Box 521
Belize City, Belize, C.A.
011-501-45841

U.S. contact:
Princess Charters
16730 El Camino Real
Houston, TX 77062
(713) 486-6993
(800) 331-2458

Belize Barrier Reef and coral atolls.

Sail Belize/Dive Belize

P.O. Box 997
Belize City, Belize, C.A.
011-501-45798

U.S. contact:
P.O. Box 9182
Treasure Island, FL 33740
(800) 237-3483
(813) 367-1592

Ventana 52'
Oagny 52'

Tropical Adventures
170 Denny Way
Seattle, WA 98109
(800) 247-3483
(206) 441-3483

These two boats will bring you unlimited diving along the Belize Barrier Reef.

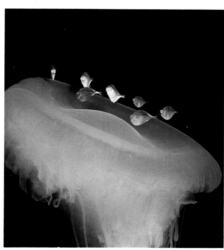

Wes Wright

British Virgin Islands Live-Aboard Dive Boats

Lammer Law 95'

Trimaran
P.O. Box 362
Roadtown
Tortola, B.V.I.
809-49-41490
800-648-3393
800-448-8866

U.S. contact:
Yacht Charters International
1686 Union St., Suite 302
San Francisco, CA 94123
(415) 775-2266

Enjoy diving in the B.V.I. off the "larges trimaran in the world," the Lammer Law.

Tropic Bird

Easy Adventures
The Anchorage
Estate Nazareth
St. Thomas, U.S.V.I. 00802
(800) 524-2027
(800) 526-1394

Throughout the British Virgin Islands.

Bay Islands Live-Aboard Dive Boats

Reef Runner

CoCo View Resort
P.O. Box 877
San Antonio, FL 34266
(800) 282-8932
FL-(904) 588-4131

Anchored at CoCo View Resort, the Reef Runner will explore all the great diving of Honduras Bay Islands.

CSY Dive/Sail

5936 Benjamin Road
Tampa, FL 33614
(800) 237-1131
(813) 886-6783
NJ or Canada (201) 568-0390

Based in Roatan CSY, Caribbean Sailing Yachts' Dive/Sail offers "a custom-designed, uninterrupted diving vacation all along the 35-mile reef along Roatan's south coast."

Cayman Islands Live-Aboard Dive Boats

Cayman Aggressor 90'
Cayman Aggressor II 100'

c/o See & Sea Travel
50 Francisco St., Suite 205
San Francisco, CA 94133
1-(800) 348-9778
1-(415) 771-0077

Either one of these modern cruisers will take 13 to 16 divers to Little Cayman and the North and South Wall for a week of unlimited diving.

M/S Ports of Call 112'

U.S. contacts:
Tropical Adventures
170 Denny Way
Seattle, WA 98109
(800) 247-3483
(206) 441-3483

Prospect Promotions, Ltd.
7322 SW Freeway
Suite 850
Houston, TX 77074
(713) 541-0915

Based on Cayman Brac, this live-aboard will take up to 20 divers diving off Little Cayman.

U.S. Virgin Islands Live-Aboard Dive Boats

Tropic Bird
Ovasion 60'
Tri-World 55'

Easy Adventures
The Anchorage
Estate Nazareth
St. Thomas, U.S.V.I. 00802
(809) 775-7870
(800) 524-2027

USVI. & BVI

My Way 60'
Ocean Pearl II 61'

Virgin Island Water Safaris
(Div. of Regency Intl. Yacht Charters)
Yacht Haven Marina, Long Bay Road
St. Thomas, U.S.V.I. 00802
(809) 774-5950
(800) 524-7676

My Way & Ocean Pearl II are just 2 of the many boats offered by Virgin Island Water Safaris that take you diving around St. Thomas.

V.I. Scuba/Sail Charters

P.O. Box 10966
St. Thomas, U.S.V.I. 00801
(809) 776-2860
(800) 524-2005

''Their boats vary in length from 40 to 80 feet and sleep 2 to 12 guests.'' They offer unlimited diving in the USVI.

Susan Speck

Caribbean Invertebrates

Steve Rosenberg

Gallery of Caribbean Coral Reef Invertebrates

By George S. Lewbel, Ph.D.

The marine life on coral reefs is similar throughout the Caribbean. Though there are important local differences, most of the beasts are cosmopolitan. In fact, reefs all over the world have much in common. Most groups of coral reef animals have worldwide warm-water distributions, although individual species in the Caribbean are not frequently found in the Indo-Pacific or the Red Sea, and vice versa. However, if you recognize the animals in the Caribbean and then dive coral reefs elsewhere you will see the faces have changed a bit, but they are familiar.

There are about one million identified invertebrate species and probably several times that number await discovery. On coral reefs most organisms which are not fish are invertebrates, though many invertebrates are mistaken by divers for plants or rocks. Some invertebrates move around and are obviously animals. Others are attached to the reef and do not move, so plants cannot be told from animals simply by their mobility or lack thereof.

Now let's begin a tour through the major coral reef invertebrate plyla.

Sponges (Phylum Porifera)

Sponges are permanently attached animals belonging to the phylum Porifera, meaning "hole-bearing." Some common sponges are large and conspicuous, such as the hard, gray barrel sponge *Xestospongia muta*, the bright yellow-green candle sponge *Verongia fistularis*, and the bluish-pink fluorescent sponge *Callyspongia plicifera*. They are found on reefs all over the Caribbean. Other less visible, but even more abundant, are the boring sponges,

147

various species of the genus *Cliona*. They live in cracks and holes in coral. Boring sponges dissolve the calcium carbonate skeleton of corals, eventually eroding coral heads from the inside and causing them to crumble.

Sponges are filter-feeders, pumping seawater through tiny pores all over their outsides. The water travels through internal canals to microscopic chambers where O_2 and fine particles of food are removed, and CO_2 and metabolic wastes such as ammonia are dumped. The water is then pumped back outside. In large sponges, the water exits from the central cavity. If you dribble a few sand grains into that cavity, you will often see them suspended by the current of waste water. In small sponges, the water exits from a number of smaller holes. Sponges are extraordinarily efficient filters, removing particles below 1/25,000 inch in size. They can pump very large volumes of water, given enough time. For example, an average-sized sponge can filter 400 gallons of water in 24 hours!

Sponges are reinforced internally by protein fibers and spicules, usually made of crystallized silicon compounds. Therein lies the rub. Have you ever patted a fuzzy-looking cactus, only to discover some spines too small to see individually? Many species of sponges have microscopic spicules that can easily penetrate your skin or stick in your wetsuit and gloves. You will find them when you unsuit and touch bare skin. Also, some chemicals secreted by sponges are highly irritating to humans. Several species of sponges cause severe dermatitis. For instance, one dark brown, large sponge is called *Neofibularia nolitangere*. Its species name means ''do-not-touch-me'' in Latin, a subtle hint from the biologist who named it. *Tedania ignis*, the red fire sponge is also aptly named. Ignis is Latin for fire. Sponges are difficult even for experts to identify, and the safe ones can look a lot like the nasty ones.

If you do touch sponges, don't even think of touching spicule-bearing gloves or hands to any important part of your body. If you get spicules in your skin they will cause mild to severe itching and dermatitis. Some people try to remove them with sticky tape, but scraping them off on a sharp edge seems to do as much or as little good. Others advocate rinsing with vinegar, mild ammonia, or meat tenderizer. Once in a while these remedies seem to reduce chemical irritation. You usually have to live with the spicules until they drop out after a couple of days, just as those little cactus spines do. In most cases, the problem goes away after a while. Cortisone cream often helps. If the itching gets worse, see a doctor.

Anemones, Corals and their relatives (Phylum Cnidaria)

Anemones, corals, gorgonians, and jellyfish are all in the phylum Cnidaria, the name derived from the Greek *cnidos*, or thread. All cnidarians have thread-like microscopic structures in their tissues. These structures include tangling, adhesive loops that snare prey, and hollow hypodermic tubes that pump stinging, toxic chemicals into animals that touch them. The stinging threads are called nematocysts, and are fired upon physical contact. Most nematocysts are harmless to humans, but there are a few exceptions such as those described below.

Cnidarians have soft, hollow, bodies with a centrally located mouth surrounded by tentacles. Most of the nematocysts are on the tentacles. Cnidarians are radically symmetrical, like the spokes of a wagon wheel. Whatever they capture with their nematocysts is inserted by the tentacles into the mouth. The prey is then digested inside the hollow body, and nondigestible parts such as bones and shells are dumped back out at the mouth. Cnidarians also have nervous systems with sensors that respond to light, touch and taste. Some of them have pretty good eyes, too.

Anemones

Anemones have bodies shaped like cylinders. They are usually stuck to the reef, but they can and do occasionally move about. Most anemones have nematocysts that cannot penetrate the thick skin of the palms of your hands or your fingertips. When you touch them, they feel sticky because they've fired their nematocysts into—but not through—this thick skin.

The most conspicuous large anemone is the giant Caribbean anemone, *Condylactis gigantea*. It comes in a variety of colors, including purple, pink, green, and yellow, and has low-powered nematocysts that won't sting your fingers. It has fat tentacles with bulbous tips, and grows to a diameter of about a foot.

If you look closely in empty conch shells or at the base of coral heads, you will eventually see the ringed anemone, *Bartholomea annulata*, which has thin, pointed, clear tentacles ringed with white spiral bands. The bands bear the nematocysts. It will retract its tentacles rapidly if you touch them lightly. *Bartholomea annulata* almost always has one or two pistol shrimps living among its tentacles. If you try to touch one of them, they will loudly snap their claws and probably make you jump about a foot.

You may also see the Caribbean mist anemone, *Heteractis lucida*, an animal with thin transparent tentacles covered with tiny white balls that look like a cloud of mist. The balls are batteries of nematocysts. *Heteractic lucida* is as sensitive about being touched as *Bartholomea annulata* and will pull in if you disturb it. Photographers will want to keep their frames from touching either anemone until they're ready to shoot.

There are at least two large Caribbean anemones capable of stinging you vigorously. One is the sun anemone, *Stoichactic helianthis*. It has short, stubby tentacles all over its face, and gets up to a foot across. It is usually pale green or yellow and generally found in shallow water, near the shoreward side of reefs or in areas with freshwater runoff. The other is the stinging anemone, *Lebrunea danae*. It usually has soft, brown, highly branched tentacles which protrude from between coral heads and stick out of crevices. It looks like the fringe of a rug. See the section below on cnidarian stings for treatment recommendations if you get stung.

Though most anemones are solitary, there are some very interesting colonial anemones that live in sponges. Next time you see a sponge that appears to be covered with tiny white or yellow dots, take a closer look. See the tentacles? Each of those dots is a little zoanthid anemone, usually a *Parazoanthus parasiticus* or *Parazoanthus swiftii*. Chemical extracts of zoanthid anemones are poisonous to some species of fish, and the combination of sponge spicules and anemones is probably a difficult meal to digest! This may be one reason why you rarely see sponges with bites taken out of them.

Corals

Corals are colonies of interconnected animals similar in structure to anemones. Individual coral animals have mouths and tentacles with nematocysts and feed as anemones do. Within colonies, the individual corals are genetically identical, since members of each colony occasionally divide in half or bud off to produce new members on the edges of the colony.

Corals are dependent upon microscopic internal plants called *zooxanthellae*. These supply organic compounds and aid corals to crystallize calcium carbonate from which they make their hard skeletons. To learn to identify corals, take a waterproof copy of the Greenbergs' *Guide to Corals and Fishes of Florida, The Bahamas and The Caribbean*, or one of the waterproof plastic cards that show pictures of reef invertebrates, on your next dive.

There are about 65 species of corals on Caribbean reefs. In shallow water, the most common corals are often the staghorn (*Acropora cervicornis*) and elkhorn (*Acropora palmata*). Elkhorn are particularly good at withstanding and recovering from wave damage. Staghorn have one of the fastest growth rates among the corals, though it is still less than one foot per year. It can form huge thickets and usually grows in deeper water than does elkhorn.

Below the Acropora zone there is usually a mixture of corals. In relatively protected areas and on shallow patch reefs, various leaf and ribbon corals of the genus *Agaricia* often predominate. They are thin and somewhat fragile. Most of them prefer quiet waters. Their close relatives,

148

the plate corals, are even more fragile, and form big sheets in deeper water or under overhangs and in caverns.

Moving down the slope, most large reef complexes are dominated by the mountainous star coral, *Montastrea annularis,* and its relative *Montastrea cavernosa,* the cavernous star coral. The star corals are the main reef builders in most areas of the Caribbean. Both of these star corals can form huge mounds or heads in shallower depths, or big flattened plates in deeper water. Buttresses are often formed by star corals and, as divers swim down along their faces, it can be seen how star corals change gradually from mounds to plates. This is an adaptation to changing environmental conditions. In deeper water corals do not need the thick structures to survive waves. Rather, they need more surface area to expose their internal plants to as much of the diminishing sunlight as possible. Some versatile species, such as the star corals, have a massive growth form for strength in shallow water and a platelike form for increased surface area in deeper, darker water. Other species are specialized for either shallow or deep water.

For example, the fast-growing staghorn coral can replace broken parts so rapidly that it does well in shallow water despite suffering occasional storm damage. In deep water, fragile species survive because they are rarely exposed to heavy weather. One can find huge, translucent colonies of lettuce and plate corals below 75 feet that are almost paper-thin yet over three feet wide. They face upward to collect the sun. Other thin, platelike forms flourish in protected spots under overhangs in shallow water, soaking up the rays despite low light levels.

Rounded, massive corals are abundant on Caribbean reefs. The most common are the giant brain coral *Colpopyllia natans,* and three species of the genus *Diploria:* the grooved brain coral, *Diploria Labryinthinformis,* the smooth brain coral, *Diploria strigosa,* and the knobby brain coral, *Diploria clivosa.* The rough and smooth starlet corals, *Siderastrea radians* and *Siderastrea siderea,* form basketball-sized round heads here and there. Brain and starlet corals grow very slowly, often less than an inch a year, but they are sturdy and their roundness gives them a tremendous resistance to wave shock. Some brain coral are well over a century old.

One of the showiest corals is the pillar coral, *Dendrogyra cylindricus.* These form spectacular white colonies up to ten feet high. Pillar corals usually have their tentacles out during the day, giving them a fuzzy appearance. If you touch them gently, they will retract in waves passing over the surface of the coral. This demonstrates that the individual coral animals in the colony communicate with one another through a nerve network. Bother one and all will pull in.

There are some interesting, less conspicuous corals on Caribbean reefs. The

Alan Davis

Margo Nelson

fungus or pizza corals, genus *Mycetophy-llia*, are easy to find. Their beautiful, brightly colored plates look like pizzas and grow on steep, deep surfaces.

In crevices divers sometimes spot something that looks like a glowing green donut or flying saucer. It is either *Scoloymia lacera* or *Scolymia cubensis*, the solitary disc corals. They have nematocysts which can zap their fellow corals and they specialize in dissolving their neighbors to clear space around them. They, too, are fluorescent. Their yellow-green color is due to absorbing blue light then re-emitting it at longer wavelengths.

In the sand channels between patch reefs you may come across *Manicina areolate*, the rose coral, a free-living coral which can crawl. It starts out life attached, but later breaks off and goes it alone. It looks like a brownish mouth resting on the sand and can be up to six inches long. You may see the skeletons of dead ones, too. These look like smiling white mouths, grinning up at you from the sand.

Most corals have nematocysts, but they are too short to penetrate human skin. However, if you bang into corals, their skeletons will cut you and the cuts often infect, especially if you stay wet. For shallow cuts and abrasions, clean the scrape with soap and water. Follow this with a mild antiseptic such as hydrogen peroxide. Cover the wound with Neosporin ointment and a bandage. Get a doctor to clean any deep cuts, and keep your tetanus shots current.

Fire Coral and Stinging Hydroids

Fire coral will become familiar to you after a few Caribbean dives. There are at least three common species of it there: *Millepora squarrosa*, *Millepora alcicornis*, and *Millepora complanata*. Fire coral can grow as flat sheets or boxlike formations. It can encrust gorgonians, coral heads and even concrete surfaces. Strictly speaking, it isn't coral. It is more closely related to the Portuguese man-of-war, but it will get your attention, however you

classify it. Fire coral has nematocysts which cause immediate stinging, and can produce dermatitis on sensitive skin. If you do not touch anything that looks like dull tan paint, you will avoid most fire coral.

Closely related to fire coral are the stinging hydroids, a group of similar species that form lacy, black fan-like colonies. Stinging hydroids usually grow under overhangs and in caverns. They have high-powered nematocysts with a sting sometimes described as "electric."

If you do brush against fire coral or stinging hydroids, and if the affected spots do not stop stinging in a few minutes, follow the same advice given below on how to treat cnidarian stings.

Gorgonians and Black Coral

Gorgonians include sea fans, sea rods and sea fingers. Their drying skeletons frequently stink up people's suitcases on the way to their mantles. They, too, are colonial cnidarians. The Caribbean is one of the world's best spots for gorgonians and nurtures more than 55 species.

Gorgonians have flexible skeletons made of protein and calcium carbonate spicules. Some species have internal plants, as do corals. The more spicules, and the more closely fused to one another, the harder the skeleton. In other parts of the world, species with hard skeletons are harvested, sliced, polished and sold as jewelry. Red coral from the Mediterranean, for example, is a gorgonian skeleton.

Sometimes Caribbean gorgonians are passed off as black corals. Black corals are colonial cnidarians not closely related to gorgonians, but very similar in appearance. Many Caribbean governments have banned the collection of black corals, which are very scarce where not protected. Gorgonians and black coral grow very slowly. If you take or break a colony, years, if not decades, of growth is destroyed.

Jellyfish and Portuguese Men-of-War

Jellyfish are cnidarians that swim through the water. Jellyfish have hollow bodies with a single, central mouth facing downward. Their nematocysts are borne on tentacles and mouthparts that hang down from the main part of the body. The body pulsates rhythmically to propel the jellyfish through the water in search of fish and plankton. There are about 200 species of jellyfish in the world. Most of them live in cooler waters, but there are many tropical species. Jellyfish are also called medusae, due to the similarities between their dangling, stinging, venomous tentacles, and the mythological monster named Medusa, who had poisonous snakes on her head instead of hair.

Despite their blobby appearance, jellyfish are more complicated than they look. At the base of their tentacles are gravity receptors to keep them right-side-up, and light detectors. Sea wasps even have eyes with corneas, lenses and complex retinas, which can probably form pretty detailed images.

The most common large jellyfish seen above coral reefs is the moon jelly, *Aurita aurita*. It is usually a foot or two in diameter with small tentacles around the rim and a large, dangling set of mouthparts. It is a slow swimmer and fairly easy to avoid. Simply stay away from the bell and you will not bump its stinging, transparent tentacles.

Sea wasps are small, clear jellyfish which swim near the surface at night. They spend the day in very deep water and are of no danger to divers then. Sea wasps have squarish, transparent bodies, are usually from two to six inches long, and trail one or more tentacles from each lower corner of the body. The nematocysts on those tentacles can cause severe reactions, including local tissue destruction, extreme pain and even respiratory difficulties.

When diving at night, be aware of sea wasps, but do not be intimidated by them. Remember, thousands of dives are logged all over the Caribbean every night without anyone's getting stung. Furthermore, a little knowledge can greatly reduce your chances of getting stung. Here are some techniques which can keep you sting-free.

First, ask local divers where and when sea wasps are most abundant. Even if you get the OK, don't assume that there aren't sea wasps present. Look before you leap. Scan the surface carefully before jumping off a boat or pier. When you ascend, look up before you come up. Sea wasps are most often sighted in the upper six feet of water. It is a good idea to avoid snorkeling on the surface at night, and to stay well below the surface during your dive. Wear full wetsuits and gloves at night in the Caribbean, and keep your eyes open. Sea wasps can swim as fast as 20 feet per minute and may be attracted to lights. If you spot one with your light and it swims toward you, point your light elsewhere and get moving.

There is some good news about Caribbean sea wasps: they are worse somewhere else! Most Caribbean sea wasps are members of the genus *Carybdea,* and are mild-mannered compared to *Chironex fleckeri,* not found in the Caribbean. *Chironex fleckeri,* an Australian species, is jam-packed with a neurotoxin that could stop a clock. It has caused dozens of known fatalities. Most deaths occur from total respiratory arrest within several minutes after a person is stung.

Portuguese Man-of-War

The Portuguese man-of-war (*Physalia* species) is not a true jellyfish, being related more closely to fire corals and stinging hydroids. The man-of-war has a gas-filled sac that floats on the surface. The float is up to eight inches long, and has a little sail which causes the man-of-war to travel with the wind. There are even right- and left-handed men-of-war; the angle of the sail causes some to move consistently about 45° to the right side of the direction of the wind, and others to the left. Every man-of-war has long, trailing tentacles hanging below it. These tentacles are covered with nematocysts that are capable of catching fish, and you know that anything that can stop a fish cold in its tracks can penetrate human skin. The floats will tip you off to the danger. If you see them, stay well clear; the tentacles can be many yards long.

How to Treat Cnidarian Stings

Small stings such as those from fire coral usually just hurt for an hour or so and go away on their own. Some divers claim that meat tenderizer can detoxify the venom and reduce the pain. Some get relief from cortisone cream on mild stings, but severe stings may require a shot from the doctor. If you get stung by a jellyfish or man-of-war, bits of tenacle will probably stick to your skin. Some of the nematocysts in these tentacles will have already fired, while others are still waiting their turn. If possible, try to avoid firing the nematocysts that haven't yet been triggered adhering to your skin. If you can lift the tentacles off gently and carefully with gloves, you will minimize the damage. Do not try to rub the tentacles off with sand; you will fire everything that is left on and into your skin.

Some biologists claim that alcohol can prevent nematocysts from firing, and the Australians keep big barrels of the stuff on their beaches to pour over sea wasps victims. However, some recent evidence indicates that alcohol may cause unfired nematocysts to fire! If you get badly stung by any cnidarian, you may need medical assistance, especially if you are prone to allergic reactions. If you are subject to severe allergic reactions from animal venom such as insect stings, it might be wise to skip night-diving in the tropics.

Corallimorpharians

Corallimorpharians are small but astonishingly sensual cnidarians overlooked by most divers, but beloved by a few and common as dirt. They are sometimes called false corals, an injustice to both the corallimorpharians and the corals. Closely related to both corals and anemones, the most abundant species (*Ricordea florida* and *Rhodactis sanctihomae*) look like mashed or flattened greenish-brown anemones two to three inches across and only ¼ to ½ inches high. They often grow in colonies, forming sheets on vertical surfaces. You will see a tiny nipple-like mouth in the center of each individual, and tiny bumps or tentacles on its "face." Be sure to stroke one gently with a bare fingertip. They are smooth, slippery and indescribably nice to feel! A less common corallimorpharian is known as the orange-balled anemone. Seen only at night, it is highly sensitive and retracts quickly if you shine a light on it. It looks like a small transparent column up to about six inches long and one inch in diameter. Its tentacles are transparent, and have fluorescent orange balls on their tips!

Segmented Worms (Phylum Annelida)

Non-divers often roll their eyes when told of the beauty of marine worms. That's because they have not seen them, and would not recognize them if they had. The worms most divers see on Caribbean coral reefs are feather duster worms, Christmas tree worms, and fire worms. These animals have long, segmented bodies divided into sections like a train. They are much more complicated in structure than the cnidarians. The worms have longitudinal nerve cords, circulatory systems with blood, primitive kidneys, muscles and intestines. With a mouth at one end and an anus at the other, marine worms are unlike cnidarians which have but one opening to eat and excrete through.

Feather Dusters

Feather dusters, *Sabellastarte magnifica,* live in a soft, membranous tube. They never leave their tube. Their spectacular, fluffy brown and white plumes grow up to four inches across. Their plumes are combined respiratory and feeding structures. The worms pump blood through their plumes which take up oxygen and release CO_2, and catch plankton and tiny food particles from the water. If you startle feather dusters, they will pull back into their tubes faster than the eye can follow. Both the Christmas tree worm and the feather duster worm have light-sensitive eyes just below the plumes. The mere shadow of a diver's hand is enough to make them retract rapidly.

Christmas Tree Worms

Christmas tree worms, *Spirobranchus giganteus,* live in a hard tube of calcium carbonate. These worms come in a variety of colors, including white, yellow, brown, and red. Their two spiraled plumes are for feeding and respiration. Christmas tree worms can plug the opening to their tubes when disturbed. After they pull in their plumes they fill the holes with hatch covers attached to the outermost part of their body. These covers are the purple and white structures you can see between the spirals.

Fire Worms

The fire worm, *Hermodice carunculata,* looks like a red and white centipede and should be treated with similar respect. Along its side are thousands of tiny white

Ted Nizialek

bristles. When the fire worm is disturbed, it flares them out in a threat display. If you ignore the threat and touch a fire worm, these bristles will be embedded in your skin, producing immediate pain and irritation. Treatment is similar to that for sponge spicules.

Fire worms are tough customers. They eat living corals and breed in huge piles, pouring clouds of eggs and sperm into the water around them.

Sea Stars, Urchins and Their Relatives (Phylum Echinodermata)

The word "echinoderm" means spiny skin. The echinoderms include sea stars and sea urchins. As are the cnidarians, echinoderms are radially symmetrical. Most of them have five similar sections radiating out from their centers, like the segments of an orange. Echinoderms have hard internal parts made primarily of calcium carbonate. In echinoderms such as sea cucumbers, these pieces are not connected to one another, allowing the animals a great deal of flexibility. In other groups such as the urchins, the pieces are fused together for strength, forming a rigid sphere that sometimes is

reincarnated in shell shops as a night light.

Perhaps the most striking anatomical feature of the echinoderms is their hydraulic system. Many of them, such as sea stars and urchins, have tiny tubular feet between their spines. These tube feet can be extended by changes in water pressure within them. The animal takes water in through a filtering screen and pumps it through internal channels to wherever it is needed for locomotion. The hydraulic system supplements the muscles. It is used by urchins to rotate their spines, by cucumbers to pull back into their holes, and by brittle stars to move their legs.

Reticulated Sea Stars

The most common sea stars in the Caribbean are reticulated sea stars, *Oreaster reticulatus*. They usually have five arms, but sometimes have as many as seven or as few as four. They range in color from red to green, though orange ones are most often seen. They get up to a foot wide and six inches high. Reticulated sea stars are stiff bodied and covered with a fine net-like pattern. Once abundant in shallow grassy areas, they are probably now more often seen in shell shops for sale. Look for them when you swim offshore en route to the reefs, and please resist the temptation to take "just one." They produce an incredibly bad smell when drying, and you and your luggage will be sorry if you bring one home. You will probably have to burn your clothes.

Caribbean Sand Stars

If you look in the sand, you may also see the Caribbean sand star, *Astropecten duplicatus*. The sand star has five long, pointed arms and a set of square plates along the outer edges of each arm. It is usually about the size of your hand.

Sea Urchins

There are many kinds of sea urchins in the Caribbean. Urchins have a tarnished reputation because some can cause immense pain with their spines, but most cannot puncture human skin. For example, *Eucidaris tribuloides*, the pencil urchin, has thick, blunt spines frequently used for wind chimes and jewelry. *Tripneustes ventricosus*, the West Indian sea egg, has a black body and very short white spines, and can be touched barehanded. Its eggs are often eaten by islanders. Another harmless urchin is the sea pussy, *Meoma ventricosa*. Sea pussies are fat, reddish-brown urchins about the size and shape of flattened grapefruits. They have five radial grooves on their tops, and stiff little spines all over their bodies. They are usually seen on the sand by night divers. They hide just under the

sand during the day, but emerge to graze at night. You can safely pick them up to look at them.

On the other end of the urchin spectrum is the long-spined sea urchin, *Diadema antillarum*. This is the animal feared most by Caribbean divers. Some divers feel that *Diadema* was put here just to remind them not to bang into coral reefs! It comes in basic black, as well as white, and black-and-white varieties, and gets as large as a basketball in some places. *Diadema antillarum* rests quietly during the day under ledges and in holes, and comes out at night to graze.

There is evidence that these urchins are essential to the health of coral reefs, by grazing away microscopic organisms that would otherwise overgrow living corals. The long-spined sea urchin has good light sensors, and can detect fish or divers swimming overhead. When it does this, it swings its spines into position, pointing directly at the possible threat. This response is not just to keep divers from bothering it. *Diadema antillarum* has other enemies, such as triggerfish and Spanish hogfish, that try to turn it over so the spines are not in the way, then eat it.

Diadema antillarum has spines sharper than needles. They will penetrate a wetsuit as easily as a knife will go through butter. Even if you touch them lightly, you'll probably get stuck. Don't be tempted to test your new gloves. They won't stop these spines which have even poked through leather welding gloves! If you do get stuck, expect some immediate pain. The spines are back-barbed. They usually break off in the wound and are virtually impossible to dig out.

Some people advocate urinating on the wound or soaking it in vinegar to dissolve the spine. Others suggest pounding the tissue around the spine to break it into tiny bits, while others just leave it alone. The spine—or its crushed products—will eventually dissolve in the body and/or fester and be rejected, but it takes a couple of weeks or more.

Urchins are another good reason to have a current tetanus shot before you dive. If you are prone to allergic reactions, or if the wound is deep, you should visit a doctor. There is a mild toxin on the spines that seems to cause much of the local pain. Little can be done to disinfect urchin punctures, but Neosporin or other similar products may help.

Brittle Stars and Basket Stars

Brittle stars and basket stars are echinoderms that have long, skinny arms which catch particles drifting in the water. Brittle stars are often seen on the outside of sponge, looking like spiders. They take advantage of the feeding currents that the sponges produce (see above). One of the most common, *Ophiothrix suensonii*, the sponge brittle star, is usually draped all over purple vase sponges. It has a small, soft disc in its center, and five very thin, hairy-looking arms that wriggle around if you touch them.

Basket stars have five arms also, but they are highly branched, making them look like huge birds' nests. The Caribbean basket star, *Astrophyton muricatum*, gets up to three feet in diameter when fully expanded at night. During the day, they are often found tightly wrapped around gorgonian branches in balls the size of your fist. At night, they expand into the current to catch their prey. They can capture small fish, shrimp as well as plankton. If you touch them gently (do it only once, please!) when they are expanded, they feel sticky and will writhe and wriggle their arms. Lights will also make them contract into a ball.

Crinoids

Crinoids or feather stars are often seen but not always recognized by divers in the Caribbean. Those fluffy-looking, long orange branches that stick out of cracks in reefs and are curled like a fiddle head at the tip are the arms of the orange crinoid, *Nemaster rubignosa*. The arms feel sticky because they are used to catch plankton. The black-and-white crinoid, *Nemaster grandis*, actually crawls around. It can be seen perched on top of sponges and coral heads, looking like a stiff bouquet of black feathers with white tips, almost a foot high.

Crustaceans (Phylum Arthropoda)

On the basis of sheer numbers and diversity, the arthropods are the most successful group of animals ever to have evolved on earth. There are 750,000 arthropod species, about three times as many as there are of all the other animals put together. Most members of the phylum are insects, which are very poorly represented in the ocean. Nearly all of the arthropods which live in the ocean are crustaceans, a group with about 30,000 species. Crustaceans include groups such as barnacles, shrimps, crabs, and lobsters.

The crustaceans have jointed legs (arthropod means 'jointed foot'), a hard outer covering called an exoskeleton that is periodically shed, and complex nervous, digestive, circulatory, reproductive and excretory systems. They reproduce sexually, and many of them have internal fertilization followed by external broodings of eggs. Crabs and lobsters "in berry" are females carrying fertilized eggs on the outside of their body. Their eyes are excellent, as any diver who has tried to sneak up on a lobster during the day knows. Crustaceans are about as complicated in structure as invertebrates get. There are hundreds of species of crustaceans associated with coral reefs, but the largest and tastiest ones usually are of most interest to divers.

Reef Spider Crabs

The largest crab you will find is the reef spider crab, *Mithrax spinosissimus*. This reddish-brown, fuzzy crab has long legs and a body that can get almost as large as a volleyball. You won't see it in the daytime except in caves and under overhangs. It is usually out at night looking for plants to eat. It cannot be mistaken for any other crab on Caribbean reefs; it is similar in shape, and is closely related, to Alaskan king crabs.

Coral Crabs

Another common large crab out mainly at night is the coral crab, *Carpilius corallinus*. It has a bright red, smooth body with fine lines and spots on top. The tips of its claws are darker red, or sometimes purple.

Arrow Crabs

Arrow crabs, *Stenorhynchus seticornis*, have probably been in more underwater photographs than any other marine organism. Arrow crabs look like big spiders. They have spindly legs up to about four inches long and little bodies the size of a dime with a long, spear-like rostrum that sticks out on the head between two beady stalked eyes. Arrow crabs are tan with brown and white stripes, and there are two little purple claws on the front legs. Divers most often see them on sponges, but they are so common that if you are on a reef, you are probably within ten feet of an arrow crab.

Cleaner Shrimps

Cleaner shrimps are crustaceans that live on or near other, larger animals, and make their living picking up scraps or eating parasites. There are many species of cleaner shrimps associated with anemones, for example. They use the protection offered by the anemones against larger predators, and are immune themselves to the anemones' nematocysts. They clean parasites from fish that stop nearby. Other cleaners—usually less than an inch long—include *Periclimenes pedersoni*, Pederson's cleaning shrimp, which is transparent with purple and white stripes, and often found on anemones; and *Lysmata grabhami*, the redbacked cleaning shrimp, which is clear with a wide red band down its back and a thin white stripe down the middle of the band. Both species will try to clean your hand if you hold it still near them.

The largest cleaner is the red-banded coral shrimp, *Stenopus hispidus*, which looks like a mini-lobster. It has long claws and a red-and-white banded body. Its very long, white antennae will tip you off to its presence in crevices, and it can be induced to come out and pick at your fingernails if you have enough patience.

Pistol Shrimps

The pistol shrimps, which are also called snapping shrimps, are usually heard but not seen. They are generally less than an inch long, and hide deep in holes or beneath anemones. If you pause momentarily between inhalation and exhalation while near the bottom of a coral reef in calm seas, you may hear a series of little snaps or pops. These sounds are generated by members of the genus *Alpheus*, the pistol shrimps. They make the snap by cocking one tiny claw like the hammer on a pistol, then holding it in place with an internal locking mechanism while muscles that normally close the claw are tightened. When the muscles are maximally contracted, the shrimp releases the lock and the claw slams shut. It's such a powerful snap that it can stun small fishes that the shrimps then eat! More than one diver poking an anemone has been startled by this snap, too.

Red Coral Shrimps

If out at night over a coral reef, you will see thousands of glowing red eyes reflecting the light of your flashlight back at you. These eyes belong to red coral shrimps, *Rhynchocinetes rigens*. They are up to four inches long and are out only at night. Once in a while you can spot them in crevices during the day, but even at night they are very easily disturbed and hard to get near enough to photograph.

Slipper Lobsters

Cousins to spiny lobsters, slipper lobsters look like a cross between a squashed bulldog and a lobster. There are a number of Caribbean species of slipper lobsters; most are members of the genus *Scyllarides*. They have no claws or long antennae, and are flattened. They get up to a foot long, but most are smaller. Like the spiny lobsters, they hide during the day and feed at night. If you find something that's not quite a crab or a lobster, and is tan or brown, it's probably a slipper lobster.

Spiny Lobsters

There are two different species of spiny lobsters on Caribbean reefs: the common spiny lobster, *Panulirus argus*, and the spotted spiny lobster, *Panulirus guttatus*. They are easy to tell apart: the common spiny lobster has a light tan or orange body with light-colored spots on it. Both of them spend their days nestled under coral heads and in caves, and come out at night. Neither has claws, but the long antennae, body, and tail are covered with sharp spines to protect them against predators, and the two sharp "horns" above the eyes can draw blood from a careless diver. They can also make a startling noise that sounds like rubbing a violin string with rosin; the noise is made by scraping their antennae against ridges on their exoskeletons.

Spiny lobsters are probably the single most desirable food sought by divers. If you take lobsters, be sure you know the local game laws and the local politics with respect to commercial lobster fishermen. If lobsters are in season where you are diving, there is probably a minimum size limit on them and a maximum bag limit, and most likely a prohibition against taking females carrying eggs. Even if there isn't, it is bad sport to take small lobsters or females in berry. Many Caribbean areas prescribe the gear that may be used to take lobsters, too. A number of islands do not permit taking of lobsters with scuba, or with any tools other than your hands.

Molluscs (Phylum Mollusca)

Molluscs are complex organisms and share some features with the arthropods. They have circulatory systems with a heart, a nerve cord and good eyes, a gut with mouth at one end and anus at the other, and a file-like structure in the gut called the radula that grinds their food. Some molluscs, such as squids and octopuses, have eyes that rival our own in their ability to resolve images. The octopuses in particular have fine wiring; they can be trained, and their brains are capable of abstract problem solving and learning to recognize geometric shapes.

Most of the molluscs in coral reefs are hidden from view. The majority of them are clams, tucked deep into holes they have bored in coral skeletons, or down in the sand. The few molluscs that are often seen are some of the most spectacular representatives of the phylum, fortunately. Coral reefs are good places for divers to spot squid and octopus, and the sandflats near reefs are usually inhabited by conchs and other large snails.

Molluscs are very popular with divers who collect shells. The essence of collecting is that collectors should, ideally, not be able to collect everything in their field of interest—there should always be that one additional item needed to complete the collection. Mother Nature has been kind to shell collectors; there are over 100,000 species of living molluscs known, and most of these have shells. Recently, this has worked to the detriment of some beautiful species. When shell collectors were limited to whatever washed up on beaches, their impact on marine life was minimal. However, since divers can easily get at many previously rare shells, some species have been driven nearly to extinction in a few decades. Even if local regulations permit you to take living shells, please consider bringing home a photograph instead, and leave the animal alive and well on the bottom.

Chitons

Everyone who dives from ironshore will wonder sooner or later what those inch-long oval depressions are next to the water, and what those little creatures that look like pill bugs in each depression might be. They are chitons, creatures which have been on Earth for about 600 million years. They are among the most primitive of molluscs. Chitons have eight overlapping calcium carbonate plates on their backs, making them look a bit like pill bugs, and a fuzzy band around their outer edges. On the West Coast, plates from chitons were used as wampum by North American Indians.

Those depressions are exactly the right size for their inhabitants because chitons customize the rock a bit at a time, leaving their spots at high tide to graze, and returning to nestle down into the same location. Over a period of years, they grow and gradually enlarge their depressions.

It is a mystery as to how each chiton finds its way back to its own depression after feeding. Some biologists have theorized that the bits of iron-containing minerals that chitons have in their radulas allow them to sense the earth's magnetic field. If this is true, a chiton's radula is an internal compass which directs the chiton home.

Marine Snails

Conchs are large snails that crawl slowly along in sandy areas, especially in seagrass beds. Their shells often grace gift shops and their muscular feet often grace restaurant platters. The conch taken most often for food, and the one that divers in the Caribbean are most likely to see, is the queen conch, *Strombus gigas*, which has a whitish-pink shell that is bright pink on the bottom, and grows up to a foot long.

Flamingo Tongues

The flamingo tongue, *Cyphoma gibbosum*, is a small snail almost always seen up on gorgonian stalks. It is a yellowish blob up to an inch long with dark colored spots. If disturbed, it slowly retracts its spotted mantle, revealing a smooth pink shell. Flamingo tongues feed on gorgonians, eating their living tissues and leaving bare patches on their hosts.

Nudibranchs

Nudibranchs are closely related to snails, but have no shell. They carry their gills exposed on their backs—hence the name "nudibranch," which means "naked gill." Despite their apparent vulnerability to predators due to the lack of any hard protection, nudibranchs are rarely bothered by other marine animals. The reason for this is that nudibranchs seem to be highly repulsive or poisonous to many animals that might otherwise eat them. In fact, a number of nudibranchs actually eat cnidarians, but somehow keep their nematocysts from firing during the digestive process. These unfired nematocysts are then transferred by the nudibranchs to their gills, where they pro-

Steve Rosenberg

154

Susan Speck

vide additional protection. Cold-water divers probably know that many nudibranchs are brightly colored. Biologists call this "warning coloration," which tells a predator he is dealing with a nasty "don't-bite-me" nudibranch.

There are several common nudibranchs on Caribbean coral reefs, but the one that is easiest to find is the lettuce slug, *Tridachia crispata*. The lettuce slug is usually about two inches long, pale green or blue, and has fluffy white gills all over its back. It looks like a garden slug on its way to a wedding. Next time you're near shore at the end of the dive, look around the staghorn coral, where they are most abundant.

Squids

The only squid that divers are likely to see on Caribbean coral reefs is the reef squid, *Sepioteuthis sepioidea*. It is a small squid, generally less than a foot long, with a fat little body and ten short arms. They are commonly found swimming in groups of three or four, changing colors rapidly from white to green to brown.

You have a better chance of getting a close-up photograph by skin-diving rather than using scuba. They seem to be spooked by bubbles. Don't bother to try to sneak up on them. Their eyes are probably just as good as yours. Just swim slowly along and edge near them. If you try to rush them, you may get close for a

kick or two, but they will sometimes pump out a burst of ink and jet away.

Octopuses

Octopuses are the undercover camouflage champions of the reef. They crawl along the bottom, changing their colors and patterns to match their surroundings. They can go from near black to white and back as fast as you can blink, and can reproduce the appearance of cobbles, sand and almost anything they are near. They are active predators, seeking out fish, lobsters, crabs, and other large prey at night, and hiding during the day. When they catch something with their eight sucker-bearing arms, they can bite it with a beak that lies in the center of the arms on the underside. The most common octopus that divers see is *Octopus briareus*, the reef octopus. You are most likely to see them at night.

The beak of an octopus can inject venom. If you choose to handle octopuses, avoid the mouth area. Caribbean species don't often bite humans, and their bite is not especially dangerous (if compared to the blue-ringed octopus of Australia, which can inject enough neurotoxin to be deadly to humans), but it can cause a severe infection. A bite will probably ruin your dive trip, not to mention your hand, nose or whatever it gets.

The invertebrates of the Caribbean add to the fascination of the underwater

world. As a diver you may find the more you learn of that world, the more enjoyable it will become for you and the more at home you will feel in it. But remember—the undersea is not separate from your world, it is another part of it. Through learning and exploring it you may begin to feel the way many veteran divers feel—that they and the sea are parts of one another, too.

Sources

This article uses common and scientific names from several published sources: Idaz and Jerry Greenberg's *Guide to Corals and Fishes of Florida, The Bahamas and the Caribbean* (Seahawk Press); Charles C.G. Chaplin's *Fishwatchers Guide to West Atlantic Coral Reefs* (Harrowwood Books); F. Joseph Stoke's *Handguide to the Coral Reef Fishes of the Caribbean* (Lippincott and Crowell); Patrick L. Colin's *Caribbean Reef Invertebrates and Plants* (T.F.H. Publications); Eugene H. Kaplan's *A Field Guide to Coral Reefs of the Caribbean and Florida* (Peterson Field Guides, Houghton Mifflin); and Norman A. Meinkoth's *Field Guide to North American Seashore Creatures* (The Audubon Society, Alfred A. Knopf).

Scientific names were included as a way to help you identify the common names and give them more meaning. Scientific names are easy to learn and much more useful if you get more into coral reef literature.

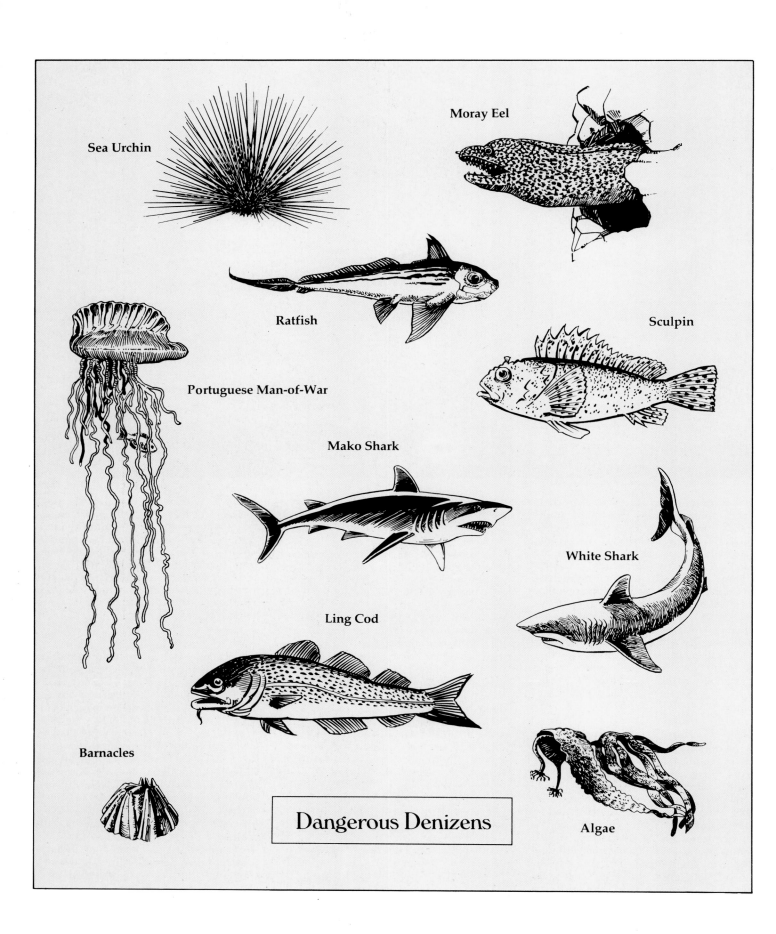

Sea Urchin

Moray Eel

Ratfish

Sculpin

Portuguese Man-of-War

Mako Shark

White Shark

Ling Cod

Barnacles

Dangerous Denizens

Algae

Wreck Diving

Stan Strauss

Anyone who has ever discovered a wreck has experienced the intoxicating call of adventure. Countless shipwrecks lie like sleeping historical witnesses waiting to be awoken by the curious and adventuresome. There are no limits to the wealth of history and actual treasure which are yet to be discovered in even the most famous shipwrecks. Divers often explore these vessels for the sheer pleasure of beholding the colorful underwater creatures inhabiting them.

The excitement experienced by the wreck diver should be tempered with an awareness of the potential danger involved. Building one's skills upon a few simple rules will help keep this sport a safe and enjoyable one.

Diving That Wreck

You're skimming over the bottom at 60 feet, turning the corner of a rocky outcropping as you explore, when suddenly you notice something unusual jutting up from the ocean floor. A little digging reveals a bit of brass, and you begin searching the area. Your adrenaline pumps as you anticipate the realization of the diver's foremost fantasy: finding an undiscovered wreck.

Whether you dive for the sheer pleasure of underwater tranquility, to capture underwater life with camera, speargun or hand, every diver, at some time or another, has dreamed of finding the treasure of a sunken ship that plied the waters centuries ago.

Most divers find joy in exploring known wrecks and bringing back some souvenir of their visit. Such casual salvage is rarely contested and offers many fun-filled hours of underwater pleasure, if proper precautions are taken.

As exciting as it is, wreck diving can be dangerous. Rusting metal hulks and disintegrating wooden galleons are constantly decomposing beneath the water, and the mere presence of a diver may accelerate the process. The *unwary* diver might just meet the fate of the ship's crew. The first rule of wreck diving is obvious: never go alone.

Diving a known wreck offers the advantage of careful preparation. Take extra tanks; experienced wreck divers use two sets of doubles and a pony tank. It allows you more time to explore and provides a back-up system in the case of trouble. Also, when the excitement of a good find has you using air more rapidly, or pushing your bottom time to the limit, the extra air can be a lifesaver. A decompression meter and decompression line are essential, since wreck diving necessarily involves a lot of bottom time. Buddy divers should each wear meters and compare readings, using the more conservative meter in the case of any discrepancy. A light is also a necessity, both for exploring and keeping in touch with your partner. Many wrecks have dark holes and overhangs that can't be explored safely without a light, and it will be helpful in investigating points of interest. A knife is also essential, and a second knife is advised. Entanglements on wrecks are more common than not; a calm, well-prepared approach will keep them from getting you in serious trouble. Finally, carry a spool of line to mark your exit should you decide to explore inside the ship's carcass.

Many experienced wreck divers carry a tool kit, both for safety and to help them explore. Lines with floats for making objects you wish to return to, hammers, an adjustable wrench, and a small file are among the items in these kits.

Once you've found something you want to take to the surface, you'll have additional needs. If it's small and you can carry it, all well and good. Heavier, bulkier items need lift bags. Attached to your find-end-down, the bag is given air from a separate tank (using your mouthpiece can be dangerous) and the bag lifts the item to the surface.

Stay clear of your find if accompanying it to the surface with lift bags, and don't put more air in the bag than necessary to get moving toward the surface, as it will accelerate as it goes up.

The final question for wreck divers is, "Who owns the find?" A good rule of thumb is to figure the more valuable the find, the more touchy the legalities. Small souvenir hunting on known wrecks is usually a finders-keepers situation, but if you're lucky enough to discover an unknown wreck, you'll have to stake your claim and do some research to learn who has jurisdiction, what claims exist, and what your rewards might be. All of that becomes easier, however, if you decide to take on the challenge of a known wreck that has never before been subjected to salvage. Pre-salvage contracts are the best approach in this case.

Once you discover the joy of wreck diving, it can be addictive. Whether your first find is a small brass plate from a recent wreck or the ship's bell from a centuries-old galleon, the thrill of finding and recovering the legacy of the sea is something you'll want to repeat.

Wreck Dive Safety

A. All basic safety rules applying to ordinary sport diving should be followed, including the buddy system. You and your partner should be familiar with each other and rehearse emergency ascents and other vital procedures in advance.

B. Remember to ascend with a good supply of air remaining, keeping in mind that more active diving necessitates more air. Bottom time should be adjusted accordingly to compensate for increased air usage.

C. Be cautious when entering a wreck, checking for stability and making certain it will not cave it. Examine the structure as you would check handholds for security when mountain climbing. Special caution is called for when exploring rotting timber shipwrecks. Include in your equipment two reliable lights and a return line to guide you out of the wreck should your lighting fail.

D. When diving a wreck, don't attempt to carry more than you are able to comfortably. Be certain your flotation device can easily support your "treasures." Remember that you are endangering those divers below you if your load is not secure in your ascent. The usual procedure in wreck diving is to gather all items into one area and then take them up in your "lift" sack.

Caribbean Shipwrecks

by Ellsworth Boyd

"Serendipity" was coined by Horace Walpole from a Persian tale about the mythical island of Serendip where the heroes "were always making discoveries . . . of things they were not in quest of."

That's the way it is when you're shipwreck-diving in the Caribbean, one of the few places in the world where a diver might be looking for one wreck and accidentally discover another! Thousands of wrecks are scattered throughout the Caribbean, lots of them charted, but many yet to be discovered. The best part is that most Caribbean shipwrecks are in warm, clear, shallow waters with tropical fish.

Another heap of serendipity for shipwreck buffs is the wealth of history gleaned from Caribbean wrecks: galleons, gun-runners, frigates, schooners, freighters, sloops and a host of others spanning four centuries. No one dares estimate the number of wrecks off the 700 islands and cays of the Bahamas, but many divers agree that one of the most interesting lies only a half-mile from Paradise Island, Nassau.

The **CANDACE**, a magnificent 200-foot steam yacht built in 1881 for a prominent English playboy, was sold several years later to the British Royal Navy. Renamed **FIREQUEEN**, she put some "steam" into the fleet as the flagship for the admiral commanding Portsmouth. She was proud and elegant, the reigning belle of the Portsmouth fleet until 1919 when **FIREQUEEN** was struck from the admiralty list.

Altered, but not stripped of her beautifully proportioned bell-shaped funnel, she arrived in Nassau in 1920 with a new name: **FIREBIRD**, and a new job: lighthouse tender. Seven years later she was sold to a local merchant who named her **BAHAMIAN**, and put the once-stately ship into routine cargo service between Nassau and the United States. In 1934 she was condemned and scuttled on the reef off Paradise Island.

The **CANDACE**, alias **FIREBIRD**, **FIREQUEEN**, and **BAHAMIAN**, is scattered over the bottom in 30 to 40 feet, inhabited by lobsters, groupers and tropical fish, all milling around like shoppers in a bargain basement. When a Hollywood movie company was searching for a suitable reef to film an underwater scene for the James Bond thriller, "Thunderball," they stumbled on the old wreck . . . more serendipity! Her rotund boilers, rising from the sand like oil-storage terminals, formed a perfect backdrop for the conclusion of "Thunderball" where the good guys do in the bad guys.

Many other movies and television shows have been filmed on her over the years and she stars today—in the hearts of divers and historians who have had the good fortune to make her acquaintance.

The United States Navy Underwater Photo Team and hundreds of sport divers are well acquainted with the wreck of an LCM—a Navy medium landing craft—sunk intact off the northeast shore of Andros Island. The 80-foot-long coral-covered craft sits upright on the reef and provides a convenient catwalk where divers sit to feed pet groupers and snappers. Photographers perch on the stern and shoot diagonally into the pilot house or hover over the wreck, securing the entire panorama: wreck, reef and fish—all in one serendipitous portrait.

A little further north of the LCM lies the remains of the 100-foot square-rigged schooner, **CUTTYSARK**, wrecked in a hurricane in 1960. Running rum and whiskey illegally from Cuba to Nassau, the captain lost his bearings and ran his ship into a sand bank. If he had waited, the tide would have risen and washed the schooner over the reef, but it was nighttime and he abandoned ship. No lives were lost, but the vessel eventually crashed into the reef and all the booze washed ashore. The natives had the biggest party (glorious serendipity) in the history of the island. The **CUTTYSARK** is spread all over the sand and reef, ten to 15 feet deep. A variable pitch bronze propellor, about three feet across, and part of the cabin are interesting remains. The wreck is only a quarter-of-a-mile from shore where part of the wooden deck is washed up on the beach.

Southeast of Bimini, near Gun Cay, is a phenomenon called **SAPONA**, a shipwreck divers find fascinating because she is made from cement! Built and launched in Wilmington, North Carolina in 1919, she was one of 12 ships poured from concrete in order to save on steel. She saw valiant service during World War I, hauling cargo from Florida to Virginia, but her cement hull began to crack prematurely. In 1922, an eccentric entrepreneur named Carl Fisher bought the vessel and towed it to Fisher's Island in Miami where he used it as a warehouse. When it started to list, Fisher sold it to a famous one-armed character from Miami named Bruce Bethel.

Bethel had **SAPONA** towed to Bimini and grounded offshore where he planned to convert her into an international night club. But the hurricane of 1926 ended his plans when the ship took a savage beating. She was only good for a turtle kraal in the late 20s, but a convenient hiding place for booze during the rum-running days of prohibition. During World War II she was used as target practice for aerial gunners.

Resting in only 20 feet of clear seas, the **SAPONA**'s bow and midship stand erect while her stern is broken free and lists sharply. Above the surface, gaping holes reveal rusting steel reinforcing rods and chipped cement. But below the surface thousands of marine tropicals glide through cargo hatches and over the coral-covered engine and boilers. Sponges, hydroids and tunicates cling to cables, ladders and debris in the engine room and main cargo hold. Beneath the boilers, a 50-pound grouper peers out, then disappears in the darkness where other critters also make their home.

Spanish Wells on St. George's Cay, just off the northern tip of Eleuthera, was a fresh water haven for Spanish vessels exploring the New World. It is also the last resting place for the **ARIMORA**, a 260-foot Lebanese freighter that ran aground in 1971. Three-fourths of the rusting hulk sits above water, affording a leeward side for diving in windy weather. Angelfish, parrotfish, snapper, barracuda and thousands of small tropicals call the **ARIMORA** home. Only 25 feet deep, the waters abound with anemones, arrowcrabs, urchins, banded coral shrimp and many other exciting macro photography subjects.

Eleuthera is also the site of the famous Train Wreck on Devil's Backbone, North Coast. A ship transporting a steam engine in the mid-1850s foundered on the

160

reef, leaving one of the strangest underwater sights in the Bahamas. Three sets of locomotive wheels and axles, plus three carriages lie in 15 feet in the sand, surrounded by coral ridges which lie at the surface at low tide. Divemasters feed pet fish while divers ogle the remains of a Philadephia-built train that became an underwater express.

The Underwater Explorers Society (UNEXSO) at Freeport, Grand Bahama Island, features a dive on **THEO'S WRECK**, a 230-foot steel cargo ship sunk in 100 feet, 30 minutes from shore. Christened **M/V LOGNA**, the vessel was built in Norway in 1954 and transported various cargoes between Spain and Norway for 15 years. The Bahama Cement Company purchased her in 1969, renamed the ship **M/V ISLAND CEMENT**, and used her to transport sand, gravel and cement throughout the Bahamas. Time took its toll on the ship and when the company decided to scuttle her, marine engineer Theo Galanoupoulos, suggested she be used as a dive site.

The sinking took four hours. The vessel settled on the port side, her stern resting near the ledge of a 5,000-foot drop-off. Divers perch on the prop or rudder and gaze into deep blue infinity, attesting to one of the most ecstatic experiences in wreck-diving. The cement ship wasn't supposed to sink that close to the drop-off, but wrecks have a way of bestowing serendipity, even as a scuttling.

Great Abaco—near Treasure Cay—is a haven for the remnants of a Civil War gunboat, the **SAN JACINTO**, the Union vessel that ran aground in 1865 while stalking a Confederate blockade runner. The prop, boilers, crankshaft and parts of the deck of the steelhulled steamer remain. Strewn in 20 to 50 feet of water, the wreck is overrun by coral and tropical fish.

South of Treasure Cay, near Marsh Harbor, Great Abaco, lies the **USS ADIRONDACK**, a 200-foot steam sloop. Another Union gunboat that ran aground—this one in 1862—leaves a historic legacy on the bottom, only 20 feet deep. Two Dahlgren cannons, each 15 feet long, cast with an 11-inch bore—the largest guns mounted on a warship of that era—are grim reminders of hostilities between the North and the South over 100 years ago.

The ABC islands—Aruba, Bonaire and Curacao—offer shipwrecks as part of their Caribbean dive packages. A wreck in Bonaire, **LA MACHACA**, sunk a stone's throw from the dock at Captain Don's Habitat Hotel, is not only legendary, but "immortal," according to divemaster Dave Serlin. A fishing vessel, turned upside down, **LA MACHACA** rests on a slope 35 feet deep. The wreck is home for two friendly margates and a tiger grouper whose mouth and body are constantly manicured by a school of gobies.

Sometime in the 1920s the small, speedy **LA MACHACA** slipped out of a Brazilian port at midnight carrying an illegal cargo of large Spanish flies. The captain was transporting the flies to Trinidad where they would be sold as an aphrodisiac. But a Brazilian gunboat intercepted **LA MACHACA** and riddled it with machine-gun bullets whose holes are still visible on the sunken craft. The vessel escaped the Brazilian military, but a combination of heavy seas and bullet

161

damage forced her into the harbor of what is now Habitat, where she sank.

The southwest coast of Bonaire has a new wreck, the **HILMA HOOKER**, a 236-foot freighter resting on her starboard side in 90 feet. The port rail is at 50 feet and the wreck can be reached by boat or from shore. A Columbian ship carrying 25 tons of marijuana, she docked at Bonaire for repairs, was discovered carrying narcotics, and confiscated by the Netherland Antilles government. Due to bulkhead and decking leaks, she was scuttled and now rests in a narrow sand channel between two beautiful reefs.

Aruba claims the **ANTILLA**, a 400-foot German freighter scuttled by her captain in 1940 when Dutch marines surrounded the vessel at dockside. Built in 1939, the **ANTILLA** was brand new when the captain set fire to her and opened the seacocks before abandoning ship. The Dutch towed her to the northeast coast where she sank in 50 feet. Part of the ship protrudes from the surface at low tide.

The stern section of the **PEDERNALES**, an American oil tanker torpedoed by the Germans in 1942, is one mile south of the **ANTILLA** and approximately one mile offshore. The ship was attacked off the south coast of Aruba but towed by the marines to the northeast coast where she was used for target practice.

Curacao's dramatic shipwreck is outside the mouth of Willemstad Harbor and St. Anna Bay. The 200-foot **SUPERIOR PRODUCER**, sunk in a storm in 1977, sits upright on a sandy bottom in 100 feet. The hull is intact and the mast rises to within 25 feet of the surface. Black coral grows from the hull. Its hatches, crew's quarters and companionways are open for exploration. Very careful scrutiny might uncover a souvenir from the **SUPERIOR PRODUCER'S** Christmas cargo of perfume, rum, leather goods and assorted trinkets.

Fort-de-France, Martinique, French West Indies—"a little bit of Paris in the Caribbean"—offers the chic big-city life you would expect in a capital city with a population of 100,000. But a one-hour drive to Carbet—on the northwest shore—generates a South Seas setting with tropical palms and white sand beaches. Here, divers from the Latitude Hotel host small groups for a dive into history.

St. Pierre, a few miles north of Carbet, is the oldest city in Martinique and nicknamed the Pompeii of the French West Indies. In 1902, the 4,656-foot Mt. Pelee erupted, killing over 29,000 residents in less than five minutes. Fourteen ships anchored in the harbor fell victim to the fiery mountain. Eleven of them rest 60 to 160 feet deep, some only 600 yards from the wharf.

In St. Pierre, Martinique, lies **GABRIELLE**, strewn with human bones, telltale evidence of the fury and devastation of Mt. Pelee. **RORAIMA**, a 300-foot Canadian cargo vessel sits upright in the sand. Looking like a phantom ship underway, it is scorched from three days of burning before sinking. A museum on the hillside houses many charred momentos of that tragic day and is well worth a visit.

Barbados is home for the **STAVRONIKITA**, a 350-foot Greek freighter saved from the scrap metal pile in 1978. That is when she was sunk by the U.S. Navy after sport divers had talked the government of Barbados into purchasing the burned hulk for an artificial reef. A prime dive site, she is a quarter of a mile off the western shore. The ship is upright, her stern at 130 feet and bow at 120. Her hull rises 50 feet from the sea floor and one of her two masts comes to within 20 feet of the surface.

The most popular wreck off St. Thomas in the U.S. Virgin Islands is the **CAR-**

TANSER SENIOR, a 140-foot freighter scuttled in 40 feet in the protective cove at Little Buck Island. Her hull is split in two, the forward section resting against the reef. Photographers have captured her engine room, railings, deck, winches, hatches and doorways. She remains a "senior" subject for underwater shutterbugs who shoot her daily.

Bolongo Bay is off the south shore of St. Thomas where Packet Rock—a submerged rock ledge is the site of an early 1800 wreck. The **WARRICK** was carrying china and tile and divers still find broken bits and pieces in the sand.

The **MAJOR GENERAL ROGERS**—a 120-foot steel-hulled Coast Guard vessel was sunk as an artificial reef between Thatch Cay and the north shore of St. Thomas. It is 45 feet deep to the deck and 70 feet to the sand bottom. Grunts and snappers swarm on the stern while sponges and hydroids cover the prop. The hull is overgrown with feather duster worms, tunicates and small clusters of star coral.

Off Kyona Beach, a little north of Port-Au-Prince, Haiti is a small group of islands called the Arcadines. Not far from these islands is an unnamed steamship that sank 25 years ago. Partially intact in shallow water, her anchor, ship's wheel and brass fittings are spread over the reef. Closer to Kyona is the "Cannon Site" where several cannons were found, but there is no trace of a wreck. The cannons could have been tossed overboard during a storm to lighten the load aboard ship.

Cap Haitien, 150 miles north of Port-Au-Prince, is haven for the **TROLLA**, a 300-foot Norwegian freighter sunk in the harbor in the early 60s. Its bronze prop and superstructure lend an aura of mystery to the massive hulk that lures divers to the north coast. The harbor contains the remains of the **BULLDOG**, a Haitian vessel that went down in 1865 during a

battle with the British. Somewhere in the vicinity of the **SANTA MARIA**, Columbus' flagship ran aground and was wrecked in 1492. This area is one of the most historically significant ocean realms in the Caribbean.

Grand Cayman divers revel over two wrecks: the **BALBOA** and the **ORO VERDE**. The **BALBOA**, resting in 35 feet of water in Georgetown Harbor, is a 375-foot freighter that went down during a hurricane in 1932. The boiler, propellor and two vertical steel girders nicknamed, "Roman Columns," are popular photographic subjects. Schools of sergeant majors wait to be fed on the **BALBOA** while soldierfish, morays and margates hide in the shadows beneath twisted wreckage. The freighter is a popular night-dive, too. Octopus, basket stars and other nocturnal creatures appear when darkness calls. Closer to shore, not far from the **BALBOA**, is the **CALI**, a 200-foot freighter—a nice snorkeling site only 10 to 20 feet deep.

The **ORO VERDE**, a Panamanian cargo ship confiscated while smuggling drugs, was sunk in 1980 about 400 yards off Seven Mile Beach. Grand Cayman divers bought her salvage rights and put the vessel down as an added underwater attraction. She is 180 feet long, intact and tipped to her port side in 50 feet. **ORO VERDE** translates to "Green Gold" in Spanish and she now offers divers a multi-colored gold mine of marine life in crystal clear seas.

Roatan offers some of the best diving in the Bay Islands of Honduras. At Anthony's Key Resort, on the northwest coast of Roatan, divers go to the **GWENDOLYN**, a 200-foot Honduran minesweeper that smashed into the reef in 1955. She sank in a channel not far from the resort in what is called "The Cut." Because of The Cut's location, where changing tides disperse plankton and silt, the visibility is limited to 20 feet. This is quite a contrast to the rest of the reefs where visibility averages 100 feet. **GWENDOLYN** rests upside-down at 120 feet, with gears, pipes, chains and twisted metal covering her bow and stern. This is not one of the resorts' regular dives, but the resort will take divers-upon-request on a tour of the ghostly looking **GWENDOLYN.**

"Ghostly" is the way to describe many shipwrecks, whether they rest in the Caribbean or other seas of the world. Resurrecting the ghosts of bygone days through exploration and underwater photography remains a favorite pastime of shipwreck aficionados. They keep encountering new things on old wrecks while blazing watery trails to new wreck sites. Horace Walpole would have loved it. He might have found a way of marooning all wreck-divers on the mythical isle of Serendip—which of course would be in the Caribbean—where unforeseen discoveries are commonplace.

Tourist Board Numbers/Addresses

Jamaica

Jamaica Tourist Board
New Kingston Office Complex
P.O. Box 284
Kingston, Jamaica
Tel. 92 9 80 70

Jamaica Tourist Board Office
1320 South Dixie Highway
Suite 1100
Coral Gables, Miami, Florida 33146
Tel: (305) 665-0557

Netherland Antilles

Aruba Toeristenbureau
A. Schuttestraat 2
Oranjestad, Aruba
Tel. 2 37 77

Aruba Tourist Bureau
399 NE 15th Street
Miami, Florida 33132
Tel. (305) 358-6360

Puerto Rico

Puerto Rico Tourism Company
Old San Juan Station
Box 3072
San Juan, Puerto Rico 00903
Tel. (809) 7 24 71 71

Puerto Rico Tourism Company
1290 Avenue of the Americas
New York, NY 10019
Tel. (212) 541-6630

Turks & Caicos Islands

Turks and Caicos Tourist Board
Cockburn Town, Grand Turk
Turks and Caicos Islands, B.W.I.
Tel. 23 21

Turks and Caicos Tourist Board
P.O. Box 592617
Miami, FL 33159
Tel. (305) 592-6183

U.S. Virgin Islands

U.S. Virgin Islands Division of Tourism
P.O. Box 1692
Charlotte Amalie, V.I. 00801
St. Thomas, USVI
Tel. (809) 7 74 13 31

Tourist Office
7270 N.W. 12 Street
Suite 620
Miami, Florida 33126
Tel. (304) 591-2070

Bay Islands (Honduras)

Honduras Information Service
501 Fifth Avenue
Suite 1611
New York, N.Y. 10017
Tel. (212) 490-0766
Tel. (212) 683-2136

Cozumel, Mexico

Infotur (Travel Agency)
5th Avenue
San Miguel
Tel: 21451

Mexican Government Tourism Offices
100 N. Biscayne Blvd.
Suite 2804
Miami, Florida 33132
Tel: (305) 371-8037

Bahamas

Ministry of Tourism,
Nassau Court
P.O. Box N 3220
Nassau, Bahamas
Tel. (809) 3 22 75 05

Bahamas Tourist Offices/Southern Area
Miami Sales Region
255 Alhambra Circle
Coral Gables, Florida 33134
Tel. (305) 442-4860

Belize

The Belize Tourist Board
P.O. Box 325
12 Regent Street
Belize City, Belize, C.A.
Tel. 02-7213

U.S. Tourist Office
Belize Embassy
Washington, D.C.
Tel: 1-800-368-5909

British Virgin Islands

B.V.I. Tourist Board
Box 134
Road Town, Tortola
British Virgin Islands
Tel: (809) 494-3134/3489

B.V.I. Tourist Board
370 Lexington Avenue
Suite 412
New York, N.Y. 10017
Tel: (212) 696-0400

Cayman Islands

Cayman Islands Department of Tourism
Government Building
P.O. Box 67
George Town, Grand Cayman
Tel: 9 48 44

Tourist Office
250 Catalonia Avenue
Suite 604
Coral Gables, Florida 33134
Tel: (305) 444-6551

UPON A CALM NIGHT

If you've only dived by day, you're in for a magical experience . . .

Imagine . . . a calm, gentle night with the full moon riding high in the dark, star studded sky. The motion of the sea barely rocks the boat as you and your buddy finish checking out each other's equipment. He steps to the side of the boat . . . and launches himself into the black water below. As he makes contact with the water a luminous cloud erupts around him, creating a minor milky way. Descending, he appears ghostly in a bluish-green aura which fans out behind him in a widening contrail. You smile, put your mask down, your regulator in your mouth . . . test . . . breathe deeply . . . and plunge after him into the magical kingdom of the night-time underwater world. As you descend you glance up to see the bright friendly orb of the full moon glistening on the surface, lighting your ascending bubbles and giving them life. You are free . . . .

This light from the sea may seem magical, yet many marine animals have the power to generate light chemically — by a process called biolumin-escence — without heat. The disturbance of the water excites the animals and causes them to emit light. Jellyfish are one variety of zooplankton which is particularly light-productive. Startled, small crustaceans will give off luminous clouds. Many squid and deep-sea shrimp emit a haze of luminous ink when threatened, in order to confuse the enemy. The night sea, for those who are willing to venture and look, offers the experience of *many* life times.

Night diving does require more skill than daytime dives and training is a must and highly recom-mended. Once you're ready for that first openwater ocean night dive, pick your spot carefully. No cur-rents, rips, surf or other swift water conditions. A calm full-moon night is best. Use a beach with easy entry or dive from a well-anchored boat that is tended. Avoid deep dives, caves, wrecks and other underwater obstructions.

If you go from the shore you should leave a light burning at your point of departure . . . *two* in-line will allow you to return to the exact spot with precision. Both lights should be amber, since many marine navigational aids are white, red or green.

When diving off a boat it's a good idea to have lights on the boat and a light *underwater* on the anchor chain . . . low watts are fine and won't interfere with your night vision.

If you wish for security, use a buddy line 6 to 8 feet long with loops at both ends. A note of caution here, though — the use of a buddy line at night can be hazardous.

Most divers choose the free approach of being highly visible by the use of a PML, or Personal Marker Light — a chemical light at-tached to the snorkel or regulator valve so as to be visible when you're on the surface. These lights come in a twelve-hour variety — three hours useful-work-bright and nine hours marker-only-bright. There is a high-intensity PML which is 3 to 4 times brighter than the general purpose, but lasts only for a short time.

As to the basic night diving equipment, it's the same as day plus a good diving light, a compass and a PML. It's a good idea to insure your knife is with you, and you should carry a plastic whistle attached to your BC . . . just in case you can't be seen from the boat. Pick your light carefully. Rechargeable lights are cheaper and brighter but tend to not burn as long as disposable dry cells. Make sure you use fresh batteries or your rechargeable

---

is fully charged . . . with enough juice to keep your light going for a while on the surface. Back-up lights should be brought along as a precautionary measure.

Once your turn-on to this new underwater experience you may want to improve the ability of a tender to see you by attach-ing a highly reflective material — called SOLAS Grade Sheeting — to your wetsuit, hood, tank, snorkel or boat. This material has been coast guard tested and is said to be easily visible from a helicopter at 1,500 feet, compared to 40 feet for an unmarked object.

As to the dangers at night, they really aren't too different from those during the day, although a close call can more readily create panic in the novice night diver. Don't let your body settle down on sea urchin spines. Shine your light into any holes you plan to stick your arm or body into. Eels may be swimming freely at night and should not bother you unless you box them into a crevice. Be careful of rays laying in depres-sions on the bottom; swimming over them too close may flush them out. Again, use your light to see what's in your path.

The main things to remember:

1. Dive at night where you've been in the daytime. Know the area well. Plan your dive; dive your plan.
2. Know your light signals: Circle pattern, all ok. Rapid up and down pattern, help.
3. Don't shine your light in your buddy's face. Your eyes take awhile to become accustomed to the dark. Turn off your light and you'll be amazed at how well you will be able to still make things out. You might try wearing dark or red sunglasses prior to a dive . . . just like pilots do.
4. It's good practice to follow the anchor chain to the bottom, stop and check all equipment, buddy up, then head out. Keep your compass bearing in mind and write on your slate.
5. As with any dive, avoid alcohol prior to the dive.
6. Avoid greasy or heavy foods.
7. Since it will still be dark and possibly cooler when you finish your dive, don't forget to bring along warm clothes.
8. If you get lost and separated from your buddy —
   a. Turn off your light — look for his PML.
   b. Surface and wait.
   c. Make sure your PML is visible.
   d. Scan the surface periodically with your main light — blow your whistle — don't panic.

Again, just imagine . . . a still, quiet, full moon night. You've seen more colors than ever, caressed sleeping fish, watched the characters of the deep out for a stroll and a bite to eat, each of them, just like humans, doing things at night they never do in the day . . . and you follow your bubbles . . . up . . . up . . . to that big friendly moon shimmering just above the surface. What a good night!

Navigating at night:

- **Use compass.**
- **Watch depth–the farther out from shore, the deeper it is.**
- **Sand bottom ripples run parallel to shore.**
- **The moon is up, and so go your bubbles.**
- **The sounds from the boat will be louder the closer you get.**
- **Use lights on shore and boat.**
- **Best of all – know the area.**

BOAT DIVING

A reputable boat will have a boat dive master or, on a smaller craft, require someone in your group to serve in that capacity. The boat dive master should be a Certified Advanced Diver, preferably the most experienced aboard. He should not participate in the dive and should only enter the water if necessitated by an emergency. His job is to coordinate the dive, both with the divers and with the skipper and crew of the vessel, to see to the safety of the divers, and to keep things going smoothly so that the purpose of diving, fun and a good time is realized. The dive master should be completely familiar with the dive site and brief the divers before entering the water. He will draw up the teams, keep the logs, check certification, licenses and oversee legal matters such as waivers, and catch limits.

Once you've found an acceptable craft and dive master, there are certain courtesies and rules of etiquette to boat diving that you should observe to make it a pleasant experience for all involved.

Be prepared and be on time. Once out of port you may find yourself paying for a dive trip and unable to dive through your own forgetfulness. Use a checklist to make sure you have all your equipment, that your tank is full, and that your gear is all in order. Be sure to carry your certification card and a current fishing license if you plan to take game. And don't forget money to pay for the charter, to cover refilling your tank, galley fees, etc. Also, mark your equipment. This not only helps you, the other divers and the crew to prevent mix-ups, but it can be an aid in identifying you in the water.

Plan to arrive at least a half-hour before departure, and sign the boat roster as soon as you're on board. Then check in with the dive master and follow his instructions for those of a designated crew member in stowing your gear. Most dive boats have racks for tanks and weight belts; use them. A classic no-no is the unthinking diver who drops his heavy tank or weight belt on the deck. This is second only to the problem of people putting their gear in a convenient corner. Stowing your gear in an organized manner at the designated place not only helps you keep better track of it, but keeps it from interfering with others' enjoyment. If carrying a speargun, remember that loaded spearguns are not allowed on or near a boat, and tips should be covered to prevent accidental injury to yourself or others.

Enroute to the dive site you'll have a chance to get to know your fellow divers, the ship and the crew. You should also get a briefing from the dive master or skipper on the dive site and prevailing conditions. Many dive boats will require you to sign a waiver, a legal document that should be treated seriously. If you've determined that you've chartered an acceptable craft with trained personnel, the waiver should cause you no reservations. It is your statement that you are aware of the risks of diving and will not hold the charter operators liable for anything that goes wrong that is not caused by their negligence.

At the dive site, use caution when suiting up. Naturally, everyone is anxious to get in the water, but by using a buddy system to suit up and by being aware of others on deck with you, you can avoid embarrassing entanglements that could delay the dive. The buddy system is also recommended for checking your gear to be sure everything is in order, and a conscientious dive master will make a final check before you enter the water. Don't walk around the boat with your fins on; they should be put on just before you enter the water. Enter the water only when given the o.k. by the dive master or designated crew member. Once in the water, swim at least 20 feet from the craft before making any equipment adjustments.

Be sure you are familiar with signals that will be used between divers, between divers and the boat, and particularly the boat's underwater recall system. Common signals are a raised right arm to signal pick-up, and any erratic arm movements to indicate a problem.

If you are new to boat diving be sure to let the dive master know. Don't be embarrassed; everyone has a first time. It will alert him and the crew to watch for the problems that first-time boat divers can experience. For one thing, from shore you can gradually condition yourself to the depth; from the boat you are committed with no pre-conditioning once you jump. Relax, accustom yourself to your surroundings and make sure you're over the dive site described in the briefing. Vertigo can also be a problem, where you have lost association with the surface and have not yet reached bottom. Use your depth gauge to make sure you're descending and watch the bubbles from your regulator to make sure they are vertical. Finally, if you're doing a current dive, don't struggle against a current if you become disoriented. Remember your briefing and surface if you can't get your bearings.

To surface when boat diving you should always stop 10 feet below the surface and listen, then surface, make a 360-degree turn and signal for pick-up.

Divers are not usually picked-up according to a first-up system, but rather according to the current, with the most down-current diver being first. When waiting to be picked up, stay back from the craft, and never get underneath another diver going up the ladder or otherwise getting on board. Dropped equipment at this point can be quite hazardous.

Once back in the craft, stow your gear in the designated place(s) and put any game or souvenirs where told. Don't embarrass yourself or the crew by trying to bring aboard illegal game. Clean your fish only in a designated area and never throw waste overboard while other divers are still in the water.

Common dense dictates that no alcoholic beverages should be consumed prior to diving, and bringing illegal drugs of any kind on board puts you, the vessel and your fellow passengers in jeopardy.

After a dive, relaxing with a hot drink or taking a shower can contribute to decompression sickness and therefore should not be suggested. With the consideration of the few simple rules outlined here, boat diving will certainly be a most memorable experience.

Darren R. Douglass

Diving From a Small Boat

A small boat is probably the most common surface-support platform used by divers with scuba equipment. Configurations and types vary greatly and range from small inflatable boats to larger solid-hulled vessels. A boat used as a platform should:

• Provide a means for divers to enter and leave the water easily and safely.

• Be seaworthy and not loaded beyond the capacity recommended by the manufacturer for the expected water conditions.

• Be large enough to accommodate adequately all members of a dive party, the diver's life-support equipment, and any special equipment being used in support of the dive.

• Provide some shelter in cold or inclement weather for the dive party en route to the dive site and after they leave the water and are returning to shore.

• Be maintained properly and in good repair.

• Carry a diver's flag.

Small boats used to tend divers can be either anchored or un-anchored. When anchored, the boat should be positioned downstream of the site for easy access when divers surface, and a life-ring should be streamed off the stern. The operator in the boat should keep a constant watch on the diver's bubbles. When tending without an anchor, the operator should drop the divers off upstream of the site. The boat should then remain downstream of the site during operations. Drift-diving with a surface float provides an effective method for keeping the boat in position for pickup. It is best to mark the dive site with a buoy or float to help orient the operator to the location of the divers. During pickup, the boat operator should not approach the divers until the entire dive team is on the surface, except in planned or emergency situations. The operator should bring the boat alongside the dive party on a downwind or down-current site for pickup, and the dive tender should assist the divers aboard. In most cases, the boat's motor should be in idle during pickup, with the propellor in neutral.

Entering the Water

Entering the water can be accomplished safely from a small boat by several methods. Sitting on the gunwale and rolling into the water is considered best. The diver should sit on the gunwale facing the center of the boat with both feet inside and extend as much of the body as possible over the water while leaning forward to counterbalance. When ready to enter the diver should simply sit up, lean backward, and let the weight of the diving equipment carry him over the side. A second method of entry is the "step-in" method generally used when entering the water from a larger boat. The diver should step onto the gunwale, bend slightly forward at the waist, and step off into the water while holding the face mask firmly in place.

Also, any equipment that cannot be carried conveniently and safely should be secured to a piece of line, hung over the side, and retrieved after entry.

As a general rule, the diver should always enter the water slowly, using the method that will result in the least physical discomfort and disturbance to equipment. Each diver should determine the method best suited to various water conditions.

Exiting the Water

When exiting the water into a boat, there are two general rules to remember and follow. First, exiting begins while the diver is still submerged. While ascending, the diver should continually look up and around to ensure that the boat is not directly overhead and that he will not strike it when surfacing. Holding an arm over the head is a good practice. Exhaling on ascent will give a clear indication to the surface that the diver is ascending. Second, after surfacing the diver should not attempt to enter the boat wearing tanks or other heavy equipment. The diver should remove them and gain assistance from someone in the boat or from another diver in the water before climbing aboard.

Probably the most widely used method for returning to a small boat is via a diver's ladder. Ladders also provide a secure point for a diver to grasp while still in the water.

Another method of assisting a diver into a small boat is the use of a platformed rigged to the stern or side of the boat and suspended just below the surface of the water. A diver can swim onto the platform, sit securely while removing equipment, and then stand up and step safely into the boat.

WARNING DISPLAYS				
TYPE OF WARNING	DAYTIME SIGNALS	NIGHT SIGNALS	EQUIVALENT WIND SPEEDS	
			KNOTS	M.P.H.
SMALL CRAFT	▷	● ○	UP TO 11	UP TO 38
GALE	▷▷	○ ●	34 - 47	39 - 54
STORM	■	● ●	48 - 61	55 - 73
HURRICANE	■ ■	● ○ ●	64 OR GREATER	74 OR GREATER

Tips for Current Diving

1. Have a thorough understanding of tides and currents.
2. Plan your entry and exit points.
3. Enter and swim against the current for the first half of the dive and then return to your exit point with the current.
4. Study the topography using a hydrographic chart.
5. Seek advice of local divers.
6. When diving from a boat ensure a tender is left onboard.
7. A marker buoy or bright coloured gloves may assist in keeping contact with the divers.
8. Descend and ascend on the boat's anchor line.
9. Attach a line from the bow to stern and a floating line from the stern of the boat to assist divers descending and ascending.
10. Watch your bottom time.
11. Use a low volume mask and secure fins and hoses to avoid them being ripped off.
12. Diving in the currents at night is dangerous.
13. Always plan your dive and dive your plan.

EQUIPMENT

EQUIPMENT MAINTENANCE
A Pre-trip Checklist

MASKS: Check for cracks, or wear around the buckle, and treat with rubber preservative; buy spare; check for any loose screws; pack and wrap carefully.

SNORKEL: Check for cracked or broken keeper; buy spare; attach mouthpieces firmly; look for cracks or tears; test easy movement of parts; check for air flow, mark tip with fluorescent or reflective tape.

FINS: Check for splitting or cracking of strap and fins; buy spare; treat with preservative.

BUOYANCY COMPENSATOR: Inflate and check for leaks in the bladder; check all valves for operation or sticking; lubricate all moving parts; check the C_O2 cylinder and buy extra C_O2 cartridges; lubricate inflator mechanism; check Velcro to ensure stitches are OK; check entire BC and straps for wear; insure auto inflator mates properly and works.

WETSUIT: Check for wear, tears and split seams; seal seams, knees and other worn areas; check and lubricate zippers; buy extra neoprene cement; check hood, boots and gloves.

REGULATOR: Check for corrosion or discoloration (if found, have checked by qualified professional); check rubber parts for cracking or wear; attach to full tank and ensure proper functioning; check hose fittings; buy extra second stage attachment.

PRESSURE GAUGE: Check for water leakage or interior corrosion; check gauge for smooth needle movement; check gauge against another; check hose fittings; check console for wear.

DIVE KNIFE: Check for rust or corrosion; sharpen; lubricate with silicone grease; check ring and straps for cracking; buy extra ring and straps; treat with preservative.

DIVE LIGHT: Check for corrosion and good seals; replace batteries or charge; buy spare batteries and bulbs; check lanyard.

TANK: Check annually at shop for internal corrosion; check last hydrostatic date and do if needed; check valve for corrosion and smooth operation; turn off and submerge to check for leak; check O-ring and get spares; remove boot and look for external corrosion; check tank pressure. (Tanks must be empty to be boarded on airplanes.)

BACKPACK: Check for signs of wear, cracks, splits in pack, tank strap and body straps; check band bolts; check for missing parts; insure smooth operation of all buckles; lubricate moving parts.

MISCELLANEOUS: Pack spare parts for all equipment; check dive flag and float; check slate and pencil, compass, watch strap, speargun, goody bags; camera gear, etc.; update fish and game gauges.

ance should be done every *six months* or once a year, depending on how often and where you dive. Generally, a good internal cleaning (ultrasonic or acid dip), by an experienced regulator repair technician, costs only about $35, and will take care of 90% of the performance problems.

Always, Always, Always . . .

- mark each piece of equipment
- insure it under a household policy, having photographed it and recorded serial numbers, brand and identification marks, etc.

Never, Ever, Ever . . .

- use earplugs or goggles to dive under any circumstances. Earplugs make it impossible to equalize water pressure on both sides of the eardrum; the plugs could be forced into the outer ear canal, or an internal squeeze could result.
- There is no way of equalizing pressure inside goggles; at increasing depths, the goggles squeeze into the flesh, forcing out the eyes . . . .

And, we're talking pain.

Flags

North Americans have learned to respond to a red square, divided diagonally by a white bar, to mean "diver down," and legislative efforts to convert them to recognizing the international blue and white symbol have been disbanded recently.

Either flag should be displayed, stiffened on a float, and boaters should respond by keeping clear by at least 100 feet, and by slowing down. Divers should always surface within 50 feet of their flags.

Regulator Maintenance Diagnosis Tips

"What if . . . ?"

. . . You experience *hard breathing* with your regulator! Most likely saltwater has corroded it, and the internal moving parts, which have become encrusted and scaled, now stick or operate sluggishly.

Rust clogging of the first stage's sintered filter, or carbon dust clogging also create resistance to smooth airflow.

. . . Your regulator mouthpiece *leaks water!* No doubt the second stage exhalation valve has deteriorated, from chlorinated water, ozone or normal aging. If it slows, dirt, sand or dust particles may have irreversibly married or dented the high pressure valve seat in the first stage.

. . . Your *O-rings leak!* Buildup of salt corrosion inside the regulator, or from the lubricant drying out, can cause tiny cracks, tears or splits, which eventually will break the seal completely.

How can you prevent these things from happening? No amount of washing or careful use can prevent your regulator from getting out of tune. Routine mainten-

Susan Speck

How to Pack Dive Gear For Travel

For scuba gear, use a "whale-sized" dive bag. If you are packing for two, this can be a good idea, as a seventy-pound bag is less likely to appeal to thieves than two more easily lifted bags.

The fins go in first, to help protect the rest of the gear from beneath. Then the suits go in.

Take your own back packs and weight belts. Using your equipment on a trip means that you are better able to concentrate on getting good pictures instead of fiddling around with unfamiliar dive gear.

Protect your console gauges by putting them into booties and packing them in the center of the bag. The same goes for the regulators. Use a couple of good straps around the bag. If the zipper goes, the contents will stay in place.

Always carry your prescription masks with you.

Bill Holderman

Basic Maintenance

1. Rinse equipment in warm, rather than cold, water to help dissolve accumulated salt. Rinse the regulator's second stage under a stream of fresh water, allowing it to run freely through any open ports, but *do not push the purge button.*
2. Minimize exposure to the sun of neoprene rubber items, such as masks, snorkels and fins; also chlorine and ozone. Keep them away from paint, gas fumes and suntan lotions.
3. Use silicone spray sparingly, and never on regulators.
4. Store equipment at a constant temperature, away from smog and electric motors. For extended periods dry thoroughly and seal in plastic bags.
5. Care for rips, fraying, sticking valves, rust, etc. as they appear.
6. Have gear professionally checked, regularly. Never disassemble a regulator yourself.

Equipment Check List

Equipment Hardware Bag
- Regulator with pressure gauge– and extra second stage
- Depth gauge
- Compass
- Decompression meter
- Knife
- Light
- Repetitive dive tables
- Slate & pencil
- Thermometer
- Lights (chemical) PML

Suit and Accessory Bag
- Mask and snorkel
- Fins
- Gloves
- Boots
- Hood
- Wetsuit jacket
- Wetsuit pants
- Drysuit
- B.C.
- Dive flag and float
- Gear line
- First-aid kit

Carry-On Equipment
- Weight belt & weights
- Tank
- Backpack

Repair Equipment
- Mask straps
- Fin straps
- O-rings

- Batteries
- Bulbs
- Neoprene cement
- Zipper wax
- Silicone spray
- CO_2 cartridges
- Electric tape
- Knife scabbard strap
- Low pressure regulator port plug
- Crescent wrench
- Pliers
- Screw driver
- Plastic zip-type bags
- Zip-slip tube "silicone gel"

Personal
- Watch
- Swim suit
- Towel
- Hat
- Jacket
- Sunglasses
- C-card
- Money w/change for phone
- Fishing license
- Log book
- Sunscreen lotion
- Toiletries
- Skin lotions
- Motion sickness medication
- Insect repellant
- Change of clothes
- Tickets
- Directions

- Food and drinks
- Emergency numbers

Specialty Gear
- Camera
- Lenses
- Strobes
- Film
- Batteries for camera & strobe
- Film protection bag (from x-ray)
- Light meter
- Speargun
- Speargun tips & extras
- Ab iron (approved w/gauge)
- Lobster gauge
- Crab gauge
- Goodie bag w/clip
- U/W housing
- Photo guide books
- Extension tubes
- Framing devices
- Flashbulbs
- Flash U/W housing
- Camera cases
- Watertight boxes
- Lens brush
- Lens tissue
- Lens cleaner
- Repair kit –
  - jewelers screw drivers
  - housing seals
  - O-rings
- Marker buoy
- Lift bag

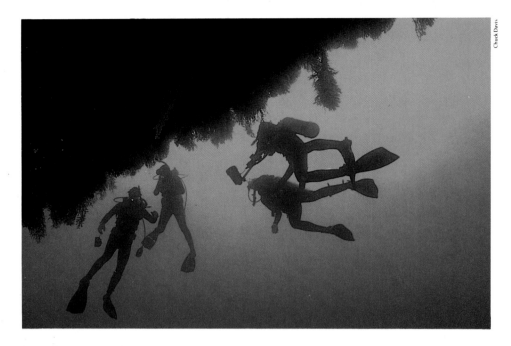

DIVE SAFETY

With all the responsibilities that a divemaster carries, he or she has little time to be concerned about your personal diving profile. Usually the divemaster will plan the dives so that the first of the day is the deepest, followed by a shallower dive later, especially when the dives are separated by only an hour or two of surface interval.

Although planning the dives this way lessens potential problems, it is up to you to keep track of and record your own bottom time and maximum depth, and to calculate your repetitive dive status. These are important personal statistics that should be carefully noted in your diving log.

When it comes right down to the crunch, your personal safety is your responsibility. Don't expect anyone else, your buddy and divemaster included, to 'look after you.'

Don't be afraid to question the divemaster about the site or conditions if you are unsure, and know when to say 'I'm passing on this one' when you feel that diving conditions are beyond your abilities. Never feel compelled to follow the crowd — perhaps they've never heard of the 'Ship of Fools.'

Most scuba enthusiasts packing for a diving holiday will think to include a basic maintenance and repair kit for their equipment But often one piece of gear gets overlooked and that's *you.*

Consider what preventive steps can be taken to ensure that you 'work' properly while abroad. Here are a few thoughts that may prove useful:
- Try to rest for a day or two before your departure. Avoid over-eating and excessive drinking during the flight. This helps minimize the effect of jet lag.
- Allow your body to acclimatize before getting into non-stop diving, drinking, discos, etc. In some tropical countries the temperature is a constant 85°F or more night and day with humidity of 90 percent.
- Determine before you go where the nearest recompression chamber is located and what emergency procedures/ transportation exist to get you to it. Emergency air evacuation, chamber treatment and hospitalization can be extremely expensive so be sure your medical insurance is sufficient in both type and amount of coverage. Be sure to get all necessary receipts for medical treatment for proper claim documentation.
- Be prepared to administer first aid. The objectives should be to sustain life, to prevent the condition from worsening and to promote recovery. Attend a qual-ity program in safety-oriented emergency first aid. It's invaluable knowledge to have all year round. Be especially clear on procedures to follow in the event of any diving-related accident.
- Always think preventive medicine. Flush out ears with clean, fresh water and dry them after every dive. Ear infections can start more easily in humid conditions. Treat all cuts and abrasions no matter how minor they might be. Don't let infections start.
- Wear a 'Medic Alert' bracelet or necklace if necessary. As well, travelling divers should carry their own personal medical alert card at all times. Make it up on an index card (and have it plasticized). Include name, address and telephone number of yourself, your next of kin and your doctor; medical/hospitalization insurance numbers and a brief medical history that includes allergies, diseases or conditions, prescription drugs used in past and present, special precautions to be taken in event of an emergency (i.e., check for contact lenses, avoid use of penicillin, etc.) and any other pertinent information.

Line Pull, Audio, and Visual Signals for Diver-to-Diver Communication		
Signal Title and Meaning	Hand Squeeze/ Line Pull/ Light Flash/ Tank Tap	Answer
OK? or OK	One	Same
Go	Two	Same
Stop	Three	Same
Surface	Four	Same
Emergency or Come Here Quickly	Five or More	Go Quickly to Signaller
All signals, except the emergency signal, should be answered, by repeating signal, when received.		

Darren R. Douglass

HAND SIGNALS

Stop	Go Down/Going Down	Go Up/Going Up	OK! Ok?	OK! Ok?
Ok?	Something is Wrong	Distress, help	Low on air	Out of Air
Let's Buddy Breathe	Danger	OK? OK (on surface at distance)	OK? OK (one hand occupied)	Which direction?
Get with your buddy	You lead, I'll follow	Hold hands	Go that way	Me, or watch me
Come here	Under, over, around	Level off, this depth	Take it easy, slow down	Yes / No
Ears not clearing	I don't understand	What time? What depth?	Look	I am cold

Ropes & Knots

A variety of natural and synthetic fibers are used to make rope. All rope materials have characteristics which can be either an advantage or disadvantage, depending upon how the rope is used. Nylon, for example, is very elastic; it is great for towing boats. Because of its elasticity, though, it can snap with tremendous force when its breaking strength is exceeded.

The knot you use for a job is partly determined by the type of rope you have. A knot that holds fast in manilla rope may untie in nylon. Ropes are tools. They will serve you well if you know how to use and treat them. Knowing when and how to tie the knots described here should help you be an asset to any dive team.

KNOT TYING TERMS
End – loose or working part of a rope.
Bight – a curve in a rope or line; usually where the knot is tied.
Standing Part – unused section of rope in knot tying.
Loop – a closed curve in a rope or line.

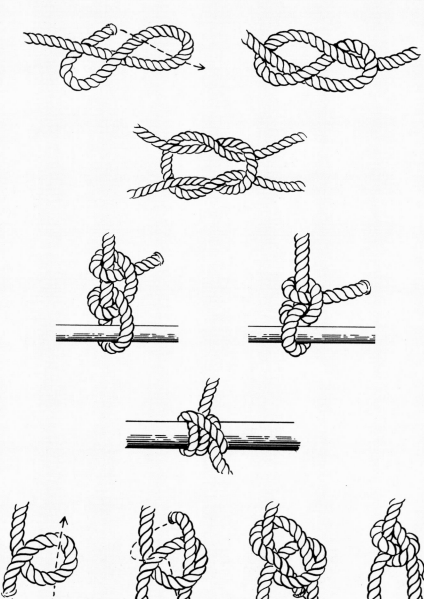

1. The figure eight knot is most often used as a stopper knot. It is used more than the overhand knot because the figure eight does not tighten as much under pressure.

2. Square knot. This knot is used to tie rope ends of the same size together. It is a quick way to join rope, but since it reduces rope strength by almost 50%, it should not be used under great tension.

3. Two-half hitches. Easy to tie and effective, two-half hitches are used to secure line to a stationary point or grommets.

4. Rolling hitch. When you cannot afford to have a rope slip sideways on a rail or rope, use a rolling hitch. The rolling hitch is also good for tying a line to a rope secured (attached) at both ends.

5. Bowline. Every diver needs this knot. It is easy to tie with a little practice. Use it any time a loop is needed at the end of a line.

Ropes & Knots

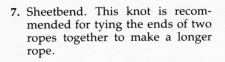

6. Ring knot. The ring knot can be tied when you have to join two ropes in a hurry. Keep in mind it can jam under a moderate strain.

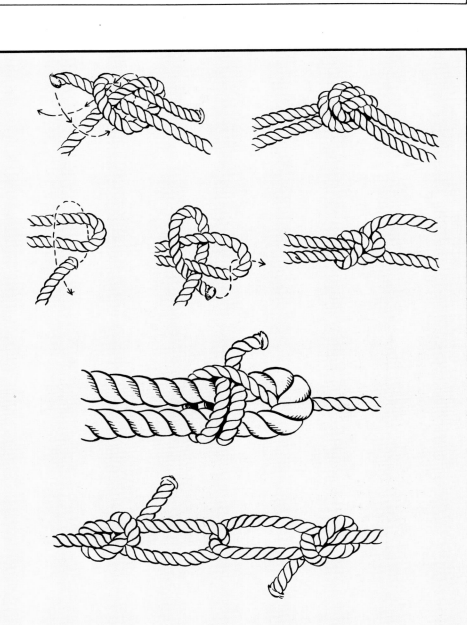

7. Sheetbend. This knot is recommended for tying the ends of two ropes together to make a longer rope.

8. Double Sheetbend. This one can take more strain than the sheetbend without jamming. It is highly recommended for tying ropes of different diameters together.

9. Bowline Bend. This knot is two bowlines which interlock. It can also be used to tie ropes of different diameters together. It is the preferred knot when a boat or vehicle has to be towed.

10. Sheepshank. When a shorter rope is needed, or a weak spot in the line has to be strengthened, tie a sheepshank.

11. Slipped overhand knot. This knot is ideal for a temporary stopper knot. To untie it, simply pull at the end.

ADAPTATION
THE KEY TO SAFE DIVING

The scope of changes you undergo while diving is far more extensive than most people realize. Environmental changes in visibility, temperature, pressure, water movement and bottom conditions are obvious. But physiological changes in heart rate, blood pressure, respiration, temperature, stress fatigue and body weight are taking place, and all senses are significantly altered. So how do people not only survive, but accomplish so much underwater?

Be Cool, Stay Warm

Underwater adaptation usually comes first with special equipment and skills, then with training and experience. The skills are essentially the same. Capable divers:
- move in a slow and relaxed manner
- move through the water in a horizontal attitude
- only move arms and legs when necessary
- often crawl along the bottom, gently using fingers and fin tips rather than swimming
- avoid surface swimming as much as possible
- breathe in a slow, deep, relaxed manner
- often pause during the dive
- control buoyancy to be neutral or just slightly negative when moving horizontally in midwater; slightly negative when on the bottom or descending, and positive when ascending or on the surface
- use natural aids to underwater orientation and navigation
- stop, breathe easily, think and get control before taking action during difficulty
- solve problems on the bottom if possible, or on the surface using positive buoyancy
- end or modify dives when they are cold, tired, low on air, not feeling well, having a difficulty, injured, uncomfortable, under undue stress, or not having a good time
- always surface slowly and never rush to exit point
- make equipment and water movement work for them
- are aware of themselves, the equipment

"Man has always displayed a stubborn ambition to do what nature never intended him to do." (Drew Middleton, **Playboy**, 1976)

and their surroundings
- recognize and deal with stress
- are able to coordinate several skills at once, such as equalizing pressure, controlling buoyancy and swimming

Don't Be A Drag

Moving efficiently through the water is a very important aspect of adaptation. In order to dive, however, you must be equipped with the appropriate gear, which creates a lot of water resistance. Some equipment-related causes of drag are:
- large, bulky gear
- dangling or protruding accessories
- drysuits, especially when inflated
- irregular or flat surfaces
- extra equipment such as camera
  Some procedures that increase drag are:
- swimming out of trim
- excessively inflating a buoyancy compensator
- kicking with excessively bent legs, using hands to maneuver
- swimming fast
- swimming on the surface

What to do instead?

- use simplest equipment available for type of diving you do
- streamline equipment
- carry as little as possible
- secure everything
- wear as complete and smooth an exposure suit as possible
- maintain neutral buoyancy and horizontal trim
- use an efficient kick
- swim at a slow, steady pace
- swim on the surface as little as possible
- use water currents or surge to propel yourself
- crawl along bottom
- use buoyancy control for ascents and descents

Finally, what does all this achieve for the diver? It improves safety and enjoyment of the sport. It is clear that you use less air and become less fatigued by moving efficiently through the water, and that you will see more, be less cold, be under less stress, not have as many difficulties, and will be better able to keep a sense of orientation.

DIVING ACCIDENTS

Some Causes

A familiar chain of events often appears: the diver is cold and tired. Stress levels increase, and the diver makes a mistake. He panics and dies. The key link in this chain is the *mistake* or human error that may have been anything from entering heavy surf to not properly maintaining a regulator.

Human Error

This stands out as the primary cause of the vast majority of diving accidents. The largest single category of causes, however, is that of medical/psychological factors. These include problems of stress and panic, cold and fatigue, cramps, drug abuse *(including alcohol)*, decompression sickness, contaminated air, heart conditions and other medical problems, along with poor physical and psychological fitness.

Either by their behavior or by allowing things to happen to them, people cause the problems that lead to diving accidents.

Environmental Conditions

Another large group of causitive factors include environmental conditions such as deep water, waves, currents, cold water, poor visibility, entanglements, and so on. Some divers attempt to blame accidents that involve environmental conditions on "acts of God," or claim that conditions are

beyond their control. Yet the divers chose to dive in these conditions, or the conditions changed and the divers chose not to deal effectively with them. In any case, it generally leads back to human error.

Equipment Failure

Ascent difficulties occuring after "out of air" and "low on air" situations are a type of accident unique to sport diving. Actually, the error is one of equipment misuse or improper breathing procedures — both human errors.

Equipment failure is insignificant as a primary cause of fatal scuba diving accidents. Equipment can cause problems, but they are more likely to inconvenience the diver than threaten his life. The accident also may be caused by the diver's misuse of the equipment. Other major problem areas are the failure of the buddy system, lack of buoyancy control and lack of training — again, all human errors.

Key Trends

Other trends in scuba diving accidents show that on a dive-for-dive basis the earliest dives (first dozen) in a person's diving career are most likely to lead to difficulties. Also, nearly all fatal accidents occur while using scuba in open water. But an accident is most likely to be a near-miss if qualified people such as instructors, guides, divemasters or boat crews

are readily available.

Putting these trends together indicates that sport divers should dive with professionally qualified people or in supervised activities while gaining their early experience. This would also be a wise recommendation for anyone who has been away from diving for several months.

Learning Control

Develop the ability to make the *no-dive* decision based on changing medical, physical, psychological or environmental conditions. Along with this goes the right for either diver at any time to abort the dive without embarrassment. Divers should get out of the water when they are cold, tired, low on air, under undue stress, injured, uncomfortable or having difficulty. Diving is not enjoyable or safe under these conditions.

If you are having difficulties during a dive, it is best to stop, think and get control. Then take corrective action. Use your equipment to help control buoyancy and maintain orientation.

Diving is a demanding activity, but an extremely rewarding one. The key to enjoyment is *control.* Maintain control of yourself, your equipment, and the situation so you and your buddy can function within the existing conditions, whatever they may be.

U.S. CERTIFICATION ORGANIZATIONS

IDEA (International Diving Educators Association)
P.O. Box 17374
Jacksonville, FL 32245
(904) 744-5554

Los Angeles County Department of Parks and Recreation Underwater Instructors Association
419 192nd St.
Carson, CA 90745
(213) 327-5311

NAUI (National Association of Underwater Instructors)
P.O. Box 14650
Montclair, CA 91763
(714) 621-5801

NASDS (National Association of Scuba Diving Schools)
P.O. Box 17067
Long Beach, CA 90807
(213) 595-5361

PADI International (Professional Association of Diving Instructors)
1243 E. Warner Ave.
Santa Ana, CA 92705
(800) 722-7234
(714) 540-7234

PDIC (Professional Diving Instructors Corporation)
P.O. Box 772
Scranton, PA 18501
(717) 342-1480

SSI (Scuba Schools International)
2619 Canton Ct.
Ft. Collins, CO 80525
(303) 482-0883

YMCA (Young Men's Christian Association) Underwater Activities Program
6083-A Oakbrook Pkwy.
Norcross, GA 30092
(404) 662-5172

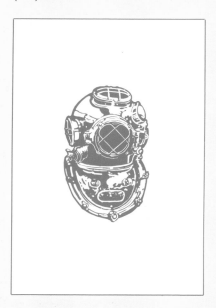

INTERNATIONAL CERTIFICATION ORGANIZATIONS

ACUC International (Association of Canadian Underwater Councils)
460 Brant, Suite 207
Burlington, ON L7R 4B6
Canada
(416) 639-2357

BSAC (British Sub Aqua Club)
70 Brompton Rd.
London, SW3 1HA
England

CMAS (Confederation Mondiale des Activities Subaquatiques)
34 rue du Colisee
75008 Paris
France

IDEA Canada
5647 Yonge St., Suite 405
Toronto, ON M2M4E9
Canada
(519) 742-5415

NAUI Canada
Box 510
Etobicoke, ON M9C 4V5
Canada
(416) 677-3817

PADI Canada
243 Mary St.
Victoria, BC V9A 3V8
Canada
(604) 381-3613

INSTRUCTOR CERTIFICATION INSTITUTIONS

Florida Institute of Technology
1707 N.E. Indian River Dr.
Jensen Beach, FL 33457
(800) 433-0116 in FL
(800) 241-7826
(305) 334-4200

PADI International College
1243 E. Warner Ave.
Santa Ana, CA 92705
(800) 223-8697 in CA
(800) 235-3434
(714) 540-7234

NASDS Instructors College
4004 Sports Arena Blvd.
San Diego, CA 92110
(619) 224-3228

NAUI Instructors College
2400 West Coast Hwy., Suite M
Newport Beach, CA 92663
(714) 631-4282

NAUI Professional Development Center of the Florida Keys
1688 Overseas Hwy.
Marathon, FL 33050
(305) 743-5929

Ocean Tech
129 Miracle Strip Pkwy. S.E.
Ft. Walton Beach, FL 32548
(904) 243-4600

Underwater Careers International
6023 Hollywood Blvd.
Hollywood, FL 33024
(305) 981-0156

DRUGS AND DIVING

In a word, drugs and SCUBA diving don't mix. In a culture which is drug-oriented, chemicals are used for prevention and cure of every malady, from the common cold to cancer. For the scuba diver, many drugs are effective and safe on the surface, but at depth, side-effects may be serious and even dangerous. Several categories should be mentioned. They are summarized in Table A. These are: analgesics, antihistamines and decongestants, anti-nausea drugs, cardiovascular drugs, anticonvulsants, sedatives, stimulants and abused or street drugs.

It is generally accepted that persons with seizures, asthma, diabetes, serious cardiovascular or psychiatric disorders requiring medication should not dive. On the other hand, commonly used drugs such as caffeine, aspirin and Tylenol do not jeopardize divers.

Without question, abused, mind-altering substances such as cocaine, marijuana, alcohol, amphetamines, narcotics, downers, minor tranquilizers (valium, etc.) and sedatives like Quaaludes, do not mix with diving and are dangerous, even on the surface.

Decongestants are probably the most commonly used medications for the diver. Although they are stimulants, and can cause disturbances in heart rhythms, medications such as Sudafed are considered safe in the healthy diver. The 60 mg tablet should be taken about 30 minutes before diving; Sudafed-SA capsules are recommended if delays or repetitive dives are contemplated as they may prevent reverse squeezes.

Antihistamines cause sedation, and should be used with caution. Topical decongestants, such as Afrin nasal spray, are safe, but can cause a type of dependence if overused.

Anti-nauseants all cause sedation to some extent, as well as other side-effects, which may cause nitrogen narcosis. Always test topside and use with caution. Shallow dives (less than 60 feet) are recommended.

Cardiovascular drugs include beta-blockers, such as Inderal, which decreases one's ability to handle stress. Antihypertensives, which lower blood pressure, have numerous serious side-effects. It is prudent to say that patients requiring these medications should not be diving at depth, both because of the underlying disease process and the medication involved. However, each case can be individualized; a physician knowledgeable in the effects of pressure should be consulted in these patients. Diuractics (water pills) are usually okay.

Of the abused drugs, alcohol is the most common. It is a depressant and involved in about one-half of adult drownings. In addition, the dehydration effect can make decompression sickness worse, and heat loss is increased, adding to hypothermia. Marijuana is an extremely dangerous drug at depth, causing many "bad trips" through paradoxical effects and severe cold intolerance. Other mind-altering substances cause greatly impaired performance and altered perceptions *all of which are increased* at pressure. Diving creates enough of a "high" itself. Use of these substances is only to be condemned.

TABLE A

Drugs in Diving

SAFE DRUGS
(OK to Dive)

Aspirin
Acetaminophen
   (Tylenol, others)
Caffeine
TOPICAL decongestants

RESTRICTED DIVING
(With Caution)

Antihistamines
Decongestants
Diuretics
Anti-Motion Sickness
   Medications
Steroids

NO DIVING

Anticonvulsants
Asthma Medications
Antihypertensives
Alcohol
Depressants (Barbituates, etc.)
Stimulants
   (Amphetamines, Cocaine)
Hallucinogens
   (Marijuana, LSD, PCP,
   Mescaline, etc.)
Tranquilizers
Antipsychotic Medications
Narcotics

Note: When taking any drug and diving, REMEMBER to consider whether the condition itself is hazardous when diving.

Steven G. Rosenberg

DIET

A proper diet, which includes daily portions of the four major food groups with minimal amounts of highly saturated fats, is adequate for the recreational diver and does not need to be elaborated upon here. Generally, those susceptible to motion sickness should avoid heavy, greasy meals prior to diving from a boat and, despite tradition among some divers, large amounts of rum or other alcoholic beverages should not be consumed the night before (or the day of) diving. It is best to avoid gas-producing foods. Reverse intestinal squeeze may become a problem. Any foods containing substantial amounts of sugar, honey, glucose, etc., taken prior to the dive, are not recommended. Likewise, vitamins have not been shown to have any specific benefit (with a few minor exceptions such as the role of Vitamin E in protecting against oxygen toxicity), and are usually contained in adequate amounts in a well balanced diet. The dietary goal of divers, as that of other healthy active people, should be to maintain proper lean body weight with an adequate intake of nutritional foods providing the vitamins, minerals and calories needed to maintain health. This should include avoidance of excessive amounts of salt, saturated fats and refined or simple sugars, and include adequate amounts of protein, complex carbohydrates, and fresh fruits and vegetables.

Proper nutrition, physical conditioning, positive emotional attitude and cognizance of environmental conditions are the keystones to enjoying safe diving. Factors which influence the diver at increased pressure are outlined in Table B. These are obviously important determinants in the individual's basic capacity for exercise and endurance in stressful or physically demanding situations.

TABLE B
Factors affecting individual response to physiologic changes at increased pressure:

1. Age	6. Drugs, including alcohol.
2. Physiologic condition.	7. Ambient temperature.
3. Weight.	8. Fatigue.
4. Sex.	9. Prior diving within 12 hours.
5. Acute or chronic illness.	10. Smoking.

Food: Do's And Don'ts For Divers

DO . . .
• Eat a normal breakfast before diving, in order to have sufficient energy to keep warm. Heat is conducted away by the water at a rate 25 times that of air. Also, high activity levels require large amounts of energy.
• Drink a lot of water, especially in hot, humid weather. The body loses a significant amount of water in diving through perspiration, which can lead to dehydration and increase the likelihood of decompression sickness.
• Have a high protein meal two to three hours before entering the water, then
• Eat carbohydrates a half-hour before diving, for quick energy;
• Between dives take in more carbohydrates such as apples, honey, or candy, and fluids

Chuck Davis

(especially hot sugared tea or soup) to replenish energy and moisture).
• Eat regularly, slowly and sensibly so as not to produce gases.
• Bring along antacid remedies for somewhat common sour stomachs.
• Make sure you eat foods supplying you with enough Vitamins A and E. A is helpful for seeing in low light levels, and aids lung functions; E assists A and helps reduce the body's need for oxygen.

DON'T . . .
• Take drugs; the effects of which are not well understood and could be hazardous. (Even non-prescription drugs.)
• Eat mucous-producing foods such as chocolate, milk or dairy products if you have trouble equalizing due to mucous.
• Eat gas-producing food such as onions, beans, cabbage or carbonated drinks.
• Touch hot and spicy foods.
• Consume fatty foods, which are bulky and difficult to digest. Too much energy would go to your digestive system, and fats take too long to become an energy source.
• Drink alcohol after diving, especially if you are cold, went deep, or if you are near the decompression limits.

Basic Conditioning

A body in good physical condition is as important to safe diving as it is to any other vigorous physical activity, be it skiing, board sailing or rock climbing. Emphasis should be on good nutrition, avoidance of drugs (including excessive alcohol), avoidance of smoking, maintaining lean body weight and a good emotional attitude. The conditioning should include strength exercises (the diver should be able to don and carry a tank and weights without difficulty) and aerobic conditioning. Ideally, aerobic conditioning includes a minimum of three workouts per week of at least 30 minutes in which the pulse is elevated *continuously* to a target level. A simple formula for the "target pulse" is:

$$P = (220 - \text{age in years}) \times 0.8$$

example:
40 yrs. $P = (220 - 40) \times 0.8$
$ = 180 \times 0.8 = 144$

Swimming, jogging and cycling are considered excellent aerobic exercises. As the majority of sport divers do not venture out in the cold of winter, a common problem is loss of conditioning during the off months. An occasional trip to the ski slopes is not adequate to keep in shape for diving. Ideally, two or three sessions per week in the local pool and/or diving once or twice a month will help the diver maintain skills as well as keep the pounds off. It's far more beneficial to maintain a level of fitness through regular exercise, than to vigorously attempt to "get back into shape" two weeks before that big trip. Individuals over the age of 40, and those over 35 with cardiovascular risk factors (smoking, obesity, etc.), should have a complete physical exam, including a stress electrocardiogram, before entering into any vigorous exercise program. Good physical conditioning may mean the difference between a minor injury or a serious accident in the water.

While the diver does not have to be an Olympic athlete, he should be able to meet minimum swimming standards such as those outlined in the NOAA Diving Manual: (1) able to swim the crawl 300 yards without difficulty, (2) able to swim 50 yards underwater, (3) able to stay afloat 30 minutes. Maintaining oneself in good physical condition is important in providing the reserve that may be necessary to prevent unforeseen events from turning into disastrous accidents and in this way, continue to make the wonders of diving not only enjoyable, but as safe as possible.

REF: (1) Davis, J.C., et al.: Medical Examination of Sport SCUBA

TABLE C

Tips for Maintaining Condition for Sport Diving

1. Watch your weight (less than 15% body fat is ideal).
2. Do regular aerobic exercise at least three times weekly.
3. Avoid smoking and excessive alcohol use.
4. Avoid recreational drugs.
5. Eat a nutritional diet including the four basic food groups.

TABLE D

DON'T DIVE IF YOU ARE:

1. Hung over.
2. Under the influence of drugs of alcohol. Prescription drugs such as antihistamines or antimotion sickness medications should be given a "trial run" prior to diving.
3. Severely motion sick.
4. Have an acute infection which would prevent or impair clearing of ears, sinuses or contribute to a pulmonary overpressure accident.
5. Unfit physically (dangerous situations may arise quickly and become catastrophes due to fatigue, hyperventilation and panic because the diver was not prepared physically for an emergency.
6. Unfit emotionally — apprehensive regarding conditions, angry at partner; depressed over finances, etc.
7. Excessively fatigued, dizzy, short of breath or having pain which may be the result of acute DCS or other injury from a prior dive.
8. Without proper equipment or preparation for dive.

REMEMBER: Panic and drowning kill more divers than all causes combined.

Getting And Staying In Shape For Scuba Diving

Experts agree that the best conditioning program for divers is diving. No other activity, not even swimming, comes close to approximating the motion of functional muscle groups — primarily flexors and extensors of the knee, hip and ankle.

Cardiovascular fitness is critical to a diver's performance. Circulatory efficiency is likely to make divers more alert, and thus better at problem solving. Plus, the fitter you are the less air you require and the longer you can explore on one tank of air. Although aerobic activities such as swimming, jogging and cycling won't automatically prepare you for specific underwater pressures, they will ease some of the strain. And, because divers are continually ventilating the air they breathe, aerobic fitness helps guard against carbon dioxide retention.

Dr. Art. Bachrach, director of the Environmental Stress Program Center at the Naval Medical Research Institute in Bethesda, Maryland, draws a close parallel between physical and psychological fitness as they pertain to diving. Bachrach feels that anyone who can snorkel can probably feel comfortable scuba diving. "But people who have fears should avoid situations in which they put themselves in danger." The best weapon against fear, he adds, is "information gathering. Do thorough dive planning, research the site, know what kind of wildlife to expect."

Thermal Conductivity Is 24 Times Greater In Water Than In Air

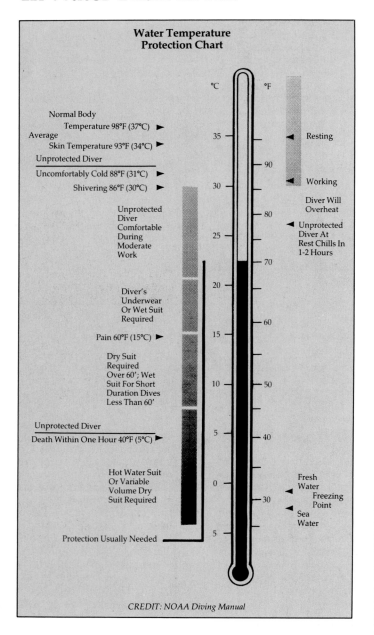

Water Temperature Protection Chart

Normal Body Temperature 98°F (37°C) ►
Average
Skin Temperature 93°F (34°C) ►
Unprotected Diver
Uncomfortably Cold 88°F (31°C) ►
Shivering 86°F (30°C) ►

Unprotected Diver Comfortable During Moderate Work

Diver's Underwear Or Wet Suit Required

Pain 60°F (15°C) ►

Dry Suit Required Over 60'; Wet Suit For Short Duration Dives Less Than 60'

Unprotected Diver
Death Within One Hour 40°F (5°C) ►

Hot Water Suit Or Variable Volume Dry Suit Required

Protection Usually Needed

°C   °F

35   90

30   80

25

20   70

15   60

10   50

5   40

0   30

5

◄ Resting

◄ Working

Diver Will Overheat

◄ Unprotected Diver At Rest Chills In 1-2 Hours

◄ Fresh Water Freezing Point
◄ Sea Water

CREDIT: NOAA Diving Manual

Seasickness

This poorly understood malady has not only ruined many a dive or fishing trip, it has probably changed the course of history. Most assuredly, some of the greatest sea captains and admirals have been seriously afflicted. Almost everyone, at some time or another, is susceptible; especially if unaccustomed to the erratic rocking motions of a boat in open water.

Motion sickness is caused by discordant stimuli to the part of the inner ear which controls balance. Factors contributing to motion sickness are genetic susceptibility, age, sex, prior evening's activities, previous meals, noxious stimuli (engine exhaust) and emotional factors. There is some adaptation in most people: that is, symptoms may decrease with repeated stimulation — a positive note! There are as many ways to prevent seasickness as there are cures, and none are completely successful. Depending on your background, you may have tried various herbs, including garlic and ginger, vitamins (B6 was recently touted by the Russians), wearing of various charms, eating, not eating, and numerous drugs. If one is faced with impending symptoms, he should move to the boat's centerline, amidship, as close to the waterline as possible to minimize motion stimulus. Look at the horizon or shut your eyes and sleep, if possible. Avoid engine exhaust and other adverse sensory input. Don't repeatedly console or chide others who are afflicted; this only makes things worse! Frequently, getting in the water as soon as possible helps.

For those highly susceptible to motion sickness, attention should be given to three things: prior night's activities, diet, and medications which block or prevent symptoms. A good night's rest, and absence of a hangover, will help greatly to minimize chances for motion sickness. Your diet should be light, low in fat and acid or gas producing foods. Eat three or four hours before the dive. Of the numerous medications used, Scopolamine is probably the most effective. Available in a skin patch (Trans-derm Scop), it is available by prescription only and *should be tried* prior to diving to assess severity of side-effects, which may include dry mouth, drowsiness, blurred vision and hallucinations. Over-the-counter drugs include Dramamine, Marezine, and Bonine — all antihistamine derivatives which vary in results, duration and side-effects. Other prescription medications such as Phenergan, alone or in combination, should probably be avoided when diving because of possible side-effects.

Although getting into the water quickly may abort an attack, one should not SCUBA dive if severely seasick.

The cause of motion sickness is still somewhat of a mystery. If the above measures are ineffective, the best advice is to avoid rough weather in a boat and to keep tabs on the latest medical advances either through publications or one's physicians.

TIPS FOR TREATMENT OF INJURIES

There are numerous good first-aid manuals available which are quite adequate for treatment of common injuries. This section will attempt to outline the first aid for minor injuries specific to diving or snorkeling.

External Ear Canal Infection (Swimmer's ear)

Signs/Symptoms: Pain, redness, tenderness of outer ear, discharge from ear canal.

Treatment: Prevent - Avoid trauma (Q-tips, etc.) Vinegar/alcohol drops after diving/swimming, or boric acid — 3% plus 70% isopropyl alcohol — 50/50 mix.
Clear ear canal (ENT specialist): Cortisporin drops*
*See First Aid Kit.

Sinus Squeeze

S and SX: Pain in sinuses, nosebleed

Treatment: Prevent - Don't dive with a cold, clear sinuses, topical and oral decongestants 30 minutes before dive.
Treatment - Don't dive until Sx clear, decongestants (Afrin spray), Sudafed (120 mg SA capsule twice daily) steroids.

Ear Squeeze

S and SX: Pain in ear, headache, dizziness, vomiting, hearing loss if rupture of ear drum. *The* most common cause of diving accidents.

Treatment: Prevention - Same as sinus squeeze.
Treatment - Same as sinus squeeze. If rupture of eardrum or severe symptoms see ENT specialist.

Stings (Jellyfish, Fire Coral, sea anemones, bristle worms, starfish). Sea cucumbers can ingest toxic hydroids and may cause stings, with possible blindness resulting.

Signs and Symptoms: Wide range: welts; swelling, redness; numbness of skin; pain (mild - severe); cramps; nausea/vomiting; respiratory difficulty; paralysis; convulsions; shock.

Prevention: Avoid touching animals, including dead jellyfish on beach.

Treatment:
1. Remove victim from water.
2. Treat for shock and respiratory collapse.
3. Rinse with sea water (*not* fresh water), then with 70% alcohol or ammonia solution (vodka or shaving lotion in a pinch).
4. Apply paste of Adolf's meat tenderizer or bicarbonate/alcohol or bicarb/ammonia (or shaving lotion in a pinch).
5. Cortisone cream (0.5% available without prescription).
6. Seek medical help for severe cases
7. Remove bristle worn bristles with adhesive tape.
8. Ice packs to reduce swelling and pain.

NOTE: Man-O-War stings require immediate treatment.

Sea Urchin/Venomous Spines

Symptoms: Pain, swelling, blanching or redness (infection) or granules (late).

Prevention: Avoid, wear protection.

Treatment: Remove spines with sterile needle/forceps; wash with antiseptic; apply ammonia solution.

Venomous Fish (Stingrays, scorpionfish, weaverfish, stonefish, etc.)

Symptoms: Pain at puncture site, blanching, swelling, redness, dizziness, nausea, respiratory problems, pulse alterations, shock, coma, death.

Prevention: Avoid, wear protection.

Treatment: Remove from water. Remove spines, foreign material. KEY: Soak injured area in HOT water (110-115 deg. F = 43-46 deg. C) for 45 to 90 minutes. Relieve pain (narcotics are usually necessary). Cleanse wound. Seek medical attention.

Dangerous Fish Bites
(sharks, barracuda, moray eel, wolf eel)

Symptoms: Laceration, may be severe; victim usually dies from blood loss and shock.

Prevention: Avoid; sharks are ubiquitous and unpredictable, greatest danger to surface swimmers. Slowly leave water if dangerous shark sighted

Treatment:
1. Control bleeding (direct pressure; tourniquet only if absolutely necessary; loosen every 20 minutes).
2. CPR if necessary.
3. Remove from water.
4. Treat shock (head down, warm; IV fluids if available).
5. Seek immediate medical attention.

Barnacle or Coral Cuts/Abrasions

Treatment: Cleanse thoroughly with betadine/H202. Apply Betadine or Neosporin ointment. See physician for signs of infection.

Sunburn

Symptoms: Redness, pain, swelling, blister formation of skin.

KEY-Prevention: Protective clothing, increase time in sun gradually; use sunscreen with SPF 8-15 containing PABA 5% in alcohol or water-resistant ase.

Treatment: Avoid further exposure, cool compresses, Aspirin, cortisone creams if severe.

✚ Diver's First Aid Kit ✚

Several pre-packaged first aid kits are available commercially today, varying from poor to excellent when utilized for diving related accidents. The following list has been compiled for those who wish to either save a few dollars or customize a kit, and start with the basic necessities. As new products become available, the kit should be updated. Don't forget to restock used items. Most items are available from your local drug store. Prescription drugs are marked with an (*) and should be obtained through your personal physician.

1. **One-Tackle/Tool Box** as a container. Plastic or metal. The Pelican@ Camera Box is ideal although quite expensive.
2. **Adhesive Tape/Assorted Bandages.** Cloth or silk tape is best.
3. **Alcohol Solution.** 70% to 95% isopropyl.
4. **Ammonia Solution.** Useful for treating stings.
5. **Antibiotic Ointment.** Betadine@, Neosporin.
6. **Antibiotic Powder.** Neosporin.
7. **Antihistamines.** (Benadryl*) Oral, (injectable).
8. **Aspirin.** Useful for sinus squeeze headaches, fevers as well as decompression sickness.
9. **Assorted Dressings.** 4 x 4 sterile gauzes, roll gauze 4" x 5 yd., Non-adherent (Telfa, Adaptic).
10. **Baking Soda**
11. **Decongestant.** Oral (Sudafed +), +120mg SA Recomm, Topical (Afrin nasal spray)
12. **Diarrhea Medications.** (Lomotil*, Pepto Bismol (Septra*)
13. **Dive Tables.** An extra copy of the tables should be included as a backup and can be used in the event of an emergency.
14. **Ear Drops.** Vinegar 1 tbsp. in 4 oz. 70% alcohol or 3% boric acid in 70% alcohol 50:50; Cortisporin*.
15. **Emergency Numbers.** Make up a self-adhering sticker with emergency numbers for your area on it. Include the National Diving Accident Network (DAN) phone number (919) 684-8111. U.S. Coast Guard (at sea VHF 16), local rescue number and the number of the nearest recompression chamber. Also tape dimes (2) and quarters (2) to lid for phone calls.
16. **Eye Drops.** 10% Sulfacetamide*, neosporin*.
17. **Flash Light.** Include extra batteries bulb; disposable penlights work well, are compact and inexpensive.
18. **Hydrogen Peroxide. (H202) for wound cleansing.**
19. **Ice Packs.** To reduce swelling/pain. Instant wet/dry mixture which are activated by squeezing are best.
20. **Insect Repellant.** (Cutters, Off).
21. **Meat Tenderizer.** (Containing Papain) Adolf's *Unseasoned*. Use for jelly fish and coral stings.
22. **Oxygen.** With appropriate device for administration should be available for treatment of DCS or gas embolism.
23. **Pain Medication.** (Aspirin, Tylenol, Narcotics*).
24. **Pencil, Pen and Paper.** Include a standard and a grease pencil for documentation of changes in a divers condition, times, instructions from rescue/medical personnel, etc.
25. **Saline Solution.** 0.9 saline (NA C1) is the normal physiologic concentration can be used for anything from burns to ear/eye flushes. If not available contact lens solution may be used; assure that it does not contain irritants.
26. **Scissors and forceps (tweezers).** A good quality stainless steel set is well worth the money. They will stay sharp and won't rust. Forceps are useful for sea urchin spine removal.
27. **Scrub Brush**
28. **Soap Antiseptic Scrub.** Betadine, Hibiclens for cleansing wounds.
29. **Sun Screen.** Should contain PABA in alcohol base.
30. **Sea Sickness Medication.** Transderm Scop*, Dramamine, Bonine, Marazine.
31. **Space Blanket.** Packaged foil blankets work well and take up little space. Available at sporting goods or drug store.
32. **Thermometer.** A must. Preferable is one that will read in hypothermic range.
33. **Triangular Bandage.** Use for a sling or to control bleeding.
34. **Tourniquet.** Know how to use and indications!
35. The kit should also contain important prescription medications by the diver on an individual basis.

**Drugs such as injectable cortisone or adrenalin may also be included but generally should be administered under the auspices of a physician.

Cardiopulmonary Resuscitation (CPR)

IF UNCONSCIOUS **1** AIRWAY OPENED	• Lift Neck • Extend Head **Danger:** Beware of Cervic Spine Injury.	Airway Obstructed	
		Airway Opened	
IF APNEIC (Not Breathing) **2** BREATHING RESTORED	• Pinch Nose • Open Mouth • Seal Around Lips • Inflate Lungs Watch Chest Rise • (4 Quick Breaths) • Repeat 12 Times/Min. • 20-30 Times/Min. For Children	Mouth to Mouth ALSO Mouth to Nose Mouth to Adjunct Mouth to Mask Bag Valve Mask Check Pulse	

IF PULSELESS (Carotid) **3** CIRCULATION RESTORED	• Compress Lower 1/2 of Sternum
	• 60-80 Compressions/Min.
	• Two Rescuers:
	  • 5 Chest Compressions
	  • 1 Interposed Lung Inflation
	• One Rescuer:
	  • 15 Chest Compressions
	  • 2 Quick Lung Inflations
		Depress Lower Sternum 1-1/2 to 2 in. Keep Arms Straight Check Pupil

DO NOT INTERRUPT CPR			

THE EFFECTS OF PRESSURE

Dave Boaz

These are the most interesting and significant external phenomenon that affect the physiology of the SCUBA diver. The tissues of the body as well as the surrounding liquid of the oceans follow the gas laws of physics and account for many of the medical problems encountered by those venturing into the deep. Basically, these (collectively known as "bubble trouble") fall into two categories: those due to direct effects of pressure and those secondary to indirect effects. They are the most common diving malady encountered and have a wide range of severity.

Direct effects of ambient pressure are mechanical in nature and, in accordance with Boyle's law (volume at depth is inversely proportional to pressure), may cause difficulty during descent (ear, sinus or lung squeeze) or during ascent (pulmonary overpressure accidents such as the middle ear or sinus) when surrounding pressure exceeds that of the space through failure of equalization. This causes swelling, engorgement and eventual rupture of blood vessels and can result in severe pain and other symptoms.

Reverse squeeze is usually the result of poor timing of a dose of decongestant. The diver clears easily during descent but, because the medication taken too early wears off at depth, clearing is impossible during ascent. This can result in incredible

pain, eardrum rupture, etc. If decongestants must be taken use the long acting type and *never* dive with a cold. Lung squeeze is a problem only in very deep breath-hold diving and is rarely encountered in the sport SCUBA DIVER.

Pulmonary overpressure accidents (POA), also termed air or gas emboli, are a second, and potentially more serious class of diving accidents, caused by the mechanical effects of pressure. They can occur only if a breath is taken beneath the surface (compressed air tank, air pocket of wreck, etc.) and the expanding air cannot be normally vented during ascent to the surface. This blockage is usually the result of breath holding but may be caused by local air trapping in a defective lung. Asthmatics,

smokers and those with congenital lung blebs are at increased risk. The increasing pressure causes rupture of the delicate air sacs (alveoli), or pleural lining, and gas bubbles are forced into the circulation. The disasterous symptoms outlined in Table A are usually very serious, causing more deaths in a compressed air diver than any other pressure phenomenon.

POA can usually be prevented by normal breathing (not forced exhalation) during ascent. It is important to remember that embolism can occur at depths of less than four feet of seawater. Most POA's are potentially serious and require recompression in a suitable hyperbaric chamber.

Indirect effects of pressure follow the Laws of Dalton

(total pressure exerted in a gas is equal to the sum of the partial pressures of each individual gas) and Henry (the amount of gas dissolved in a liquid is proportional to the partial pressure of that gas) and explain disorders such as decompression sickness (DCS, "bends") and nitrogen narcosis. At depth tissues may become saturated with dissolved inert gases (e.g. nitrogen). If barometric pressure is lowered too rapidly, the gas separates from the liquid medium and forms bubbles in blood or other tissues. This evokes a complex series of chemical changes which result in the various DCS syndromes. Treatment of DCS are outlined in Table B and Fig. 1. REMEMBER: Any symptom, including that of joint pain or extreme fatigue, following compressed air diving is considered serious and should be treated aggressively! **Mild symptoms often progress to more serious ones.**

A second effect of indirect pressure is that of Nitrogen narcosis, or, as Cousteau termed, "rapture of the deep." This may occur at depths of much less than 100', and is greatly potentiated by various drugs as well as individual and day-to-day variation among divers.

REMEMBER: the Martini Rule: Each 50 feet depth = one Martini. Contamination of breathing air with carbon monoxide, etc., may be influenced by pressure changes only.

TABLE A

Signs and Symptoms of Pressure Related (Dysbaric) Diving Accidents

NOTE: Mild S/Sx often progress to more severe.

AIR EMBOLISM

1. Headache	6. Seizures
2. Visual defects	7. Bloody, frothy, Sputum
3. Numbness	8. Unconsciousness
4. Chest pain	9. Cardiovascular collapse
5. Paralysis	

NOTE: Victim frequently is unconscious, treat as gas embolism until proven otherwise.

ALSO: Usually rapid onset of symptoms; may resemble a "stroke," i.e., paralysis in one side of face or body.

Decompression Sickness (The Bends)

"Mild" Signs/Symptoms
1. Fatigue
2. Weakness
3. Skin rash
4. Personality change/indifference

"Moderate/Severe" S/SX
1. Joint pain
2. Above 1-4 with progression despite initial first aid
3. CHOKES
   a. Shortness of breath
   b. Cough (severe)
   c. Chest pressure
d. Bloody sputum
4. Neurologic symptoms:
   a. Visual difficulty
   b. Dizziness
   c. Loss of balance
   d. Staggering
   e. Low back or abdominal pain
   f. Mental confusion
   g. Numbness
   h. Paralysis (face and limbs)
   i. Convulsions
   j. Coma/unconsciousness
5. Shock

NOTE: S & Sx of DCS and POA may occur together. POA can cause bubbles which "seed" the blood stream and precipitate or cause DCS S & Sx of DCS are usually more gradual onset; majority occur within six hours; may occur up to 72 hours.

TABLE B

Emergency Treatment of Dysbaric (Pressure) Diving Accidents

(Bends, pulmonary, air emboli)

1. Determine if an emergency exists. Recognize signs (appearance of victim) and symptoms (subjective complaints) of Decompression Sickness (DCS) and Pulmonary Overpressure Accidents (POA). *ANY DIVER USING COMPRESSED AIR WITH PRESSURE-RELATED SYMPTOMS/SIGNS HAS POA OR DCS UNTIL PROVEN OTHERWISE.*

2. Support respiration and circulation if necessary (CPR).

3. Give 100% oxygen by tight-fitting mask.

4. Place in head-down position on left side (Durant's position).

5. Give two aspirin tablets by mouth.

6. Give oral fluids by mouth if victim is able to drink. Avoid coffee, carbonated drinks or alcohol. Give 6-8 ounces every 15-30 minutes if tolerated.

7. Keep warm if cool; cool if warm.

8. Arrange transportation to the nearest recompression chamber AS SOON AS POSSIBLE. This should be done while above resuscitation is being carried out. Transportation should be in aircraft pressurized to less than 1,000 feet (preferably sea level). Information concerning chamber location can be obtained through DAN 1-(919)684-8111 (collect if necessary) or USCG VHF 16 at sea or local number.

9. Record victim's vital signs and neurologic function noting any changes. Include time. Also measure urine output.

10. Prevent aspiration of stomach contents.

Flying After Diving

If you fly too soon after diving, you could be in for a painful, if not dangerous, experience. Excess nitrogen remaining in your system can cause decompression sickness (bends) that would not occur at sea level.

Reduced pressure does exist in modern jets flying at high altitude. That's why your ears pop. Commercial aircraft are only pressurized to a maximum of 8,000 feet above sea level. Problems with flying after diving, at such reduced pressures, are obvious. A similar condition to diving at altitude would exist, and similar precautions should be made. Remember, bends have occurred merely by driving over mountains after diving. Recommendations by the Undersea Medical Society include: (1) For no-decompression dives, when total bottom time for all dives in the preceding 12 hours is less than one hour ("D diver"), wait at least four hours before flying in a commercial jet. (2) If bottom time is four hours or less, wait at least 12 hours. (3) If more than four hours have been spent in the water in the previous 12, you should wait at least 24 hours before flying.

If symptoms do develop during your flight home, notify the flight crew immediately. One-hundred percent oxygen should be given and cabin pressure increased, if possible. Emergency landing may be necessary if symptoms persist.

Here again, prevention is the best cure. Planning a day of topside activities the last day of your diving vacation is the recommended way to prevent "bubble trouble" on your flight home.

Cramps

Divers, like runners and other athletes who use their legs a lot, are subject to cramps, usually from one of three causes. Your body could be lacking some nutrient, usually potassium. Eating bananas can increase your potassium intake. More than likely, though, you're out of condition. A good exercise program, begun several weeks before your expected dive, can help. You should check out several routines used by runners, whereby you stretch your leg muscles prior to diving. The last major cause is improper kicking. Have a buddy check your kick. If you're bending your knees in a 'bicycle type' kick, you're putting undue stress on muscles. A good kick should be slow and long-sweeping, moving from the hips. Once you're kicking correctly, begin a regular routine of practice. If problems persist, have a doctor check you over, just to be on the safe side.

Divers Alert Network (D.A.N.)

The Divers Alert Network (DAN) is a membership association of individuals and organizations sharing a common interest in diving safety. DAN operates a 24 hour national hotline, (919) 684-8111 to provide advice on early treatment, evacuation and hyperbaric treatment of diving related injuries. Additionally, DAN provides safety information to members of DAN to help *prevent* accidents. For $10 a year every member receives: the DAN *Underwater Diving Accident Manual* which describes symptoms and first aid for the major diving related injuries, plus emergency room physician guidelines for drugs and i.v. fluids; a membership card listing diving related symptoms on one side and DAN's emergency and non-emergency phone numbers on the other; 1 tank decal and 3 small equipment decals with DAN's logo and emergency number; and a newsletter,

"Alert Diver" describing diving medicine and safety information in layman's language along with articles for professionals, case histories, and medical questions related to diving. Special memberships for dive stores, dive clubs, and corporations are also available. Posters and brochures for dive stores, dive clubs, dive boats, and emergency rooms are free. The DAN manual is available separately for $4.

In an emergency a diver or his physician dials (919) 684-8111 and asks for DAN. (Collect calls are accepted in actual emergencies.) The caller is answered by an operator at Duke University Medical Center in Durham, North Carolina, the site of DAN Headquarters. Suspected diving accidents or emergencies are connected to a diving medicine trained physician available 24 hours a day. The physician may advise the caller directly or

refer him to one of DAN's 6 other Regional Coordinators. DAN divides the U.S. into 7 regions, each coordinated by a specialist in diving medicine who has access to the skilled hyperbaric chambers in his regions. Non-emergency or information calls are connected to the DAN office and information number, (919) 684-2948. Non-emergency, information callers should dial this number direct, between 9 a.m. and 5 p.m. Monday-Friday eastern standard time. Divers should *not* call DAN for chamber location information for general knowledge. Chamber status changes frequently making this kind of information dangerous if obsolete at the time of an emergency. Instead, divers should contact DAN as soon as a diving emergency is suspected. DAN does not *directly* provide medical care. All divers should have comprehensive medical insurance and check

to make *sure* that hyperbaric treatment and air ambulance services are covered internationally.

Diving is a safe sport and there are very few accidents compared to the number of divers and number of dives made each year. But when the infrequent injury does occur, DAN is ready to help. DAN, originally 100% federally funded, is now largely supported by the diving public. Membership in DAN or purchase of DAN manuals or decals provides divers with useful safety information and provides DAN with necessary operating funds. Donations to DAN are tax deductible as DAN is a legal non-profit public service organization.

For further information write:
DAN
Box 3823
Duke University
  Medical Center
Durham, NC 27710

A Word For Pregnant Would-Be Divers — Don't!

In 1980 a workshop was held by the Undersea Medical Society (UMS). Their findings suggest that even though the expectant mother doesn't experience any decompression problems, the fetus might. Also, if the expectant mother does need recompression, the common practice of treatment with 100% oxygen can harm the fetus. The UMS recommendation is that pregnant women refrain from diving. Perhaps while in care of this new life, an expectant mother should practice her surface snorkeling skills only and wait until after the birth

to introduce her young to the joys of scuba. Japanese female pearl divers have almost three times the rate of premature births as compared to nondiving women. On the other hand, there have been anecdotal reports of healthy infants born to mothers who have dived extensively during pregnancy. Species differences and experimental technique differences account for some of the conflicting research results. There are ongoing studies which will hopefully elucidate this important problem; however, until accurate information is

available, the recommendations of the Undersea Medical Society should be followed. That is, prospective moms in charge of previous new life practice their snorkeling skills, soak up the sun and wait until after the birth to enjoy the pleasures of SCUBA.

Points To Remember

1. NEVER attempt recompression in the water.
2. REMEMBER *drowning* frequently is associated with pressure accidents.
3. Dive buddy and equipment should be taken with accident victim to recompression chamber.
4. Victim may be stabilized in nearby emergency facility — IV fluids, foley catheter, etc., ONLY while awaiting transportation. While great strides in physician education have occurred in recent years, the local ER doc may know less than you about diving injuries. INSIST the patient be given oxygen and that DAN be notified.
5. When in doubt — recompress.

DIVING ACCIDENT MANAGEMENT FLOW CHART

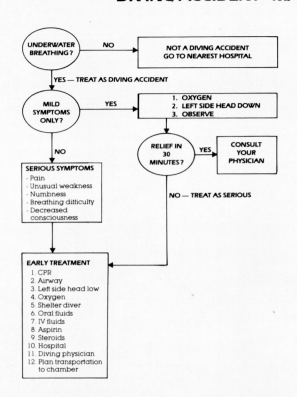

UNDERWATER BREATHING? — NO → NOT A DIVING ACCIDENT GO TO NEAREST HOSPITAL

YES — TREAT AS DIVING ACCIDENT

MILD SYMPTOMS ONLY? — YES → 1. OXYGEN / 2. LEFT SIDE HEAD DOWN / 3. OBSERVE

NO ↓

SERIOUS SYMPTOMS
- Pain
- Unusual weakness
- Numbness
- Breathing difficulty
- Decreased consciousness

RELIEF IN 30 MINUTES? — YES → CONSULT YOUR PHYSICIAN

NO — TREAT AS SERIOUS

EARLY TREATMENT
1. CPR
2. Airway
3. Left side head low
4. Oxygen
5. Shelter diver
6. Oral fluids
7. IV fluids
8. Aspirin
9. Steroids
10. Hospital
11. Diving physician
12. Plan transportation to chamber

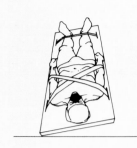
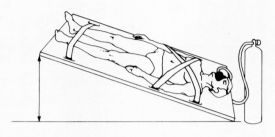

LEFT-SIDE-DOWN-HEAD-LOW DIVING ACCIDENT POSITION (TRENDELENBURG)

YOU NEED DAN DAN NEEDS YOU!

Join the DIVERS ALERT NETWORK

DAN FILLS A NEED

DAN unites hyperbaric chamber facilities into a nationwide communications network to help divers and their physicians arrange consultation, transportation, and treatment by using a single central emergency telephone number.

FOR DIVING EMERGENCIES CALL (919) 684-8111
24 HOURS   7 DAYS A WEEK
FOR INFORMATION CALL **(919) 684-2948** MONDAY-FRIDAY 9-5 E.S.T.

DAN NEEDS YOU

The cost of providing this invaluable national service is high. Startup funding was provided by the federal government but not continued. Do your part by becoming a member of DAN which will help insure the continuing existence of DAN as well as provide you with **diving safety information**

JOINING DAN—$10

Individual membership in Dan is $10 per year—a small sum to insure there will be somebody able to help you immediately in the event of an accident.
On joining you will receive:
- **MEMBERSHIP CARD** with the DAN phone number and a list of diving injury symptoms.
- **TANK DECALS** with the DAN emergency phone number.
- The DAN **UNDERWATER DIVING ACCIDENT MANUAL** which describes symptoms and first aid for the major diving related injuries plus guidelines a physician can follow for drugs and i.v. fluid administration.
- **A NEWSLETTER, "ALERT DIVER"**, presents information on diving medicine and diving safety. Actual DAN case histories and questions are presented in each issue.

☐ Yes, I wish to join the National Divers Alert Network (DAN), and enclose my membership fee of $10. Please send my new member's package as soon as is possible (Please allow 3-6 weeks for delivery.)

☐ I am enclosing an extra tax deductible donation of $ _____

Tax deductible corporate membership is encouraged. Please write for more information.

NAME _____

ADDRESS _____

_____

AGENCY _____

Check if you are a
☐ instructor ☐ dive shop operator ☐ physician

Mail to **DIVERS ALERT NETWORK**, Box 3823, Duke University Medical Center, Durham, N.C. 27710

NARCOTIC EFFECTS OF COMPRESSED AIR DIVING

(30-100 ft.) . . . . Mild impairment of performance on unpracticed tasks. Mild euphoria.

(100 ft.) . . . . Reasoning and immediate memory affected more than motor coordination and choice reactions. Delayed response to visual and auditory stimuli.

(100-165 ft.) . . . . Laughter and loquacity may be overcome by self control. Idea fixation and overconfidence. Calculation errors.

(165 ft.) . . . . Sleepiness, hallucinations, impaired judgment.

(165-230 ft.) . . . . Convivial group atmosphere. May be terror reaction in some. Talkative. Dizziness reported occasionally. Uncontrolled laughter approaching hysteria in some.

(230 ft.) . . . . Severe impairment of intellectual performance. Manual dexterity less affected.

(230-300 ft.) . . . . Gross delay in response to stimuli. Diminished concentration. Mental confusion. Increased auditory sensitivity, i.e., sounds seem louder.

(300 ft.) . . . . Stupefaction. Severe impairment of practical activity and judgment. Mental abnormalities and memory defects. Deterioration in handwriting, euphoria, hyperexcitability. Almost total loss of intellectual and perceptive faculties.

(300 ft.) . . . . Hallucinations (similar to those cuased by hallucinogenic drugs rather than alcohol).

CREDIT: Derived from Edmonds, Lowry, and Pennefather 1976.

TYPICAL TOTAL AIR DIVE DURATIONS

■ **TIME IN PARENTHESES EXPRESSED AS:**
(HOURS : MINUTES)

Depth, feet	15	20	30	40	50	60	80	90	100	120	150	160	200	220	250	300
190	29 MIN (:29)	51 MIN (:51)	93 MIN (1:33)	143 MIN (2:23)												
180	27 MIN (:27)	46 MIN (:46)	83 MIN (1:23)	133 MIN (2:13)	178 MIN (2:58)											
170	25 MIN (:25)	42 MIN (:42)	76 MIN (1:16)	122 MIN (2:02)	160 MIN (2:40)	213 MIN (3:33)										
160	23 MIN (:23)	37 MIN (:37)	71 MIN (1:11)	112 MIN (1:52)	149 MIN (2:29)	193 MIN (3:13)										
150	21 MIN (:21)	32 MIN (:32)	65 MIN (1:05)	100 MIN (1:40)	139 MIN (2:19)	173 MIN (2:53)	254 MIN (4:14)									
140	19 MIN (:19)	28 MIN (:28)	58 MIN (:58)	86 MIN (1:26)	126 MIN (2:06)	157 MIN (2:37)	235 MIN (3:55)									
130	18 MIN (:18)	26 MIN (:26)	53 MIN (:53)	77 MIN (1:17)	113 MIN (1:53)	146 MIN (2:26)	211 MIN (3:31)									
120	NO DECOMP	24 MIN (:24)	46 MIN (:46)	72 MIN (1:12)	98 MIN (1:38)	131 MIN (2:11)	187 MIN (3:07)	222 MIN (3:42)	250 MIN (4:10)							
110	NO DECOMP	NO DECOMP	39 MIN (:39)	65 MIN (1:05)	86 MIN (1:26)	116 MIN (1:56)	169 MIN (2:49)	198 MIN (3:18)	226 MIN (3:46)							
100	NO DECOMP	NO DECOMP	35 MIN (:35)	57 MIN (:57)	78 MIN (1:18)	99 MIN (1:39)	153 MIN (2:33)	175 MIN (2:55)	198 MIN (3:18)	253 MIN (4:13)						
90	NO DECOMP	NO DECOMP	NO DECOMP	49 MIN (:49)	70 MIN (1:10)	87 MIN (1:27)	135 MIN (2:15)	158 MIN (2:38)	177 MIN (2:57)	222 MIN (3:42)						
80	NO DECOMP	NO DECOMP	NO DECOMP	NO DECOMP	61 MIN (1:01)	78 MIN (1:18)	114 MIN (1:54)	137 MIN (2:17)	158 MIN (2:38)	194 MIN (3:14)	260 MIN (4:20)					
70	NO DECOMP	NO DECOMP	NO DECOMP	NO DECOMP	NO DECOMP	69 MIN (1:09)	99 MIN (1:39)	114 MIN (1:54)	134 MIN (2:14)	172 MIN (2:52)	221 MIN (3:41)	246 MIN (4:06)				
60	NO DECOMP	NO DECOMP	NO DECOMP	NO DECOMP	NO DECOMP	NO DECOMP	88 MIN (1:28)	105 MIN (1:45)	115 MIN (1:55)	147 MIN (2:27)	199 MIN (3:19)	209 MIN (3:29)	271 MIN (4:31)			
50	NO DECOMP	NO DECOMP	NO DECOMP	NO DECOMP	NO DECOMP	NO DECOMP	NO DECOMP	NO DECOMP	NO DECOMP	126 MIN (2:06)	172 MIN (2:52)	182 MIN (3:02)	236 MIN (3:56)	261 MIN (4:21)		
40	NO DECOMP	NO DECOMP	NO DECOMP	NO DECOMP	NO DECOMP	NO DECOMP	NO DECOMP	NO DECOMP	NO DECOMP	NO DECOMP	NO DECOMP	NO DECOMP	NO DECOMP	232 MIN (3:52)	262 MIN (4:22)	320 MIN (5:20)

Bottom Time, minutes

CREDIT: US Navy Diving Manual

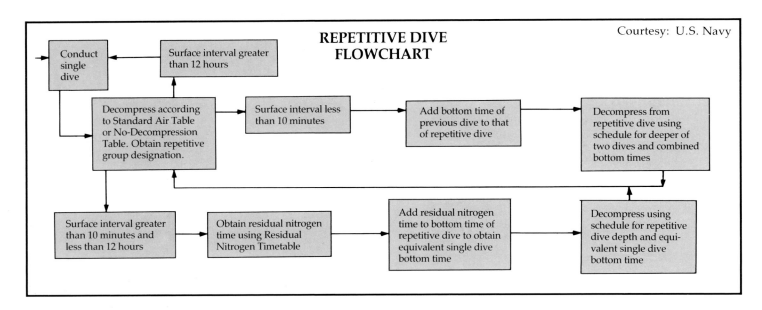

REPETITIVE DIVE FLOWCHART

Courtesy: U.S. Navy

REPETITIVE DIVE WORKSHEET – NOAA

I. PREVIOUS DIVE:

_____ minutes

_____ feet

_____ repetitive group designation

II. SURFACE INTERVAL:

_____ hours _____ minutes on surface.

Repetitive group from I _____

New repetitive group from surface

Residual Nitrogen Timetable _____

III. RESIDUAL NITROGEN TIME:

_____ feet (depth of repetitive dive)

New repetitive group from II. _____

Residual nitrogen time from

Residual Nitrogen Timetable_____

IV. EQUIVALENT SINGLE DIVE TIME:

_____ minutes, residual nitrogen time from III.

+ _____ minutes, actual bottom time of repetitive dive.

= _____ minutes, equivalent single dive time.

V. DECOMPRESSION FOR REPETITIVE DIVES:

_____ minutes, equivalent single dive time from IV.

_____ feet, depth of repetitive dive

Decompression from (check one):
☐ Standard Air Table ☐ No-Decompression Table
☐ Surface Table Using Oxygen ☐ Surface Table Using Air
☐ No decompression required

Schedule used_____

Repetitive group_____

Decompression Stops:

_____ feet _____ minutes

_____ feet _____ minutes

_____ feet _____ minutes

_____ feet _____ minutes

_____ feet _____ minutes

REPETITIVE DIVE TABLES

No-decompression limits and repetitive group designation table

DEPTH (feet)	NO-DECOMPRESSION LIMITS (Min.)	A	B	C	D	E	F	G	H	I	J	K	L	M	N	O
10	—	60	120	210	300	—	—	—	—	—	—	—	—	—	—	—
15	—	35	70	110	160	225	350	—	—	—	—	—	—	—	—	—
20	—	25	50	75	100	135	180	240	325	—	—	—	—	—	—	—
25	—	20	35	55	75	100	125	160	195	245	315	—	—	—	—	—
30	—	15	30	45	60	75	95	120	145	170	205	250	310	—	—	—
35	310	5	15	25	40	50	60	80	100	120	140	160	190	220	270	310
40	200	5	15	25	30	40	50	70	80	100	110	130	150	170	200	—
50	100	—	10	15	25	30	40	50	60	70	80	90	100	—	—	—
60	60	—	10	15	20	25	30	40	50	55	60	—	—	—	—	—
70	50	—	5	10	15	20	30	35	40	45	50	—	—	—	—	—
80	40	—	5	10	15	20	25	30	35	40	—	—	—	—	—	—
90	30	—	5	10	12	15	20	25	30	—	—	—	—	—	—	—
100	25	—	5	7	10	15	20	22	25	—	—	—	—	—	—	—
110	20	—	—	5	10	13	15	20	—	—	—	—	—	—	—	—
120	15	—	—	5	10	12	15	—	—	—	—	—	—	—	—	—
130	10	—	—	5	8	10	—	—	—	—	—	—	—	—	—	—
140	10	—	—	5	7	10	—	—	—	—	—	—	—	—	—	—
150	5	—	—	5	—	—	—	—	—	—	—	—	—	—	—	—
160	5	—	—	—	5	—	—	—	—	—	—	—	—	—	—	—
170	5	—	—	—	5	—	—	—	—	—	—	—	—	—	—	—
180	5	—	—	—	5	—	—	—	—	—	—	—	—	—	—	—
190	5	—	—	—	5	—	—	—	—	—	—	—	—	—	—	—

REPETITIVE GROUPS (AIR DIVES)

INSTRUCTIONS FOR USE

I. No-decompression limits:

This column shows at various depths greater than 30 feet the allowable diving times (in minutes) which permit surfacing directly at 60 feet a minute with no decompressions stops. Longer exposure times require the use of the Standard Air Decompression Table (table 1-10).

II. Repetitive group designation table:

The tabulated exposure times (or bottom times) are in minutes. The times at the various depths in each vertical column are the maximum exposures during which a diver will remain within the group listed at the head of the column.

To find the repetitive group designation at surfacing for dives involving exposures up to and including the no-decompression limits: Enter the table on the exact or next greater depth than that to which exposed and select the listed exposure time exact or next greater than the actual exposure time. The repetitive group designation is indicated by the letter at the head of the vertical column where the selected exposure time is listed.

For example: A dive was to 32 feet for 45 minutes. Enter the table along the 35-foot-depth line since it is next greater than 32 feet. The table shows that since group D is left after 40 minutes' exposure and group E after 50 minutes, group E (at the head of the column where the 50-minute exposure is listed) is the proper selection.

Exposure times for depths less than 40 feet are listed only up to approximately 5 hours since this is considered to be beyond field requirements for this table.

"No decompression" limits and repetitive group designation table for "no decompression" dives.

U.S. Navy Standard Air Decompression Table

DEPTH (ft)	BOTTOM TIME (min)	TIME TO FIRST STOP (min:sec)	50	40	30	20	10	TOTAL ASCENT (min:sec)	REPET GROUP
40	200	0:30					0	0:40	(*)
	210	0:30					2	2:40	N
	230	0:30					7	7:40	N
	250	0:30					11	11:40	O
	270	0:30					15	15:40	O
	300	0:30					19	19:40	Z
50	100	0:40					0	0:50	(*)
	110	0:40					3	3:50	L
	120	0:40					5	5:50	M
	140	0:40					10	10:50	M
	160	0:40					21	21:50	N
	180	0:40					29	29:50	O
	200	0:40					35	35:50	O
	220	0:40					40	40:50	Z
	240	0:40					47	47:50	Z
60	60	0:50					0	1:00	(*)
	70	0:50					2	3:00	K
	80	0:50					7	8:00	L
	100	0:50					14	15:00	M
	120	0:50					26	27:00	N
	140	0:50					39	40:00	O
	160	0:50					48	49:00	Z
	180	0:50				1	56	57:00	Z
	200	0:40				1	69	71:00	Z
70	50	1:00					0	1:10	(*)
	60	1:00					8	9:10	K
	70	1:00					14	15:10	L
	80	1:00					18	19:10	M
	90	1:00					23	24:10	N
	100	1:00					33	34:10	N
	110	1:00				2	41	44:10	O
	120	1:00				4	47	52:10	O
	130	1:00				6	52	59:10	O
	140	1:00				8	56	65:10	Z
	150	1:00				9	61	71:10	Z
	160	1:00				13	72	86:10	Z
	170	1:00				19	79	99:10	Z
80	40	1:10					0	1:20	(*)
	50	1:10					10	11:20	K
	60	1:10					17	18:20	L
	70	1:10					23	24:20	M
	80	1:10				2	31	34:20	N
	90	1:10				7	39	48:20	N
	100	1:10				11	46	58:20	O
	110	1:10				13	53	67:20	O
	120	1:10				17	56	74:20	Z
	130	1:00			3	19	63	86:20	Z
	140	1:00			8	26	69	104:20	Z
	150	1:00			12	32	77	122:20	Z
90	30	1:20					0	1:30	(*)
	40	1:20					7	8:30	J
	50	1:20					18	19:30	L
	60	1:20					25	26:30	M
	70	1:10				7	30	38:30	N
	80	1:10				13	40	54:30	N
	90	1:10				18	48	67:30	O
	100	1:10				21	54	76:30	Z
	110	1:10				24	61	86:30	Z
	120	1:10			3	32	68	104:30	Z
	130	1:00			10	34	74	119:40	Z
100	25	1:30					0	1:40	(*)
	30	1:30					3	4:40	I
	40	1:20				2	15	18:30	K
	50	1:20				9	24	34:30	L
	60	1:20				16	34	51:30	N
	70	1:10			5	19	39	64:30	O
	80	1:10			10	23	48	82:30	O
	90	1:10			18	23	57	99:30	Z
	100	1:10			18	34	65	118:30	Z
	110	1:00			24	37	72	134:40	Z
110	20	1:40					0	1:50	(*)
	25	1:40					3	4:50	H
	30	1:30				3	6	10:50	J
	40	1:30				10	21	32:50	L
	50	1:30			3	14	32	50:50	M
	60	1:20			9	17	44	71:40	N
	70	1:20			16	23	55	95:40	O
	80	1:20			19	28	63	111:40	Z
	90	1:20			23	34	72	130:40	Z
	100	1:20		2	31	37	84	155:40	Z
120	15	1:50					0	2:00	(*)
	20	1:50					2	4:00	H
	25	1:50					6	8:00	I
	30	1:50				5	14	21:00	J
	40	1:40			2	16	25	44:10	L
	50	1:40			10	24	43	78:10	M
	60	1:40			19	33	56	109:10	N
	70	1:30		2	23	41	68	135:20	O
	80	1:30		11	30	50	79	171:20	Z
130	10	2:10					0	2:20	(*)
	15	2:10					1	3:30	F
	20	2:10					4	6:30	H
	25	2:10				3	10	16:30	J
	30	2:00			3	18	25	...	M
	40	2:00			10	23	45	...	N
140	10	2:20					0	2:30	(*)
	15	2:20					2	4:30	G
	20	2:10				2	6	10:30	I
	25	2:10			2	14	18	34:20	K
	30	2:10			5	16	24	46:20	N
	40	2:00		2	6	24	44	76:20	O
	50	2:00		6	16	23	56	97:20	Z
	60	2:00		16	19	32	68	125:20	Z
	70	1:50	1	23	22	34	79	155:20	Z
150	5	2:30					0	2:40	C
	10	2:30					1	3:30	E
	15	2:20				3	3	5:30	G
	20	2:20			2	7	7	11:30	H
	25	2:20			4	17	24	23:30	K
	30	2:20			8	19	33	30:30	L
	40	2:10		5	19	33	51	59:30	N
	50	2:10		12	23	51		88:30	O
	60	2:00	3	19	26	62		112:30	Z
	70	2:00	11	19	39	75		146:30	Z
	80	1:50	1	17	19	50	84	173:30	Z
160	5	2:40					0	2:50	D
	10	2:40					1	3:50	F
	15	2:30				1	4	7:40	H
	20	2:30			3	7	11	16:40	J
	25	2:30			7	20	23	29:40	K
	30	2:20		2	11	25	39	40:40	M
	40	2:20		7	23	30	55	71:40	N
	50	2:10	2	16	23	55	69	98:40	Z
	60	2:10	9	19	33	55		166:40	Z
170	5	2:50					0	3:00	D
	10	2:40				2	3	6:00	F
	15	2:40			2	5	6	12:00	H
	20	2:40			4	15	25	26:00	J
	25	2:30		2	7	20	27	40:00	L
	30	2:30		4	17	27	50	53:00	M
	40	2:20		10	24	37	74	93:00	O
	50	2:20	3	17	24	50	81	128:00	Z
	60	2:10	9	19	30	65		168:00	Z
180	5	2:50					0	3:10	D
	10	2:50				3	4	7:10	G
	15	2:50			4	6	14	14:10	I
	20	2:40		1	6	20	31	31:10	K
	25	2:40		6	11	20	55	44:10	L
	30	2:30	1	8	19	32	72	63:10	N
	40	2:30	8	14	23	55		103:10	O
	50	2:20	5	17	22	57		147:10	Z
	60	2:20	10	13	37	72		183:10	Z
190	5	3:00					0	3:20	D
	10	2:50				3	5	8:10	G
	15	2:50			5	11	14	14:10	I
	20	2:40		2	6	20	31	31:10	K
	25	2:40		5	11	25	55	44:10	M
	30	2:30	1	8	19	32	72	63:10	N
	40	2:30	8	14	23	57		103:10	O
	50	2:20	1	8	23	33	72	147:10	Z
	60	2:20	10	13	37	84		183:10	Z

197

REPETITIVE DIVE TABLES

REPETITIVE DIVE DEPTH (Ft.) (AIR DIVES)

REPET. GROUPS	40	50	60	70	80	90	100	110	120	130	140	150	160	170	180	190
A	7	6	5	4	4	3	3	3	3	3	2	2	2	2	2	2
B	17	13	11	9	8	7	7	6	6	6	5	5	4	4	4	4
C	25	21	17	15	13	11	10	10	9	8	7	7	6	6	6	6
D	37	29	24	20	18	16	14	13	12	11	10	9	9	8	8	8
E	49	38	30	26	23	20	18	16	15	13	12	12	11	10	10	10
F	61	47	36	31	28	24	22	20	18	16	15	14	13	13	12	11
G	73	56	44	37	32	29	26	24	21	19	18	17	16	15	14	13
H	87	66	52	43	38	33	30	27	25	22	20	19	18	17	16	15
I	101	76	61	50	43	38	34	31	28	25	23	22	20	19	18	17
J	116	87	70	57	48	43	38	34	32	28	26	24	23	22	20	19
K	138	99	79	64	54	47	43	38	35	31	29	27	26	24	22	21
L	161	111	88	72	61	53	48	42	39	35	32	30	28	26	25	24
M	187	124	97	80	68	58	52	47	43	38	35	32	31	29	27	26
N	213	142	107	87	73	64	57	51	46	40	38	35	33	31	29	28
O	241	160	117	96	80	70	62	55	50	44	40	38	36	34	31	30
Z	257	169	122	100	84	73	64	57	52	46	42	40	37	35	32	31

INSTRUCTIONS FOR USE

The bottom times listed in this table are called "residual nitrogen times" and are the times a diver is to consider he has already spent on bottom when he starts a repetitive dive to a specific depth. They are in minutes.

Enter the table horizontally with the repetitive group designation from the Surface Interval Credit Table. The time in each vertical column is the number of minutes that would be required (at the depth listed at the head of the column) to saturate to the particular group.

For example: The final group designation from the Surface Interval Credit Table, on the basis of a previous dive and surface interval, is "H." To plan a dive to 110 feet, determine the residual nitrogen time for this depth required by the repetitive group designation: Enter this table along the horizontal line labeled "H." The table shows that one must start a dive to 110 feet as though he had already been on the bottom for 27 minutes. This information can then be applied to the Standard Air Decompression Table or No-Decompression Table in a number of ways:

(1) Assuming a diver is going to finish a job and take whatever decompression is required, he must add 27 minutes to his actual bottom time and be prepared to take decompression according to the 110-foot schedules for the sum or equivalent single dive time.

(2) Assuming one wishes to make a quick inspection dive for the minimum decompression, he will decompress according to the 110/30 schedule for a dive of 3 minutes or less (27+3 = 30). For a dive of over 3 minutes but less than 13, he will decompress according to the 110/40 schedule (27+13 = 40).

(3) Assuming that one does not want to exceed the 110/50 schedule and the amount of decompression it requires, he will have to start ascent before 23 minutes of actual bottom time (50−27 = 23).

(4) Assuming that a diver has air for approximately 45 minutes bottom time and decompression stops, the possible dives can be computed: A dive of 13 minutes will require 23 minutes of decompression (110/40 schedule), for a total submerged time of 36 minutes. A dive of 13 to 23 minutes will require 34 minutes of decompression (110/50 schedule), for a total submerged time of 47 to 57 minutes. Therefore, to be safe, the diver will have to start ascent before 13 minutes or a standby air source will have to be provided.

Repetitive dive timetable for air dives

REPETITIVE DIVE TABLES

REPETITIVE GROUP AT THE END OF THE SURFACE INTERVAL (AIR DIVE)

Begin ↓ / End →	Z	O	N	M	L	K	J	I	H	G	F	E	D	C	B	A
Z	0:10 / 0:22	0:23 / 0:34	0:35 / 0:48	0:49 / 1:02	1:03 / 1:18	1:19 / 1:36	1:37 / 1:55	1:56 / 2:17	2:18 / 2:42	2:43 / 3:10	3:11 / 3:45	3:46 / 4:29	4:30 / 5:27	5:28 / 6:56	6:57 / 10:05	10:00 / 12:00*
O		0:10 / 0:23	0:24 / 0:36	0:37 / 0:51	0:52 / 1:07	1:08 / 1:24	1:25 / 1:43	1:44 / 2:04	2:05 / 2:29	2:30 / 2:59	3:00 / 3:33	3:34 / 4:17	4:18 / 5:16	5:17 / 6:44	6:45 / 9:54	9:55 / 12:00*
N			0:10 / 0:24	0:25 / 0:39	0:40 / 0:54	0:55 / 1:11	1:12 / 1:30	1:31 / 1:53	1:54 / 2:18	2:19 / 2:47	2:48 / 3:22	3:23 / 4:04	4:05 / 5:03	5:04 / 6:32	6:33 / 9:43	9:44 / 12:00*
M				0:10 / 0:25	0:26 / 0:42	0:43 / 0:59	1:00 / 1:18	1:19 / 1:39	1:40 / 2:05	2:06 / 2:34	2:35 / 3:08	3:09 / 3:52	3:53 / 4:49	4:50 / 6:18	6:19 / 9:28	9:29 / 12:00*
L					0:10 / 0:26	0:27 / 0:45	0:46 / 1:04	1:05 / 1:25	1:26 / 1:49	1:50 / 2:19	2:20 / 2:53	2:54 / 3:36	3:37 / 4:35	4:36 / 6:02	6:03 / 9:12	9:13 / 12:00*
K						0:10 / 0:28	0:29 / 0:49	0:50 / 1:11	1:12 / 1:35	1:36 / 2:03	2:04 / 2:38	2:39 / 3:21	3:22 / 4:19	4:20 / 5:48	5:49 / 8:58	8:59 / 12:00*
J							0:10 / 0:31	0:32 / 0:54	0:55 / 1:19	1:20 / 1:47	1:48 / 2:20	2:21 / 3:04	3:05 / 4:02	4:03 / 5:40	5:41 / 8:40	8:41 / 12:00*
I								0:10 / 0:33	0:34 / 0:59	1:00 / 1:29	1:30 / 2:02	2:03 / 2:44	2:45 / 3:43	3:44 / 5:12	5:13 / 8:21	8:22 / 12:00*
H									0:10 / 0:36	0:37 / 1:06	1:07 / 1:41	1:42 / 2:23	2:24 / 3:20	3:21 / 4:49	4:50 / 7:59	8:00 / 12:00*
G										0:10 / 0:40	0:41 / 1:15	1:16 / 1:59	2:00 / 2:58	2:59 / 4:25	4:26 / 7:35	7:36 / 12:00*
F											0:10 / 0:45	0:46 / 1:29	1:30 / 2:28	2:29 / 3:57	3:58 / 7:05	7:06 / 12:00*
E												0:10 / 0:54	0:55 / 1:57	1:58 / 3:22	3:23 / 6:32	6:33 / 12:00*
D													0:10 / 1:09	1:10 / 2:38	2:39 / 5:48	5:49 / 12:00*
C														0:10 / 1:39	1:40 / 2:49	2:50 / 12:00*
B															0:10 / 2:10	2:11 / 12:00*
A																0:10 / 12:00*

REPETITIVE GROUP AT THE BEGINNING OF THE SURFACE INTERVAL FROM PREVIOUS DIVE

INSTRUCTIONS FOR USE

Surface interval time in the table is in hours and minutes (7:59 means 7 hours and 59 minutes). The surface interval must be at least 10 minutes.

Find the repetitive group designation letter (from the previous dive) on the diagonal slope. Enter the table horizontally to select the surface interval time that is exactly between the actual interval times shown. The repetitive group designation for the end of the surface interval is at the end of the vertical column where the selected surface interval time is listed. For example, a previous dive was to 110 feet for 30 minutes. The diver remains on the surface 1 hour and 30 minutes and wishes to find the new repetitive group designation. The repetitive group from the last column of the 110/30 schedule in the Standard Air Decompression Tables is "J." Enter the surface interval credit table along the horizontal line labeled "J." The 1-hour and 30-minute surface interval lies between the times 1:20 and 1:47. Therefore, the diver has lost sufficient inert gas to place him in group "G" (at the head of the vertical column selected).

*NOTE: Dives following surface intervals of more than 12 hours are not considered repetitive dives. Actual bottom times in the Standard Air Decompression Tables may be used in computing decompression for such dives.

Surface interval credit table for air decompression dives

T·I·D·E·S

Types of Tides

Diurnal: A tide is considered diurnal if there is just one high and one low water during a lunar day. Diurnal tides are caused primarily by the changing declination of the moon. (See figure .) Such tides are found in the northern Gulf of Mexico and Southeast Asia.

Semidiurnal: The semidiurnal is the most common tide in the world. It is characterized by two high waters and two low waters in the lunar day. The elevations of succeeding high waters and succeeding low waters are nearly the same. The East coast of the United States has a semidiurnal tide.

Mixed: Just as with a semidiurnal tide, the mixed tide is marked by two high waters and two low waters in a lunar day. They are generally of a different height, however. This diurnal inequality is caused by the changing declination of the moon. Mixed tides are common to the west coast of the United States.

In each ocean basin, a tidal wave is created by tide generating forces. Tidal waves occur every 12 hours and twenty-five minutes, which is half the lunar day, but the wave direction, amplitude, speed and wavelength are influenced by the earth's rotation and the specific geometry of each basin.

Sandy Frame

The Oceans

No one knows for certain how the oceans were created, but many geologists today believe that they came slowly into existence beginning roughly 4.5 billion years ago. At that time, the still-molten Earth is thought to have flung out plumes of carbon dioxide, nitrogen, and water vapor. Together these gases formed a thick atmosphere around the globe, which condensed as the Earth's crust began to harden and cool. The ensuing rains lasted for millions of years until, as C.P. Idyll describes it, "the clouds thinned slowly and then broke, and the sun glinted on the fresh new sea."

Courtesy: Neil Spitzer

In the open ocean, the semidiurnal tidal wave generally has a length of several thousand kilometers, but the height averages only fifty centimeters. Undercurrents beneath the tidal wave are less than .2 knots, or .5 kilometers/hour. These figures increase dramatically when the tidal wave travels onto a continental shelf; There the waves pile up and the speed of the undercurrent increases. Tides between adjacent bodies of water have an additional effect. As the tidal wave advances, it can be reflected by another body of water, and pile up the tidal wave even more. The Bay of Fundy and the English Channel are examples of these so-called resonant tides.

All these and other astronomic movements go on simultaneously in cycles whose lengths vary one from the other. Winds, storms and barometric pressures affect the amplitude of tides as well, but it is the predictable movements of the moon and the earth which help us to predict tides accurately.

Ocean Forces

The Tides

Although a number of forces interact to produce tides, consider for now only the Moon and the Earth. The gravitational attraction between the two is balanced by centrifugal force — caused by the rotation of the earth and moon in space.

On the side of the earth nearer the moon, the gravitational pull between the earth and moon is greater than the centrifugal force. On the side of the earth farther from the moon, the centrifugal force is greater than the gravitational pull between the earth and the moon. These forces create two "tidal bulges" on opposite sides of the earth. (See figure .) Because there are two bulges, there are generally two tides per lunar day — every 24 hours and 50 minutes. The difference between the tides created by these forces depends largely upon where the tides occur on the earth.

Because the sun is so far away from the earth, its effect on the tides is only about half that of the moon. Anyone who has observed tides has noticed that the difference between a high and low tide may vary from day to day. This difference, between successive high and low waters, varies primarily because the sun and moon change position in relation to the earth. (See figure .) If the moon is in line with the earth and sun, we have either a full or a new moon. When this happens, the attractive forces of the sun and moon are aligned and reinforce each other. This causes an increase in the tidal bulge making the high tides higher and the low tides lower and producing what is known as spring tides.

If the moon is at a right angle to the sun, we have a first quarter or third quarter moon. When this occurs, the attractive forces of the sun and moon counteract one another, and consequently, high tides are lower, and low tides are higher, than average. These are called neap tides.

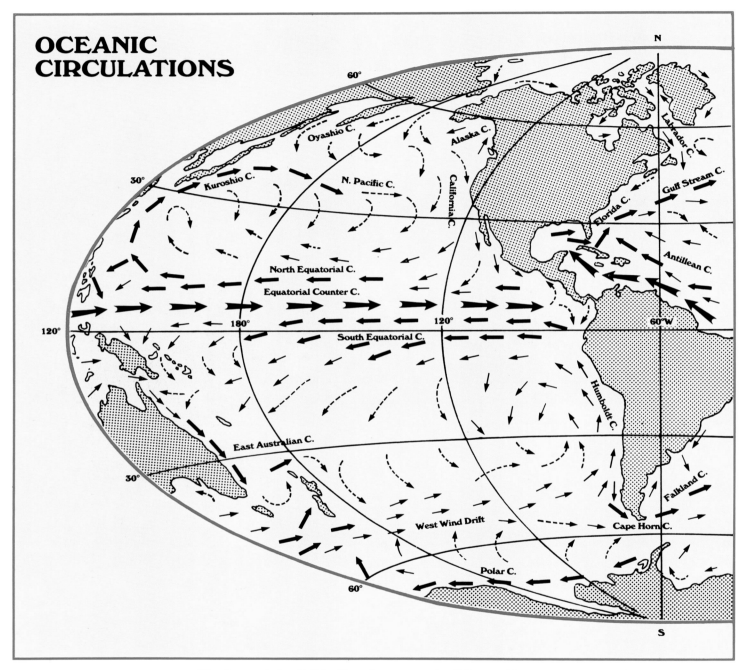

OCEANIC CIRCULATIONS

Northern winter (left half) surface currents of the world ocean.

The Oceans and Climate

Weather (which exists in the short-term and changes quickly) and climate (which exists in the long-term and changes slowly) are determined by the interactions among water, air, land, and ice. The oceans, vast reservoirs of solar energy, play a generally stabilizing role. Slow to gain or lose heat, they warm the atmosphere during winter and cool it during summer, moderating extremes of temperature.

Oceanic Circulations

Although man's knowledge of the processes which produce and maintain ocean current is far from complete, he does have a general understanding of the principal factors involved. The primary generating forces are wind and the density differences in the water. In addition, such factors as depth of water, underwater topography, shape of the basin in which the current is running, extent and location of land, and deflection by the rotation of the earth all affect the oceanic circulation.

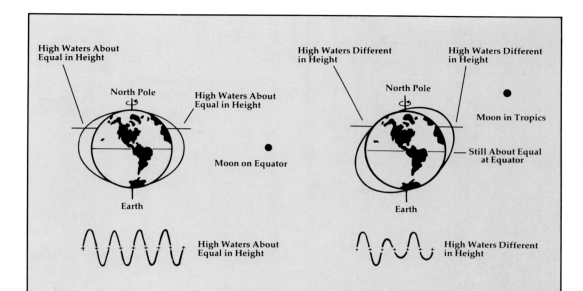

The sun's effect on tides, because it is so far away from the Earth, is only about half that of the moon. Anyone who has observed tides has noticed that the difference between a high tide and a low tide may change from day to day. The difference between successive high and low waters varies primary because the Sun and moon change position in relation to the earth.

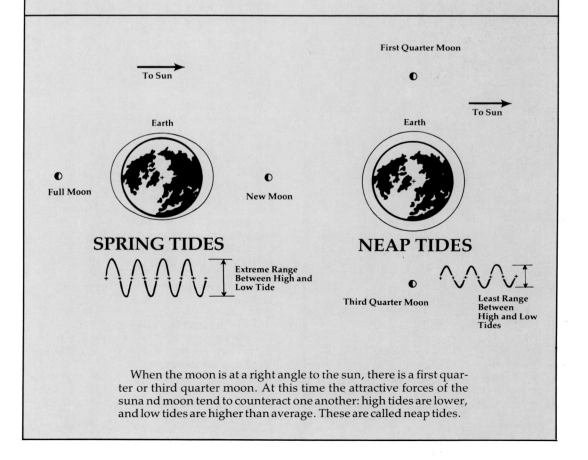

When the moon is at a right angle to the sun, there is a first quarter or third quarter moon. At this time the attractive forces of the sun and moon tend to counteract one another: high tides are lower, and low tides are higher than average. These are called neap tides.

SIMPLE FORECASTING

Wind Direction From-To	Sea-Level Pressure Millibars (Inches)	General Forecast
SW to NW	1022.7 (30.20) or higher and steady	Continued fair with little temperature change.
SW to NW	1022.7 (30.20) or higher falling slowly	Fair for 2 days with slowly rising temperature.
S to SE	1019.3 (30.10) to 1022.7 (30.20) falling slowly	Rain within 24 hours.
S to SE	1019.3 (30.10) to 1022.7 (30.20) falling rapidly	Increasing winds and rain within 12 to 24 hours.
SE to NE	1019.3 (30.10) to 1022.7 (30.20) falling slowly	Increasing winds and rain within 12 to 18 hours.
S to SW	1015.9 (30.00) or below rising slowly	Clearing within a few hours. Then fair for several days.
S to E	1009.1 (29.80) or below falling rapidly	Severe storm within a few hours. Then clearing within 24 hours—followed by colder in winter.
SE to NE	1019.3 (30.10) to 1022.7 (30.20) falling rapidly	Increasing winds and rain within 12 hours.
SE to NE	1015.9 (30.00) or below falling slowly	Rain will continue 1 to 3 days, perhaps even longer.
SE to NE	1015.9 (30.00) or below falling rapidly	Rain with high winds in a few hours. Clearing within 36 hours—becoming colder in winter.
E to NE	1019.3 (30.10) or higher falling slowly	In summer, with light winds, rain may not fall for 2 to 3 days. In winter, rain within 24 hours.
E to NE	1019.3 (30.10) or higher falling rapidly	In summer, rain probably within 12 to 24 hours. In winter, rain or snow within 12 hours and increasing winds.
E to N	1009.1 (29.80) or below falling rapidly	Severe storm (typical Nor'easter) in a few hours. Heavy rains or snowstorm. Followed by a cold wave in winter.
Hauling to W	1009.1 (29.80) or below rising rapidly	End of the storm. Followed by clearing and colder.

BEAUFORT WIND SCALE

	Knots	Pressure lbs./sq.ft.	Name	Description	Wave Height (ft.)	Wave Action
0	0-1	0	Calm	Smooth, mirror-like seas, smoke vertical.	0	Calm
1	1-3	.1-.5	Light Air	Ripples w/o foam crests, smoke drifts, vanes don't move.	Under 1	Smooth
2	4-6	.5-1	Light Breeze	Small short wavelets, crests don't break, wind felt, vanes just move.	1	Slight
3	7-10	1-2	Gentle Breeze	Large wavelets, some crests break, glassy foam, small flags extended.	2-3	Moderate
4	11-16	2-3	Moderate Breeze	Longer small waves, numerous white foam crests, leaves and paper raised.	4-5	Rough
5	17-21	3-4	Fresh Breeze	Long form waves, many white foam crests, some spray, small trees sway.	6-9	Heavy Seas
6	22-27	4-6	Strong Breeze	Large waves, wide foam crests, spray. Whistle of wind in wires.	10-13	Heavy Seas
7	28-33	6-8	Moderate Gale	Sea heaps, streaky blowing foam, spray from waves begins, resistance from wind when walking, large trees in motion.	14-19	Very Rough
8	34-40	8-11	Gale	Longer moderately high waves, crest edges break to spray, foam blown in well-marked streaks, branches break from trees, hard to move into wind.	18-25	Very Rough
9	41-47	11-14	Strong Gale	As above but more intense, slight structural damage.	23-32	High
10	48-55	14-18	Storm	High waves, foam crests, large foam patches.	29-41	Very High
11	56-63	18-25	Violent Storm	Intense wind pressure, air filled with spray, streaky form, large ships hidden in troughs, considerable structure damage.	37-52	Mountainous
12	56-63	18-25	Hurricane	More severe than above, widespread damage.	45 +	Mountainous

Knots x 1.151 = MPH   MPH x .869 = Knots
NWS Forecasts: "Moderate" Swells = 3'-5' "Heavy Seas" = 6' +

Weather Rules For Safe Diving

Before setting out:

Obtain the latest available weather forecast for the diving area. Where they can be received, the NOAA Weather Radio continuous broadcasts (VHF-FM) are the best way to keep informed of expected weather and sea conditions. If you hear on the radio that warnings are in effect, or see flags at warning display stations, don't venture out on the water unless you are confident you can navigate safely under forecast conditions of wind and sea.

While Afloat:

1. Keep a weather eye out for: the approach of dark, threatening clouds, which may foretell a squall or thunderstorm; any steady increase in wind or sea; any increase in wind velocity opposite in direction to a strong tidal current. A dangerous rip tide condition may form steep waves capable of broaching a boat.
2. Check radio weather broadcasts for latest forecasts and warnings.
3. Heavy static on your AM radio may be an indication of nearby thunderstorm activity.
4. If a thunderstorm catches you while afloat, you should remember that not only gusty winds but also lightning poses a threat to safety.
– stay below deck if possible.
– keep away from metal objects that are not grounded to the boat's protection system.
– don't touch more than one grounded object at the same time (or you may become a shortcut for electrical surges passing through the protection system).
– put on a life jacket and prepare for rough sea conditions.

Doug Cameron

Old Wave's Tale

Take note: it is *not* always true one big wave will follow after 6 or 7 smaller ones. Many visitors to coastal tide pools have been swept away when counting on this old wive's tale. Large waves can break at any time and should be watched for; use caution when diving from coastal rocks, and take along a guide who knows the quirks of the area.